From Pampas to Hedgerows and Downs

Photograph from the Smithsonian Institution

Hudson at the age of twenty-six

From Pampas to Hedgerows and Downs

A STUDY OF W. H. HUDSON

by

Richard E. Haymaker

It is the worshipers of beauty . . .
who have done the real pioneer work
of the world.

— THOREAU

Bookman Associates : New York

Copyright, 1954, by Richard E. Haymaker

MANUFACTURED IN THE U.S.A.
BY RECORD PRESS, NEW YORK, N. Y.

FOR

Emma Vogelgesang Haymaker

Schweitzlerian in her feeling for animals, extraordinarily sensitive to the appeal of many places and peoples, and an inveterate foe of the forces threatening the humanities

Preface

My approach in this study has been much more from the literary than the scientific point of view. One of my main purposes has been to present a unified picture of Hudson's total experience, for the form in which he gathered most of it—that of the out-of-door essay—tends toward the loosely episodic. Such a picture, to be of much service, must be painted in some detail, even though it involves a considerable amount of mere description and, if something of the original vividness is to be preserved, a generous use of quotation.

Because of the way I have patterned the book, some repetition is inevitable. Though each path taken through the outer and inner realms of Hudson's experience is a fresh one, we occasionally come upon a prospect already seen. Approached from a different direction or more leisurely viewed, such a prospect, I hope, will produce a new or a deeper impression.

I wish to express my gratitude to my mother and Dr. Lloyd Davidson for their thorough and illuminative reading of my manuscript and, most of all, to Dr. Raymond D. Havens, who embodies the truth that the greatest teaching is inspired by friendship, for his lively interest and searching criticism throughout the various stages of its writing.

E. P. Dutton & Company, through the courtesy of their president, Mr. Elliott B. Macrae, have most generously given me permission to quote from Hudson frequently and at length.

R. E. H.

July 1954

Acknowledgements

The permission granted me by E. P. Dutton & Company includes the use of the following books by or on Hudson: *The Purple Land, A Crystal Age, The Naturalist in La Plata, Fan, Idle Days in Patagonia, British Birds, Birds in London, Nature in Downland, Birds and Man, El Ombú and other South American Stories, Hampshire Days, Green Mansions, A Little Boy Lost and Various Poems, The Land's End, Afoot in England, A Shepherd's Life, Adventures among Birds, Far Away and Long Ago, Birds in Town and Village, The Book of a Naturalist, Birds of La Plata, A Traveller in Little Things, A Hind in Richmond Park, Dead Man's Plack, An Old Thorn, and Miscellanea, Men, Books and Birds* (edited by Morley Roberts), *Letters from W. H. Hudson, 1901-1922* (edited by Edward Garnett), and Morley Roberts' *W. H. Hudson: A Portrait.* I am indebted to the Golden Cockerel Press for permission to quote from *W. H. Hudson's Letters to R. B. Cunninghame Graham, with a Few to Cunninghame Graham's Mother, Mrs. Bontine* (edited by Richard Curle) and to the Houghton Mifflin Company for permission to quote from the following books by or on Burroughs: *Under the Maples, Ways of Nature, Leaf and Tendril, The Summit of the Years, The Heart of Burroughs's Journals* (edited by Clara Barrus), *My Boyhood,* Clara Barrus' *Our Friend, John Burroughs* and *The Life and Letters of John Burroughs.*

Contents

Biographical Sketch

Optima dies . . . prima fugit.

—V<small>IRGIL</small>

*Der ist der glücklichste Mensch, der das Ende seines Lebens
mit dem Anfang in Verbindung setzen kann.*

—G<small>OETHE</small>

WHEN WILLIAM HENRY HUDSON was about to embark for England on the fifteen-hundred-ton *Ebro,* his younger brother, with whom he was closer than anyone else then living, uttered these revelatory words: "Of all the people I have ever known you are the only one I don't know." The greater part of his personality was later laid bare, for many of the things he was "loath to tell" his "dearest friends" (to use the phrasing of Montaigne) were given "to the whole world." But not all. In order to keep some reaches of his soul inaccessible, he was, like Browne and Doughty, extremely reticent about certain of the more intimate experiences of his life. And to thwart whosoever might not heed the injunction in his will against a full-scale biography, he called in thousands of letters shortly before his death and fed them to the flames. Even Morley Roberts, as intimate as he was with him in later years, could add little to his portrait that was not already public property.

One of the reticences concerned his age, about which he was as sensitive as Whistler and Davidson and George Moore. Wishing to be of "no age at all," he generally avoided precision in dating the events of his life. As a result of what Roberts calls "a deliberate mystification" in certain chapters of *Far Away and Long Ago,* the date of his birth on the bookplates of the collected edition of his works makes him appear five years younger than he actually was. It has now been established that he was born, the fourth of a family of six, on August 4, 1841, in a rancho at Quilmes, and baptized at the English Methodist Church of Buenos Aires, which lay eleven miles to the west.

Hudson described himself as "a Dumnonian, if not a 'swart Belerian,' with an admixture of Irish blood." Roberts noted that in "his power and size, the roundness of his skull, its shape and index" there was much "of Beaker ancestry, those powerful men . . . whose . . . barrows . . . are found from Torquay to Caithness, men whose descendants are still strong . . . and are not born to be hewers of wood and drawers of water. . . . " And from them, as we shall see, he inherited some of his most profound characteristics. From the Celtic strain, which was strong in both his parents, came, in large measure, his whimsicality, the richness of his emotion, with its melancholy and its sensitivity to the magical qualities of nature, and

14

also his imaginative power. His high-pitched voice and cackling laugh, much of the looseness of his frame, "which made him seem a little awkward as he flopped across the road like a winged eagle," and a certain shrewdness of mind were probably a heritage from the New England environment. For his father, Daniel, though the son of a Devonian, was born in Massachusetts and his mother, Caroline Augusta Kimble, in Maine, of Pilgrim ancestry.[1]

On a voyage to South America, Daniel had reached Buenos Aires, and thus when tuberculosis threatened him, he and his wife decided to leave the harsher climate of New England and seek their fortunes in the Argentine as sheep-ranchers. At first they met with some success, but later, owing primarily to Daniel's "childlike trust in the absolute good faith of every person with whom he came into business relations," with deepening failure. Except for this trust and for a certain defect in the instinct of self-preservation, strikingly illustrated by the aplumb with which he met the menacing demands of various fragments of Rosas' broken army for fresh mounts, there was little to distinguish him from the ordinary. Among the traits he at least strengthened in William were a distaste for money-grubbing and a hatred of wanton destructiveness. "I never saw him angrier," so his son has written, "than once when a visitor staying in the house, going out with his gun one day suddenly threw it up to his shoulder and brought down a passing swallow."

There was in William much more of the essence of his mother. The four hundred books she brought along with her to the Argentine reflect a cultivated mind, and it was she who became largely responsible for the early education of her children. A very religious woman, she was deeply concerned about the effect the alien, primitive society that enveloped them would have upon their moral and spiritual well-being. While reading Leigh Hunt's autobiography late in life, Hudson was struck by the strong resemblance between their mothers, particularly their compassion for those outside the family circle. (Until someone else could be found, Caroline once nursed the baby of a native who had died in childbirth.) What drew him closest to her were their love of nature—his mother's love for wild flowers being "little short of adoration"—and their quick response

---

[1] Through his mother's family, Hudson was pleased to claim kinship with Florence Merriam, the author of *A-birding on a Bronco*.

to the beautiful in all things. "Thus, besides and above the love of mother and son," he tells us, they "had a spiritual kinship, and this was so much to [him] that everything beautiful in sight or sound that affected [him] came associated with her to [his] mind."

Throughout Hudson's youth, the Argentine was an extremely romantic place in which to live. The pampas—a sea of tall, waving grass—stretched away from the gates of Buenos Aires to the far horizon, broken only by atoll-like clumps of trees round widely scattered ranchos and, following the heavy downpours of winter, by broad lagoons. In the spring the color of the grass was creamy-white changing to a deep green; in summer, yellow toning down to yellowish brown; and in autumn, a rusty thistle-brown. Over its free expanses roamed at will an incredible multitude of half or wholly wild cattle and horses. The droughts of summer often maddened the herds, and made tremendous thistle fires a constant threat. Throughout the year, but most frequently during the hot season, the *pampero*, a wind blowing from the interior with hurricane force, would suddenly burst upon a landscape that was the embodiment of serenity and cause terrific damage. In the everglades along the Rio de la Plata and other scattered coverts, the two "cat-monarchs" of South America, the jaguar and the puma, were ready to spring like lightning upon their prey, and,

> Stationed always in the skies,
> Waiting for the flesh that dies,

were "the lordly carancho, almost eagle-like in size, black and crested, . . . and his humble follower and jackal, the brown and harrier-like chimango."

The chief human figures in these vast, lonely spaces were the gauchos—on horseback, like centaurs; on foot, going about in their ponchos, *chiripas* and ponderous spurs, like "certain tardigrade mammals of arboreal habits when removed from their tree." Descendants of the conquistadores and the girls of conquered Indians, these nomadic herdsmen inherited from them many of their inner as well as outer characteristics. From the Spaniards (and through them, the Moors) came their strong individuality and melancholy; from the Indians, their sense of kinship with the soil and fanatic love of liberty; and from both, their ability to endure the greatest hardships, their fatalism, and, as is characteristic of those in whom passion dominates the will, their ferocity and cruelty. On the slightest provocation, gauchos were as ready to flash their dirklike *facones* at a person's throat as a cat to unsheathe its claws. Knife-duelling, particularly in a wayside *pulperia* after several glasses of gin or rum, was not uncommon, for in order to be permitted to live in peace (as the hero of Eandi's "Dangerous Men" had to learn) they felt it necessary to prove their "prowess by killing a few of [their] opponents." As soldiers, they "loved to kill a man not with a bullet but in a manner to make them know and feel that they were really and truly killing." Prisoners were often slashed from ear to ear as in cattle-slaughtering, the performance over a young man with a good neck being done "in a leisurely, loving way." It was largely because of their skill at soldiering, so essential in a land continually harassed by savage Indians, that, in the course of time, they came to acquire, in the imagination of their fellow-countrymen, a certain aura of heroism. Besides this estimable quality and a strong sense of hospitality, there was in the gauchos a remnant of Old World culture, especially noticeable in their passionate love of song. As *payadores*, wandering like medieval troubadours from one estancia to another to sing wild songs and improvise ballads to the cadences of the guitar, they were most romantic.

At the time of the arrival of the Hudsons, the Argentine was under the dictatorship of the gaucho Rosas, "the Nero of South American adventurers." Though the Indians continued to raid the frontiers, killing and taking captives, he at least brought some order to the country, which, since the throwing off of the Spanish yoke, had been torn with internecine strife between the various *caudillos* or large ranch owners, who gathered men around them like feudal lords. In 1852, after the Hudsons had been there almost twenty years, his dictatorship was broken by the equally ferocious Urquiza— a defeat brought home to William not only by the demand for horses made upon his father but by the cutting of the throat of a young officer by his own men—the usual fate of officers in a fleeing army. It was only after Urquiza, in turn, had been vanquished by Mitre that the Argentine, in 1862, set up a constitutional government and became truly a nation.

Such was the more general milieu in which Hudson passed his youth. The first five years were spent at *Los Veinte-cinco Ombúes,* a small estancia lying along the Conchitas, a rush-filled stream that serpentined its way to the Rio de la Plata, some six miles to the east. The century-old, low brick house, built on the highest ground, dominated the undulating sea of wild lands. As was the custom, the place took its name from its stand of trees—a row of ombús, one of the four species indigenous to the pampas. The scene that painted itself most hauntingly upon Hudson's memory of these early years was an evening one of "the green quiet plain extending away from the gate to the horizon, the western sky flushed with sunset hues, and the herd of four or five hundred cattle trotting homewards with loud lowings and bellowings, raising a great cloud of dust with their hoofs, while behind gallop the herdsmen urging them on with wild cries."

In order to engage in more general trade, Daniel moved his family to *Las Acacias*, which lay to the southeast on the flat, dislike plains of Chascomús, some seventy miles from Buenos Aires. It was at this estancia that the most interesting part of William's life was passed, and to it, more than to any other dwelling-place on earth, his memories swarmed. Though more within the pampean desert, it had as its chief glory thousands of trees, among them, mulberry, red willow, rare black acacia and white, ailanthus, chinaberry, and, on the outside, a double row of Lombardy poplars. There was also a large orchard of quince, pear, apple, plum, cherry, and from four to five hundred very old peach trees—like a gigantic bouquet when in bloom at springtime. Since there was little shelter on the open pampas, woodland birds thronged to these trees and to the interspersed bushes and thickets as to an oasis. The large house, beneath the flooring of which snakes glided about ghostlike, was formerly occupied by the Jesuits, and round it were many outbuildings and huge woodpiles. Both trees and buildings were encircled with a forty-foot-wide moat, whose waters attracted teal and widgeon and whose banks, like the hide-filled barns, were a paradise for rats, which filled the nights with terrifying noises and occasionally even crept between the sheets of the beds. Here, in the midst of abundance, the Hudsons lived for a decade in lavish primitive style, delighting in hospitality to casual wayfarers.

During this period, the family circle was a very happy one. The children were given the utmost freedom to follow each his own bent. Since their mother (perhaps remembering the strictness of her own upbringing) thought that nature was a brighter lexicon for youth, the rigors of the improvised classroom were usually relaxed "when sun and wind and the cries of wild birds called insistently [for them] to come out and be alive and enjoy [themselves] in [their] own way." Seldom were they punished or even chided. When their first tutor attempted to enforce his tyranny with a horse-whip, he was summarily dismissed. Such casual training involves of course certain moral and social risks in the development of character, but it is excellent for the unfoldment of personality. Though the four brothers became extremely unlike in character and in mind, they shared deep within them a spiritual quality that made them one, a quality inherited from their mother.

Hudson early showed the makings of a naturalist. More than most children, he found the natural world, with its many different plants and animals, enormously exciting. So much did this little Robinson Crusoe stand and stare in curiosity and amazement that his mother, for a time, thought him a bit daft. In his continuous reconnaissance, there were sounds and scents as well as sights that intoxicated him with delight. Doglike, he would roll on green, fresh-smelling clover, and crush and rub the young leaves of the Lombardy poplar in his hands and on his face in order "to get the delicious balsamic smell in fuller measure." At the age of six he was given a pony, and allowed to ride out upon the plains whithersoever his exploring spirit would take him. Soon he acquired the habit, so valuable to a naturalist, of roaming about alone, filling every day with fresh discoveries.

Dogs (there were usually about a dozen in the Hudson pack), cattle, horses, romping lambs, yellow deer, vizcachas, armadillos (one of which was kept as a mouser), bats and serpents—all aroused his interest; but, with the first sight of flamingoes, it was the magic of birds that swung his universe. Many species, frequently in immense numbers, were found in the boscage around the neighboring estancias, along the watercourses, and in the lagoons. In such multitudes did cowbirds flock to *Las Acacias* that in winter the bare trees would suddenly "put on an inky-black foliage." Hidden amidst the grass, whose spikes often reached the height of eight to ten feet, were many rheas, their plumage "hanging like a picturesquely-worn mantle" about their bodies and their call "at intervals loud as the summer humming of insects, then decreasing and at last so faint as to be scarcely audible, so that . . . you almost came to think it an imaginary sound." In the vast reedy marshes were ibis, crested screamers, spoonbills, geese, courlans, jacanas, storks, swans, spurwing lapwings, and great and varied flocks of ducks and troupials. Hudson's first meeting with a large owl while exploring in a dimly lighted barn made his hair stand up as if he "had received an electric shock." The calls and songs of birds, such as the deep, humanlike note of the yellow-billed cuckoo, the carillon-like concert of a charm of stilts, and the wild musical cry 'of the upland plover, "mellowed and made beautiful by distance and the profound silence of the moonlit world," were as the finest music to his listening. And when migratory flocks were on the airways or resting for a while on the plains, he would mount his pony and gallop to witness the spectacle. The desire for flight, "to circle upwards" like the crested screamer "to a great height and float on the air without effort," first came to him after "the wild arboreal mood" had taken him aloft his favorite climbing tree, a big red willow.

Possessing as he did the rare faculty of intimacy with wild creatures, William's early observations of them, as in his ability to distinguish many species of birds, were remarkably accurate. And unlike most boys, who have little more than "a monkey-like, prying curiosity about things, especially . . . living things," he developed a certain respect and love for them. The "little action" that an escaped pet cardinal had of lingering longer on the feeding-ground than other birds "went far to reconcile" him to the loss, changing his "boyish bitterness to a new and strange kind of delight in [the bird's] happiness." By causing him "to reflect on a subject which had not previously seemed one for reflection," several incidents were later to have considerable influence upon him. Once, while seeking with his *bolas* some plovers on a neighboring estancia, he was shamed by a gaucho shouting at him: "Why do you come here, English boy, frightening and chasing away God's little birds? Don't you know that they do no harm to anyone, and it is wrong to hurt them?" And on another occasion he was impressed by the strange joy that shone from the face of a woman after she had rescued a snake from the blows of her companions. Though its growth was retarded for some time by the necessities of frontier life and scientific investigation, the feeling that sparing rather than killing is "better not only for the animal spared but for the soul" ultimately led him to resign from the British Ornithologists' Union, which had refused to stay the hand of the collector.

At first his enjoyment of nature was largely one of the senses, but even as early as his eighth year a change came over him, not unlike that which had come over Wordsworth at a somewhat later period in his development. "It was," he says, "as if some hand had surreptitiously dropped something into the honeyed cup which gave it at certain times a new flavour. . . . When the feeling was roused by the sight of a small and beautiful or singular object, such as a flower, its sole effect was to intensify the object's loveliness." On other occasions, it became "so poignant as to frighten" him. The sunsets on the pampas, like those on the ocean, were often spectacular, and the sight of them "was sometimes almost more than [he] could endure and made [him] wish to hide [himself] away." Trees, with their annual resurrection and the murmurous language of their leaves, are among the most impressive of living things, and so it is not surprising that this feeling, as with Phillpotts and William Sharp, was evoked by them, especially when made unearthly by the pale shafts of the moon.

> Frequently, after I had first begun to experience it consciously, I would go out of my way to meet it, and I used to steal out of the house alone when the moon was at its full to stand, silent and motionless, near some group of large trees, gazing at the dusky green foliage silvered by the beams; and at such times the sense of mystery would grow until a sensation of delight would change to fear, and the fear increase until it was no longer to be borne, and I would hastily escape to recover the sense of reality and safety indoors, where there was light and company. Yet on the very next night I would steal out again and go to the spot where the effect was strongest, which was usually among the large locust or white acacia trees. . . . The loose feathery foliage on moonlight nights had a peculiar hoary aspect that made this tree seem more intensely alive than others, more conscious of my presence and watchful of me.

Later this feeling was also powerfully evoked by serpents and bird migration, and it is quite possible that the qualms of conscience Martin (the "little boy lost") felt after killing a spoonbill corre-

spond to some of Hudson's own when he was of much the same age.[2]
So deeply affecting were these experiences, he could not communicate them to anyone else, not even to his mother.

> The reason of my silence was, I think, my powerlessness to convey
> in words what I felt; but I imagine it would be correct to describe
> the sensation[s] . . . as similar to the feeling a person would have
> if visited by a supernatural being, if he was perfectly convinced that
> it was there in his presence, albeit silent and unseen, intently regard-
> ing him, and divining every thought in his mind. He would be
> thrilled to the marrow, but not terrified if he knew that it would
> take no visible shape nor speak to him out of the silence.

This animistic feeling, which, under the constant inspiration of
the immensities of the pampas, broadened into a panpsychic philosophy, became the guiding light of all his days. Impregnated with the
unfathomable spirit of the universe, many of the most familiar things
took on an air of mystery. By giving him a sense of oneness with all
things, it deepened his intimacy with the tangible world, particularly with animals. And by giving him the power to apprehend
nature mystically as well as sensuously, it urged him on to creativity
and became, as we shall see, the touchstone of his art. Moreover,
since the feeling of an indwelling spirit is "the root and essence of
all that is wonderful and sacred in nature," it early plumbed depths
beyond those reached by his mother's teachings about "the Supreme
Being," and led to states of mystical exaltation.

    This heightened awareness of nature did not isolate him from his
fellows. A robust lad, he could "easily outrun and out-jump" any
of his gaucho playmates, "even those . . . three or four years older,"
and readily acquired the knack of throwing the *bolas*. Afloat in a
cattle-trough and armed with home-made javelins, he and his
brothers once quested in a shallow winter lake near *Las Acacias* for
the venomous toadlike creatures that filled the night with croakings.
Eager to go duck-hunting, he chafed with impatience until allowed
to possess a gun. His two elder brothers made him the butt of many

---

2 In a letter to Roberts (March 29, 1917), Hudson says, "I had that feeling
[the instinctive idea of a monster 'that doth close behind (one) tread' in any
dark solitary place] so strongly in childhood that if I were a good artist with a
pencil I could make a startling portrait of the one who used always to follow me—
at nights among trees. . . . Out on the plains the sense of his presence was quite
faint and hardly frightened me."

a practical joke, but they were taken in good spirit. Only a severe wound brought to an end their practice sessions in the art of slashing with the *facón*. Occasionally called upon to do the chores of shepherd and herdsman, he, like the narrator of *Don Segundo Sombra,* soon became adept at most of them. He gloried in horseback-riding, finding its rhythmic, flightlike motion exhilarating not only to the body but also, as did Montaigne and others, to the mind.

As time went on, he found an increasing interest and pleasure in grown-ups. The search for birds took him to neighboring estancias, and often the persons met there were such as one finds only in out-of-the-way places: barrel-chested Blas Escovar, whose raised voice carried his words a quarter of a mile and whose mad yell at an intractable ox dropped the creature in the furrow stone-dead; Don Gregorio, with his toadlike gravity of expression and his mania for piebalds; Don Anastacio, the exquisite—putty in the hands of sycophantic poor relations but stubborn in his passion for breeding half-wild pigs; patriarchal Don Evaristo, helpful to those in distress and living peacefully with six wives and numerous offspring; and, among his English neighbors with their apathetic native wives, George Royd, who dreamed of making a fortune with sheep's-milk cheese and died a suicide. Though resenting many of their acts of cruelty, William came to accept the gauchos as fairly good human currency. "I was accustomed to ruffians even as a child," he later declared, "and did not find that they differed much from other men. . . ." He enjoyed their songs, ballads and tales, and was once an excited spectator at a recital in a *pulperia* that threatened to end in a duel with *facones.*

At the age of nine, William became "desperate[ly]" infatuated with a gaucho girl—delicately-featured, sprite-like Anjelita. Almost every day he would see her, with loose-hanging, jet-black hair caught in the wind, galloping bareback over the plain, always on some errand bent: driving in horses, rounding up sheep, or coming to his father's *pulperia* for provisions. He often yearned to say something that would lighten her expression and make her forget, if only for a moment, "the many cares and anxieties which made her so unnaturally grave. . . ." But before he could summon the courage, Anjelita and her anomalous kinsfolk vanished from the scene. Even if appropriate words had come, it is unlikely that he could have brought himself to utter them, for most boys are inarticulate in the expression of their deepest feelings, particularly in the presence of a girl.

Through exposure to many of the same influences as well as through intimate association, Hudson came to possess, in large measure, the spirit of the gauchos, including much of their primitive simplicity of mind, their rhythm of thought, and, especially in Spanish, their manner of expression. He had something of the Spanish graciousness of manner and the gaucho camp-fire wisdom, so close to that of nature. His tendency toward mysticism may have come from the Irish blood and the Quaker upbringing of his mother, but some of it came, as it did to the gauchos and their Moorish progenitors, from long acquaintance with the night and its constellations, which served as beacons over the lonely plains and as companions during a bivouac. There was also ingrained in him much of their melancholy, which found its chief expression in music. Most of all, he possessed the essential wildness of these primitive children of nature, their sense of identity with broad open spaces, their passion for freedom, their hatred of class distinctions, and their rebelliousness against the encroachments of civilization. Though he later associated with many sophisticated people, wherever he wandered (to use the phrasing of Don Segundo) these qualities of soul went before him, leading him like a bell mare.

In comparison with his experiences outdoors, those of the schoolroom (if such it may be called) and of books seemed tame indeed. After a while, his mother turned over instruction to occasional tutors, who were hired by the month like shepherds and herdsmen; but, since teaching was to them merely a stop-gap between more congenial employments or the easiest way of keeping body and soul together, William's formal education remained extremely desultory. One of the tutors, a former actor, delighted his small rancho audience, to whom novels were almost unknown, with dramatic readings from Dickens. Occasional visits to Buenos Aires were of some educational value, for, though it was then little more than a large frontier town, it brought him in touch with the wider world of men, including art galleries with their landscapes, and churches with their organ and orchestral music. It was perhaps well that his schooling was little and the visits to the capital infrequent, for education, as Thoreau has remarked, "often . . . makes a straight-cut ditch of a free, meandering brook" and sophistication is a great destroyer of the sense of the wonder of the world, which is one of our most precious possessions.

Until his mid-teens, this son of the pampas lived "in a paradise of vivid sense-impressions in which all thoughts came . . . saturated with emotion, and in that mental state reflection is well-nigh impossible." When he looked into books, it was to seek out something about nature, especially some expression of the ecstasy it evoked in him. And this expression he found mainly in poetry. Amongst the volumes his mother had brought with her was one of Shenstone, which, despite its artificiality and tameness, was continually reread, so desperate was he for any literature dealing with the outdoors. He learnt of the existence of many nature poets through long excerpts scattered in old natural history compilations, and it was in this way that acquaintance was made with Akenside and Hurdis. As with John Clare, his earliest real discovery among such poets was Thomson, whose *Seasons* he chanced upon while browsing in a second-hand shop in Buenos Aires. It was the first book in English that he ever purchased, and few were to bring him greater pleasure. Most of the other books on the shelves of his home—among them, Addison's and Leigh Hunt's *Essays,* Chesterfield's *Letters,* Rollin's *Ancient History,* Gibbon's *Decline and Fall,* Carlyle's *French Revolution,* and an eighteen-volume *History of Christianity*—held little interest for him until several long convalescences brought with them opportunities for reflection. Some years later, when again suffering from poor health, he read so omnivorously (probably in Spanish as well as in English) that he nearly went blind.

Unlike the typical child of Wordsworth's poem, William did not provoke the years to bring the inevitable yoke. What he dreaded most in early adolescence, we are told, was lest the "everlasting delight and wonder, rising to rapture, which was in the child and boy would wither away and vanish, and in its place there would be that dull low kind of satisfaction which men have in the set task, the daily and hourly intercourse with others of a like condition, and in eating and drinking and sleeping. [He] could not, for example, think of so advanced an age as fifteen without the keenest apprehension." In other words, he did not want to grow up into mere prose, to see the dreamlike freshness and glory of the world fade into the light of common day.

Unfortunately, at the most critical period of adolescence, when this dread of the loss of rapture was keenest, he had to endure a series of calamities. In 1856, his father suffered severe financial reverses, and the family was forced to return to their former home, *Los Veinte-cinco Ombúes,* which was all that was left. A year later, before fully recovering from an attack of typhus contracted in pestilential Buenos Aires, William was prostrated by rheumatic fever, which had been caught from a midwinter drenching while driving in cattle from a distance. In addition to a lengthy convalescence, there followed years of ill-health, with constant attacks of sharp pain and violent palpitations of the heart, and he was bluntly told by physicians that he "had a permanently bad heart and might drop down at any moment." This blow, coming when the mind is in its "most receptive stage" and "when the foundations of character and the entire life of the man are laid," and intensified as it was by still further ordeals, produced a psychological shock that left an indelible impression upon his spirit. As a result, there came into his imaginative vision of life, most noticeably in his romances, a sense of the beauty of the world fluttering like a bird upon the ground, wing-shattered. That the prognosis of these incompetent physicians proved in the end to be largely wrong does not matter, "since the injury had been done and could not be undone if [he] lived a century."

While in a weakened physical condition, he was assailed more violently than ever by the fear of death, which soon became enmeshed with religious doubts. Like the little boy in "Birds in a Village" who turned into a wryneck, he had early come upon the archenemy in the Eden of his pure joy in nature, and been terrified. No words ever affected him more, he says, than those of his tutor at the burial of their dog Caesar—words indicating the finality of death. Later, when Margarita, the beloved nurse of the household, died of consumption, he alone had hung back from the open coffin. "It was not grief," he confesses, "that gave me this sensation, much as I grieved; it was solely my fear of death." The sight and sound of cattle being slaughtered—the blood spurting from their throats and the dreadful moans and suffocating sobs—had brought the terror back in full force. His first direct encounter with death occurred at the time of the attack of typhus, but since he had not yet begun to reflect upon its true character, it was still regarded as "a person, a monstrous being who had sprung upon [him] in [his] flowery paradise and had inflicted a wound with a poisoned dagger in [his] flesh." A renewed belief in the immortality of the soul had at least temporarily closed the wound.

But the illness that left his heart impaired, and made him feel like a captive condemned to death by torture, opened and deepened the wound. So eager was Hudson for immortality that he would (he says) have accepted life among the eternally damned in preference to annihilation, if only his earth memories were vouchsafed him and he could "perhaps meet and have communion there with others of like mind . . . and with recollections like" his own. To dispel his agonizing doubts, he steeped himself in religious literature; but instead of encouraging him with some sign, it merely broadened the basis of his scepticism. The voice of "the supposed Evil One" often turned out to be nothing more than that of his "own reason striving to make itself heard." The absolute scepticism of an old gaucho and a passage chanced upon in a book of physiology contending that the desire for life in another world is not universal and therefore not a spiritual instinct were painful blows to his already distraught mind. Had religious doubts assailed him when not under the sentence of death, he might (so it seemed to him later) have thrown off all belief in revealed religion with the lightness of heart of his strong, sporting brother, Edwin, for when one is in perfect health, the mind refuses to admit the thought of death. Instead, however, the struggle went on, and became further intensified in 1859 by the passing of his mother, to whose nursing he probably owed his recovery.

The return of Edwin from the United States after an absence of five years led to its partial resolution. One of the first questions he put to William concerned his position in regard to the theory of evolution—a question that dumbfounded him, for he had not read a single line of *The Origin of Species*. The reading of his brother's copy led only to passionate rejection, "solely because [he] could not endure to part with a philosophy of life . . . which could not logically be held, if Darwin was right, and without which life would not be worth having." But though resisting the theory for years and always remaining critical of some parts of it, especially that dealing with natural selection, he "insensibly and inevitably" grew into an evolutionist, for, besides Wallace and Huxley and Spencer, Nature herself kept continually thrusting upon him proof upon proof, the most dramatic of which was the cruel way some species prey upon others.

Unable to reconcile an old faith with the devastating disclosures of the physical sciences and unwilling to embrace any "hope that asks less than a total courage," he became, somewhat in the manner of several of his characters in *Fan*, very much the sceptic—one though who contemplates the mysteries of life in the spirit of natural piety. Certain practices of the church came to grate upon his sensibilities, such as the "button-holing" of the Deity and the emotional barbecues of the "chapel people," which reminded him of a gigantic kite making "little tentative swoops to set" the congregated fowl "fluttering and screaming." Yet he always regarded Christianity, despite its shortcomings, as a beautiful exfoliation of the religious sensitivity of man. And frequently he went to church, not merely as a naturalist keeping in touch with the folklore of a people but for rest and companionship and some spiritual nourishment.

Though coming to terms with most of the conditions of life, he remained to the very end vulnerable to the fear of death. To a certain extent, this failure to reconcile himself to so natural a phenomenon may be regarded as a defect of character, for serenity of mind can scarcely be achieved until this fact has been assimilated. Because birth involves death should not make the interval between them less desirable, particularly if one has had some measure of fulfilment. Yet this fear (for varying reasons) has come to the strongest of men—to Cicero and Johnson, to Borrow and Morris and Tolstoy. With them, as with others who possess an enormous vitality and to whom the sensible world means much, it was but an expression of their profound love of life, a love that is innate and essentially unaffected by the rational faculty. Emotionally, the fear of death heightened still more the intensity of Hudson's delight in nature, just as encompassing blackness intensifies the qualities of almost every color.

There were other values derived from this period of crises. The photograph taken in his mid-twenties shows a man alive in every fiber of his being; and all who met him in later years, seeing his large, strongly sinewed frame and his indomitable energy, thought Nature had fashioned him for a life of strenuous physical adventure. As his essay "The War with Nature" indicates, he would have found much satisfaction in the activities of a pioneer. Toward the "still-life" of most artists, he often displayed the irritation of the man of action, declaring on one occasion that to him the career of any adventurer would have been preferable to that of Tennyson. By making such a career impracticable, his rheumatic heart deprived him not only of a sense of security but of easy access to what should have been his most natural source of happiness. On the other hand, it gave him many and long intervals of leisure in which to think and feel as well as to read, and thereby released in him aspects of personality that might otherwise have remained hidden—the reflective and the artistic. Besides, is not happiness the prime enemy of art?

Although he had to be careful for some time, the intervals between the bouts of ill-health lengthened. Longer and longer periods were spent in the outdoors, Nature in her cyclic loveliness becoming for him, as it did for Abel in his great sorrow, the principal *"vis medicatrix."* After a while, his old mystical joy in the sights and sounds of earth returned, coming often "like a sudden ray of sunlight in a dark place," particularly during the periods of bird migration. The reading of Thomas Brown, the philosopher, and some of the early nineteenth-century nature poets convinced him that he need fear no longer the loss of rapture upon stepping across the threshold of manhood. No matter how wearisome the ways of the workaday world that lay before him, he felt assured that nature would remain an opening wonder and that he could always find kindred spirits, if not among the living, at least among the dead.

Heretofore, one of the main shortcomings in Hudson's training as a field naturalist was his failure to take notes—the best way of "remembering not to forget." Once he and his brothers started a journal—each depositing his contributions in a tin box, from which they were collected by their tutor and copied out on a large sheet of paper—but, since the youngest of them could not be wangled out of any of his pocket-money, the project soon collapsed. It was probably not until after his long convalescence that he began the practice of recording his observations, a practice which proved to be a valuable apprenticeship in the art of writing. The reading of Gilbert White suggested to him the possibility of making La Plata his "parish of Selborne." And in order to assist him in this task, he kept supplementing his watchings and ponderings with a fuller and fuller reading in the various provinces of natural history.

From the going-out of youth until the meeting with Roberts in 1880, little is known of Hudson's life.[3] At eighteen, he trained with the National Guard for Indian-fighting;[4] and at nineteen, for a while took charge of the sheep-shearing at a bankrupt estate, keeping the books, weighing the wool, and paying the shearers. From time to time he lent a hand at cattle-markings and partings, and, admiring the natural grace and dignity of manner to be found in most women of Spanish descent, joined wholeheartedly in the accompanying festivities. The driving of large flocks of sheep and visits to his brother's ranch took him across the Rio de la Plata to the Banda Oriental, over the western pampas of La Plata, and southward to Cape Corrientes and the Sierra de la Ventana. Most of his leisure was spent in observing the various modes of wild life, especially those of birds, which by this time, so much did they gladden his heart, were probably becoming something of a symbol. His "dreams by night," he tells us, "were often of some . . . bird . . . which had never been named and never ever seen by any appreciative human eye"—dreams that were "a grief to wake from." In order to watch them in one of their most secluded haunts, he spent a summer at a herdsman's hut in a swampy forest bordering the Rio de la Plata. By his early twenties, his activities as an ornithologist had brought him in touch with Burmeister, the director of the National Museum at Buenos Aires.

Through Burmeister, he met H. R. Helper, the American Consul to the Argentine, who by letter introduced him to Baird of the Smithsonian Institution. It was for the Smithsonian that from 1866 to 1868 he collected over five hundred bird-skins, most of them from the district around *Los Veinte-cinco Ombúes*. So eager was Hudson "to give [his] whole time to a pursuit that afford[ed him] so much pleasure" that he offered to furnish "a concise account" of the habits of each species and, besides, to collect fossils and specimens of indigenous insects and plants. Nothing came of this proposal, for in the meantime Baird had sent some of the skins to Sclater,

---

3 To avoid repetition, I have omitted or merely alluded to some of the material that might have been included in the remaining pages of this chapter. The biographical sketch, therefore, should not be considered complete until the end of the book has been reached.

4 His being ill much of the time so worried his captain that, despite a liking for the budding ornithologist, he occasionally wished him dead.

secretary to the London Zoological Society and an authority on neo-tropical ornithology, who soon opened to Hudson wider opportu-nities as a field-worker. From 1869 until his arrival in England, he kept sending Sclater, along with some birds and mammals, an inter-esting series of letters and articles, which, after being edited, were published in the *Proceedings* of the society and thus launched him on his literary career.

In one of these letters, he asserted that Darwin was wrong in adducing from the habits of carpinteros "an argument in favour of his theory of the origin of species. . . . It is not only the erroneous account of this bird's habits that makes" Darwin's mention of it "peculiarly unfortunate, but also because this bird rather affords an argument against the truth of [his] hypothesis. . . . Natural selec-tion has done absolutely nothing for our Woodpecker." Darwin rarely paid any attention to such attacks, but to this one he made immediate rebuttal. While admitting the error in regard to the climbing of trees, he supported the rest of his statement by stress-ing the fact that habits vary somewhat according to the locale. Later, after observing the carpintero in Patagonia, Hudson realized he had been generalizing from too limited a purview, and in *Birds of La Plata* incorporated Darwin's conclusions. Because of this attack and certain other criticisms scattered in his writings, Darwin's son avoided making Hudson's acquaintance, but when at length confronted by so large-spirited a man, he was soon disarmed.

The voyage to the Rio Negro region of Patagonia in late 1870 was undertaken not only to collect animals and extend his knowl-edge of bird migration but also to explore the burial-places of Stone Age man. When chancing upon some relic of the Indians who had once roamed over La Plata, he was accustomed to try to recreate in his imagination the sort of life they had lived, but since such memorials were few, their ways remained for him little more than a tradition or a fable. The evidences of paleolithic and neolithic man along the valley of the Rio Negro were however so many and im-pressive that, with Dumnonian memories surging strongly in him, he could more readily project himself into their more remote world and dwell there. This reaching out of the imagination, coming as it did when (because of his profound affinity for the desolate plains) his unconscious primitive self was revealed to him in its "original nakedness," brought a permanent sense of fellowship with these long-vanished and forgotten peoples. And this sense strengthened the monolithic quality in his personality, often making him appear, especially in later years, as old as humanity. Besides these influences and a general deepening of certain other characteristics acquired on the pampas, his stay in Patagonia, as we shall see later, was important in his artistic development. On his homeward journey, he had, like Alfred Wallace, the misfortune of losing the finest specimens of his collection—a blow harder to bear, so he claimed, than the gunshot wound that had laid him up for several months.

Just why he left South America in 1874 one cannot be sure. The death of his father six years earlier had cut the remaining parental tie, and all but his youngest sister had left *Los Veinte-cinco Ombúes*. If he had been inclined to possess a ranch of his own, the want of money and the uncertainty of his health would have held him back. His journal kept growing fuller and fuller, and, with two decades of memorabilia in it, must have become voluminous. How all these memorabilia, some of them not of strictly scientific interest, were to be presented to the public must have become a matter of some concern. He was probably unable to find round him the sort of friends who could have been of much help in such a presentation, nor were there, in so Spanish-speaking a country, many opportunities for publication, let alone wide circulation. In England, as his correspondence with Sclater and his articles in the *Proceedings of the London Zoological Society* seemed to indicate, there were such opportunities. Perhaps, too, he was thinking already of turning to other kinds of writing, which would find a far better market in England.

Besides—and this must have been an important strand in his thinking—he had for long regarded Great Britain as his spiritual home. Since there was in his day little immigration from the United States, the English-speaking neighbors and friends of his family were in the main English and Scotch, whose love for the Old Country frequently became intensified by distance into a romantic attachment. And since there was little American literature exported during his youth, his reading had been primarily of British authors. Still more subtly persuasive was the call of blood and ancestral home.

> Before I knew it the Exe was a beloved stream. . . . My forefathers had dwelt for generations beside it, listening all their lives long to its

music, and when they left it they still loved it in exile, and died at last with its music in their ears. Nor did the connection end there; their children and children's children doubtless had some inherited memory of it; or how came I to have this feeling, which made it sacred, and drew me to it? We inherit not from our ancestors only, but, through them, something, too, from the earth and place that knew them.

Had Hudson remained in South America, he would probably have become a greater naturalist. Perhaps he might also have become the author of *The Purple Land, Tales of the Pampas,* and *Far Away and Long Ago,* but since his artistic sensibilities would not have been so finely quickened, these books may not have turned out to be quite so impressive as works of art. There is little likelihood, however, that he would have become a fellow of Montaigne and Thoreau, for an essayist in the Argentine of that day, because of the economic pressure, would have lacked the "shelter to grow ripe" and the "leisure to grow wise." Had he come to the United States instead of to England, he might have gained earlier recognition, but at least a part of his personality would not have been so charmingly revealed, for though there is more wildness and sublimity in America, the English have a more thorough appreciation of their countryside, where man and nature have for many centuries been living in harmony.

From time to time, even after gaining recognition, he would grow "sick with longing" for the scenes of his youth,

> Where dwells unsullied loveliness,
> With calm and peace divine,
> Far in the untrodden wilderness.

Having experienced the freedom of life on the pampas, he became so galled by the demands of an industrialized society that it assumed in his imagination the form of "a huge Clapham Junction, with human creatures moving like trucks and carriages on cast-iron conventional rails, which they can only leave at the risk of a destructive collision." And when he thought of the great variety of birds in the land of his birth, England seemed almost a country "of glorified poultry-farms." Then, too, with pampean roots continually tugging within him, transplantation became a slow process. It is possible to interpret his failure to take out naturalization papers until after twenty-five years of residence as further proof that he looked upon himself for a long time as somewhat of an alien.

But he never went back. At first, poverty and an unwillingness to admit defeat prevented him. By the end of the 'eighties, when one of his brothers, living in western Argentina, offered to finance him should he care to continue his South American adventures, it was too late. He was in the midst of publishing a book, and had several others in the throes of composition, one of which was to point him the way to his finest achievements. Moreover, he did not like the changes that were transforming the pampas—the giant grasses giving way to the plough; the large estancias fenced off into small farms, which were worked not by gauchos but by miserable peons; and the flooding of the land with a "withering stream of Italian emigration." The gauchos had killed few birds except the rhea, which was hunted with the *bolas*, but the Italians appreciated "Dame Nature's minstrels" merely "for [their] flavour"—a reputation that has followed them round the world. To have beheld the pampas again so changed would have meant the shattering of the picture that had long been treasured in his memory.

In the meantime England was gaining a stronger and stronger hold upon him—the astonishingly brilliant hue of its greenery, the patchwork-quilt of tilth, pasture and woodland, the downs of the southern and western counties, the many secluded villages and earth-loving villagers. Especially attractive to one with such profound atavistic moods were the many evidences of a rich and immemorial past—cathedrals, ancient monuments, and barrows. Though he might have lived a fuller life emotionally and adventurously in South America, there was stimulation in the mental climate of Europe and deep satisfaction in artistic achievement—in the knowledge that he was capturing in volume after volume much of the beauty fast vanishing both from the pampas and from the face of England. In the end, he came to feel a passionate love for his adopted country, many parts of which were to his eyes "demi-paradise."

As he soon realized, "success in almost any calling in England, unless the aspirant happens to be endowed with energies and talents almost superhuman, depends in a great measure on the possession of money." And so, after a few happy months of wandering about the countryside, he found himself caged in "lurid London," unable for years to make more than an occasional short flight to wild, green places. Because of his dependence upon personal intimacy with living creatures in their native habitats as the basis of his knowledge, he, like Fabre, was usually ill-at-ease with those whose knowledge was derived primarily from books, museums and zoos; and "remote control" naturalists and specialists were, in turn, suspicious of him because of his interest in the poetic as well as the prose truth of observation and in the relationship of each object to the whole of experience. Chafing in tandem harnessing, he soon discovered collaboration with Sclater far less congenial than anticipated. He ran afoul of John Gould, one of the chief collectors in a period dominated by collecting, and also "the doyen of the Ornithological world," Alfred Newton, both of whom regarded him as a trespasser upon their preserves. Laborious writer that he always was, the projects that occupied most of his attention for the first decade and a half, a long history of the House of Lamb (of which *The Purple Land* is only a part) and *Argentine Ornithology*, were a long time in the process of composition. Thus, instead of making much headway toward recognition as an ornithologist and as a novelist, he found himself struggling just to keep body and soul together. He had to resort to short articles on birds for various periodicals and such miscellaneous writing as the essay "Wanted, a Lullaby," which often appeared anonymously or pseudonymously. For a while he was even secretary to an archaeologist who, finding little remuneration in his chosen field, "made a somewhat precarious living by discovering, perhaps concocting, genealogies for Americans who were ready to pay for ancestors real or spurious." Becoming a victim of his employer's chronic insolvency, he was in great danger of being cast adrift on the dark waters of London poverty.

In his essay "On the Want of Money," Hazlitt lists among its consequences: "to be a thrall to circumstances, . . . to forego leisure, freedom, ease of body and mind, . . . [to] earn a precarious and irksome livelihood by some laborious employment, . . . [and] to marry your landlady." Within almost two years after his arrival in England, all these things came to pass in Hudson's life, even to the marrying of his landlady, Emily Wingrave, a former concert and opera singer. Though some fifteen years his senior (a fact he did not know until much later), she still possessed a voice that seemed to him, so deeply was he moved by it, even more beautiful than that of her friend, Adelina Patti. It was natural that Emily, on her part, should have been strongly attracted to this tall, bronzed Argentinean, with his romantic background and his scientific and literary gifts. Time revealed, however, that neither of them was truly in love with the other, and that their marriage was primarily one of companionship.

In order to provide him with the necessary leisure for writing, she took upon herself the main burden of making a livelihood, continuing to run the boarding-house and giving lessons in music. Hudson was always grateful for her faith in him and for her humble, unselfish devotion. Though slower of foot "than the poor proverbial snail or tortoise," she was occasionally, as we see in his letters and in *Afoot in England,* his companion on his walks about the countryside, and together they shared many experiences with nature. "That bond uniting us," he once declared, "unlike all other bonds, was unbreakable and everlasting." She is the one referred to in "The Return of the Chiff-Chaff" who "led [him], waist-deep in the flowering meadow grasses, to look for" the bog-bean, "and called it our 'English edelweiss.' " Whenever parted from her, he wrote daily; when she became an invalid, he forwent many of his pleasures in order to be with her, and until his own health gave way, attended her with devoted care.

Yet, as almost all who have written portraits of them realized, the marriage was a blunder, since his wings were fledged for a wide sweep of sky and hers, for hardly more than an aviary. Beyond the gift of a lovely voice, an abundance of golden hair, and a "beautiful look of kindness," she was just an ordinary woman, who could give her husband little mental or, except in the presence of nature, spiritual companionship. They enjoyed evenings of music with his, rather than her, friends, but after her voice faded and the conversation turned to scientific or literary matters, she, being unable to take part, would withdraw to her own nook. Later, when Hudson became famous and was sought after by feminine admirers, she grew resentful of any attention he might show them—a resentment that prompted him to have inscribed under her name on their tombstone the words "I will not fail thee." As for him, though attracted to women and in possession of normal instincts, he was not by temperament the marrying sort. He loved all nature as his bride, and probably no woman, even had she come earlier into his life, could have kept him close for long.

Poverty continued to hound them for over a quarter of a century. Since Emily, partly because of her ready sympathies, was a poor business woman, boarding-house after boarding-house went bankrupt. Between such failures, she "trudged about teaching girls without voices and temperaments to howl opera, and those without music to beat a wretched piano." Still groping about as an artist and plagued not only with a "stammering" heart but by attacks of bronchitis, pleurisy and pneumonia, he could not help much toward filling the larder. After real privation—one week there was nothing to eat but "a tin of cocoa and milk"—they were at last able to settle down in a large but drab house near the Paddington Station, which had been left, heavily mortgaged, to Emily by a sister. Here they eked out an existence by renting the lower rooms as flats. A pathetic revelation of the difficulties of these years is to be found in *Afoot in England*:

> When life had little or no other pleasure for us on account of poverty and ill-health, [walks] were taken at pretty regular intervals two or three times a year. It all depended on our means; in very lean years there was but one outing. It was impossible to escape altogether from the immense unfriendly wilderness of London simply because, albeit "unfriendly," it yet appeared to be the only place in the wide world where our poor little talents could earn us a few shillings a week to live on. Music and literature! but I fancy the nearest crossing-sweeper did better, and could afford to give himself a more generous dinner every day. It occasionally happened that an article sent to some magazine was not returned, and always after so many rejections to have one accepted and paid for with a cheque worth several pounds was a cause of astonishment, and was as truly a miracle as if the angel of the sun had compassionately thrown us down a handful of gold. And out of these little handfuls enough was sometimes saved for the country rambles at Easter and Whitsuntide and in the autumn.

Hudson had to wait almost twenty years for recognition, and still another decade before the specter of the ultimate workhouse was removed. Though his first volume, *The Purple Land,* published in 1885 at the age of forty-four, was applauded by Professor A. H. Keane—"the first taste of praise [he] ever had"—it was in general indifferently reviewed, and a large number of the copies had to be remaindered. *Argentine Ornithology,* finally completed four years later, brought him recognition as a specialist, but Sclater received the lion's share of the royalties. His out-of-door essays were finding their way only slowly into periodicals, being "always [so he remarked] 'too' something for editors—or else not 'too' something enough." How desperate was his plight even after the publication of such distinguished books as *The Naturalist in La Plata, Idle Days in Patagonia,* and *Birds in a Village,* we may glean from Gissing's letters, in one of which, written in 1901, he exclaims: "I do hope his friends will not allow him to end his life in the workhouse." As late as 1916, he was without sufficient funds to send his wife to an invalid home.

Over these years, he made some valuable friendships. In 1880 began his long intimacy with Morley Roberts, a good anvil upon which to fashion his thoughts. Among the artists to whom Roberts introduced him, he was attracted to the etcher Alfred Hartley, who did some of the illustrations for *Idle Days* and acquainted him with the advantages of Shoreham. It was in his studio that in 1889 he met Gissing, whose spirit had also been bruised by London poverty and who, though a bookish man, was an amateur botanist and an ardent lover of nature. The four of them, despite considerable differences of temperament, felt congenial in each other's company, as may be judged from a letter Gissing wrote to his sister in the autumn of that year: "I had a great party here the other evening. Roberts, Hudson and Hartley. Great was the talk, portentous the tobacco-smoke; huge the laughter; boundless the scorn of critics and the public." It was he who "dubbed the quartette the Quadrilateral, after the Italian fortresses." A year or so later, through the appearance of an essay of his on the Argentine, Hudson met Cunninghame Graham, that *"singularisimo escritor inglés"* (as he is described in one of the few dedications), who likewise had known the pampas before they were invaded by a locustry of immigrants. Shortly afterwards, he became acquainted with the Greys of Fallodon, who gave him the occasional use of their Hampshire cottage and were instrumental in securing for him, in 1901, a Civil List pension of £150, which, so he declared to Gissing, made him "a rich man."

Next to his own wife and Viscount Grey, it was Edward Garnett who saved him from poverty. One of the leaders of literary London, he gave Hudson, as in the rewriting of *Green Mansions,* excellent critical advice, championed him in the reviews, and marketed him well. With the countryside made increasingly accessible by the bicycle and the automobile, his books began to find a wider audience; but until *A Shepherd's Life,* which plumbs deepest into the English rural heritage, none of them sold more than a thousand copies. It took *Green Mansions* twelve years to reach popularity, and then primarily through a foreword by Galsworthy. Appealing as this romance does to some of the most fundamental yearnings of "a generation self-shut out of Eden," its sale in America became large enough to put a new publisher on his feet. With editors now beginning (as he put it) to throw "money at him with both hands," he insisted upon giving up his pension.

Yet adversity, like a toad, ugly and venomous, wore a precious jewel in its head, for it brought with it some important compensations. The early sense of exile in England, like that of Jefferies in London, deepened him emotionally and quickened his imagination. The impact of a mechanized society and drab surroundings, like the grain of sand in the flesh of an oyster, gave him the impulse to conceive *A Crystal Age* and to choose the most primitive of settings for *Green Mansions.* From his unfortunate marriage, we gain Rima, the greatest of all his character creations, and also some of the poignancy there is in his essays on little girls. The sense of nostalgia that came with the continual surge of memories of his native land, making him feel at times that his life had indeed ended with his departure, aided him in vintaging them well. Then, too, if he had found early success as a novelist, some of the rareness in the man might have been lost in the professional writer, and his true métier, the out-of-door essay, never fully explored. And so intense did his "green thirst" become in the brick wilderness of London that when he took his outings at Easter and Whitsuntide and in the autumn, his awareness of nature was considerably heightened.

Though leaving scars, the long delay in recognition and, later, the failure to receive much of the fruit along with the flowers of praise did no damage to his spirit. Rather than truckle to popular taste or shift to another way of life, he chose to live, so he wrote to Cunninghame Graham in the mid-'nineties, "on 'rather' less than £100 a year and be free—yes, free even from life's 'pleasures.'" He kept following the vision within, and before the preparation of each volume, was careful that the springs of observation and of wisdom had filled up again and were overflowing. As to the value of his various writings, he was, from the beginning, quite willing to let "the wise years decide." Hostile criticism that was beside the mark he attributed, not, as did John Davidson, to the malignancy of the critic but rather to his ignorance, and it was a rule with him never to reply. To keep his spirit refreshened and poised, there was always the companionship of Nature, who "is immortal and has green hair and green eyes, and her body and soul are green, and to those who live with and love her she gives a green soul as a special favour."

Frequently Hudson disclaimed any great interest in books or knowledge of them. "I am not a great reader, and know few books"; on most literary matters "I therefore speak as a fool, or, at all events, an ignorant person." But reading nourished his depths more than he realized, and the long periods of ill-health made him even something of a man of letters. Preferring to make discoveries of his own rather than document those of others (as many were doing for Darwin at that time), he used books in his special field of knowledge primarily as aids to his own observations, and thus, though well-read, never became, in an academic sense, learned. He did not want to lose his originality, as many have done, through too keen an admiration for the writings of others. In poetry, if not in philosophy, he ranged widely. He was acquainted with many Continental authors besides the Spanish—finding especial pleasure in the company of the great Russian novelists, who were being steadily translated by Constance Garnett, the wife of his friend. His knowledge of contemporary literature, some of the best of it written by friends, was remarkably broad and catholic. Always he read critically, and never suffered from literary flatulence.

As many have testified, Hudson was an extraordinarily full and well-rounded human being. To a marked degree, most of the major as well as many of the minor virtues were his: vitality and zest for life, despite ill-health; curiosity as to the nature of the physical universe; courage, both moral and intellectual; a wide spread of mind that could irrigate many provinces of thought; a certain mystical power to see into the heart of things; and a Schweitzer-like reverence for life in its myriads of forms—all harmoniously integrated in his personality. Never losing his simplicity amidst the complexities of existence, he seemed completely unconscious of being amongst the elect of literature. "He could and would play," says Roberts, "with a child or bird or dog or cat as if he were upon their level, and then turn swiftly to things of intuition and philosophy and deep speculation without any strain or pose or affectation." The most remarkable quality of his personality—the flower of the man—was the reconciliation in him of much of the best of civilization with the wild in nature and the primitive in man, giving to his life and work the appearance of a Doric edifice on prehistoric foundations.

Though by temperament and pursuits a solitary, he often enjoyed companionship. With an interesting fellow-traveller, he was always ready to strike up an acquaintance. It was his practice to live intimately with the cottagers at whose homes he stayed, eating at their tables and even attending family prayers; and their "glad welcome" he found to be, as did Cobbett and Hardy, "one of the sweetest things in life." The only outstanding man of science he ever really warmed to was Sir Arthur Keith, but among his literary friends (besides those already mentioned) were Wilfrid Blunt, Joseph Conrad, John Galsworthy, Norman Douglas, Hilaire Belloc, Henry Salt, Ford Madox Ford, T. E. Lawrence, H. J. Massingham, W. H. Davies, Robert Lynd, and Edward Thomas. (The keenness of his insight into the essential genius of some of them is evident in his urging Masefield, before the appearance of *The Everlasting Mercy,* to turn from fiction to narrative poetry and Roberts to abandon the novel, and in his early recognition of the poet in Thomas.) Very enjoyable to him was lunching with those who went to *Mont Blanc* and having them foregather of an evening in his own home.

What he valued most in people were depth of feeling, strength of character, familiarity with country things, adventurous living in the open, and originality, which, particularly in authors, "is after all the main thing." In women, by far the chief requirement was charm. If there was no real basis for sympathy or at least a flow of fresh observations, an acquaintance was quickly—and sometimes rudely—dropped. Where there was sympathy, and friendship freely offered, he was generous and faithful, though not in a demonstrative way. Because of his frequent failure to acknowledge affection and his faculty of instantaneous detachment, some of his acquaintances thought him indifferent or cold, and a certain irritability, largely the result of recurring illness and the coming-on of old age, alienated others. Rarely did he care to have any of his friends with him when "in the woods or any wild place." Once, in a moment of for-

getfulness, he invited Richard Curle to watch geese on the marshes
near Wells-next-the-Sea, but even before his guest's arrival, he was
troubled with regrets. Curle did not watch with him long, and
after this experience it seems quite probable that "no one else ever
was asked."

Hudson's presence was in itself impressive: great height somewhat reduced by a "thoughtful stoop of [the] head, as though he
for ever leant to hear what lesser folks had to say"; small, grave,
weathered face, with a peaked Spanish beard accentuating its beak-
like sharpness and "always slightly screwed together like the faces
of men looking to windward in a gale"; a shock of wavy, wind-
blown hair; and hazel-brown eyes peering from beneath prominent
brows eagle-keen or, from time to time, suffused with a kindly
sparkle. Though, like most outdoor men and Nature herself, slow
and deliberate in expression, he possessed an inexhaustible store of
anecdotes and brought to bear upon any subject a fresh and unconventional mind—the unpredictability of his comments being one of
his charms. Masefield met only one person who was his equal as
a teller of tales; Galsworthy thought his talk "the most truly original [he had] ever listened to"; and through all the years of their
friendship Garnett never heard him repeat himself. His sense of
humor—grave or whimsical or puckish—was peculiarly his own,
and his sense of the ridiculous became most acute when an egotist
could be espied in a grotesque posture. Being what he was, his very
silences were pregnant.

Many are the evidences of his concern for others. Once he was
eager to adopt a girl who had become alienated from her fanatically
religious parents—probably the model for Constance Churton in
Fan. Seeing that one of his nurses at a Catholic hospital, a novitiate
about to take final vows, was not following the real bent of her
personality, he persuaded her to return to the fuller, more natural
life—counsel for which she lived to thank him. At the risk of his
own life, he aided Roberts in the rescuing of three girls, whom a
current off the Shoreham beach had carried out beyond their depths.
Toward Thomas he felt as toward a son, and when the news of
his death in the Arras battle came, he was moved to tears. And
there was in him not only the creative influence of a rich and singular personality but also the power to inspire love in others. Thomas
once said, "Except William Morris there is no other man whom I

would sometimes like to have been, no other writing man"; and Massingham has declared, "He laid his hands upon me. He did more than give a meaning to my pilgrimage into wild places." The feeling of villagers toward him is suggested by their carving these words upon a stone: "W. H. Hudson used to sit here."

Yet he was essentially a lonely man, feeling, as did Montaigne, that one "must eftsoons love this or that, but wed nothing but himself." Earlier than most of us, he had learnt "that in all our most intimate thoughts and reflections concerning our destiny and our deepest emotions, we are and must be alone." In such matters, as his letters clearly indicate, he never desired a confidant. Much of this sense of isolation came as a result of being often alone with nature, but there was also "something in his character," as Roberts remarks, "which forbade him to abandon his soul to others. He kept it in a strong secret place, as those fabled giants in ancient myths keep theirs." Curle's portrait of him watching geese amidst the Norfolk marshes shows him against one of the most suggestive of backgrounds: "a lone figure blending into the universal gloom and seemingly an integral part of the tragic landscape."

Thanks to the vitality of his senses, which his mystical faculty kept quickening to rapture, and to the insatiable curiosity of his mind, he remained, like Hardy, Bridges and Freud, fresh to the very end of his life. As the prospect of dissolution thrust itself more and more upon his attention, he often repeated to himself a line from Melendez: *Es amargo al final de la vida caminar triste y solo.* "I hate the thought" of dying, he wrote to a friend, "as much now as when I was a boy—when this visible world looked a very wonderful and beautiful place to spend an eternity in." He had warmed both hands before the fire of life, but, unlike that other untrammeled octogenarian, he was *not* ready to depart. At the end of his last book, he had written, "No sooner have I finished a book, than I come, rover-like, to hate it: a proper instinct." But there was to be no more roving. Death would have been more acceptable to him, so he believed, had he been able to count on a few more score years of friendship with earth and sky, insects and beasts and birds. Eighty-one springs seemed too few before having to dwell in an eternally silent village.

Bitter though such thoughts were, there must have been others to assuage them. The country of his youth had become transformed in his memory to the beauty of dream, and the dream of his youth—the England of the nature poets and landscape painters—had become a reality. And he had been able to catch in essay after essay the dream as well as the reality. Moreover, he had been instrumental in establishing throughout England many sanctuaries for birds, and had willed the bulk of his earthly substance for the fuller appreciation and preservation of them. Like Wordsworth and Thoreau, he had devoted much thought to the bringing of men into a closer alliance and harmony with nature as a whole, so that "the religion of humanity" might have "a deeper, tougher, woodier root in our soil." And, though a cairn or a barrow on a down would have made a more appropriate grave than that in the Broadwater Cemetery at Worthing, he died, as he wished, like a stricken deer or guanaco—alone.

The Out-of-Door Essay

God hath spread the earth for you like a carpet, that ye may walk therein along spacious paths.

—KORAN LXXI

Nature consists not only in itself, objectively, but at least just as much in its subjective reflection from the person, spirit, age, looking at it, in the midst of it, and absorbing it—faithfully sends back the characteristic beliefs of the time or individual—takes, and readily gives again, the physiognomy of any nation or literature—falls like a great elastic veil on a face, or like the molding plaster on a statue.

—WHITMAN

THE ROOTS OF our appreciation of nature extend deep into Mediterranean antiquity. Hellenic religion, which sprang from the worship of the sensible world, kept the people in close and imaginative touch with its various forms, metamorphosing many of them into such figures as hamadryads, nymphs, oreads, Proteus rising from the sea, old Triton blowing his wreathèd horn, and Aurora making the welkin flash with her tremendous team. The early philosophers of Ionic Greece discovered nature as a theme for meditation, and soon became engrossed in the physical interpretation of the universe. Their influence was sufficiently strong to make Aristotle the first great student of natural history, many of whose findings, such as those on the migratory habits of mackerel and tunny, the sound-mechanism of the cicada, and the egg-laying of the working-bees, show remarkable powers of observation. In classical literature there are passages on nature that linger in the memory: sensitive vignettes of landscape and seascape in Sappho, Aeschylus, Catullus and Ovid; intimate sights and sounds of the countryside in the Greek Anthology and in Theocritus; such generic portraits of animals as those of the nautilus by Aristotle and the cock and the nightingale by Pliny; many everyday incidents of animal life in Aesop's fables; glimpses of Horace's farm amidst the Sabine hills; various arts of husbandry in Hesiod, Xenophon and Virgil, along with delineations of flowers, trees, insects, birds and beasts; and the vast, elemental panoramas of Lucretius, with heavy surf pounding against rocky shores, mountainous masses of clouds flashing bolts of lightning, and hurricanes hurling themselves against "the ramparts of the mighty world." Occasionally, as in the Plinys, Virgil and Lucretius, there is even some suggestion of a Wordsworthian feeling for Nature.

Yet, all told, such passages do not bulk large in the art of the times. For Socrates, rarely moved to thought by animals or plants or countryside, focussed his attention upon man. Discovering a soul there, he bifurcated the universe into spirit and matter, and made the mind of man the earthly citadel of the spirit. He and Plato and their followers so effectively fortified the frontiers of the human and the divine against those of the natural world that they were able to deflect Greek philosophy from nature to the realm of man. With the later assistance of the Ptolemaic theory of the universe and the spiritual aspiration of Christianity, the direction they gave to thinking persisted, almost unchallenged, into the Renaissance. Man, given heroic stature only a little short of that of gods or angels, became the preoccupation of art, and nature, however much it might have meant in everyday life, was brought in primarily as background. The landscapes most enjoyed were cultivated ones smilingly subservient to human demands, and, though domestic animals found place in their affections, most wild ones were looked upon with a hunter's eye and there was little sense of kinship with the brute creation as a whole.

For many centuries, the Christian church remained extremely hostile toward nature. Never having identified her own deities with natural objects,[1] she regarded the creatures of classical mythology as demons; and though animals play a prominent rôle in the biographies of the saints and were frequently kept as pets in nunneries and monasteries, to have referred to the "spirit" of any of them would have opened oneself to the charge of witchcraft. Even St. Francis, since he knew little animal psychology, appreciated them in the main sentimentally—as celebrants of the goodness and grandeur of God rather than for their own selves. Later, Protestantism, which appeals to the more northern mind, considerably modified or overcame this hostility. But to this day, the Catholic Church, significantly, withholds her blessing from groups seeking the protection of animals.

During the Middle Ages, there was little intellectual interest in the external world, and as a result natural history lost much of the ground that had been gained. Peasants, it is true, still retained some of the lore of the husbandman and woodsman, and the nobles delighted in falconry and in hunting the deer and the boar; but, even with the clergy, the interest was almost entirely utilitarian. Instead of adding to their inheritance from Dioscorides and Theophrastus, botanists became fascinated by certain plants with supposedly magical properties and by the theory of signatures; and, in most minds, the zoology of Aristotle and Pliny shrank to a few

---

1 "The proudest boast of [the] highest intellects" of the Jews, so Hudson reminds us, "was that they had never bowed in reverence or kissed their hand to anything in nature" (*The Book of a Naturalist,* p. 168).

distortions of memory, some of which are preserved for us in the bestiaries, where whimsically they are made to serve a moral turn. Even so learned a man as Bartholomew, who was not incapable of fresh and loving observation of domestic animals, made statements in his *De proprietatibus rerum* (c. 1250; in English, 1397) that could have been corrected by the most casual use of the eye. Some of them, such as the one that bees load themselves with small stones as ballast against a strong wind, were mere echoes of Aristotle, whose infallibility it was dangerous to question. Centuries were to elapse before the large accretions of legend could be removed from natural history.

As long as nature was regarded as a foe to be overcome, most people remained cold to its aesthetic appeal. By the time of the troubadours and minnesingers, when many parts of northern Europe had been brought under control, nature began to appear again in literature, usually in the form of trim castle gardens, meadows star-scattered with flowers, and, in England and France, an occasional woodland—all seen as backgrounds for human activities. Since there is little evidence of close observation in these scenes, it is difficult to tell how much of the enjoyment they represent was genuine and how much merely conventional. Now and then, however, we do come upon some vividly intimate description and even a pleasure in the sterner aspects of the earth, especially in the more northern poets: the author of *Pearl* and *Sir Gawain and the Green Knight,* Henryson, Dunbar, and Douglas. Many later writers on the out-doors have been attracted to Chaucer's "child-like delight in sights and sounds and smells" and the broadness of his sympathy for many forms of life, Burroughs asserting that "there is more of spring in a line or two of [his] . . . than in the elaborate portraits of her by Thomson," and Hudson, that while in "Wordsworth and Ruskin, nature appears . . . as a picture—it has no sound, no smell, no *feel* [—] in Chaucer you have it all in its fullest expression; he alone is capable of saying, in some open woodland space with the fresh smell of earth in his nostrils, that this is more to him than meat or drink or any other thing, and that since the beginning there was never anything so pleasant known to no earthly man." Though we have still a long time to wait for much real interest in animals for their own sake, there are to be found, here and there—in choir stalls and the illuminations of manuscripts as well as in literature—striking delineations of them, Hudson noting, for example, the "wonderful onomatopoetic lines" of Dunbar describing the tempest of noise that comes from an aroused gathering of birds.

The Renaissance brought with it a very different concept of the relationship between man and the rest of the universe. By pointing out that the sun and not the earth was the central body of our sidereal system, Copernicus pricked the bubble Ptolemy had blown; and, with the later discoveries of Kepler, Galileo and Newton, the heavens became at last truly astronomical. From a figure large against the sky, man found himself deflated to the size of a midge. Belief in an ever-mindful God had to be considerably modified or abandoned, and, to bolster his ego against such a stunning blow, man began to make greater efforts to understand and thus gain mastery over the world about him. The chief means at his disposal were inductive inquiry and mathematics, the former stressed by Bacon, who did much to rid the mind of tradition and prepare it for scientific pursuits, and the latter by Descartes, whose idea of the universe as a series of mechanisms proved stimulating not only to physiology but to science in general. Though not without distinguished predecessors, Spinoza impressively resolved the dualism of Hellenic-Christian thought into the monism of pantheistic philosophy. The realm of matter and that of spirit were believed to be aspects of both God and Nature, and in all their ramifications exactly parallel with each other. It was not long before Nature assumed in many minds some of the qualities of the medieval God.

One of the results of this new awareness was the appearance, after the middle of the sixteenth century, of an increasing number of volumes on natural history, which provided a good foundation for subsequent nature writing. Gesner, often called the German Aristotle, was able to enrich his own observations with those of many and well-scattered correspondents. His *Historiae animalium* (1551-87), beautifully illustrated with woodcuts, some of them by Dürer, was creatively translated by Topsell, whose delightfully intimate English gave it wide circulation. Upon reading it two and a half centuries later, Thoreau was led to reflect that the early naturalists, unlike many of his own contemporaries, gave their animals an existence in their imagination: "These men . . . will describe and will draw you a cat with four strokes, more beastly or beast-like" than "Ruskin's favorite artist draws a tiger." Turner, a friend of

Gesner, was the first scientific naturalist among the English, and four generations later came the first great one, John Ray, whose descriptions of animals, especially birds, fishes and insects, were well-arranged and unusually full. In their inquiries into the structure, growth, properties, behavior, and relationships of various living things, these men were prompted not only by intellectual curiosity but a love of nature for its own sake.

Hudson bears witness to several of the defects and virtues of some of the other natural histories of this period. In reference to *Sylva*, the first book on forestry in English and to a certain extent responsible for the patterning of England with hedgerows and woodlands, he exclaimed to a friend: Evelyn "looks at trees and thinks of nothing but the use that can be made of them! . . . He looks at [a field of broom] and says the proper thing to do is to cut it and chop it up small and feed donkeys with it!" On the other hand, for Gerard's descriptions of the various plants in old English gardens, which also charmed Thoreau, he has penned one of the finest encomiums:

> Next to the delight of flowers themselves is to me that of listening to the old herbalist discoursing of the same; and this would I say of no other work on plant-lore, for these are mostly a weariness to read. The old author is simple, not concerning himself overmuch about the reason of things, or, as he would say, he loveth not to dance in quagmires. And sometimes he is almost childlike in his repetitions and reaffirmations; but the colour of his style is never overworn, and he is for ever fresh and full of variety and agreeable surprises, like Nature herself. . . . Indeed, there is not seldom a lustre in his words that serves to remind one of the red whortle he greatly admired, which is full of juice of so orient and beautiful a colour to limn withal that Indian lacca cannot be compared thereunto. Nor let it be forgot that it was he who invented the name of Traveller's Joy; and by increasing the pleasure which all have in that green and silver adorner of our country waysides and hedges, may even be said to have added something to nature.

More and more, nature became a theme in Renaissance art. The backgrounds in Italian painting were rendered with closer attention to natural forms and particular locales. Among northern painters—Patinir, Breughel, Rubens, Hobbema, Ruisdael, Lorraine, and Poussin—landscape came to be a satisfying source of inspiration. With his emphasis upon the wilder aspects of the Calabrian countryside, Rosa pointed the way to some of the more extravagant forms of romanticism in the following century. Though painters were to become thoroughly aware of the English countryside, it is in the poetry of Spenser and Drayton, Shakespeare and Herrick and Milton, Marvell and Traherne and Vaughan, that we now see and feel it memorably. In the latter trio, there was even some anticipation of Wordsworth and the more pantheistic attitude toward nature, Vaughan, for example, perceiving a sentience in the whole of nature (trees "resent" great storms "before they come") and a power to arouse the best in mankind, who often "hath not so much wit as some stones have. . . ."

In the main, however, the artists of the sixteenth, seventeenth, and early eighteenth centuries did not go much beyond the recovery of the classical enjoyment of nature. The pastoral tradition, brilliantly revived in England by Spenser and Sidney, remained strong for over a century. Charming as its world must have been to the contemporary imagination, it possesses as a description of any part of the natural scene little relief, and, with the inexpressiveness of most of its details, is wanting in conviction. The most popular landscape painters of the latter part of this period were Lorraine and Poussin, who sought to bring nature into more intimate relationship with man by imposing on it classical attitudes. The immediate experience with nature most relished by the cultivated man was that found in a garden, preferably located in the country. "The purest of human pleasures," said Bacon, is the planting of a garden, and that of his choice was a formal one, even if it did include a heath, and some of its alleys were to be set with burnet, wild thyme, and watermints in order to perfume the air when trodden upon. Later in the century the attractions of a garden were given just as notable expression by Marvell, Cowley, and Temple. Foremost among them was the retreat it afforded from "the busy companies of men," where one might relax and commune with oneself. There was little or no desire to draw closer to Nature and learn more of her secrets.

Occasionally, animals were appreciated solely for themselves. Montaigne reminded his readers that "it is not long of a true discourse, but of a foolish hardiness and self-perfuming obstinacy, we prefer ourselves before other creatures, and sequester ourselves from their condition and society." Sir Thomas Browne showed exceptional catholicity of taste when he declared: "I cannot tell by what logic we call a toad, or bear, or an elephant ugly; they being created in those outward shapes and figures which best express the actions of their inward forms. . . . There is no deformity but in monstrosity. . . ." Pisanello discovered animals, particularly dogs and birds, as a major theme for an artist, and Potter, though possessing more of an eye for details than essences, even dared to devote a large canvas to the portrait of a bull. Bird-song inspired many of the poets, and at times their sympathies were touched for the individual creature, as Skelton for a sparrow, Herrick for a robin, and Marvell for a fawn. Yet, by and large, the Renaissance, with its bear- and bull-baiting and such hunts as those depicted by Rubens and Snyders, was cruel toward many of the rest of nature's family. Especially provocative of cruelty was the Cartesian theory that animals are only "machines"—like plants, incapable of feeling. Though opposed by such philosophers as More, Cudworth, and Locke and by that modern Aesop, La Fontaine, this theory not only gave sanction to the most wantonly brutal sort of vivisection but, by widening the gulf already placed between human and animal life, set back the full appreciation of animals for almost a century.

The first book that comes fairly well within the bounds of the out-of-door essay is *The Compleat Angler* (1653-76). Since Walton was sixty when it was published, his observations, aside from those supplied by friends or culled from predecessors (among whom were Aristotle, Pliny, Gesner, Bacon and Gerard), were the fruit of many holidays in the open. Wishing to make "a recreation of a recreation," he put into it much of the countryside of Merry England—her rivers gliding between velvety or flowery banks, her dewy meadows chequered with water-lilies and lady-smocks, and her honeysuckle hedges, graceful willows, sturdy beeches and sycamores, under which there was shelter against both the noon-day sun and the frequent shower that "falls so gently upon the teeming earth and gives a sweeter smell to the lovely flowers that adorn [the] verdant meadows." Enlivening the various landscapes are many figures: otters, sheep with their gambolling lambs, cattle, song birds (his "simple expressions of delight" in the nightingale gave Hudson "ever-fresh pleasure"), children gathering cowslips along the streams, dairy maids singing at their tasks, friends of Piscator, with pith and marrow in their speech, and, to cast some shadow on the portrait of rural humanity, thieving gypsies lurking along the by-ways. To these out-of-door-essay qualities, Walton added another necessary to this genre and wanting in natural histories—a companionable, meditative personality. Thankfulness that his soul had been fashioned by many joyous days of angling along a beautiful, quiet countryside permeates all his pages, and is expressed with engaging simplicity. Moreover, despite the large element of dialogue, the form of the book, reflecting as it does an enthusiastic reading of Montaigne, comes close to that characteristic of the out-of-door essay.

There is, however, too much of the pastoral dream or nostalgia for Elizabethan times in the scenes presented, even though they are, to a certain extent, given a local habitation—the countryside along the Thames, the "delicate" Dove, the meandering Shawford Brook, and the sedgy Lea. And despite the large amount of dependable information on the characteristics, the breeding, the seasons and the methods for the catching of chub and grayling and carp, pike and trout and salmon—the massing of which gives portions of *The Compleat Angler* the appearance of a manual—Walton was capable of many inaccuracies and some sheer superstitions, such as his entertainment of the idea that some salmon turn into trout, that toads are engendered from leaves submerged in ponds, and, what Ray was disproving, that insects are born from decaying vegetable matter. More serious, as indicated by his attitude toward otters and the catching of herons with baited hooks, his angle of vision was too much that of the sportsman. (Though sportsmen acquire considerable knowledge of animals, their sympathies are much narrower than those of the naturalist or the out-of-door essayist.) And finally, there is in Walton no deep reading in "Nature's mystic book."

At least as a field naturalist, Sir Thomas Browne deserves mention. His most original contribution to science, for which Grew is usually given credit, was his discovery of the sexuality of plants. Along with Malpighi, Swammerdam and Ray, he helped to arouse an interest in insects, noting, for example, "the wisdom of the pismire" and, like Marvell, the beauty of the glow-worm, in which there may be, he thought, "some original in the seed and spirit analogous unto the element of stars." As an ornithologist, his views on migration were more advanced than those of White. Though occasionally showing a cautiousness toward "forewriters" that amounts to timidity, he despatched a large number of "old and grey-headed errors" in *Pseudodoxia Epidemica* (1646), many of them in the domain of natural science. Yet little of his writing comes strictly within the purview of the out-of-door essay. What excludes it more than anything else is Browne's failure to make the setting of his plants and animals a part of the telling (we rarely get a glimpse of Norfolk) and to give a continual sense of his own presence, such as is to be found in the account of his raking for ambergris in the paunch of a whale.

The eighteenth century took an immense stride forward in the appreciation of nature. Browne had declared that man has been given two volumes for the understanding and worship of God—the Bible and the scriptures of nature, a "universal and public manuscript that lies expansed unto the eyes of all." Many of those who depended on the former began to realize, as the title of Ray's popular philosophical book indicates (*The Wisdom of God Manifested in the Works of the Creation*), that they might find evidences of divinity in other modes of being besides the human; while those who depended on the latter, including many of the deists, came to regard themselves more and more as a link in the vast "Chain of Being," in which all creatures, even the minutest of them, have an indispensable place—the main core of thought in the first epistle of the *Essay on Man*. An earlier spokesman than Pope for such a concept was Shaftesbury, who, with his strong susceptibility to the appeal of the outdoors and his pantheistic feelings, impressed upon his readers that they could communicate with God through nature, the more sublime objects and forces giving a sense of His majesty. This new intellectual and emotional attitude, combined as it was with the realistic trend of the times, gave such an impetus to the study of natural science that before the century was half over it became an important element in education and led many men, particularly clergymen, to devote some of their leisure to its advancement.

Concomitantly, the feeling toward animals became much more sympathetic. Influential voices, such as those of Mandeville, Addison, Hume, Hartley and Adam Smith, continued to be raised against Cartesian psychology. Besides emphasizing the interdependence of all forms of life, the theory of the "Chain of Being" taught that (as Pope put it) "man alone" does not "engross . . . Heaven's high care."

> [He] sees with equal eye, as God of all,
> A hero perish or a sparrow fall.

Believing that "compassion is the supreme form of moral beauty," Shaftesbury and Hutcheson laid the philosophical foundation for the humanitarian movement, which encouraged a more friendly regard for the other tenants of this planet. Later in the century, there was even some discussion as to whether animals possess souls and are destined to share with man a future life, the affirmative side (as Hudson noted) finding considerable support in Wesley. The great interest in natural history, which was increasingly inspired by a love of all life in and for itself, strengthened this humaneness. The sense of compassion was intensified by certain portraits and episodes that began to appear more and more frequently in various forms of art, such as Hogarth's *Four Stages of Cruelty,* Sterne's caged starling and sundry asses, Cowper's spaniel and pet hares, Blake's fly and lambs, and Burns's auld mare Maggie, the ewe Mailie, and the "wee, sleekit, cow'rin', tim'rous" field mouse. By the beginning of the next century, when their cause had been given further momentum by an awareness of the right of the individual to life, liberty, and the pursuit of happiness, the humanitarians were ready to marshal their forces for legislative action. In our own day, there has even been some suggestion that we help animals free themselves from overspecialization so that they may respond to their environment in a more creative way.

From the immediate popularity of *The Seasons* and its great vogue throughout the century both in England and on the Continent, one may gather how much people were waiting for a portrayal of rural life reflecting these various tendencies. Whenever Thomson records what he has actually seen, as in many of his descriptions of flowers and insects and birds, he rivals the greatest of nature poets in the steadiness of his eye, a steadiness that won the admiration of White. Most of the animals are presented in connection with the daily and seasonal activities of country folk: horses pulling the plough, sheep being washed and sheared, and cattle ruminating in the pastures or in their stalls. Except for trout, he shows a genuine pity toward all that breathe: for the ox slaughtered by "the cruel hands even of the clowns he feeds" and birds robbed of their eggs or confined in cages; for all the hunted, stag or fox or hare beset by "dark snares, and dogs and more unpitying man"; and even for the least of them, bees plundered of their winter store and cast out from "their honey'd domes" to die by the myriad and (what Walton would have regarded as sheer sentimentality) angling worms twisting "in agonizing folds." Alive as he was to the varying effects of the floral world, his figures, including those of many countrymen, are set in the midst of vivid landscapes, in which he sought to rival with words,

> Whate'er Lorraine light-touch'd with softening hue,
> Or savage Rosa dash'd, or learned Poussin drew.

The more philosophic aspects of the new sensibility toward nature are reflected in the many outbursts of praise to the Author of all creation.

In the poetry that followed, there were an increasing accuracy and subtlety of observation and a more conscious love for the wild and elemental. Gray had gifts as a naturalist, and, though he expressed a fuller and deeper love of nature in his letters and journals, his verse reflects much of the essential appeal of the English countryside, with some of its wilder prospects. The melancholy grandeur of Argyleshire is sensitively, if vaguely and incidentally, presented in *Ossian*. How much nature might have meant to Cowper (as Hudson points out) is revealed in "Yardley Oak," in which there is a confession that were it not for the restraints of his religious upbringing he would yield to an instinctive desire to bow down to this famous tree in worship. Being, however, a "stricken deer," he turned to nature primarily to be soothed, and so gave most of his attention to a faithful rendering of the tranquil, humanized countryside around Olney, with the osier-edged Ouse winding slowly through ploughland and spacious meadows, "with cattle sprinkled o'er." These poets, along with many others, helped to train the eighteenth century toward a more subtle and emotional response to the open-air world. An indication of the extent of their influence upon the out-of-door essay is to be found in the twenty-fourth letter of *Selborne*, which is written largely in verse.

Though lagging somewhat behind the poets, English painters began to participate more and more in the artistic return to nature.

For his patrons, Wilson painted dull canvases in imitation of Lorraine, but for himself, inspired by the Dutch, he occasionally anticipated later achievements, even those of Cézanne. In Gainsborough there was an intensely subjective, if not profound, feeling for several countrysides. In Marshall and Stubbs and Morland, the eighteenth century found skilful delineators of animals, wild as well as domestic. One of the most important developments in the whole history of English art was the appearance of water-colors, the best medium in which to catch the evanescent moods of nature and the spontaneous emotions of the painter. At first they were largely topographical in inspiration, but with the Sandbys, Girtin, Cozens and Cotman, the scene and the artist often became one. Just as the poetry of Thomson and Cowper culminated in that of Wordsworth and Shelley, landscape painting culminated in Crome and Constable and Turner—Crome, with his large and profound simplicity, giving spirituality and grandeur to the most ordinary Norfolk scenes; Constable, with a wider color range and more emotional temperament, faithfully recording the low, rain-swept countryside he had known since boyhood; and Turner, so familiar with nature's various forms that he could take the liberty of rearranging them without falsifying her effects. Landscape became, indeed, the most characteristic expression of the painter throughout the nineteenth century, even as the human figure was in the eighteenth and the abstract is in our own.

One of the most valuable contributions of the late eighteenth century was the appreciation of mountains—of value not only because it added another province to the imaginative conquest of the earth but also because, through its stimulation of the sense of awe, it played a large rôle in shaping the general attitude toward nature. The Chinese, from the beginning of their culture, had a passion for such extravagant wildness, their very word for landscape, *shan-shui*, meaning mountains and waters; but for a long time the Western world looked upon them with abhorrence, for the recognition of a beauty "that hath terror in it" was slow of growth. Among the few attracted were Hesiod, Pindar and Lucretius in ancient times, Petrarch, Gesner, Montaigne and Vaughan in the Renaissance, and Ray, Dennis, Shaftesbury and Addison in the neo-classical period. Of his journey up to the Grand Chartreuse in 1739, Gray wrote in one of his letters, "I do not remember to have gone ten paces without an exclamation, that there was no restraining: not a precipice, not a torrent, not a cliff, but is pregnant with religion and poetry." Particularly prominent amongst the increasing number of enthusiasts in the same generation was Rousseau, who, in the presence of mountains, was moved to heroic and sublime meditations. These "solemn temples" became a leading passion in the lives of Wordsworth and Turner and, later, in those of Ruskin, d'Indy, and Muir.

Even though travellers were often so intent upon exploration and adventure as to neglect the aesthetic qualities of their surroundings, they made important contributions to nature writing. In earlier centuries there had been Marco Polo, Gilles, Belon, Oviedo, Acosta, and, in England, Raleigh, whose *Discoverie of Guiana* received for its natural history the praise of Humboldt and Schomburgk. In the eighteenth century, Dampier, La Condamine, Cook, Bruce, Azara, and Mungo Park made purchase of still other portions of the globe. From a literary point of view, one of the best was the American naturalist, William Bartram, whose *Travels through North & South Carolina, Georgia, East & West Florida* (1791) had an influence upon Wordsworth, Coleridge, and Chateaubriand. In it there are lively descriptions of plants and animals and Indians—all set well against the semi-tropical scenery of these states. He himself becomes a part of all that he sees, responding especially to scenes of grandeur. There is a certain leaven of philosophical romanticism in his account, most noticeable in the introduction. "The great Author," he says, "has impartially distributed his favours to his creatures, so that the attributes of each one seem. to be of sufficient importance to manifest the divine and inimitable workmanship." This belief helped him to an imaginative sympathy for animals, even for the "magnanimous" rattlesnake, and to an awareness of the beauty of forests and swamps as well as that of mountains. Forests were indeed the chief characteristic of the American landscape, and Bartram, along with Chateaubriand, Cooper and others, did much to make their mysterious depths also an important element in the experience with nature.

Among the few prose writers who gave much attention to the scenery of Great Britain was Gilpin, the eighteenth-century Ruskin. As the illustrations in his books demonstrate, he looked upon it with a painter's eye, sensitive to the forms of shrubs and trees and hills, the relationship of the various components of a panorama, the value of animals in accentuating its spirit, the many colors and tones, and the varying effects of light and shadow. Indeed, being without any deep feeling for the wild or for what lies beneath the aesthetic surface, he subjected landscape too rigidly to the rules of picturesque art, speaking scornfully of a countryside that does not "compose" well and thus opening himself to such criticism as that of Hudson, who called him a "glorified landscape gardener." Despite all his limitations, he did, nonetheless, aid many besides his contemporaries to look at nature with more aesthetic enjoyment, Thoreau, in the first flush of discovery, finding in his *Forest Scenery* "some of the cool wind of the copses converted into . . . graceful sentences." And by including a sense of mystery and awe in his conception of the picturesque, he pointed the way toward a more romantic susceptibility.

The great interest in natural science resulted in momentous advances. Linnaeus, with his binomial system of nomenclature, blazed many a trail through the vast wildernesses of fauna and flora for succeeding naturalists to explore exhaustively. Amongst those of his own century were Frisch, Trembley, Roesel, Ellis, Kalm, the Bartrams, de Saussure, Pallas, Banks, Fabricius and Forster, some of them journeying to the far corners of the earth. The supreme genius of the age, Goethe, giving much of his time to scientific research, made notable discoveries in the comparative anatomy of plants and animals. Some of the best and surely the most brilliant writing came from France. Réaumur, with his *Mémoires pour servir à l'histoire des insectes,* gave an immense impetus to the study of entomology. Buffon took more pride in his gift for bold hypotheses than in that for descriptive writing, but it is because of the descriptions, which were strongly influenced by the seventeenth-century "character" writers, that the many volumes of his *Histoire naturelle* gained their widest fame. Though the fullness and the arrangement of them depend upon the artificial principle of the animal's relative importance to mankind and though they are wanting in any real sympathy, he became one of the foremost popularizers of science that the world has produced—the modern Pliny.

The book that had the most telling influence on the out-of-door essay, itself a masterpiece of the genre, was *The Natural History*

of Selborne (1789), which blossomed, quite unexpectedly, out of
a period given over largely to description and classification.[2] White
realized that it was "no small undertaking for a man, unsupported
and alone, to begin a natural history from his own autopsia"; yet
that is exactly what he did, when, at the age of thirty-one, he started
to record in a journal his observations of the life of the fields. Sixteen years later, he was ready to draw off, from time to time, the
best of them in letters to Barrington, an antiquarian and lawyer
as well as naturalist, and Pennant, the author of *British Zoology*
and the *History of Quadrupeds.* Subsequently, they were revised
into more essay-like form and, with a specially written introductory
and closing group, gathered into a volume.

"Why does this 'little cockle-shell of a book,' " asks Hudson,
"come gaily down to us over a sea full of waves, where so many
brave barks have floundered?" One likely reason is that its maker,
seeking to enlarge his mind through intimacy rather than novelty or
vicarious knowledge, confined his observations to the limits of his
own small Hampshire parish, and saw all things there in close
relationship, one with the other. "All nature is so full," he declared,
"that that district produces the greatest variety which is the most
examined." His eye and ear were attracted to the minutest details:
the shrilling of field crickets, which fills the mind "with a train of
summer ideas of everything that is rural, verdurous, and joyous,"
the differences between the chiffchaff, wood- and willow-wrens, the
protective coloration of stone-curlews, the diverse ways in which
field mice, squirrels, and nuthatches open hazel-nuts, the strange
effects of certain echoes, the "conversation" of birds, and the eco-
nomics of earthworms, those "great promoters of vegetation."
When a French anatomist claimed that cuckoos do not hatch their
own eggs because the disposition of their intestines "incapacitates
them for incubation," he proceeded to dissect both a cuckoo and a

---

2 Two of the *Letters from an American Farmer* (1782) come within the
limits of the out-of-door essay, for in them various animals, along with the joys
of the settler on the frontier, are presented in an intimate way with exciting episodes. Though not a naturalist or philosophically inclined, Crèvecoeur possessed
a sense of literary form, derived, in large measure, from a reading of the *Spectator*
papers, and his quietly idiomatic style is eminently suitable for this genre. Since
the letters went almost unread for several generations, they had no effect upon
its development.

nightjar and proved him wrong. He did, it is true, allow himself to
believe, like most of his contemporaries, that swallows "lay themselves up like insects and bats, in a torpid state, and slumber away
the more uncomfortable months," but he refrained from giving
anyone the impression that there was any real evidence of this sort.
"As to their hiding, no man pretends to have found any of them in
a torpid state in the winter."

His primary interest was in birds, especially swallows, martins
and swifts, and his pages on them are not only the most vivid but
the most valuable to science, which for long had been ignoring
ornithology. There are many sketches of other animals, some of
whom become almost like personal acquaintances. Who does not
remember Timothy, the tortoise, hobbling "towards its benefactress
with awkward alacrity," as apprehensive of the rain "as a lady
dressed in all her best attire," and withdrawing every November to
its dormitory near "a great turf of hepaticas" until the following
April? In order to illustrate sociability amongst animals and the way
natural affection "sublimes the passions, quickens the invention, and
sharpens the sagacity of the brute creation," he introduces us to the
doe that was protected against her canine assailants "with [the]
fierce lowings and menacing horns" of cows, among whom she had
been reared, and the field mouse who, upon the uncovering of her
bed, was able to carry her infants to safety by not disturbing their
hold upon her teats. Human beings are included in his chroniclings,
though one might well wish, as did Jefferies, that they had been
given greater prominence. Among the more interesting ones is the
village idiot, whose "strong propensity to bees" made them "his
food, his amusement, his sole object." Much attention is paid to
superstitions, such as the prognostication of "ill or good luck, . . .
the death of a near relation or the approach of an absent lover"
by the actions of a house cricket. And one is made aware of the
surroundings of all these various creatures: the secluded village,
with its humble cottages, its trees, and its low-towered church;
meadows watered with brooks and dotted with cattle; Wolmer
Forest, where the poor of the village gathered wood; and downs
stretching to the far horizons, with their grazing flocks and the
mysteriously-fed ponds on their summits. From a scientific point
of view, the terrain around Selborne is described in the manner
employed by explorers for a whole continent.

Another reason why this cockle-shell of a book has come down to us is that its author had a sense of form and style, and, "in spite of his modest and extreme reticence" (as Hudson puts it) "his spirit shines in every page. . . ." Though the conditions under which the letters were written imposed restrictions—probably keeping him from presenting more of the texture of his personality—they at least account for some of the effect of artlessness. The style, with its scholarly precision and sobriety of tone, is in a lower key than that of *The Compleat Angler,* but it has something of its exquisite simplicity and is not without many happy turns of phrasing. While wanting somewhat in poetic sensibilities and philosophic impulses, which kept him from the full aesthetic and spiritual response of his great successors, White reveals himself as a friendly sort of person, regarding the creatures of the fields and hedgerows as individuals possessing, like human beings, their own unique biographies, and fascinated by certain strange phenomena, the explanation of which kept eluding him. So well did he succeed in identifying himself with all things Selbornian, he has become its *genius loci.*

The romanticism of the late eighteenth and early nineteenth centuries, finding the greatest inspiration in nature, had a profound effect upon its appreciation. A more extensive and passionate perception, particularly of the mysterious aspects of the natural world, brought with it a renascence of wonder, and the large use of imaginative insight gave to the things perceived deeper meaning. Because of the emphasis upon the subjective, men took delight, far more than ever before, in discovering in nature correspondences of their own personalities, and these correspondences not only led to the exaltation of certain objects and forces but became a theme for philosophic discourse. Beyond all others, Rousseau, with his immense ego, had given a great impetus to this sort of response. One of its dangers is, of course, that it leaves too much to the individual and his varying moods. If he is in good countenance, like Crabbe's Orlando anticipating a tryst with his beloved, even the most sterile countryside, one that mocks "the thin-set rye," can be a subject for rapture; if he is out of countenance, as Orlando was after learning that his beloved had gone to visit "a friend," hedgerows, flower-banked streams, lush meadows, and hills high-crowned with trees pall him with their "eternal green." Though often revealing more of the observer than the thing observed,[3] such a response considerably enhanced the emotional and imaginative possibilities of nature, fact being quickly raised (in Thoreau's phrase) to the temperature of blood heat.

As we have seen, earlier writers on the outdoors had occasionally been moved by pantheistic feeling, but the Romantics brought it more thoroughly and suggestively into the experience with nature. Since, according to the philosophy from which it emanates, divinity is diffused throughout the universe, man can find affinities in all things and, if sufficiently sensitive, hear accents of its eternal language in even the least of them. In the grain of sand or a blade of grass, as well as in the flower in the crannied wall, there is embodied the mystery

> Which shakes the spheres conjoint—
> God focussed to a point.

Nature was something more than a stimulus to the senses, the emotions, and the mind; it spoke directly to the soul and thus became, even more than with the deists, a religion. Since divinity was felt most intensely in those aspects that awakened the sense of awe, romanticists brought to bear upon the presentation of them their profoundest craftsmanship. Yet they could, like the Graces, make the most familiar things seem "strangely remote" and "wondrous near."

The poet who, in England, best illustrates the romantic approach is, of course, Wordsworth. Though the "substantial lineaments" he gave to various forms of nature helped considerably toward raising still higher the general cultural interest in natural history, he owes his supremacy to his revelations of the emotional depths to which man is moved in the open air, particularly the deep joy that comes to the one who "watches and receives" in "wise passiveness" the spirit that abides behind all "outward show." Thus, in so typical a poem as "Tintern Abbey," after anchoring it in direct observation as well as in that recollected in tranquillity and after testifying

---

[3] Something of the same charge might be made against the transcendental approach to nature, made popular by German idealism. Regarding man as the world in epitome and his mind as sovereign over the rest of nature, the transcendentalist thought he could largely ignore the empirical method and, through the use of intuition or reason, penetrate to the heart of nature.

to the ecstasy to be found in a purely physical relationship with nature, he dwells upon her soothing and wise companionship for those who love her and the exaltation she brings to the spiritually susceptible, allowing them, at rare moments, to "see into the life of things." Those who look upon her with too scientific an eye, so he thought, receive only a small measure of these values,[4] and those who seek too eagerly for the aesthetic are in danger of missing the spiritual.

Another important influence of Wordsworth on nature writing was his dignifying of rustic folk, whose features are "moulded in the cast of Earth, their infinite companion." Though enriching the landscapes of Walton, Gay, Thomson and Gray, they are portrayed in too idyllic or condescending or remote or moralizing or academic a manner. Goldsmith, Cowper, and Crabbe are more convincing, but it was Burns, peasant born and more in tune with the democratic spirit of the times, who presented them with complete sympathy, fully perceptive of the universality of their emotions. Countryman that he was, Wordsworth knew many kinds of rural folk, and, when placing them in his Cumberland and Westmoreland landscapes, emphasized their innate nobility, their resolute independence, their intuitive grasp of the basic issues of life, their awareness of natural beauty, and the depth of their piety.

Many of the Romantic poets added new vistas to the general appreciation of landscape: Scott, the glens, moors, lochs, bare crags, and misty mountain-tops of his native land; Byron, views of Continental landscape, usually melodramatic in content and painted in bravura style, with a lordly sweep of the brush; and Shelley, ethereal effects of forests, mountains, seas, and the immeasurable sky, whether lighted by the sun or the moon or myriads of stars glowing "like a swarm of golden bees." Though tending to sentimentalize animals by interpreting them in the light of their own moods, they intensified the pleasure found in certain species and orders as well as the sympathy felt for all the children of life: Wordsworth, Keats, Hunt and Clare giving fuller emotional relief

---

4 This is one of the main reasons for the hostility felt by many romanticists toward those who "peep and botanize." As Thoreau put it, "Man cannot afford to be a naturalist, to look at Nature directly, but only with the side of his eye. He must look through and beyond her. To look at her is fatal as to look at the head of Medusa. It turns the man of science to stone" (*Journal*, March 23, 1853).

to insects; Scott, Wordsworth and Byron, to the dog and various other mammals; and Coleridge, Wordsworth, Shelley and Keats, to the nightingale, the cuckoo, the linnet, the skylark, and the albatross. The humanitarianism of the time was well summarized by Blake and Coleridge:

> A robin redbreast in a cage
> Puts all heaven in a rage.
>
> He prayeth best who loveth best
> All things both great and small. . . .

Just as mountains had been one of the most original creations of the eighteenth-century imagination, so the eternally restless ocean became, with some of the Romantics, a correspondingly fine embodiment of the love of the wild and the sublime. Though there are sensitive marine vignettes in Homer, Aeschylus, Virgil, Ovid and Catullus, and the Romans flocked to the beaches in summer, the open sea was, on the whole, a place of foreboding and lay beyond the imaginative sympathies of the ancients. The early English and Irish poets were profoundly affected by its moods, but from the Norman period until the nineteenth century only rarely did it engage the attention of an artist or draw people in large numbers to its shores. While losing none of its terror for Turner and his contemporaries—witness *The Slave Ship,* Shelley's "A Vision of the Sea," and Byron's *Don Juan*—they recognized its grandeur and its protean beauty. Byron found in its boundlessness and changelessness the image of eternity, a "glorious mirror, where the Almighty's form glasses itself in tempests," and, identifying his ostracized self with its lawlessness, invoked it to "roll on" even though it swallows "oak leviathans" in its "yeast of waves." Chateaubriand, Whitman and Melville, Hugo and Swinburne, Conrad, Dougherty and Masefield, MacDowell and Debussy, in their several ways, were also to come under its spell.

Almost every decade of the nineteenth century saw advances in natural science through the achievements of such botanists as Brown, Hooker and Gray, such entomologists as Lubbock, Kirby and Spence, such marine biologists as Forbes, Gosse and Thompson, such ornithologists as Wilson, Yarrell, McGillivray and Gould, and such general zoologists as Cuvier and Agassiz. Of great influence upon Hudson as well as upon other nature writers were the ex-

plorers, particularly the brilliant group attracted to the opulent life
of the South and Central American jungles. Humboldt charted the
course of the fabled Casiquiare, gave full descriptions of a number
of animals hitherto only partially known, and was immensely interested in Indian anthropology and the remains of Incan civilization.
Waterton was primarily concerned with the behavior of animals in
habitats undisturbed by man—his best-known study being that of
the sloth, which he proved to be, not one of Nature's vagaries, as
it had been regarded by naturalists from Oviedo to Buffon, but an
amazing example of functionalism—actually, at times, belying its
name. Darwin was brought near to "that mystery of mysteries—the
first appearance of new beings on this earth"—by studying the remains of gigantic prehistoric animals at Bahia Blanca and the living evidence of evolution in the Galápagos, each island of which
possesses, to a certain extent, its own distinct species of plants and
animals. (Observing a much more dramatic dividing line between
the animals indigenous to Malaysia and those of Australia, Wallace
arrived independently at the formulation of the theory of evolution.) Bates discovered that on the expanded membrane of butterfly
wings "nature writes, as on a tablet, the story of the modifications
of species," and Belt, that an intimacy exists between certain plants
and animals and, following the lead of Bates and Wallace, that
many forms of life depend upon mimetic resemblances for survival.
Among the other naturalists travelling in America and other conti-
nents were Le Vaillant, Saint-Hilaire, Nuttall, Richardson, d'Orbigny, Schomburgk, Spruce, Kane, Edwards, Dufferin, Du Chaillu,
and Im Thurn.

Although the accounts of these men belong essentially to the
literature of scientific exploration, they contain many out-of-door-
essay passages. In Humboldt, there are such episodes as the Bar-
mecidean feast of a titi monkey upon the engravings of Cuvier's
Tableau élémentaire d'histoire naturelle and Indians fishing on
horseback for electric eels and such graphic riverine scenes as those
of the journey up the Apure; in Waterton, the tolling of "the pretty
snow-white campanero" in the depths of the forest, savages brew-
ing wourali poison, and a huge alligator being ridden by the
author, its forelegs used as a bridle; in Darwin, the "snowing" of
butterflies and gossamer spiders far out at sea and lagoon islands
with their barrierlike beaches resisting the fury of the ocean; in

Wallace, two pet parrots, one of them solemn, morose, and irritable and the other "inquisitive as a monkey and playful as a kitten," and the ochre-colored, gull- and tern-haunted Amazon; in Bates, sand wasps excavating galleries and sealing in them paralyzed flies and the environs of Pará, Santarem and Ega; and in Belt, the terrorizing advance of "army" ants through a forest, two male hummingbirds displaying their charms to a quietly seated female by shooting up like rockets and, with snow-white tails expanded like inverted parachutes, slowly descending in front of her, and the pageantry and magic of the jungles: every tree different from its neighbor, each trying to overtop the other, and lianas entwining them in a "great network of coiling cables, as the serpents did Laocoon." Writing in the first person, all these naturalists give one a sense of their presence and, especially Waterton and Belt, an occasional intimate glimpse into their personalities. Some of the chapters of *The Naturalist in Nicaragua* come almost completely within the domain of the out-of-door essay.

In those naturalists who wrote largely about their experiences along the British countryside—Bewick (whose engravings themselves were a great stimulus to the aesthetic appreciation of animals), Knapp, Jesse, Howitt (who exerted some influence on Thoreau), Miller, St. John, Knox, Johns, Wood, Buckland—there are also many out-of-door-essay passages: in Knapp, vignettes of spring flowers ("cherished as private friendships") and fungi (those "fragile children of earth"); in Jesse, the massive, gnarled Burnham beeches, which carry one "back to the times of the bowmen of Harold and the days of Robin Hood"; in St. John, two lampreys anxiously employed in making triangular heaps of stones for their spawn and "the muckle hart of Benmore"; in Knox, a pair of ravens brought back after the theft of their young had driven them away and a merlin that, in order to swoop on wounded snipe, accompanied him on all his hunting trips for two months; and in Buckland, Jacko the monkey, who would splash water out of his bath upon anyone laughing at him, and an Angora cat, an old raven, a mastiff, and a remarkably large rat eating together and lying before the fire in a posthouse. The writings of some of these men, as well as those of the explorers, were marred by the insentience of the collector or the sportsman, but others were strongly imbued with the spirit humane, Waterton, for example, pleading eloquently for crow, kestrel, and barn owl and establishing on his estate the first wildlife sanctuary in England. A personal flavor permeates some of them, and occasionally there is an awareness of something underlying nature.

Of considerable aid in bringing the out-of-door essay to its finest flowering was the revival of the familiar essay after the lapse of a century. The periodical essay, especially in its epistolary form, had of course played a large rôle in its shaping, but the qualities wanting in it that the familiar essay possessed to an eminent degree were depth of feeling and completeness of self-revelation. Like the Romantic poets, the familiar essayists thoroughly screened what they found in the outer world through their own temperaments. Thus when Hunt or Hazlitt or even Wilson (who was more of a naturalist) wrote of the countryside, his picture was at least as much of himself as of a part of England or Scotland. But since the out-of-door essay is the product of the field naturalist turned artist rather than the belle-lettrist turned open-air reporter, we must look for the full embodiment of this influence among such men as we have been giving our chief attention.

Although there are familiar-essay qualities in the naturalists just mentioned, the full embodiment occurred first in the United States during its "golden day" of literary expression. For a long time, Americans, with their European traditions, had remained on guard against emotional or spiritual intimacy with nature, made still more alien by her primitiveness and vastness. But under the influence of the Bartrams, Kalm, Audubon and other charters of the wilderness, suspicion of her essential spirit was gradually allayed. Led by Cole, painters discovered the beauty of the Hudson valley and were soon recording the grandeur of the Far West. American poetry felt the impact of romanticism; and in Emerson, singer of the humble-bee, the titmouse, the rhodora, the pine, and "the frolic architecture" of snow, the external world found an eloquent interpreter. His little volume, *Nature*, in which there is much of the new philosophical point of view, helped materially in establishing at least a temporary balance between the allurements of the Green Goddess and the hold of the Greek and Christian elements in the cultural environment. Thoreau and, to a lesser extent, Burroughs were to reflect this balance, but in Melville and Whitman, nature triumphed over these elements, especially in Whitman, in whom there was rooted, deep in the unconscious, a sense of continuous identification with the most elemental forces of the earth.

In his journal for March 15, 1842, Thoreau regretted that there was no convenient book to carry with him into the woods "whose author has been there already [and] whose pages will be as good as [his own] thoughts"—evidently something by a naturalist who was also a poetically-minded familiar essayist. With the writing of "The Natural History of Massachusetts," "A Winter Walk," and "A Walk to Wasusett," he soon made a beginning toward the removal of this deficiency. Though none of these essays is an outstanding performance in the domain of art, they are important in literary history for their enfranchisement of the world of the naturalist to the form and spirit of the familiar essay. The influence of the Lyceum is to be felt in the shaping of them—an influence full-blown in many of their successors—but much more that of the familiar essay, which was becoming increasingly popular in the Concord and Boston of that day.

Throughout the rest of his life, Thoreau kept gathering golden moments into that hive, his journal, and with it fashioning lectures and volumes of essays—*A Week on the Concord and Merrimack Rivers* (1849), *Walden* (1854), *Excursions* (1863)—and three travel books, *The Maine Woods* (1864), *Cape Cod* (1865), and *A Yankee in Canada* (1866). Despite its outdoor studies and its delightful vignettes of early rural America, the first of these, with its many comments upon literature and life in general, is, like Stevenson's *Inland Voyage*, somewhat overliterary; and the travel books, not discounting their fine depictions of various locales, do not come entirely within the confines of the out-of-door essay. *Excursions*, though containing such excellent essays as "Walking" and "Wild Apples" and, like *A Week* and the travel books, revealing the more genial side of its author, is not Thoreau at his best. The best of them, *Walden*, acclaimed by Hudson as "the one golden book" of nature-writing, was surely just the sort of *vade mecum* Thoreau had been looking for. By the time of his death, the out-of-door essay, given prominence by the *Atlantic Monthly*, was fast gaining recognition in America as a new literary form.

Though remaining always, and happily, the amateur, Thoreau excelled in the fields of botany and limnology, in the one receiving valuable assistance from Gray and in the other groping his way as a pioneer. His journal is filled with the most careful observations of swamps, ponds, wriggling river-beds and snowfalls, all of which were the subject of innumerable plumbings. He pondered long on the effect of certain environments, both native and foreign, upon plants, animals, and men. Comparatively ignorant of the methodology of science and unable to generalize from the findings of others, he became, however, more and more the tabulator, overwhelming himself with detail. "I milk the sky and the earth," he declared, "at the risk of endless iteration," and the later years of his journal indicate that he was doing so without a clear sense of how all his material might be shaped into significance. It is for this reason, as well as failing health, that he could not bring off his *magnum opus* on Concord, which was to have been a greater *Selborne*, arranged according to the seasons.

Whatever may be the limitations of his science, no one can deny his excellence in pure observation, to which many scientists have acknowledged indebtedness. Of the inanimate world, he has, as a result, given us a large number of accurate yet imaginative descriptions, from lichens to forests and mountains, and from rivulets to the ocean. Grass is seen flaming up "on the hillsides like a spring fire," and, in "Autumn Tints," the foliage of trees is brilliantly painted, most notably that of the scarlet oak, the *terra firma* of whose leaf, with its "broad, free, open sinuses and . . . long, sharp, bristle-pointed lobes," is almost a petite "archipelago." Though not particularly good at rendering a large, detailed landscape, he had an extraordinary sense of milieu: there is nothing in literary geography to exceed in clarity his impression of Walden Pond, its purity and depth, its shore line and encircling forest, and its varied aspects throughout the year. Many passages in his writings, including those capturing the spirit of the different times of the day and of the seasons, are veritable lyrics or odes.

With much that was faunlike in his own personality, Thoreau could see into the minds of animals with an unprejudiced eye and feel toward them a strong sense of companionship. And they, in turn, like the fish that allowed themselves to be lifted out of the water and the partridge that led her brood past his windows, recognized in him a friend, and in his presence lost some of their fear. In the unfoldment of their little comedies and tragedies, as in that of the battle fought "with more pertinacity than bulldogs" between red and black ants amongst pine stumps, his narrative skill is superb. Of birds and beasts that linger in the memory are the dainty chickadees that, with their "faint flitting lisping notes, like the tinkling of icicles in the grass," came daily to pick a dinner out of his woodpile, one of them even pecking at the armful of wood he was carrying; the loon, making the forest ring far and wide with his wild laughter and playing with Thoreau a game of dive-and-seek; flocks of geese in perfect harrows cleaving the air; the cow moose and her calf, startled in the Maine wilderness, looking like "great frightened rabbits"; and the fox that barked "a vulpine curse" at him through his window.

Though "in moments of quiet and leisure [his] thoughts [were] more apt to revert to some natural than any human relation," he enjoyed casual acquaintanceships with those who were also in close touch with nature—farmers, fishermen, hunters, and their children. "I . . . am ready enough," he declared, "to fasten myself like a bloodsucker for the time to any full-blooded man that comes in my way." There are a number of such persons in his pages, some of the more vivid being poetically-minded farmer Minott, an old Wellfleet oysterman, his Penobscot guide in the Maine woods, and that visitor to his Walden hut, the Canadian woodchopper, "a true Homeric or Paphlagonian man," whose thinking was "immersed in his animal life" and who had such an exuberance of animal spirits that he "sometimes tumbled down and rolled on the ground with laughter. . . ." One of the most impressive features of his landscapes is the sounds—the patter of rain, the fury of storms, the booming of ice, the song of the cricket ("wiser and more mature than that of the wood thrush"), cockcrow ("surpassing the clangor of the goose"), the ululations of owls (like that of "fallen souls that once in human shape night-walked the earth and did the deeds of darkness, now expiating their sins with their wailing hymns")—particularly those strained by distance: the baying of hounds in woods at midnight, the lowing of a cow and the tinkling of her bell in a far pasture, the shouts of boys and the songs of girls, and a late supper horn.

By constantly relating his experiences with nature to those as a member of human society—thereby achieving an experience that was total—Thoreau considerably widened the scope of the out-of-door essay. The reason for his stay at Walden, so he informs us, was the desire "to live deep and suck out all the marrow of life, to live so

sturdily and Spartan-like as to put to rout all that was not life, to
cut a broad swath and shave close, to drive life into a corner, and
reduce it to its lowest terms, and, if it proved to be mean, why
then to get the whole and genuine meanness of it, and publish its
meanness to the world; or if it were sublime, to know it by experience, and be able to give a true account of it in my next excursion."
Such an account, he thought, might help to make men feel more
at home on this globe and create a better sort of society.

One of the chief things he learnt was the value of the wild in
life, which he came to love "not less than the good." "Our village
life would stagnate," he declares, "if it were not for the unexplored
forests and meadows which surround it. We need the tonic of wildness,—to wade sometimes in marshes where the bittern and the
meadow-hen lurk. . . . We need to witness our own limits trans-
gressed, and some life pasturing freely where we never wander."
This insistence upon the wild is, as we have seen, one of the major
characteristics of the romantic sensibility, but Thoreau gave it fresh
emphasis by finding as great an expansion of the soul in the presence
of deserts (of which he got some conception on Cape Cod) and
"impervious and quaking swamps" as in that of mountains, forests,
and the ocean. There had been, it is true, some anticipation of such
a feeling in Crabbe, Bartram, Wordsworth, and Byron; the bare,
solitary llanos of Venezuela had engaged the imagination of Humboldt more than the wonders of the Cordilleros; and the English
were already being irresistibly drawn to the mysterious, liberating
sands of Arabia. But, surely, never had anyone brooded over swamps
so meticulously and lovingly as Thoreau:

> Would it not be a luxury to stand up to one's chin in some retired
> swamp for a whole summer's day, scenting the sweet-fern and bilberry
> blows, and lulled by the minstrelsy of gnats and mosquitoes?

> A day passed in the society of those Greek sages, such as described
> in the Banquet by Xenophon, would not be comparable with the dry
> wit of decayed cranberry vines, and the fresh Attic salt of the
> moss-beds.

> There are no richer parterres to my eyes than the dense beds of dwarf
> andromeda . . . which cover these tender places on the earth's surface.
> . . . My spirits infallibly rise in proportion to the outward dreariness.
> . . . When I would recreate myself, I seek the darkest wood, the

thickest and most interminable and, to the citizen, most dismal, swamp. I enter a swamp as a sacred place, a *sanctum sanctorum.* There is the strength, the marrow, of Nature.

It is as if I always met in those places some grand, serene, immortal, infinitely encouraging, though invisible, companion, and walked with him.

Believing that the prime function of literature is to keep the primitive roots of mankind flourishing, he contended that it should contain much more of the wild.

In the presence of nature he continually felt, as Hudson expresses it, "a sense of an infinite and unaccountable friendliness, . . . like an atmosphere sustaining him." On the animal plane, it brought him, as when "mix[ing] his blood with sunshine" after a swim across Walden Pond, a genial sense of physical well-being. He was too much the intellectual and anti-sentimentalist to surrender himself as frequently or completely as the Romantic poets to pantheistic reveries, but he felt that nature nourished and exalted his spirit, a feeling which accounts for some of the emotional intensity in his writings. Yet puritanism and humanism kept awake in him certain suspicions, and thus, though urging men to identify themselves more with Nature, he warned that "we are not wholly involved in" her. It was his attempt to achieve a balance between these forces, along with his insistence upon the tonic value of the wild, that especially distinguishes his reading of life. As a social critic—in which realm he exerted considerable influence—he stood up stalwartly for the rights of the individual against a world going collectivistic. His various ideas, as well as the harvestings of his senses, were presented in a sinewy prose, in which there is a strong gamy flavor.

Before the heyday of Burroughs, the next major figure in the out-of-door essay, there occurred a momentous change in the concept of nature. For a long time the idea of the evolutionary growth of organisms had been entertained by a number of persons, but it was not until Darwin, with his well-documented theory of natural selection, that the world was compelled to listen. With its opening of new vistas everywhere—in philosophy and ethics as well as in the various natural sciences—it became one of the most creative ideas in the history of civilization. By impressing upon man his mammalian nature—that even his best feelings have their origin deep in the temper and instincts of the brute creation—it not only made him more a part of natural history but brought him still closer in mind and in spirit to all that breathe. This change in attitude led Hudson to declare: "Undoubtedly we are more conscious of many things, both within and without—of the length and breadth and depth of nature; of a unity which was hardly dreamed of by the naturalists of past ages, a commensalism on earth from which the meanest organism is not excluded. For we are no longer isolated, standing like starry visitors on a mountain-top, surveying life from the outside; but are on a level with and part and parcel of it. . . ." Instead of turning to the more splendid effects of inanimate nature for an understanding of the mystery of life, men turned more and more to the study of animals.

The immediate response to *The Origin of Species* was a mixed one. Wallace felt that in the explanation of the workings of natural selection too little consideration had been given to the power of the unconscious will. Fearing that the theory of evolution would rend the temple of religion, Agassiz, whom Thoreau acknowledged as his teacher in things scientific, remained aloof; and others, such as Gosse and Fabre, attacked it with all the weapons at their command. Among the poets, it deepened the disillusionment of Arnold; confirmed Tennyson's impression that Nature is often not in accord with the better impulses of man and turned him to a "higher" pantheism, in which there is a God above nature and especially close to man because of his spiritual aspirations; and was readily and joyfully absorbed in the transcendentalism of Emerson and Whitman and the pantheism of Swinburne and Meredith. In some of the naturalists who accepted evolution, as in many of the poets, there remained enough of the romantic feeling that nature has a soul and reflects some human qualities to give their writings a flavor largely absent in the generations that have grown up as evolutionists and regard Nature as indifferent to man and of interest primarily as she illustrates the laws that govern her.

The theory of evolution played a conspicuous rôle in the life of Burroughs. His early sheaves of essays, beginning with *Wake-Robin* (1870), were written largely under the influence of the spirit of Emerson and Whitman, the artistry of Thoreau and such other essayists of the *Atlantic Monthly* as Flagg and Higginson, and the natural history of Wilson, Nuttall, and Audubon. With the reading of Darwin in the early 'eighties, he became so interested in the philosophical implications as to neglect somewhat the out-of-door essay. Such volumes as *The Light of Day* (1900) and *Accepting the Universe* (1920) lie outside the limits of the genre, whilst those that remain within, like *Ways of Nature* (1905) and *Leaf and Tendril* (1908) are more scientific in spirit than the earlier ones and wanting in their freshness and poetic beauty. In laying down the laws for this new literary form, he was apt at times, as in his attack on Seton and Roberts, to draw the circle too close around fact. Though giving the chief weight of his influence to the mechanistic concept of the universe, he came for a while, late in life, under the spell of Bergson, and thus blended the Emersonian and Darwinian strains in him.

Contrary to his own belief, the current in the channel of his personality was not so strong as Thoreau's, the difference being comparable to that between a mountain torrent and a broad, placidly flowing river. In his distinctly out-of-door essays, there is not the play of ideas or the poetic intensity to be found in Thoreau, nor much opposition to the trend of the times; and in the more scientific and philosophical ones, though often well guided by his feelings, he shows little of the discipline of the logical development of thought. "I have acquiesced in things as they are," he confessed, "and have got all the satisfaction out of them that I could." In his manner of presentation, he prided himself upon his extemporaneousness. "I have never carried a notebook, or collected data about nature in my rambles. . . . What was mine, what I saw with love and emotion, has always fused with my mind, so that in the heat of writing it came back to me spontaneously." " 'Tis with thoughts as with apples; the ripest fall the easiest. When a man's ideas are fully matured, a slight effort, a gentle jogging of his branches, brings the golden pippins down." Such amiability of character and ease of manner, reminding one of Hunt and of Irving, were to assure the out-of-door essay of popularity. The epithet, "the Longfellow of naturalists," fits him well.

The countryside that he was the happiest in presenting—one that seemed to him like an outlying part of himself—was the foothills of the Catskills, a countryside similar to that which Wordsworth knew. He loved the long, undulating lines of range upon range of hills and mountains, all anciently and gently eroded, and the broad, cradle-like valleys, with their ribands of meadows and well-cultivated fields, their "patches of fragrant brakes like miniature forests," their "friendly" rocks, stone fences, and nestling farmhouses. There are few set descriptions of this countryside; rather we see it as part of the pageantry of the months and in connection with the various pursuits of the farm. Though an extraordinarily sensitive recorder of the moods of all the seasons, he is at his best with those of spring, his favorite season. Keenly enjoyed were the singing of the toads ("a kind of gossamer of sound drifting in the air"), sugar-harvesting in maple woods (the most delightful of all farmwork), leaf-buds "making a faint mist of green," the flowering of the wake-robin and the arbutus (lover of evergreens and of rocks and when in bloom "like the cheek of a maiden"), the "still, hazy, brooding mid-April mornings," in which there are freshness and sweetness and "a sort of spirituality," and, later, the blossoming of the orchards. In one of his better essays, "The Return of the Birds," he describes what was to him the most heart-warming aspect of these bridal days. Though he gives us intimate views of forests and hills and mountains in such essays as "Birch Browsings" and "The Heart of the Southern Catskills," the call of the wild never became so insistent or so profound in him as in Thoreau or in Muir. As he well put it, "The pastoral is in my veins."

Aided by the studies in ecology and animal psychology inspired by the theory of evolution, Burroughs was able to penetrate more surely than Thoreau into the minds of animals and to see them more clearly as part of the intricate web of life. Though little attention is given to insects, his essays on gossamer spiders and on bees are memorable. With trout streams gurgling "about the roots of [his] family tree," he became even more knowledgeable than the "Compleat Angler" of at least this particular kind of fishing. Many of the smaller beasts are intimately sketched: the clucking chipmunk, "clean, pert, dapper, nervous" and solitary; red, grey, and flying squirrels with their mirth and mockery; the porcupine, whose "immunity from foes [and] from struggle" has dulled his wits and made "frail and brittle the thread of his life"; the fair-weather woodchuck, "the epicure of the meadows and pastures"; the "gliding snakelike form" of the weasel, whose "methods are a kind of *Schrecklichkeit* in the animal world"; and the fearless skunk, the odor of whose terrible weapon seemed to Burroughs even bracing. Rarely has the cow, who makes "the fields friendly, the hills eloquent, [and] the shade-trees idyllic," found so appreciative an eye or ear. Birds, more prominent in his landscapes than in those of Thoreau, are the source of much of his most poetic writing. It was not so much the beauty of their form and plumage and the expressiveness of certain of their habits that charmed him as the beauty of their singing. "Indeed, I do not seem to know a bird till I have heard its voice." Many of the songs of American and British birds are well rendered, some of the better ones being those of the white-eyed vireo, the bluebird, the ovenbird, the vesper- and song-sparrows, and the hermit thrush ("the finest sound in nature," suggestive of "a serene religious beatitude").

Since the pastoral is the chief theme of his landscape art, one is often aware of the presence of human beings, especially farmers and their families performing the labors of the agricultural year. So little care, however, is taken with their portrayal that most of them, as in the paintings of Wyant and Inness, seem to blend anonymously with the countryside. There is, of course, always a sense of the serene companionship of Burroughs, finding "a perennial interest in the common universal things which all may have on equal terms" and communicating it in one of the most natural of styles, with frequent felicities of phrasing. What is of special note in the history of the out-of-door essay is the inclusion in the self-portrait of many memories of his boyhood in the environs of Roxbury, when life was "half-holiday." The essays of Lamb and Hazlitt and Hunt, as well as Romantic poetry, abound in childhood reminiscences, but, though there is some harking back to earlier scenes in his predecessors, it was Burroughs who, in such essays as "Strawberries," "Speckled Trout," "The Summit of the Years," first tapped this vein of literary ore freely for the new genre. "As I grow old," he declared, "my subsequent days slough off, or fade away, more and more, leaving only the days of my youth as a real and lasting impression." Thus, in the end, we see the Sage of Slabsides not only throughout the years of his maturity but in full temporal perspective.

It took England almost a generation longer to blend natural history completely with the familiar essay, but, in the meantime, she continued to enrich the out-of-door essay in other ways than

through her poets, scientific explorers, and naturalists. Though in
form and in spirit *Rural Rides* (1830) marks no advance over the
achievements of the eighteenth century, it is full of sheer physical
delight in the open air and a love for all wholesome ruralities.
Cobbett manifests considerable skill in sketching from memory,
after a day in the saddle, the contour of a countryside, such as
those of the valleys of the Test, the Avon and the Wylye, with their
long succession of rich meadows, ploughed fields, and orchards—
sketches done with vigorous, masculine strokes, somewhat in the
earlier manner of Girtin and the Sandbys. Despite his essentially
utilitarian point of view, he will pause to admire the leafage of a
tree and enjoy an encounter with wild creatures, such as that with
the flock of ten thousand goldfinches that flew before him between
Somerford and Ocksey for half a mile. His panoramas are dotted
with cottages and, since he was a neighborly sort of person, with
many cottagers. Wielding a doughty yeoman's lance, he sought to
save the humbler villages from THE THING, the *status quo* of Pitt,
Castlereagh, and "the barbarous and impious Malthus and his assis-
tants, the *feelosofers* of the *Edinburgh Review*," which assumed in
his imagination the form of a monster, whose chief abode was the
"Wen" (London).

The inclusion of villages in the out-of-door essay was an en-
largement of resources, for they provide the most natural setting
for the observation of rural folk. Though there are glimpses of
these metropolises of the plough in earlier literature, it was not
until Goldsmith that they were discovered as a promising theme
for poetry. Within two generations they began to assume some
prominence in prose—in the work of Galt, Irving, and, most
notably, Mary Mitford, an admirer of Walton and White and a
friend of Cobbett, Wordsworth, and Ruskin. Though none of the
individual figures of *Our Village* (1824-32) are particularly memorable nor any of her landscape vignettes, they all contribute in
giving a sense of a small community ("close-packed and insulated
like . . . bees in a hive, or sheep in a fold, or nuns in a convent,
or sailors in a ship") living in harmony with the surrounding fields
and coppices. What do more than anything else to establish these
delicate sketches as a classic of their kind are the playful and childlike
impulsiveness of their creator and her very real delight in the
outdoors at all seasons and in all weathers. "Her pleasure in every-

thing," says Hudson, "makes everything interesting, and in displaying her feeling without art or disguise she succeeds in giving what we may call a literary expression to personal charm. . . ."

Ruskin (Hudson's favorite English prose writer) seldom entered into the realm of the out-of-door essay. As the result of long absorption in the art of painting, his landscapes become too suggestive of canvases—a limitation recognized even by his admirers. The few animals to be found in his pages are almost all generalized ones and included primarily for the purpose of training the eyes of his art students. And in his attribution to all natural phenomena the paramount function of educating and pleasuring man, he was guilty, as many besides Thoreau and Muir have felt, of a sort of cosmic provinciality. Yet he was an outstanding spokesman for the naturalism that consists of a close and humble fidelity to the thing seen, the fidelity characteristic of White and Wordsworth and Burroughs. And in the delicate precision of details in his own depiction of nature and in the sweep of his canvas, he was the greatest word-painter of inanimate nature in the English language, nothing being too small or large for his brushstroke or too subdued or dazzling for his palette. Moreover, what especially attracted Hudson, he was able to quintessentialize the spirit of some of the animals—in *Queen of the Air* and *The Eagle's Nest,* for example, those of the bird and the serpent.

The influence of Ruskin, as well as that of White and many contemporary scientists, pervades Kingsley's studies in natural history, two volumes of which assure him a modest niche in the gallery of out-of-door essayists. Though essentially a travel book, *At Last* (1871) has several chapters, such as "The Northern Mountains" and "The Cocal," that might be regarded as out-of-door essays, and some memorable descriptions, such as that of calling crabs, with their "pairs of long-stalked eyes, standing upright like a pair of . . . little lighthouses" when they are active, and their "long single arms . . . brandished, with frightful menaces, as of infuriated Nelsons." *Prose Idylls* (1873) contains still better specimens of this genre, the best being "North Devon," with its descriptions of the "cyclopic masonry" of the coast line, sheep hanging "like white daisies" upon the steep hills, Ilfracombe with "its white terraces rambling up the hills and its capstone sea-walk," "the little strip of semi-tropic paradise" just beyond Morte and "between two giant wastes of sea and moor," and Lundy, with its "bright gray granite rocks, spangled with black glittering mica and golden lichens." Unlike Ruskin, Kingsley imparted to nearly all his scenes a sense of physical exuberance.

Apparently independent of Thoreau, if not of Burroughs and Kingsley, Jefferies, with his large number of out-of-door essays, established the genre in England. To gain intimacy with nature, he always took his own advice of climbing over the stile and following the footpath, and, though never bringing to bear upon his observations a particularly resourceful scientific mind, he soon acquired the habit of recording them minutely and in time became a reporter of genius. As with Cobbett, Burroughs, and many another country lad, he owed much of his lore to the instincts of the hunter, and as a result there is in his first volumes a certain callousness toward animals. He confessed, for example, to the use of the horse-hair noose in the killing of bullfinches and to the shooting of kingfishers in order to satisfy the desire of cottagers' wives for ornaments on their parlor mantels. However, he outgrew the gun, and, while continuing to uphold fox-hunting, came to the defense of other persecuted animals, such as the otter, and expressed scruples against interfering with the "harmless liberty" of insects.

The writings of his early period, from *The Gamekeeper at Home* (1878) to *Round about a Great Estate* (1880), constitute a unit. In these, many observations of Coate and its environs are grouped around the activities of various typical country figures— the farm laborer, the poacher, the gamekeeper, the yeoman farmer, and the squire. More than the others, *Wild Life in a Southern County* (1879) is an "idyll" of a whole countryside, in which there are not only cottages, orchards, and cultivated fields but much of what lies beyond human habitations: wooded streams, forests and downs, with their scaly, chitinous, furred, and feathered denizens. In these volumes and in *Red Deer* (1884), which is a return to his early manner, animals and their settings are presented with a rather unimaginative realism, and though they contain a good deal concerning his youth, there is very little of the self-revelation characteristic of the familiar essay.

The transformation of Jefferies from a reporter into an artist was brought about largely by new surroundings, mystical experiences and illness, and with them an increasing sense of the importance of including himself in his landscapes in a more revealing way. Though London, at first, while he was working on the early volumes, became something of an inspiration and though much pleasure was found in its still partially wild suburbs and along the Sussex coast, it frequently gave him the feeling of "a bird let out with a string tied to the foot to flutter a little way and return again." Then in memory he would wander back to his old home in Wiltshire, to its farmhouses with their thatched roofs, its green fields of corn and brown fallows, its broad meadows made Arcadian with roan-and-white cattle, its large pond and many copses, and the ever-beckoning slopes of the downs, where the wind occasionally brought with it the scent of the far-off sea. In some of the best essays of this later period, such as "Mind under Water," "Meadow Thoughts" and "The Pageant of Summer," he is thinking of this panorama, in which he had passed many happy, carefree days. What had formerly been matter-of-fact now became poetry, and he began to look upon his new surroundings with a deeper sensibility.

For long he had had mystical experiences in which he felt himself "absorbed into the being or existence of the universe," able to relive the life of the remote past and to apprehend the deeper meaning of things evident; but it was some time before he realized their full import. Partly interpreted in *The Story of My Heart* (1883), they intensified some of his experiences with nature and helped to ripen his knowledge into wisdom. Though tuberculosis brought into his writing occasional sentimentality and querulousness toward society, it was, as with Keats, not unproductive of good. To be kept a prisoner from the outdoors, where "all things seem[ed] possible," and to know that he, who longed so passionately and clamorously for life, was condemned to leave unread many of the pages of the great green book of nature further deepened his sensibility, making him more contemplative and more conscious of the swift passing of the perfect moment and giving to some of his last essays, such as "Hours of Spring" and "My Old Village," great poignancy. All these influences are not of course to be found in all his later work. Under the continued necessity of daily writing and of satisfying certain editors, it was inevitable that much of it should continue to be largely journalistic.

Despite the opinion of Burroughs that Jefferies' essays are "cloud-like—vague, formless, highly-colored masses of vapor"—

there is in even the later ones a "rich guerdon of the visible world."
He was sensitive to the varying beauty of the seasons, particularly,
as befits a worshipper of the sun and the author of "The Pageant
of Summer," to that in which all nature achieves fulfilment. While
less successful with large detailed landscapes than Cobbett and
Kingsley, he was skilful in evoking some of the major components
of them, such as wheat-fields spread out like cloths of deepening
gold, downs with their configurations of clouds, and the sea, with
many ships upon its bosom beckoning to unknown lands. Like
Burroughs, he was unusually susceptible to flowers (the anemone
became his signature) and to trees, most of all to oaks, firs, and
cathedral-like beeches. Though the later essays are not so enlivened
with animals as the earlier ones, we are frequently made aware of
their presence. Birds were the chief attraction, and he excelled in
the description of their song and their flight. His essay on the
swallow is based upon as vigilant observation as that of Ruskin in
Love's Meinie, and has the advantage of being better art. Even more
impressive are his descriptions of flight in "The Hovering of the
Kestrel" and "Birds Climbing the Air." As in the early essays, a
prominent place is given to human beings, some of the best portraits being those in "The Field Play" and "My Old Village," in
the latter of which he records some of the many changes that had
been wrought on the scenes of his youth, among them the passing
of certain figures who loom large in the pages of *Round about a
Great Estate*—all "gone as you might casually pluck a hawthorn
leaf from the hedge."

As to his philosophy, Jefferies reflects both the agnosticism of
his own generation and the romanticism of the several preceding
ones. It seemed to him that nature, possessing "no more feeling
than the force which lifts the tides" and devoid of consciousness,
sets no value upon life, whether that of minute hill-snail or of
human being. The proper religion for mankind, therefore, is humanity at its farthest reach, for man alone is capable of conscious
aspiration. Yet he did not deny nature an important function in
such a religion, for in the enjoyment of its beauty there often comes
a yearning for the higher life of the soul. Such was his own experience, and this feeling, as well as sheer physical ecstasy, gave a lilt
to his style and to many of his passages an impassioned quality.

Throughout the nineteenth century, the out-of-door essay continued, of course, to receive nourishment from various Continental sources, particularly from France, with such poets as Lamartine, Hugo and Leconte de Lisle, such painters as those of the Barbizon group, and such prose writers as Michelet, Maeterlinck, and Fabre. Of major importance were the many successive volumes of the *Souvenirs entomologiques* (1869-1907), which brought the growing interest in the multitudinous and inexhaustible world of insects to full artistic expression and led other essayists to devote more attention to its chronicling. Like an anthropologist amongst savages, Fabre recorded their bizarre forms, the marvellous workings of their instincts, and with dramatic vividness presented the cycle of their lives: their wrigglings out of eggs or chrysalises, their various devices for securing a livelihood, their dances and songs and insatiable loves, their guerrilla fighting ("worthy of the athletes in the ancient palaestra") and their deaths—cicadas emerging from the earth after years of tunneling; field crickets, bees, and spiders constructing their homes; glow-worms anaesthetizing snails with a few gentle tweaks and then reducing them to soup before quaffing from the shell; praying mantises and scorpions devouring their mates after pairing; and great peacock moths, guided (so Fabre erroneously thought) by scent, swarming from the far horizons about a prospective bride. What generalizations he has to make—a very cautious procedure with him—are withheld until after the unfoldment of the drama so that the reader will have the feeling of having participated in their formulation.

His Lilliputian actors are seen against a definite background, usually that of his "harmas," a natural laboratory of weedy fields on the outskirts of Sérignan, in Provence. They are considerably humanized by his referring many of their habits to similar ones in human life, including those recorded by literature and history; and so impressively described are some of their actions they assume almost symbolic significance. Fabre himself, along with the members of his family and the folk of the countryside, frequently appears in the various scenes, and, like Burroughs, he enjoys browsing on memories of the days of his youth. An amiable, devout, unworldly, and poetically-minded man, able to look upon the many horrors of insect life with hardly any repugnance, he gives one a continual sense of the wonder of the world and the feeling that "nothing is

trivial in the majestic problem of nature." Possessed of one of the
most limpid and exquisite of styles, he enclosed in the amber of his
essays a host of ephemera.

Such, in broad outline, was Hudson's heritage in his main field
of expression.

Development and Achievement

Sweet flowers are slow and weeds make haste.

HUDSON WAS NOT a weed, nor was he one of the flowers that take the winds of March with beauty. Rather, it was only in late summer that he came to blossom, but once in blossom he continued fresh and fragrant until the killing frosts of late autumn. Burroughs was likewise slow of growth, but, though born only four years before Hudson, he had made his bow to the public as an out-of-door essayist twenty-two years earlier. Jefferies, on the other hand, born seven years later than Hudson, was already six years in his grave before Hudson revealed himself in book form as a fellow-essayist. Had Hudson died at the age of Thoreau, *The Purple Land* would be his only hold upon fame, and that, a slight one. The lateness of his blossoming is, indeed, the most remarkable circumstance of his artistic unfoldment.

Some of the reasons for this lateness have already been presented in the biographical sketch. Before his arrival in England in 1874 at the age of almost thirty-three, Hudson had done the spadework of observation for several volumes. The various papers he addressed to the London Zoological Society from 1869 to 1876, containing some of the material that went to the writing of his first two books of natural history, reveal a man who, as in the account of "the Procreant Instincts of the three Species of *Molothrus*," has perfected his power of observation as a field naturalist and is reading widely in the realm of natural history. They also reveal one who, thanks to the library of standard authors a mother took with her to an isolated pampean home, has a certain command of expression and who is alive to the beauty as well as the wonder of the world about him. As a natural historian, Hudson was still in need of intimate association with those of similar interests, for scientifically the Argentine was only a colonial outpost. England (it will be remembered) made available such associations—in the beginning, largely in the person of Sclater. As an out-of-door essayist, he had a tortuous path yet to tread. It was primarily his long struggle with poverty, forcing him to fritter away much of his energy as a literary hack, that kept him from publishing the first volumes of his nature studies, *Argentine Ornithology* (1888-89), until his late forties.

Although the title page unfairly gave his collaborator the larger share of credit,[1] these two volumes once and for all established Hudson's reputation as an ornithologist, the reviewer in *Nature* asserting, "Never was there a better describer of the habits of birds. . . ." He showed himself enough of a student to make full use of the knowledge then available, particularly that of Azara among predecessors and that of Gibson and Barrows among contemporaries. But Argentine ornithology still required the labors of a pioneer, and Hudson, with his unparalleled opportunities for observation of the birds of the pampas and of the Rio Negro, was eminently qualified to be their chronicler, recording their language and rendering living likenesses. The papers sent to the London Zoological Society yielded him much of the material for his studies of the swallow, the cowbird, the scarlet tyrant, the blackbird, the woodpecker, the cuckoo, the burrowing owl, the rhea, the glossy ibis, the heron, the spoonbill, the rail, and the gull.[2]

Though his style is as yet uneven, he exhibits admirable skill with the generalized character-sketch, as in those of the ovenbird, the firewood gatherer, the rhea, and the carancho and chimango hawks, both of which are invested with some nobility. For bird-cries and bird-song, his ear is unerringly fine and discriminating. There is also ample evidence of a speculative mind, concerned with such major problems as adaptation to environment and natural selection. Always modest in his claims, Hudson nowhere in all his writings underscored his contributions to science. But one of the more obvious ones here, besides the discovery of two new species, is his study of the parasitic habits of the Argentine and the screaming cowbirds, which led him to a different conclusion from Darwin's as to their incipiency. Of special interest are his many accounts of the playfulness and the dancing performances of birds, for he was to recur to them frequently in his essays and they served in shaping his theory of the origin of the sense of beauty. The aerial dance of the black tyrant about his perch, the téru's quadrilles, and the pom-

---

[1] It reads: *Argentine Ornithology: A Descriptive Catalogue of the Birds of the Argentine Republic.* By P. L. Sclater, M.A., Ph.D., F.R.S., Etc. With Notes on Their Habits by W. H. Hudson, C.M.Z.S., Late of Buenos Ayres.

[2] The descriptions of the rufous and laughing cachalotes were first published in 1885 in the *Ibis.*

pous, military precision with which two lapwings kept conducting each arrival to and from a lagoon, as if they were the dispensers of the water—all, so Hudson insists, have little or no connection with the sexual instinct.

Although Hudson's approach in *Argentine Ornithology* is necessarily a generalized one, the out-of-door essayist in him is occasionally adumbrated. Many of the birds are individualized: the wounded chestnut-shouldered hang-nest that warbled in his hand; the little red heron who simulated a dead, yellow, tapering bulrush by stiffening its elongated body and keeping its bladelike edge toward him; and the rhea that, Niobe-like, tried frantically to shelter her young brood against a gang of fifteen caranchos, who kept striking them dead "on the small of the neck just behind the head." There are also glimpses into the world that was later to be fully revealed in *Far Away and Long Ago*: the illimitable grassy ocean of the pampas, broken by occasional rush and sedge beds and studded with innumerable brown vizcacha villages (the homes, too, of bank martins and burrowing owls); the broad swampy margins and luxuriant groves of the Rio de la Plata; the Hudson estancia, with its fragrant white acacias and its narrow, thistle-enclosed path, where the chimango hawk would swoop down to strike a terrorizing blow upon the forehead of his horse; and the colorful gauchos, pitting crested screamers against one another, hunting the rhea with the *bolas*, and snaring the tinamou with cane and noose and hovering carancho.

As in most of the incidents already mentioned, we are often made aware of Hudson's companionship. The account of his first hearing of the matchless song of the shy white-banded mockingbird, hidden in a chañar-wood along the valley of the Rio Negro, is in the very spirit of the out-of-door essay. After discovering the perfect manner in which the parasitical instinct functions in the screaming cowbird, whose eggs and young are indistinguishable from those of her victim, the bay-wing, he bubbles over with excitement: "To-day I . . . am as pleased as if I had found a new planet in the sky." And after witnessing the marvellous instinct for self-preservation of the red heron, he exclaims, "I . . . thought that never had anything so beautiful fallen in my way before. . . ." Personal touches of this sort, the great amount of intimate bird-gossip, and the sketching in of a picturesque background make *Birds of La Plata* (1920), the title to which *Argentine Ornithology* was changed after Sclater's material had been deleted, one of the most delightful books of its kind.

Its more diversified companion volume, *The Naturalist in La Plata* (1892), which also owes some of its material to the papers sent to the London Zoological Society, was immediately acclaimed by Wallace to be "a storehouse of facts and observations of the greatest value to the philosophical naturalist, while to the general reader it will rank as the most interesting and delightful of modern books on natural history." [3] It possesses certain advantages over the previous works in the field, such as *Wanderings in South America, The Voyage of the Beagle,* and *The Naturalist on the River Amazons,* for, having been written by a native, it could dispense with the often tedious connective tissue of a travel book, and, instead of presenting the observations of a naturalist in the form of isolated incidents, could group them around certain speculations. Since the chapters are of essay length, capable of separate existence, and often of essay texture—their author being "chiefly occupied with matters of personal knowledge, seasoned with a little speculation"—they savor of the out-of-door essay, particularly the last three of them. While *The Naturalist in La Plata* is closer to literature of power than its companion, *Birds of La Plata,* and superior in style to its predecessors, it is still essentially literature of knowledge.

Many of the observations are discoveries of his own, such as those on the bee that protects itself with its stench as well as its sting; the grasshopper that on taking flight becomes the facsimile of a common wasp; the venomous toad accredited with the killing of horses; the arboreal opussum thriving on the plains; the hairy armadillo that alone of its congeners has adapted itself, by its versatility, to invading civilization; and even a striking variation of *Homo sapiens,* one possessing perpetually snarling lips, sharklike teeth in an enormous mouth, and a high-pitched animal voice. No one previously had described so fully the life of the vizcacha, the most

---

[3] George Romanes, in his review of it in the *Nineteenth Century,* declared, "It is seldom that the literature of zoology has received a contribution at once so full of original observations, and presenting so great a charm of literary style" (XXXIII [1893], 886). And Karl Groos in Germany, who made considerable use of it in his *Play of Animals,* called it a "wonderful book" (New York, 1898, p. 10).

common mammal on the pampas. There are also good chapters on spiders, hummingbirds, crested screamers, and skunks, to whose effluvium "crushed garlic is [as] lavender."

The two traits that attracted most attention from the general reader were those attributed to the guanaco and the puma: the former is pictured as repairing, at the approach of death, to the Golgotha of its species in southernmost Patagonia, and the latter, as so strongly affected by the scent of man that it becomes passive and docile in his presence. Both of these attributions, the first shared by Darwin, are now discredited: the one, definitely, for the large bone deposits of the guanaco have been traced to their having starved to death in great numbers during severe winters; and the other, to a considerable extent, for Hudson, as the advocate of the allegedly cowardly puma, somewhat overstressed his gentleness toward human beings in order to reinstate him in the good graces of mankind.[4] However, since nearly all of the observations in *The Naturalist in La Plata* have withstood sixty years of fuller investigation, it was unworthy of Burroughs to say that he had come to doubt Hudson's "veracity as an observer" because of that work's "many big stories."

The speculative quality of his mind is here fully disclosed. In "Music and Dancing in Nature" he enlarges upon one of the themes of *Birds of La Plata*: the deep-rootedness in animals of a sense of beauty. He is concerned also with such questions as the amount of intelligence that can be ascribed to the various classes of animal life, at what stage of their development birds and beasts acquire fear of their enemies, how the parasitism of the gnat, tick, mosquito and bird-fly originated, the purpose of the luminous organ of the firefly, the *raison d'être* of the migratory instinct of the gossamer spider and even that of the cackling of our barnyard hen. By showing, in "A Wave of Life," how the exceptional prolificacy of mice during one season leads, as the result of the thronging of enemies to the feast, to their bare survival in the next, Hudson vividly illustrates, as Darwin had done, the interdependence of all living things.

---

[4] In his article on the puma in the *Harmsworth Natural History,* Hudson neatly parries Theodore Roosevelt's attack on his analysis of the puma's strange conduct toward man. To the very end of his life, he adherred to his original conclusions.

Of his closing chapter, he remarks that it "is not intended for the severe naturalist, but rather for such readers as may like to hear . . . about the pains and pleasures of the seeker, as well as the result of the seeking." Something of this quality, the romance of natural history, is communicated, here and there, throughout the volume. One finds it in many of the personal experiences with which he illustrates his findings and his speculations. Such a one is the sudden, unprompted charge of his horse Picaso, an untameable-looking brute with turbulently rolling eyes, upon a bull that was fleeing from tormenting gauchos, a charge that brought the rider an unmerited round of applause. In the opening chapter, the desert pampas, with its engaging disarray of stately grass, in which the wind plays a magical music, is beautifully described. And occasionally the sense of wonder all but takes his breath away. The tremendous evening chant of an incalculable multitude of crested screamers, sounding louder than the sea crashing against a rocky coast, overcame him with astonishment as he sat at supper in a lonely rancho. When lying back on his horse till head and shoulders rested almost on its crupper and gazing upon "the vast circle of the heavens glittering with innumerable stars," he had "the enchanting illusion" of soaring through space, "the muffled sound of hoofs on the soft sward" becoming "in fancy only the rushing of the wings of [a] Pegasus."

What Hudson had done for the birds of La Plata he also did for those of the land of his adoption. Since the birds there already had many chroniclers, some of them encyclopedic, and he had started to become acquainted with them only in his mid-thirties, *British Birds* (1895) is only one among many good handbooks. The composite life-histories, such as those of the throstle, rook, cuckoo, common guillemot and stormy petrel, are recorded more trimly than those of *Birds of La Plata*. There are some out-of-door essay elements: the description of the aerial exercises of the snipe and the incident of the pet kestrel that, after returning faithfully every evening for several years to perch on the shoulders of master or mistress and be fed small scraps of meat, suddenly started to attack their heads violently. But the personality in the writing is much fainter than in *Birds of La Plata,* and the volume is without the excitement of important discoveries. Both in spirit as well as in form, it is more of a compilation. Had *British Birds* been written toward the end of his career and he had drawn upon the valuable

material of his own essays, what a rich volume it would have
been!

Only twice again did he, strictly speaking, project books of
natural history, one on the serpent, which had to be abandoned late
in life even though much labor had been spent on it, and the other,
an expansion of a pamphlet on lost British birds, written in 1894
for the Society for the Protection of Birds, which Linda Gardiner,
after his death, completed for him—*Rare, Vanishing & Lost British
Birds* (1923). The preservation of birds was, throughout his life,
a matter very close to his heart, and by making the English conscious of the many beautiful and noble birds already lost to their
enjoyment or in danger of being annihilated, he thought he might
stay a few of the many hands of destruction, possibly even those of
"gamekeepers, collectors, cockney sportsmen, and louts with guns."
The book, like the obituary column of a newspaper, is very much
a compilation, the only part of some general interest being "Allusions
in Poetry."

These volumes are Hudson's main contribution to the shelves
of natural history. After sixty years, *Argentine Ornithology* still
dominates its particular shelf, and *British Birds* I have personally
found to be one of the best companions for wandering about the
fields and woods and marshes. Both, however, require direct experiences with nature to animate their pages. Of *The Naturalist in La
Plata,* a recent authority has declared, "There is no book in any
language that gives such an intelligible and lasting impression of
the animals of the Argentine." [5] It is, indeed, one of the best volumes that nineteenth-century science has contributed to literature.
In its pages, the out-of-door essayist who was to shine in *Idle Days
in Patagonia, Birds in a Village,* and *Nature in Downland* and thus
set a new luminary swinging in the literary firmament is clearly
discernible. Still, the development from *The Naturalist in La Plata*
to *Idle Days in Patagonia,* the most important in his career as a
writer, is a considerable one. And it should give us pause.

In "How I Became an Idler," one of the best essays in the latter
volume, Hudson tells us that it was a mere accident, a gunshot

---

[5] Paul R. Cutright, *The Great Naturalists Explore South America* (New York,
1940), p. 36.

wound just below the knee-cap, laying him up for many weeks, that changed him from a naturalist and ornithologist into an essayist. What had mainly attracted him to Patagonia in 1870 was the opportunity for studying birds in a region that had been ornithologically visited only by d'Orbigny and Darwin.

If things had gone well with me, if I had spent my twelve months on the Rio Negro, as I had meant to do, watching and listening to the birds of that district, these desultory chapters, which might be described as a record of what I did not do, would never have been written. . . . Seeing one class of objects too well would have made all others look distant, obscure, and of little interest. . . . Lying helpless on my back through the long sultry midsummer days, with the white-washed walls of my room for landscape and horizon, and a score or two buzzing house-flies, perpetually engaged in their intricate airy dance, for only company, I was forced to think on a great variety of subjects, and to occupy my mind with other problems than that of migration. These other problems, too, were in many ways like the flies that shared my apartment, and yet always remained strangers to me, as I to them, since between their minds and mine a great gulf was fixed. Small unpainful riddles of the earth; flitting, sylph-like things, that began life as abstractions, and developed, like imago from maggot, into entities: I always flitting among them, as they performed their mazy dance, whirling in circles, falling and rising, poised motionless, then suddenly cannoning against me for an instant, mocking my power to grasp them, and darting off again at a tangent. . . . Happily for the progress of knowledge only a very few of these fascinating elusive insects of the brain can appear before us at the same time; as a rule we fix our attention on a single individual, like a falcon amid a flight of pigeons or a countless army of small field finches; or a dragon-fly in the thick of a cloud of mosquitoes, or infinitesimal sand-flies. . . .

And after leaving my room, hobbling round with the aid of a stout stick, and sitting in houses, I consorted with men and women, and listened day by day to the story of their small unavian affairs, until it began to interest me. But not too keenly. I could always quit them without regret to lie on the green sward, to gaze up into the trees or the blue sky, and speculate on all imaginable things. The result was that when no longer any excuse for inaction existed, use had bred a habit in me—the habit of indolence, which was quite common among the people of Patagonia, and appeared to suit the

genial climate; and this habit and temper of mind I retained, with
occasional slight relapses, during the whole period of my stay.

Thus, at least by the age of thirty, he became aware of the essayist
in him, eager to observe and record more and more of the pageantry
of life. It was not, however, until over two decades later, and then
by what seems to have been a series of accidents, that he came to
make literary capital out of his essential temperament, becoming in
deed what he had already become in spirit. Why this long delay?

Hudson's only publications before leaving the Argentine several
years later were the papers sent to the London Zoological Society,
one of which, that on the vizcacha, he was able to republish as a
chapter of *The Naturalist in La Plata* with almost no alteration.
He must have taken with him, though, a sizeable journal—the
increasingly full record of his experience with nature from youth on
—and some miscellaneous writing ready, or almost ready, for publication. His association with Sclater and other ornithologists and
naturalists undoubtedly accentuated the scientist in him, aiding him in
extracting the more scientific content from his journal and in presenting it in the volumes just discussed. On the other hand, this
association bred in him a distrust for the purely scientific or museum
mind. "The scientific mind in its questing after the truth reminds
one of the stoat on the track of its quarry. . . . The difference is that
the stoat makes no mistakes, and the seeker after truth makes many."
That is, scientists, too intent on the goal in their pursuit of knowledge, are wont to ignore the attractions along the wayside, the aesthetic quality of experience; and living constantly in their presence
gave Hudson a sense of confinement or of being blinkered. He preferred the broader horizons of the versatile, old-fashioned field
naturalist, and often later, when he refers to some specialist, such as
a dipterist or a lepidopterist, a smile of condescension seems to
be playing about his lips.

There were paths of escape, along which he could occasionally
indulge the poet and the romancer in him. *Merry England*, in 1883
and 1884, accepted several of his poems—"The London Sparrow,"
"In the Wilderness," and "Gwendoline." He kept writing poems
throughout his life, and in the end had enough to fill a few volumes.
Had he devoted a lifetime to the practice of poetry, he might have
achieved a niche among the more respectable minor poets, for the

reading of poetry was a major passion of his and there was within him much of the essence of which poets are fashioned. He was conscious, however, of his limitations in the handling of the "delicate and difficult instrument" of verse, and was inclined to deem himself "too much occupied in seeing. There is no room and time for 'tranquillity,' since I want to go on to see something else." Actually, one finds in his writing much of the emotion recollected in tranquillity, but he needed the more detailed scope, the more casual melody, of prose to secure his effects. So before his death, with a courage rare among authors, he committed his poems to the flames rather than have them fall into the hands of a publisher. Perhaps he felt that the poet in him had found adequate expression in the romances and the essays.

It would have been just as well had several of his novels suffered a similar fate. But the novel, the romance, and the short story are far more liberal with the purse than is poetry—at times even lavish—and the protégé of Professor Sclater was finding it hard to keep body and soul together while dwelling so completely within the domain of natural science. Despite the miserliness of the muse of fiction toward her new votary in the beginning, he continued to serve her faithfully, after his fashion, to the very end of his days. There was a sense of release in her presence, and those offerings that were not entirely worthy of his sense of devotion long remained anonymous.

The Purple Land That England Lost (1885), even though it possesses certain defects in structure and in style, which a later revision did not entirely remove, belongs to that rare company of *A Sentimental Journey, Dead Souls,* and *A Bible in Spain.* Its series of sketches and stories, in which the free though not easy life of the open road is captured, does for the Banda Orientál what its companions do for other lands. The portrait of this wild, exotic country, drawn with freshness and verve and humor, should have established Hudson's literary reputation once and for all. But beyond some kind words in the *Academy*, this extraordinary book, probably because of the heavy historical introduction, the unfamiliarity of its locale, the apparent lack of artistic intention, and the very broadness of its humanity, received either an indifferent or harsh reception, and after a few years passed into limbo. Had it been written a decade later, when the pendulum of taste was swinging in a different direction, it might have received immediate and wide recognition. Good though it is—the only one of his books to reflect the youthful Hudson—*The Purple Land* has not the merit of the best of his volumes of out-of-door essays.

Largely as the result of the increasing pressure of industrialism, some writers sought escape in utopian romance. And Hudson, feeling the pressure more sharply than the others, imagined, in *A Crystal Age* (1887), the most idyllic of the fantasies of the future. The strength of some of the ideas, particularly the manner in which society is perpetuated, gives the book a vitality often wanting in its fellows and makes it important in the interpretation of its author's attitude toward life. In spite of a certain tightness, the texture of the writing shows the hand of an artist. Though possessing much beauty and measuring up well with the best of its genre, *A Crystal Age* likewise met with a cool reception and was soon forgotten; but Hudson thought well enough of his creation to revise it, and, in 1906, to claim it as his own. *Ralph Herne*, the first written of all his longer works and serialized in an obscure magazine (*Youth*) in 1888, was not published in book form until 1922, and then, as in his acknowledgement of *Fan*, only to increase his bequest to the Royal Society for the Protection of Birds. Except for the forceful picture of the yellow-fever plague in Buenos Aires and the quality of the style, it is little better than the run-of-the-mill fiction of its time. *Fan: The Story of a Young Girl's Life* (1892), showing the influence of Gissing, was written against the grain. Conventional in plot and awkward in dialogue, it was nevertheless, as the reviewer of the *Spectator* pointed out, "immeasurably superior to the average product of the circulating libraries." The main situation, the friendship between two women, is an unusual one, and some of the responses of the heroine indicate the workings of an original mind. But its chief interest to us of this age is a personal rather than an artistic one. The reviewer for the *Athenaeum*, deeming *Fan* "as dull and badly put together as it is coarse and repulsive," expressed the wish that what "appears to be its author's first experiment in fiction . . . may also prove his last. . . ."

Thus up to the time that he turned to the out-of-door essay, Hudson had achieved in the novel one distinct and one partial artistic success. None of the four had brought him, despite all his efforts, more than a mere pittance. Yet, even after receiving high acclaim in a different genre, he still felt impelled to write fiction, and with his next novel (it will be remembered) won through to his first real financial success as an author. The composition of poetry and fiction was not, however, without considerable value to him, apart from helping to keep alive his corruptible self while he was the servant of science: it nurtured the artist in him. Only by balancing scientific reality, in which he felt himself becoming entirely too much engrossed, with romance was he able to adjust his personality and find an outlet for his deep emotional reservoir. The training received from the craft of fiction proved valuable to him as an essayist, enlarging his knowledge of human beings and his sense of their importance not only in his own life but in the total scheme of nature. The human note grows fuller and deeper in his essays, and is more skilfully sounded. The training further encouraged him, a naturally reticent man, to speak out occasionally *de profundis*. It also aided him in sensing and extracting the dramatic in a situation, noticeably wanting, for instance, in *Selborne*, and impressive in his own essays.

There were other reasons, besides his work in natural science and his excursions into the provinces of poetry and fiction, that he did not find his true medium earlier. Though the out-of-door essay had already been established in America by Thoreau and, in the 'seventies, had received wide recognition in the writings of Burroughs, it was not until a decade later that their names began to be a force in English literature. Just how early Hudson became acquainted with Thoreau and Burroughs we do not know, but that he was familiar with them before turning to the writing of the out-of-door essay there can be little doubt. Indeed, as indicated from time to time in the last chapter, he was fairly well acquainted with the whole range of nature writing, and doubtless with much of it at this stage of his development. The spectacle of Jefferies' life was before him—in part, as a warning; in much larger measure, as an inspiration. Yet, except in a general way, Hudson derived little from his predecessors in the out-of-door essay. He did not owe his appreciation of the wild and his aloofness to Thoreau, his charm to Burroughs, nor his passionate desire for oneness with the beauty of Nature to Jefferies. He was essentially an original genius, obeying merely the laws of his own being.

Only slowly had Burroughs and Jefferies gathered an audience, for an essayist, unless he is willing to sell his birthright for a pot of message, does not easily gain a hearing. Essays are, in truth, the most aristocratic form of prose, and since aristocrats among readers are few, their authors are wont to receive little encouragement. The shabby reception editors accorded Hudson's earliest efforts in this genre has already been noted. To the customary coolness toward what did not reverberate with a challenge, there must have been added, particularly in the mind of an urban editor, a sense of confusion. How were the writings of "a traveller in little[, rural] things" to be classified? As belles-lettres? or as natural history? Were they flesh or fish or fowl? And, after all, who, except the readers of heavy scientific volumes, sporting journals or poetry, were really interested in birds? Nowadays, as F. M. Colby has wittily remarked, many an editor keeps a literary bird-dog on his staff just to flush small game for each succeeding number. Hudson did as much as, if not more than, anyone else to bring about this change of taste, but conditions were different when he began to press for a hearing. The confusion in his reception is reflected in the reviews of his first collections of essays. It is quite likely, for example, that the *Athenaeum* turned over most of these books to naturalists for reviewing, since the criticisms in its columns dwell mostly on the natural history element in them, cautioning their author not to give himself over so completely to mere "impressions" but rather to be more definite about the plants and creatures referred to; and they either ignored or hastily generalized on the aesthetic values in the essays.

It is well that Hudson did not become an editor's bird-dog, and remained only an occasional contributor to magazines. To have put himself in weekly, or even monthly, intercourse with a large, heterogeneous, and lackadaisical public would probably have meant the loss of much that is rare and beautiful in his works. True, some of his essays are of the "bread-and-cheese" variety, written not to please himself but to indulge an editor when the larder was low. For essays do not pay well until their author has attracted to himself a sizeable following, and it was not until the sudden popularity of *Green Mansions* that there was any clamoring for Hudson's essays. Although a goodly portion of most of his volumes appeared first in periodicals, he was usually able, with careful revision and the inclusion of fresh material, to arrange his chapters into something of a pattern, and, as often as not, had a book in mind either before submitting any of it to an editor or after only an essay or two had been published. Thus, far from disfiguring his essays, as they did a number of Jefferies, magazine requirements aided him in securing the proper length and provided the opportunity for rewriting.

It is fortunate, too, that some of the propaganda in Hudson— frequently he was moved to protest against the wanton destruction, among other wilding things, of bird-life—found a convenient outlet in the form of pamphlets issued by the Humanitarian League or the Royal Society for the Protection of Birds. The effectiveness of these pamphlets can still be felt, whether their purpose was to impart information, as in "Something about the Owl" (the preface to Waterton's *Barn Owl*, 1895) and *On Liberating Caged Birds* (1914), or to attack an abuse, as in the *Letter to Clergymen, Ministers, and Others* (1895) and *The Trade in Birds' Feathers* (1898). And they led to the enactment of laws. Several of them, largely because he realized that "in matters of this nature nothing but the concrete instance can take any hold on us," are valuable additions to the corpus of his essays—*Osprey: or, Egrets and Aigrettes* (1891), *Linnets for Sixpence!* (1904), and *Roff and a Linnet: Chain and Cage* (1918).

While finishing *The Naturalist in La Plata*, he began to plan a book on his Patagonian experiences. His South American journal probably could not have yielded another volume of natural history of equal importance. Besides, the spirit of rebellion against the world of science was rising within him. He had acquiesced in the collaboration with Sclater in *Argentine Ornithology* only to get his material published. What was written there and in *The Naturalist in La Plata* had come primarily out of his own intimate contact with nature; he had no desire to turn next, by means of long burrowing in the necropolis of a museum, to the compilation of "ponderous tomes which nobody reads, elephantine bodies without souls; or shall we say, carcasses, dressed and placed in their canvas coverings on shelves in the cold storage of the zoological libraries." The trouble with most natural history books is that there is too much of the author's specialty in them, and not enough of general human interest. "When a man has a good deal of science," Hudson observes, "he is apt to muffle himself up in it, even to the concealment of his natural features, so that we do not know whether he is one of us or not, or to what tribe he belongs." He himself was not going to yield his humanity for the sake of any specialty, nor become a mere stock-taker of God's possessions. In *The Naturalist in La Plata*, he had sought, by means of giving an essay-like quality to some of the chapters, to make literature out of natural science, and several of them had been accepted before book publication by the more literary magazines. His journal probably contained a fuller experience than he had chosen to reveal in this volume. The auto-biographical impulse, strong in *The Purple Land*, continued to work in him, and as early as 1886, he wrote what was to become sub-stantially the first chapter of *Far Away and Long Ago*. So it is very likely that in planning *Idle Days in Patagonia* he decided to cast aside restraint and animate the whole book with the spirit of the concluding essay of *The Naturalist in La Plata* by presenting the full experience of a field naturalist who was also very much a poet. Why not finally assert the idler in him, one capable not only of knowing Nature but of enjoying her in wise passiveness? On the plains of Patagonia his essential temperament had been revealed to him, and the experience of two decades had confirmed the truth of that revelation.

Besides, his English journal was growing apace. His adopted country, where natural history had reached the monograph stage, did not afford him, as a field naturalist, the unparalleled advan-tages of the Argentine, nor did he enjoy that intimacy with its wild life that comes with close association from childhood. "It is hard, well-nigh impossible, . . . for any one to know the shy, volatile inhabitants of any district sufficiently well to justify a book about them, . . . without that familiarity with their ways which comes only from very long and patient observation, which begins in boyhood in the country-born boy, and grows with his growth, and becomes at last a habit of the mind as well as a passion." Then how was this material to be used? He had already reached complete emotional and intellectual maturity. To the poet and the romancer in him, there had been gradually added, through wide reading, the man of letters. The style of *The Naturalist in La Plata*, though still rather matter-of-fact, was a distinct advance over that of *Birds of La Plata*. A fuller use of emotion as an interpreter of Nature would bring his writing to complete artistic maturity, and give it an occasional glow. Why not, keeping the scientist subordinate to the artist, write about himself apropos of the life of English fields and hedgerows and villages? "One must have a medium to work in," he says in apology for the appearance of his first book on the English countryside.

> There must be some way or "port" for the mind. If this one [he is speaking generally of books on English birds] happens to be "always peopled with a great multitude," I must nevertheless walk in it, having no longer that other more familiar port, "desolate and over-grown with grass," in which I formerly moved with greater ease. Blown by adverse winds from my own coast and cast on shore here for the rest of my life, as I now begin to believe, I must either hold my peace or speak of what I see, and love best to see, with only this hope and ambition, that the admiration and other agreeable emotions which all bird life in all places excite in me may not prove wholly incommunicable.

Perhaps after he had become in print most truly himself, Fortune would at last smile upon him.

In some such manner, at a time of life when most writers are well along on their course, Hudson entered, quietly but splendidly, into his own kingdom. Not that he was without some misgivings. Probably with memories of the mere *succès d'estime* accorded his first volumes of out-of-door essays, he feared while writing *Nature in Downland* that the result might be another "small unimportant book, not entertaining enough for those who read for pleasure only, nor sufficiently scientific and crammed with facts for readers who thirst after knowledge." The very quality of his genius, its simplicity, its quietness of tone, its dignity and aloofness, its wise scepticism, kept him a long time from full recognition. And occasionally there were wistful glances backward to the more profuse wild life of South America. In one of his essays he expresses the wish of having been able to spend half a lifetime there studying spiders. As late as 1920, a very short time before his death, he wondered whether, by coming to England, he had not made a mistake. "When I think of that land so rich in bird life, those fresher woods and newer pastures where I might have done so much, and then look back at . . . the little I did, . . . the reflection is forced on me that, after all, I probably made choice of the wrong road of the two then open to me." By his early fifties, however, he had reached, in the language of aeronautics, the point of no return.

Idle Days in Patagonia (1893) and *Birds in a Village* (1893), the one a record of his visit to the Rio Negro and the other the first sheaf of his harvest of English impressions, appeared within a few months of each other. The earlier of the two betrays some uneasiness in artistry, for, though well leavened with the spirit of the idler sensitively alert to the revelations of Nature, there are evidences, here and there, of the long struggle that went on in him between the scientist and the essayist. The narrative thread, which effects a dramatic opening[6] with its picture of shipwreck and a long, weary trudge over sand dunes and monotonous, gravelly plains to the nearest human dwelling-place, is dropped after having loosely held together the first half of the book. And some of the later chapters, even though Hudson has dexterously tied them in with references to specific Patagonian experiences and with the tendrils of his own personality, do not inevitably belong to a volume on Patagonia: they seem to be serving as a make-weight. Yet, when one considers the brevity of his sojourn and the bounds of his itinerary (he was in this southernmost province of the Argentine only a year, several of the best months of which saw him laid up with a wounded leg; he journeyed along the narrow valley of the Rio Negro to about a hundred and twenty miles from the ocean and made occasional short excursions into the surrounding desert), it is remarkable what a sense of fullness there is in his record. He succeeded in placing Patagonia forever upon the spiritual map of the world.

As Wallace immediately pointed out, *Idle Days* does not possess "the wealth of original observation and ingenious speculation which made *The Naturalist in La Plata* a masterpiece," but there is enough in it to satisfy the naturalist in most of us. Patagonia is not especially rich in wild life, and Hudson, for the most part, included only what was suitable for presentation in essay fashion. Thus we meet with a shy little rodent, which, in spite of its subterranean life, has, unlike the mole, bright and prominent jet-black eyes; the dreaded "serpent with a cross," which Darwin thought the ugliest of living things, warming itself against the body of Hudson as he lay wounded in an old, abandoned hut; the escaped cow with her fierce body-guard of feral pigs; and an old, blind retriever, whose drop of bad

---

6 It contains a scene similar to that aboard the *Patna* just before Lord Jim took his fateful leap.

blood made him suddenly, at the scent of geese, revert, like Seton's Wully, to the irresponsible wild dog. Birds, more abundant and the special object of search, come more conspicuously into these pages. Particularly memorable is the encounter with a Magellanic eagle-owl on an island in the Rio Negro. There is a good chapter on bird music, in which, after refuting the idea that the highest flights of melody are limited to the sober-suited, he defends the vocal talents of South American birds.

The panorama Hudson paints of Patagonia is an unforgettable one. The clear, sea-green water of the misnomered Rio Negro, flowing radiantly through a landscape of monotonous greys and greens and browns, draws the eye to it "as to a path of shining silver." The life of the settlements, as well as the remnants of an earlier civilization, is sympathetically included. Never within the scope of an essay has the essence of pioneering—its hardships and disappointments; its joys, yielding "a rill of pure water, . . . the sweetest rill in existence"—been more eloquently presented than in "The War with Nature." And certain human figures—such as Damian, who, on returning after thirty years of captivity among Indians, found himself an alien in the midst of his former fellow-villagers—remain vivid in one's memory. Beyond the borders of the narrow valley stretches monotonously the waterless, treeless, and hill-less desert, where "nothing grows except the barren things that Nature loves." This desolate, grey, brooding solitude, seen *sub specie aeternitatis*, is the theme of "The Plains of Patagonia," one of the most impressive essays in our language.

The idler that his long convalescence from the bullet wound had made Hudson is given full expression in his meditations upon some of the "unpainful riddles" of our common life. The psychology of the senses, to which he was to return again and again, most notably in the last volume of all, *A Hind in Richmond Park*, he makes fascinating beyond all other essayists. Chapters are devoted to the eyesight of the savage, which did not impress Hudson nearly so much as it had Humboldt, and to the various pigments of the eye, their use to animals and their value in the interpretation of racial characteristics. The view of El Carmen and its adjacent hills trans-figured with snow, together with the memory of a passage in *Moby Dick*, leads to a meditation on the sense of mystery and terror that the whiteness of certain flowers and animals, of white clouds and snow and the white horses of the sea, arouse in some sensitive persons; and the evening primrose suggests the theme of the power of odor to act as "a kind of second more faithful memory" in summoning vanished scenes to the mind. In ancient burial-places, where he searched for the artifacts of past cultures, he tried to penetrate imaginatively into the life of those long dead.

These meditations often take a personal turn. Thus, in illustrating what a spur an odor can be to the memory, Hudson tells how the fragrance of the evening primrose ("the sweet perfumer of the wilderness") and the Lombardy poplar brings back to him, in visionary moments that annihilate time and space, the glory and dream of his early days on the pampas. Unconsciously revealing are many of the passing comments on his experiences. After relating how the *vivora de la cruz* had crawled beside his wounded body for warmth, he says, "Had my friend's arms not been occupied with sustaining me he, no doubt, would have attacked it with the first weapon that offered, and in all probability killed it, with the result that I should have suffered from a kind of vicarious remorse ever" afterwards. The profoundest self-revelation comes in "The Plains of Patagonia," the soul and the climax of the book. Day after day he had ridden into the solitude of this desert, "going to it in the morning as if to attend a festival, and leaving it only when hunger and thirst and the westering sun compelled" him. There, with the happy combination of its evocative power and the animistic faculty with which he was endowed, Hudson experienced the mental state of the pure savage and felt himself to be the living sepulcher of the dead past. "The sweetest moment in any life . . . should be when Nature draws near to it, and, taking up her neglected instrument, plays a fragment of some ancient melody, long unheard on the earth." There are fragments of such melody in many of the volumes that were to follow, and the strength of the animistic feeling in him was to be more fully revealed in *Far Away and Long Ago.*

Idle Days, with its wide sweep of canvas for the imagination to play upon, has a corresponding epic breadth of treatment. *Birds in a Village*, with its minutely varied, gardenlike settings, is a slighter, though more artistic, achievement. The long title essay, the record of a springtime spent in the Berkshire village of Cookham Dean, is beautifully conceived, like an expanded Wordsworthian lyric. The remembrance of a girl's ecstatic delight in the birds of

St. James's Park brought Hudson the sudden realization "that only the wished sight of wild birds could medicine" his vision so long dimmed by murky London, and sent him out into the byways of the countryside. And the essay is supported at the end by another delicate caryatid, a village girl swinging lazily under a pair of apple trees and singing a simple melody in a voice that "had no earthly trouble in it, and no passion, and was in this like the melody of the birds of which [he] had lately heard so much; and with it all that tenderness and depth which is not theirs, but is human only and of the soul." Not only did he bear her music in his heart, as Wordsworth did that of the solitary reaper, long after it was heard no more, but the whole intervening experience, recollected in tranquillity, became transmuted into an idyll.

There is, of course, reference value in most of Hudson's out-of-door essays. Here, for example, he concerns himself with some of the problems of bird psychology, problems that had been generally ignored by ornithologists. Why, he asks, do some birds use, in moments of extreme agitation, "singing notes that express agreeable emotions"? Is a parent bird, when fluttering in broken-wing manner along the ground, deliberately feigning injury in order to toll off an intruder upon its nest or young?[7] As is characteristic of the out-of-door essay, there are a number of individual portraits: the wry-neck that was starved out of its nest in the hole of an old apple tree and the nightingale that, at the height of its excitement as Hudson approached its nest, burst into song. And there is a sensitive recording of bird-song, such as that of the greenfinch, with its long trillings and little chirps, its soft warbled note, and long, low, inflected scream, "as if some unsubstantial being, fairy or wood nymph, had screamed somewhere in her green hiding-place." But what gives to this essay a new note in the treatment of birds is the unique quality of the author's vision. Toward birds, as toward the rest of nature, White had remained relatively objective. Thoreau and Jefferies were often subjective in their appreciation, but birds

---

[7] This question Hudson did not answer, here or elsewhere, to the satisfaction of present-day ornithologists. It is well that he pointed out that there is no intelligence involved in the act, but he should have taken into consideration the instinct of self-preservation as well as that of parental anxiety in determining the cause. "Distraction-display" is now thought to be the product of a conflict between these two basic impulses.

never meant so much to them as to Hudson, to whom they were almost as interesting as men and women. Since his eyes and ears had been trained in another continent, he could bring to the appreciation of English birds fresher and more justly appraising senses. And his having been long in city pent only intensified his vision and made him more lyrical. His sensitivity toward birds was indeed more subtle and poetic than even that of Burroughs.

More important, Hudson was now writing of himself apropos of English birds. Next to a lover of birds and the outdoors, he reveals himself as a lover of poetry. When seeking out "shady green pavilions" for the sake of their solitude from all except birds, he chooses as his companion a sheaf of poems, such as those of elfin Melendez, "whose finest songs are without human interest; who is irresponsible as the wind, and as unstained with earthly care as the limpid running water he delights in; who is brother to bird and bee and butterfly, and worships only liberty and sunshine, and is in love with nothing but a flower." There are gleams of poetry in "Birds in a Village," which, at times, as in the transformation of a boy into a wryneck, becomes fantasy; and often the poetry of others is interwoven into the texture of his style. In *Far Away and Long Ago*, Hudson tells us that had he anticipated the writing of that book, he would have withheld from his previous volumes much of his early life on the pampas. It is fortunate for us that its writing was unforeseen and that it came late in his career, for in so doing he would have deprived us of that frequent harking back to the scenes of his youth, which intensifies the personal note in his essays and gives them a delightfully exotic flavor.

There was to come into his essays a growing interest in human beings and in villages. Besides the sketches of the two girls and group portraits of the villagers, there are other likenesses that stand out from their background: two birdcatchers who hated pigeons for having superseded starlings as targets for trap-shooting gentlemen and thus robbed them of part of their livelihood, and, especially, the old man with mottled clothing and twinkling eyes who told Hudson the story of the wryneck that lodged in his orchard. The village itself is sketched in with vivid touches, particularly the nearby stream with its pollard-willows, the only sort of "man-mutilated" things in nature that not infrequently gain "in beauty by the mutilation, so admirably [do they] fit into and harmonize with the landscape," and with its water-lilies, their polished buds "shaped like snakes' heads."

Since the title essay of *Birds in a Village* would have made too slim a volume, Hudson padded it with miscellaneous essays on birds. Later, when the volume was revised[8] and called *Birds in Town and Village* (1919), he added "Birds in a Cornish Village," which, though decidedly inferior to the title essay, somewhat balances the volume. In all this make-weight, there are some good pages on the starling, the much-maligned London sparrow, the jackdaw, and the chanticleer, whose song has "more associations for man than any other sound in nature." Chaucer and Thoreau would have delighted in his analysis of the intrinsic merits of cockcrow, which ranges from "the raucous bronchial strain" of the cochin to the "brief, piercing, and emphatic" trisyllabic crow of the bantam. And the excellent "In an Old Garden" introduces us to one of Hudson's main attitudes toward art.

Idle Days in Patagonia and *Birds in a Village* revealed in the realm of the out-of-door essay an author who possessed fresh and significant material, a master of a style that could be exquisite, vigorous and eloquent, and a poetic personality. The former, with such capital essays as "The War with Nature," "How I Became an Idler," "The Evening Primrose," and "The Plains of Patagonia," was, at the time of its appearance, the best book of out-of-door essays since *Walden*. And though he was soon to paint larger canvases of the English countryside, "Birds in a Village" remains an exquisite achievement. Both books give one the sense of complete inspiration. With so full-blown a maturity of mind and mastery of art, we can hardly expect any further important development in Hudson. Except for *The Purple Land*, he had, as an author, largely skipped his youth; he was on the older side of middle years before finishing the long period of preparation and gaining complete command of all his resources. Consequently, there could scarcely come into his writings so marked a change as appeared in those of Jefferies. And what we have mainly to look for in the volumes that follow are the expansion of old interests, the occasional inclusion

---

8 In the revision of the title essay, Hudson incorporated some of the material that appeared originally in the appendix, and added further observations on birds and several colorful incidents, which give it greater variety.

of new ones, the progressively fuller revelations of his personality, and his skill in bringing the ampler experience, with its ever-fresh, protean material, under the control of his art.

Birds in London (1898), written, like his poem "The London Sparrow," out of a thankfulness for small blessings, is one of Hudson's bread-and-cheese books. London to him was always a brick-and-mortar desert with fields of headstones and monstrous mausoleums relieved by a few oases; and, like Jefferies, he looked eagerly forward to the day when "the dust of all her people" shall have been blown "by the winds of many centuries" and "old trees" grow "again on this desecrated spot as in past ages" and thus be made "healthy at last!" Yet for his sins, so he informs us, this lover of the wild was compelled to spend the summer months of 1896 and 1897 in this desert; and, passing the time as profitably as possible, he made the rounds of the oases, beginning with the central parks and working toward the more open spaces of west and north London, to take the bird census. The meagerness of his report makes for depressive reading.

It is a practical book, with several specific purposes. Eager to preserve within the limits of London as much as possible of the wild, "our best medicine," he stresses, as Arnold had done in "Kensington Gardens," the importance of wooded parks, the "lungs" of a city. Woodman, spare that tree! becomes a constant refrain. He is against the landscape gardener, with his pruning hook, his dreary rhododendrons, and his fashionable blooms, all regimented and patterned after "the pretty, cloying artificiality of Kew Gardens." "To exhibit flower-beds to those who crave for nature is like placing a dish of Turkish delight before a hungry man: a bramble-bush, a bunch of nettles, would suit him better." Even more, he stresses the value of wild animal life for those who seek refreshment in a city's open spaces. "The spectacle of a couple of moorhens occupied with their domestic affairs" in their rushy home is infinitely more satisfying than a bed of flowers. As in *Birds in Town and Village*, he urges the establishment of colonies of small birds, both new species and those that are dwindling. Much attention is given to the protection of bird-life and to the teaching of the beauty of kindness toward our fellow-mortals. The scene of "afternoon tea" in Hyde Park, with children, accompanied by their nursemaids, playing host by scattering crumbs for the birds, and a workman tossing them the remains of his lunch, is a heart-warming one.

Except to the Londoners of that day and to city-planners, the scope of *Birds in London* does not allow for much that is of interest. There are the usual observations valuable to natural history: the depredations of the pike, "our crocodile," upon the young of duck and teal and little grebe, and the persistence of some species in spite of the disappearance of others of a sturdier build. Even so, in comparison with his other books, this one does not measure up in scientific observation. Hudson being what he was, the book is not lacking in passages of literary value, such as that on a close flock of a hundred and fifty gulls, with their white bodies and red beaks pointed in one direction, tossing up and down on the black, gale-swept waters of St. James's Park, each bird maintaining its position amongst its fellows; and that self-portrait of the author feeding them with showers of sprats, his eyes and ears made glad with the encircling tumult. But, by and large, the book is not well buoyed with Hudson's usual delight in the exercise of his senses or with his characteristic moments of rapture; and the style, though in the main pleasantly conversational in tone and occasionally forceful, tends to sag from time to time beneath the weight of facts. Of all his volumes of essays, *Birds in London* has worn least well.

In *Nature in Downland* (1900) he was again at full power. The South Downs had to wait a long time for their rightful place upon the literary map of England. John Ray pioneered in opening them up to aesthetic appreciation, but Gilpin thought them monotonous because unadorned. Though White had found "the shapely figured aspect" of them "somewhat peculiarly sweet and amusing," his art fell short of the finesse needed to do them justice. Copley Fielding, Charlotte Smith and James Hurdis, in painting, in story and in verse, gave expression to their pleasure in them. And occasionally these rhythmic chalk hills are vignetted in the out-of-door essays of A. E. Knox. Had he continued to live on, Jefferies, who loved the downs and whose spirit still haunts them, might have done even better for southwest Sussex than he did for northeast Wiltshire. But, as it turned out, it was Hudson who was ordained to become their chief interpreter, and his skill in presenting this panoramic scene is commensurate with that shown in *Idle Days in Patagonia*.

Following a suggestion from White, Hudson attributes the charm of the downs—apart from that of their wildness, their wide prospect of "unenclosed country, an elastic turf under foot, and full liberty to roam whithersoever we will"—to "their fungus-like roundness and smoothness." Isolated, they fail to attract, but seen as a succession of flowing outlines, they suggest "the most prominent and beautiful curves of the human figure, and of the 'solemn slope of mighty limbs asleep.' " And to explain their charm more fully, he applies an aesthetic theory of Burke, in which locomotion is associated with seeing. Their garment is well described: the proud, thick, close-bit turf, that, once destroyed, never grows again; the patches of shining white flints and of flowers—ragwort, squinancy-wort, forget-me-not, eye-bright, viper's bugloss, daisy, white campion, yellow furze, plume thistle, fragrant purple thyme; and, on many of their summits, groves of beeches in great masses of intense color. The silvery thistledown, seen under certain conditions, enchanted Hudson, carrying him back in memory to his old home on the pampas. And when most afloat on the air, it became for him a symbol of all the days he had passed upon the South Downs.

In his description of the animal life, he should perhaps have lingered longer over the snails, which are very profuse there. It is appropriate, however, that he devotes a full chapter to insects, the "fairy fauna," for they, of all creatures, most "impress us in all the open shelterless places." The tremendous tragedy that autumn brings to them is the inspiration of several of the most impassioned pages of *Nature in Downland*. Of beasts and birds there are many pleasing glimpses: of stoat, badger, fox, dog, sheep, linnet, swallow, swift, magpie, peewit, gull, owl, and kestrel. The abundance of moles, reputedly very thirsty creatures, on the highest parts of the downs during the summer season when no water is available leads Hudson on to an interesting inquiry. His concern with snakes, which was to find its fullest expression in *The Book of a Naturalist*, is maintained here by the prominent place accorded the adder. The cruel process of wheatear-catching is fully described, and there are good recordings of the songs of the stonechat and the whinchat. But, as should be, he gives most attention, among beasts and birds, to the coal-black, long-horned oxen—drawing ploughs or wagons across these great hills in their slow, deliberate manner, as with the tread of the years—and to the skylark, whose song, intensifying the silence of downland, has probably never been better rendered.

Human beings are given their proper place in the panorama. In these pages, we first become acquainted with Hudson's keen interest in shepherds, which was to find full expression in *A Shepherd's Life.* Coming across these solitary figures along the sheepwalks, he found many of them to be naturalists in a small, amateur way, and shepherd lads were usually worthy of a chat. Though not so greatly attracted to the peasants of these downs as to the sweeter, more graceful and beautiful people of the West Country, he admired their "rock-like stability of character, their sturdy independence of spirit, and, with it, patient contentment with a life of unremitting toil." And some of them come entertainingly into his record, such as the ponderous, dull-witted farmer's wife, "a sort of rough-hewn pre-adamite lump of humanity, or gigantic land-tortoise in petticoats," whose refusal of food to Hudson was immediately rectified by the quick sympathy of one of her lodgers. As lurid shadow to the portraiture of human beings, there is a strong indictment of the people of foul-smelling Chichester, who delight in caging blackbird, jackdaw, and white owl and who worship, in a plethora of pubs, the god of beer. In comparison to Hudson's portrait of Demon Beer, the sileni of Rubens and Jordaens are as cherubs.

While in self-revelation *Nature in Downland* is not so profound as *Idle Days in Patagonia,* it dwells upon the more human side of the author's personality. Hudson's delight in poetry, ranging from Langland to Yeats, is here given full expression. Especially noteworthy is the enjoyment derived from the reading of the minor poets, an enjoyment found here chiefly in the works of Hurdis but to be made more fully manifest in subsequent writing. "Being of that tribe myself, I have a kindly feeling for little people, not for the living only, who write in the modern fashion and are by some thought great, but also for those who have been long dead, whose fame has withered and wasted in the grave." Among the other "little people" are Gerard, Burke the aesthetician, and many a local worthy who had felt impelled to put down his impressions of his beloved native heath. We discover Hudson to be an admirer of village churches when they have been brought into harmony with their surroundings and a haunter of churchyards. Exercising an historical sense that, among his predecessors in the out-of-door essay,

Kingsley would especially have appreciated, he peoples grove, valley, and down with Danes and Romans.

Owing to the unity of the locale and the art of its author, *Nature in Downland* has almost a symphonic pattern. The opening chapter, with its initial picture of Hudson sitting on the crest of a down and gazing in wonderment at a sky filled with thistledown, has the suggestive complexity of the first movement of a symphony. The immediately succeeding chapters, in which the various kinds of life native to the downs are presented one after another—floral and animal and human—are developments of the themes it contains. So, too, are those on villages and on the maritime district (itself held partly together by the dominating spire of the Chichester Cathedral) and the concluding one, with Hudson's escape from "the Chichesters" to the purifying wind and rain of the downs. To it all, there is a quiet ending, a conversation with a South Downs man in whom the home-call was so strong that nowhere else in all the world could there be complete happiness for him. Throughout the volume the wheel of the year keeps turning, from summer to autumn and on to winter, with the contrasts that the varying seasons provide, until the thistledown of the overture become the snowflakes of the finale. In one's memory, the whole pattern of the book, with its multiplicity of themes, all subtly interwoven, has the vibrancy of the living texture of nature.

Hudson's style is here at its best—powerful, as in his indictment of the people of Chichester; eloquent, as in his realization of the tragedy that autumn brings to insects; and, in general, possessed of a quiet harmony of tone. The beauty of the world is caught in passage after passage, for Hudson was just as aware as Emerson in "The Rhodora" that "Nature herself . . . maketh her plants not for meat and medicine only, but some to be esteemed for beauty alone, and as garlands and crowns for pleasure." *Nature in Downland* is not so exceptional a book as *Idle Days in Patagonia*, nor is it so original in natural history as many of the later volumes, but it shows a mastery in the painting of a large canvas of the English countryside beyond that possessed by any of his predecessors. Other large canvases, some of them patterned after this one, were to follow, until he had covered a considerable portion of southwestern England.

One of the great purposes of Hudson's life was, by stressing the unity of all living things, to increase man's sympathy for his horizontal and winged brethren. In *Birds and Man* (1901)[9] he declares that "all animals distinctly see in those of other species, . . . sentient, intelligent beings like themselves; and that, when birds and mammals meet together, they take pleasure in the consciousness of one another's presence, in spite of the enormous difference in size, voice, habits, etc." Were man similarly inclined, his sense of the beauty of the natural world would be considerably enlarged and enhanced. By underscoring in this volume the humanlike qualities of birds, Hudson brings them even closer to the business and bosoms of men than he had in earlier writings, and his success, at least artistically, is beyond that of Michelet in *L'Oiseau*.

The sympathy that exists between living creatures is here illustrated with a wealth of anecdotes. One describes seven daws a-scramble on the back of an appreciative cow standing statuesquely in a meadow adjacent to the Bishop's Palace at Wells, busy in the search for treasure—a common sight on the pampas with cowbirds. Hudson cites examples of the rich human associations that have grown round certain birds, such as the robin, the parrot, and that genial rascal, the ecclesiastical daw. He has an almost infallible instinct for portraying birds at their best, and is constantly investing them with dignity, most notably the domestic goose, "that stately bird-shaped monument of cloudy grey or crystal white marble," whose lofty spirit makes her insist upon a "strict adhesion" to her rights. Much of the pleasure derived from the calls and songs of birds lies, he says, in "the human emotions which they express or seem to express." In one of the most interesting essays in *Birds and Man*, he attempts to read the thoughts that birds have of men. All this is done without the sentimentality that sometimes mars *L'Oiseau*.

Since Hudson was stressing the value of sympathy between all creatures, it is fitting that he should say something in denunciation of that chief persecutor of rare birds, the "cursed collector." This *bête noire* receives the author's execration repeatedly throughout the

---

9 When the book was revised in 1915, one chapter, "Birds in London" (which belongs as a postscript to the volume with that title), was omitted, and two new ones (besides other matter) added—"Vert-Vert; or Parrot Gossip" and "Something Pretty in a Glass Case."

volume, and he depressingly dominates two of the later essays—
"The Dartford Warbler" and "Something Pretty in a Glass Case,"
the latter, one of the most extraordinary of all Hudson's essays.
To make the punishment fit the crime, he envisages collectors, in
another life, mounted by taxidermists "in the most perfect life-like
attitudes, with wideawake glass eyes, blue or dark, in their sockets,
their hair varnished to preserve its natural colour and glossy appearance, . . . placed separately in glass cases," and "set up in pairs in
niches in the walls of the palace of hell." Surely by the time the
roll is called of those English birds that have now been exterminated
or are fast disappearing, the collecting instinct lurking in any reader
will have been exorcised!

To keep the book from becoming too exclusively concerned with
birds, Hudson included much of the accompanying experience.
There is, for instance, his delight—"hermit in heart" that he was—
in the secluded wildness of Savernake Forest, with its carpetings of
red, copper, and gold beech leaves that seem never to die but only
to sleep "like a bright-coloured serpent in the genial warmth."
That he should find enjoyment in towns comes as a new note, but
such enjoyment is severely limited to half a dozen, and of them only
the sight of Wells "in April and early May, from a neighbouring
hill, . . . caused [him] to sigh with pleasure." There are many
characters other than collectors in these pages, met along the wayside or in cottages. To add to the variety of the book, Hudson even
included an essay on the secret of the charm of flowers, which
contained, in the first edition, one of the few judgments that he
later found it necessary to amend.

The landscape background of *Birds and Man* is considerably
varied, but the countryside that makes the chief impression is that
of Somerset, which Hudson endeavored to pull together by his
panoramic views of Bath and Wells with their environs and, especially, by that from Brean Down, a view stretching across the
Severn Sea to the blue mountains of Glamorganshire and, in another
direction, across long leagues of the flattest land in all England
to the blue Quantock range beyond. Wanting in the unifying force
that the Rio Negro gave to *Idle Days in Patagonia* and the downs to
Nature in Downland, this book depends upon the theme implicit
in its title to hold the essays loosely together and upon the per-
vasiveness of its author's personality. Even though the last essay,

"Selborne," sheds no new light on its subject, it acts as an effective conclusion by summing up the attitude toward nature initiated by Wordsworth in poetry and by Thoreau and Jefferies in the essay. Altogether, *Birds and Man* is one of Hudson's better books.

With *El Ombú and Other South American Stories* (1902)[10] he reappeared as a writer of fiction, this time in the realm of the short story. These four tales, vivid with the bold colors of Latin America, present strong situations. Technically, they are of little interest; but within the old-fashioned narrative tradition, which, after all, was eminently suitable to the quality of the experience, Hudson can be very effective. Told with a large simplicity and impregnated with the melancholy characteristic of the author, they evoke, like many of Cunninghame Graham's sketches, a life that was vanishing. The title story, in particular, has won high praise. "Pelino Viera's Confession" and the narrative poem "Tecla and the Little Men" were added to this group when they were published in America under the better title of *Tales of the Pampas* (1916).

The success of *Green Mansions* (1904), which lay long on the anvil of composition, depends to a considerable extent upon the expert description of the primeval forests of Venezuela, which Hudson had never seen but which, after reading Humboldt, Wallace, Bates and many others, must have kept haunting his imagination. It depends more upon the presence of Rima, one of the rarest creations of fantasy in the whole of English literature. The catastrophe, with all the intensity of emotion it engenders, cuts almost as deeply into the memory as any other in contemporary fiction. Although this strangely beautiful and richly elegiac romance has brought many to a reading of its author's greater works, it has nevertheless tended to mislead the general public as to the real character of his achievement.

The story of Alma and the mist of Yí in *The Purple Land*, as well as many passages in his essays, indicated that Hudson was an excellent teller of tales for children, but for a long time he shied from doing a whole book for them. *A Little Boy Lost* (1905), in which dreams and realities are exquisitely confounded, was written by chance and as an experiment. In it he recorded many of the thrills, half-frightening and yet wholly fascinating, that nature

---

[10] The "Story of a Piebald Horse" originally appeared as a chapter of *The Purple Land*, and "Nino Diablo" was published in 1890 in *Macmillan's Magazine*.

afforded him as a child, and thus, as self-revelation, it belongs with *Far Away and Long Ago*. As a book for children, it may make too great a demand upon the imagination of a city-bred generation, but, with its large core of poetry, it deserves a place on the shelf of the second-best.

After these novels and tales, little fiction came from the pen of Hudson. It is possible that he had about written himself out of suitable material, though some of the sketches of *A Traveller in Little Things* and some of the incidents in his letters might well have been shaped into short stories. More probably, he had by this time so fully committed himself to the essay as to look upon narrative material mainly from that artistic angle. Certainly there is much of the essay quality in the last volume of his fiction, *Dead Man's Plack and An Old Thorn* (1920). The first of these two stories, which re-enacts, without an accumulation of historical data, one of the most tragic events in English history, was "forced on [him] so to speak"; but the second, which first appeared nine years earlier in the *English Review* and might almost have been incorporated into *A Shepherd's Life,* is quite within the range of his special vision. The volume as a whole, however, added little to his reputation, and is inferior, both in skill and in interest, to the *Tales of the Pampas*.

In the meantime, another volume of out-of-door essays, *Hampshire Days* (1903), had made its appearance. Compared with *Nature in Downland* in its total effect, it reminds one of the difference between a collection of vignettes and scenes, some of which are not clearly articulated with the rest, and a large panoramic canvas by an Old Crome or a Copley Fielding that Nature herself has endowed with impressive unity. In other words, we are given many glimpses of the New Forest, with its woods, heaths, bogs and farmlands, and of the valleys of the Test and the Itchen, but do not grasp Hampshire as a geographical entity, in the manner that we do the South Sussex Downs. The scattered profusion of wild life, ranging "from spiders and flies to birds and beasts, and from red alga on gravestones to oaks and yews," gives the book copiousness but also keeps any distinct pattern from emerging. Besides, many of the experiences with animals have not the special pertinency they possess in *Nature in Downland*: they might have occurred just as appropriately in many another county of England. Nor are the chapters unified by any dominant theme as they are in *Birds and Man*. Yet the restriction of his rambles to the confines of a single county makes for some artistic effect, and what *Hampshire Days* lacks in broad design is counterbalanced by the many happy moments recorded in it.

These moments came not because he felt more at home in Hampshire than elsewhere in England, for the county that was most like home was Wiltshire. And though he was indeed "fortunate in the houses that received him" there, one of them being that of Grey, he actually felt more congenial with the people of the West Country. Yet over a period of many years, when he dwelt poor and friendless in the brick wilderness that London was to him, Hampshire afforded an easily accessible retreat; and a wild, out-of-the-way corner of the New Forest, a miraculous survival of Saxon England, became his "favourite summer resort and hunting-ground." In her "sunlit emerald glades" and villages, and on her broad heaths, a wan soul might soon be made ruddy again. Many of the experiences that brought back that health, gathered over many years of saunterings, are within the covers of *Hampshire Days*, making it, by and large, one of the best of his books on England.

Nowhere is Hudson better in the presentation of animal life. There are interesting encounters with birds of the field and forest and marsh; with white-throat, swift, swallow, green woodpecker, blackbird, moorhen, peewit, coot, redshank, and grebe. The drama that ensued from the smuggling of a cuckoo's egg into a robin's nest, though accurately described a century earlier by Jenner, is as sensitive a record as can be found in natural history. Weasel, squirrel, vole, and adder are among the many other animals that wander into these pages, as though alive. And, as usual, Hudson holds many of his observations together with speculations, such as those on the power of memory in animals, the tenacity of life in some of them, their attitude toward their own dead, and the disastrous effect of fascination on chaffinch, vole, rabbit, and cat.

The considerable attention given to insects and spiders, with all the intimacy that a study of them requires, shows how leisurely were the sojourns in Hampshire. As various chapters in *The Naturalist in La Plata* indicate, Hudson had early been attracted to them. In *Nature in Downland* they were allotted their proper place in the panoramic pattern. Their greater prominence in *Hampshire Days*, corresponding to that given them in *The Naturalist in La Plata,* is quite appropriate, for this book is pre-eminently one of full summer, and the New Forest abounds in insect life, including most of "the kings and nobles of the tribe." We meet with the stag beetle, "our most majestical insect," the silver-washed fritillary, the white admiral, with its graceful unfluttering flight, the hornet, the dragonfly, like a flying serpent, the glow-worm and the firefly, the one like the light of the moon and the other a tiny rocket of the night. To insect music, as in the recording here of that of the great green grasshopper, Hudson was as sensitive as a Japanese or an ancient Greek.

There are many vignette-bright glimpses of the woodland scenery in the low-lying southwest corner of Hampshire, which Hudson considered the most beautiful in all England; of Wolmer Forest, with its dark, shaggy mantle of pines and its thick undergrowth of heather; and of the valleys of the Test and the Itchen, with their celebrated yews and their garland of flowers, especially its brightest blossom, the long-unsung wild musk, which conjured up in his memory the yellow camalote of South American watercourses, a flower as dear to him as "the wee, modest, crimson-tipped daisy" to "Burns or to Chaucer." There are some fine pages on man's preference for the open heath; and fuller expression than in earlier books is given to his delight in villages, especially in the grace that time bestows on their churches and churchyards.

Hudson the amateur anthropologist had made his appearance in *Idle Days in Patagonia,* and there are evidences of the same interest in the volumes that follow. Here, in his analysis of the four types of indigenous Hampshire folk, he raises this interest to a major theme of his essays, broadening their human quality. His sympathies are mainly with the Iberian, endowed with nimbler brains, quicker sensitivities, greater character and imagination. And his imaginative identification of himself with prehistoric man, first enunciated in *Idle Days* and repeated in later volumes, is here the inspiration of one of the most eloquent passages in all his writings. In the evening, on a lonely, furze-covered barrow near Beaulieu, one of his favorite villages, he attains a sense of complete harmony with its ancient dead, and wishes for no better company when he is at last made to lie in a grave.

The Land's End (1908), on the other hand, in spite of its many fine passages, is not Hudson at his happiest. Being a record of first impressions accounts for much of its freshness and vividness and also for some of its shortcomings in sympathetic understanding. Books on Cornwall seem to have been read by him only to be refuted. While admiring her moors, her black "granite and serpentine cliffs and seas of Mediterranean blue," and her great promontory jutting westward into the Atlantic, he was disappointed in the comparative poverty of her animal life. And Cornishmen were among his "imperfect sympathies." Had he written *The Land's End* later, its general tone would have been more genial, its appreciation fuller and mellower, for West Cornwall attracted him more and more as time went on, and, during the last years of his life, he was often to be found rambling over her many open spaces. It is, nevertheless, remarkable how quickly he was able to bring the myriad of first impressions to focus in his temperament and in the medium in which he worked.

There is a painter's sensitivity in the many sea- and land-scapes scattered through the book: the exquisite, changing Cornish sea, with its blues, greens and purples, and the gaunt grey cliffs, crowned with castle-like rocks and flecked with gannets, gulls, ravens, and cormorants—pictures that recall those of Kingsley in "North Devon: An Idyll"; the naked, wind-swept moor and rocky headland of Land's End, which has drawn generations of Englishmen to it more powerfully than any other spot in England; sand dunes, which the ocean has brought out of her depths, devouring the coastline fields; wind-sculptured trees; stone hedges cushioned with tangles of ivy looking like broods of grey serpents; long blue bands of vernal squill; and fields of furze and bracken, in summer like "yellow and orange flame . . . against the blue of the sea" and in winter, when transformed by rain, like a curious, mellow red design spread on a dark green background. Most of the scenes give one a sense of vastness and wild desolation—qualities of landscape that always brought Hudson great joy. Still more than in *Hampshire Days*, he is aware of the immemorial human associations of the countryside, "the vast ghostly multitude" of Celts, who, continually beaten and driven westward, had found in Bolerium their last refuge and their last defeat.

As there is more of the sea in *The Land's End* than in any other of Hudson's volumes, so there is also more of sea-birds. The gull and the gannet attracted him most: the one "a sort of feathered Mr. Micawber among sea-birds" and the other a living javelin-head when with closed wings it hurls itself down on its prey—both, with their aerial maneuvers, endowing the sky with sublimity. Of land-birds, there are many interesting accounts: a raven swooping savagely on a gaunt-looking fox standing defiantly on a flat-topped rock, the migration of a flock of ravens into wintry Cornwall, the inquisitive little titlark shattered wantonly by a gentleman hunter, the feathered skeleton of a crippled robin that some children brought him, and the independent jenny-wrens, the prevalence of which amid the waste places made the West Cornwall bird-life mean much to him after all. The jackdaw, as in that delightful colloquy a pair of them, perched on a smoking chimney-pot of St. Ives, seemed to engage in while they faced each other inquiringly, gives a humorous touch to some of the pages. There are also accounts of adder, seal, sow, badger, dog, cow, and donkey.

One finds the usual concern for human beings. As was his custom, Hudson lived among the peasantry; and on some of their farms, the way of life was so rough that he often had the feeling of being back on one of the primitive estancias of the Argentine. The blaze of furze in a cavernous fireplace especially stirred to life old instincts. The fishermen of St. Ives, clothed in keeping with their tasks, appealed to his eye. And there is a beautiful picture of fishing boats, "singly, in twos and threes, and in groups of half a dozen," drifting from the harbor, shaking out their red winglike sails, and going away "in a kind of procession" into the sunset, reminding him of a straggling group of flamingoes flying low over a pampean lagoon. Finest of all, though, is the portrait of several aged pilgrims to Land's End, who, obeying a deep impulse, had come to this rude foreland, only to realize how bright in the flower life is and how sad in the fruit. With its Sir-Thomas-Browne-like eloquence, the book is brought to an effective close.

What gives *The Land's End* its most distinctive human flavor is the analysis of the Cornish character, which is fuller and more original than the corresponding one in *Hampshire Days*. In spite of their county being a land of legend and their blood Celtic, Hudson found the Cornish to be the most prosaic people he had ever known, the remnant of "an ancient crystallised race with the imaginative faculty undeveloped"; and, in spite of their pleasant enough laughter, to be without a sense of humor, except a very primitive one, "the humour of children and of men in a low state of culture who delight in practical jokes." It was their cruelty toward animals, the result of "a drop of black blood in the heart—an ancient latent ferocity," that offended him most. There had been strong attacks on birdcatchers earlier in his essays, as in *Birds in a Village* and *Nature in Downland*, but rarely did he flame to the indignation of his description of the manner in which the people of St. Ives, taking advantage of a cold wave that had driven a vast multitude of birds before it to the limits of the land and made them desperate with hunger, proceeded to massacre them, beating the bushes and setting gins. The picture painted is even more haunting than *The Birdnesters* of Millet.

There has been much dispute as to the accuracy of his analysis of Cornishmen—a dispute into which I have no qualifications to enter. The chief criticism has been that his etching needle omitted certain necessary strokes and that the *aqua fortis* was allowed to cut too deeply into the plate. Perhaps Hudson relied overmuch upon the accuracy of first impressions and also suffered from the strain of too continuous an association with strangers. His divining-rod for humor, as in his questioning of a peasant as to where the stone had been got for building houses, was not always infallible. Since he was a Dumnonian and thus racially akin to the Cornish, he considered himself specially qualified to cast the penetrative shaft into their character and privileged to draw them candidly, "without the usual pretty little lying flatteries." Imperfect though his sympathy may have been, there can be no question of the effectiveness of his art in expressing the impact they made upon him. These chapters devoted to the analytical portraiture of the people of Cornwall show how broad was Hudson's scope, how well he could shape to artistic purposes material that comes as much within the domain of the familiar as it does within that of the out-of-door essay. Even in the absence of outdoor elements, Hudson could still have written excellent essays.

The genii of many scattered places are in *Afoot in England* (1909). Since its essays cover many years of composition, from the early days when an editor's acceptance of one of them was "a cause of astonishment," there is some unevenness in the writing. It is more of a miscellany than *Birds and Man*, for though it has as good an introduction, the concluding essay is not so effective. Yet, like those of *Birds and Man*, the essays are all informed with the same spirit: that of one who wanders, vagabond-like, in search of the England that had shaped itself in his mind's eye during his youth on the far-away pampas and who frequently experiences, in that search, the charm of the unknown and the joy of discovery. The essays on Cobbett, Mitford, and, particularly, Bloomfield, whom Hudson had read in his youth, are thus appropriate. In passage after passage some rare beauty of landscape or animal or of human being is captured, making *Afoot in England* one of the choicest blossoms of Hudson's genius.

There is a charming wildness about the England he explored. Especially was he drawn to the solitary open spaces: fields and downs, cliffs and beaches, familiar to him in sun, fog, wind, and storm. And the air is often filled with musical sounds: the songs and calls of many birds, the lowing of cattle, the soughing of the wind, and moan of the surf on the shingled beach. He has many unusual encounters with animals: a carrion-crow with crimson eyes, swifts kept from migration by late breeders, and a precipice-colony of gulls which, upon discovering that Hudson was a stranger, set up wave after wave of ringing and chiming cries of alarm. There is a delightful characterization of a lonely dog, Jack, whom Hudson allowed to tyrannize over him for awhile, and an essay, "In Praise of the Cow"—that "majestic, beautiful creature with the Juno eyes," "more like man's sister than any other non-human being"—which deserves a place beside Burroughs' "Our Rural Divinity."

Hudson as the lover of villages is here given still fuller expression. He possesses great skill in discovering the special genius of a place: Exford, Abbotsbury, "Norton," Winsford, and Branscombe—most of all, Branscombe—are presented with an exquisite sense of their charm, arcadian yet real. A few towns are included: Bath and Wells once again, and now Salisbury, the beauty of its cathedral enhanced by a large miscellaneous bird-colony, with its "various voices, from the deep human-like dove tones to the perpetual subdued rippling, running-water sound of the aerial martins." Especially full is the book in encounters with human beings, many of whom, warmed by his sympathetic interest, freely unbosomed themselves to him. Some of the unusual persons we meet are the vicar whose parishioners were once addicted to feeding and caressing pet toads dwelling under the flooring of their pews; the solitary old squire of "Norton," who ruined himself by opposing the prize system of cattle-breeding and, for solace, committed his inmost feelings to the strict confines of sonnets, some of which are exhumed for us; and the chapel-builders—a noble-looking father, a plebeian mother, and their many children—disturbed by their son and brother taking to tobacco. With his strong sense of oneness with "the undying human family," Hudson is ever-mindful of the dwellers in stiller villages, those long gathered into barrows. And our wayfarer pauses meditatively at Roman Calleva and at Stonehenge, once "the spiritual capital, . . . the meeting-place of all the intellect, the hoary experience, the power and majesty of the land."

A Shepherd's Life (1910) is an extraordinarily deft reconstruction of a century of life on the South Wiltshire Downs, seen through the memory of Caleb Bawcombe, an aged shepherd. A few of Caleb's reminiscences are enough to maintain a narrative thread throughout this series of essays. Often an essay is got started with one reminiscence, and several more are later casually introduced to help hold the miscellaneous material around Caleb's own life. In "Concerning Cats," two filaments of memory, those of a trout-catching cat and an old bachelor's eleven-cat ménage, are enough to maintain the narrative thread. At times, the skill in reconstructing Caleb's life is almost like that of a paleontologist modelling an animal out of a few bones and patches of skin. Caleb's pastoral lore is filled out with the experiences of other shepherds and, most of all, with the author's own copious Wiltshire observations. To present Caleb in the round and give him articulateness and to keep so much of the material of a field naturalist bound within a slight, quiet pattern of narrative, the novelist in Hudson came to the assistance of the out-of-door essayist.

Hudson was peculiarly fitted by temperament to write just such a book. The life that Caleb lived in memory was the sort that the young Hudson on the far-off pampas had conjured up in his imagination while he, too, herded sheep, talked with his English neighbors, and read Thomson's *Seasons* and Bloomfield's *Farmer's Boy*—a life wilder and more beautiful than that experienced since his arrival in England. What attracted him to this neglected part of Wiltshire, besides the harmony that prevailed between sheep and cattle and men and countryside, was the village of "Winterbourne Bishop," which, in its very barrenness when compared with many arcadian ones, was more like the home of his earliest years, *Los Veinte-cinco Ombúes*, than any other place known to him in England. And in the presence of Caleb, as in that of only "a dozen old men more or less like him," Hudson seemed to find himself among the people of his own past, and "sometimes they were so much like some of the remembered, old, sober, and slow-witted herders of the plains" that he could not help saying to himself, "Why, how this man reminds me of Tio Isidoro, or of Don Pascual of the 'Three Poplar Trees' . . . . " Just as they reminded him of these acquaintances of his youth, "so did they bring back the older men of the Bible history—Abraham and Jacob and the rest." And on Salisbury Plain he could commune with those to whom he felt spiritually most akin, for so little had life changed there that were the dead to come forth from their barrows and from Old Sarum, they would recognize, though dynasties had passed, "the same familiar scene, with furze and bramble and bracken on the slope, the wide expanse with sheep and cattle grazing in the distance, and the dark green of trees in the hollows, and fold on fold of the low down beyond, stretching away to the dim, farthest horizon." At heart, Hudson was at least half-shepherd.

Caleb is, of course, the center of human interest, and his patriarchal figure, painted large against a quiet sky, is a memorable one. Tall, big-boned, round-shouldered, with a bewhiskered, faunlike face and clear hazel eyes, he was (though when hard pressed a poacher) thoroughly trusted by his masters, familiar with the Scriptures, in which a similar terrain and mode of life are depicted, and, in a small way, a naturalist, sympathetic toward all animals. Sheep, with their "multitudinous tremulous bleatings," and sheep-dogs, with their crisp, ringing barks, he loved most among animals, and, in his old age, his dreams were alive with them. So great was his love of home, that away from Winterbourne Bishop he felt himself an exile. His return from a village just inside the nearest boundary of Dorset, where he had been shepherding for some years, is told with the simple beauty of a home-coming in the Bible. Even forty years later, Caleb was speaking of this sojourn "as the ordinary modern man might speak of a year's residence in Uganda, Tierra del Fuego, or the Andaman Islands!"

There are many vivid sketches and brief life-stories, done largely with a few sweeping strokes, of the people whom Caleb's life touched—his father Isaac, "physically a kind of Alexander Selkirk"; his favorite brother, David, the news of whose death stunned him for many weeks; his sister Martha, who suckled the puny babe of the manor house; the man who tried to keep back his sick-pay, Elijah Raven, looking, with his mass of virgin-white hair, like a gigantic white owl; his employers, the Ellerbys of Doveton, upon whom had fallen a terrible curse—and of a host of peripheral figures, such as the man who refused to have his children buried in the churchyard to the tolling of a bell; the woman who heroically opposed an earl over the right to take dead wood from his forest; nonagenarian Joan, who at the age of ten had become a girl-of-all-work under a hard taskmaster and who had remained a toiler in the fields until her eighty-fifth year. One of the most impressive scenes, in a quiet way, is that in which the husband of Martha, returning from the fields one day in his seventy-ninth year, declares, "I've done work. . . . I'll not go with the flock no more," and three days later, while laying his head on her knees, goes to his eternal rest, "like a baby that has been fed and falls asleep on its mother's breast."

In *A Shepherd's Life*, Hudson's keen sympathy for the lowly receives explicit statement. He would rather know, he says, the histories "of the humble cottagers, the true people of the vale who were rooted in the soil, and flourished and died like trees in the same place, . . . than of the great ones of the vale. . . ." Like Cobbett and the later Jefferies, he considers the agricultural laborer the sanest, as well as the healthiest and perhaps the happiest, man in England; and he condones occasional poaching, for "the law of the land does not square with the moral law as it is written in the heart of the peasant." Throughout the book, the lives of the humble are seen against a menacing background of social privilege. As illustrated more dramatically in "An Old Thorn," the law, the main support of such privilege, is the villain, transforming some of its administrators into "human devils" in black caps.

As in *Afoot in England*, animals play a subordinate rôle. Caleb's memory is, however, almost as full of dogs as of people, and he recognizes them as individuals, each with his own character and peculiarities: Jack, the expert killer of adders; Tony, of mixed blood, whom Caleb killed in a moment of anger; Rough, who mothered a lamb; and others—most of whom were valued not merely for their utility but also for their companionship. And there is pathos in the telling of their deaths. No dog-hater, as Hudson has sometimes been called, could have penned these sketches. There is not so much of the actual process of sheep-herding as a Massingham, say, or a Mary Austin would have given us. "Bird Life on the Downs," while filled with starlings, rooks, ravens and hawks, is not so good an essay as similar ones in other volumes. Hudson's skill in rendering the soul of places is demonstrated in his sketch of Salisbury, a wonder city to villagers, and in his detailed pictures of Winterbourne Bishop set in the midst of bleak, lonely downs, and of the vale of Wylye, where there is "the sense of beautiful human things hidden from sight among the masses of foliage." Thus the reconstruction of a life leads to the portrait of a whole environment.

There is nothing else quite like *A Shepherd's Life* in English literature. It depicts a way of life that has persisted through the centuries and, given great dignity by the Bible, has taken firm possession of the imagination of the Western world. There have, indeed, been many pastorals in our poetry, but most of them suffer from prettiness. Hudson sought, with a faithful adherence to facts, to present that life as it was actually lived. The choice of Caleb, with his undramatic life, as his central figure precluded the possibility of an exciting book. And, as sure as Wordsworth of the intrinsic interest of his material, he was even willing to run the risk of a certain baldness, the baldness of actuality. The telling is low-keyed and the style unadorned; the book is without the intellectual plenitude or the rapture over the beauty of the world that characterizes most of his books. Appropriately, there is little humor in it, for Caleb was not "a laughing man." Yet, like *Michael*, it is quietly impressive. Other writers in prose have seen shepherds in somewhat the same light—Jefferies and Hardy and Phillpotts—but none of them has written so rare and authentic an evocation.

With *Adventures among Birds* (1913) Hudson added a companion volume to *Birds in Town and Village* and *Birds and Man*. He was as usual careful that the material be sufficiently varied— that there be, so as to achieve the finest effects of the out-of-door essay, the right admixture of other animals (including man), of setting, and of self-revelation. Although travel threads aid in grouping some of the essays—the chief locales being the coast of Norfolk, the Peak district, eastern Dorset, Hampshire, and Somerset—they are held together mainly by the author's personality. Had he chosen to give this book a longer title, it would have read, so he remarks: "The Adventures of a Soul, sensitive or not, among the feathered masterpieces of creation." Since his was a soul poetically sensitive to many of the beauties of nature and since, in spite of the absence of such impassioned outbursts as those in *Hampshire Days* and *The Land's End*, there was no falling off in artistry, *Adventures among Birds* ranks as one of his major achievements, the last of the better volumes devoted primarily to observations of the English countryside.

In his pursuit of birds, he has many strange experiences: with a sand-martin, who, during the absence of the other males, zealously discharged his responsibility of keeping the hens on their nests, and with a group of starlings that, carried away by a sudden impulse, detached themselves from their fellows to mix with a small gaggle of wild geese crossing their path at right angles. As was his wont, he includes some observations by other persons, such as that of a wounded teal who would sit in perfect bliss at the feet of her assailant and who, after she rejoined the flock, would, for the sake of auld lang syne, leave her companions to come and greet him. Besides the songs of ring-ouzel and marsh-warbler, he beautifully records those of birds that, like the whinchat, seldom sing, and those of rare birds, like that of the Dartford warbler, with its "buzzing stream of sound . . . interspersed with small, fine, bright, clear notes, both shrill and mellow." Among other animals there is the strange action of a pet fox, Peter, who, after responding for several days to the call of the wild, expressed his joy at reunion with his mistress by running round and round her in a wide circle and then, like Bewick's otter, vaulting three times clean over her head. And among human beings there is the quaint old parish clerk of Itchen Abbas, with black skullcap and hawklike eyes, who, because of his careful enunciation of each syllable, would finish solemnly, in a high-pitched voice, several words after the rest of the congregation. Of those adventures described at greater length, two of the best are "A Tired Traveller," containing a subtle analysis of the mind of a redwing who had been forced to lag behind his fellows on their flight across the North Sea, and "Cardinal: The Story of My First Caged Bird." Just as the singing of a Wood Street thrush brought reveries of the green pastures of her early home to Wordsworth's Susan, so the loud, glad call of a cardinal, heard while walking along a London thoroughfare, transported Hudson instantly to his early days on the pampas and his experience with a cardinal finch that remained permanently handicapped by early caging.

As in all his writings, he gives us not only descriptions and anecdotes but psychological insights. One of the main themes of *Birds and Man*, the sympathy that exists between living creatures, he again emphasizes here. "Birds in Authority" shows how those of the air take "the mastership for the general good," some even extending their watchfulness over the members of other species. Considerable attention is paid to friendship amongst animals, "the highest point to which the animal's mind can rise." Pet nothing and persecute nothing was Hudson's precept, and in "The Sacred Bird" he attacks the coddling of the pheasant at the expense of much wild life, including soaring birds. A certain note of grimness comes into some of these pages, for he includes, unlike Michelet and most English bird-lovers, the raptorial order within his range of appreciation. "There is no more fascinating spectacle in wild life than the chase of its quarry by a swift-winged hawk. . . . Pursuer and pursued are but following their instincts and fulfilling their lives, and we as neutrals are but spectators of their magnificent aerial displays."

In "The Temple of the Hills," which is largely concerned with his observations of some of the few raptorial birds that England yet possesses, there is another of his many pictures of the rhythmic downs with their occasional crests of trees, this one distinguished by being sketched "on a hot, windless summer day, during the phenomenon of 'visible air.' " With the aid of Drayton's description of the undrained Lincolnshire fens and his own memories of the pampas during the time of his youth, he recreates for us in "The Lake Village" the primitive beauty of the vast peat-swamps of prehistoric Somerset. The enjoyment he received from watching wild geese in large numbers took him many an autumn to Wells in Norfolk, and gives us some good shorescapes of low sand dunes, broad, grey saltings, and a nearby pinewoods carpeted with long, grey marram grass, where the sound of the wind and of the sea are one.

As attested by *A Little Boy Lost* and the cloud of reminiscences that he trails in his essays, Hudson had often revisited the far-distant kingdom of his childhood. The reminiscences had usually come as intensely and lifelike as visions, through no effort of the memory, but they had come singly or in small groups and had dissolved quickly. Now, however, in his late seventies, while lying seriously ill in a hospital in Cornwall, he was suddenly visited by that "rare state of the mind" in which there were "all at once revealed to him as by a miracle" the first eighteen years of his life. For a span of six weeks his soul was privileged to re-enact the little drama it had performed three score and more years earlier on "the green floor of the world." And the record of its scenes in *Far Away and Long Ago* (1918)[11] is probably the best re-creation of childhood in our language and, as is fitting for one who often felt that the most momentous part of his life had come to him before the age of fifteen, his finest efflorescence.

"We cannot escape," Hudson warns us, "from what we are, however great our detachment may be; and in going back we must take our present selves with us. . . . " Yet what he says of Aksakoff's autobiography is equally true of his own: "The picture was not falsified, simply because the temper, and tastes, and passions of his early boyhood—his intense love of his mother, of nature, of all wildness . . . endured unchanged in him to the end and kept him a boy in heart, able after long years to revive the past mentally, and picture it in its true, fresh, original colours." For in Hudson, even more notably, the child was father to the man. Despite the many marks that decades amidst alien scenes had made upon him, he did not have to reorient himself to a phase of life outlived. What made him stand and stare in wonderment as a child continued to delight him throughout the years. The visionary gleam described in "A Boy's Animism" became the master-light of all his seeing, and

---

11 This beautiful title, in the first draft phrased *Long Ago and Far Away,* may have been suggested by Wordsworth's "far-off things and battles long ago." Much of the first chapter, as already noted, appeared in the *Gentleman's Magazine* of 1886, and much of the second and third, in the *English Review* of 1912. The idea of an autobiography must repeatedly have occurred to Hudson, yet he had to wait not only for the moment of inspiration but for the time when he should reach in the public mind a position of sufficient consequence to justify such egoism.

never was its brightness dimmed as it was for Wordsworth. Illuminated by this intense light, he had only to make suitable selection
from the mass of detail offered him by his vision.

Looking back over what he had written, Hudson acknowledges
some "small errors of memory . . . not worth altering . . . ; so long
as the scene or event is rightly remembered and pictured it doesn't
matter much whether I was six or seven or eight years old at the
time." Because of his sensitivity in regard to his age, some of the
errors were deliberate, particularly noticeable when the overthrow
of Rosas is brought within the background of the remembered scenes.
His memory did not take him back so far as Aksakoff's, to his
weaning, or, as Gosse's, to an event that occurred before he could
talk. The years from twelve to fifteen, usually the most confused and
the least engaging, are intentionally skipped, and those from sixteen
to nineteen, considerably telescoped. It would seem, for instance,
from his account, that his mother died shortly after he was stricken
with rheumatic fever, but actually she did not die until almost three
years later. Taken as a whole, however, the self-portrait gives one
the feeling of absolute truth.

The milieu in which he moved and had his being as a child, the
Argentine of the 'forties and 'fifties, is strikingly presented. One
difficulty with making childhood as interesting to a reader as adult-
hood is its comparative want of variety. The boy Hudson would, to
be sure, have stood out in any environment, but the exotic quality
of the one in which he found himself aided considerably in making
his record various and unique. Throughout the book, there is a fine
commingling of the exotic in setting with the familiar in psychology.
The picture of his second home, *Las Acacias*, where all his boyhood
was spent, remains unexcelled in English autobiography. The many
pungent portraits of visitors, tutors, and neighbors are among the
best of their kind. The still wider social setting, dominated for a
time by one of the bloodiest of dictators, the inscrutable Rosas, is
also vividly brushed in. Cunninghame Graham has presented this
milieu more fully and with more gusto in his many brilliant sketches
but with no more perceptiveness and authenticity.

All this is given to us impressionistically, as it actually impinged
upon the consciousness of a growing child. The moving of the family
from *Los Veinte-cinco Ombúes* to *Las Acacias* is seen through the
eyes of a child of five: the excitement at the start of the journey

(it was Hudson's first venture into the unknown); the far backward view of the home that was being abandoned; the sea-like flat
country that spread out before them, broken only by island-like
groves of trees surrounding the various ranchos; the sleep that came
upon him before the end of the journey that extended into the
night; and, next morning, the excitement of exploring a new and
strange world. When Hudson visits old Doña Pascualo, who had
once kept her St. Anthony hung headfirst down a well until he
would heed her prayer for the rain to stop, the impression given is
such as would have occurred to a child of six. The political turmoil
of the time is inserted not as a well-rounded historical background
sketch but only as it touches the lives of *Las Acacias*. As is usual
with a child, the human surroundings are taken for granted. With
the exception of an occasional implicit remonstrance against the
revelry that the half-savage gauchos found in cruelty, he passes no
judgment upon the violent and often amoral society in which he
found himself. Nature, whom the young Hudson did not take for
granted, also had her moments of cruelty, as when the *pampero*
maimed and killed a myriad of his beloved golden plovers.

Striking as was the social world in which he moved, it is kept
subordinate, as background, to the main theme of the book: the
psychology of the author's childhood and boyhood. The change from
a purely physical to a mystical response to nature is described at
some length in the central chapter, "A Boy's Animism," which
immediately attracted wide attention. More than anything else, the
sense of the numinous quality in nature made the child father to
the man, and allowed the man, in the evening of life, to erase most
of the palimpsest of many decades and recover, in all their freshness, the perceptions of a child. Not only does it account for the
unity of *Far Away and Long Ago*, as the struggle between two
temperaments accounts for that of Gosse's *Father and Son*, but, by
bringing his rapture in nature to early maturity, it gives one the
feeling that the whole of Hudson is in these pages. The misfor-
tunes that almost overwhelmed him in late adolescence—the rheumatic fever that "made shipwreck of all [his] new-born earthly
hopes and dreams" and the "obstinate questionings" that followed
—produce an effective ending. Throughout the book, the theme is
illustrated with memorable pictures and episodes, some of which
have already been presented.

Far Away and Long Ago is high achievement. The sudden surge of memories was intense and sustained enough to allow Hudson to paint the details of his large canvas as freshly as though they had come from immediate perception. "Life all past" became

> Like the sky when the sun sets in it,
> Clearest where furthest off.

Aesthetic distance, as in *The Prelude* and Lubbock's *Earlham*, had probably softened some of the outlines and given prominence to others, for the sensitivity of the artist is other than that of the photographer or the so-called objective historian. To secure unity of impression, the author did not depend, as do most autobiographers, merely on making all the events described referable to the first person singular. Factually, indeed, the book is no better than Muir's *Story of My Boyhood and Youth* or even Burroughs' *My Boyhood*, in both of which there are more of the minutiae of self-portraiture and a fuller sense of the family circle and its annals. True, we do see Hudson's father and mother vividly on several occasions, but they remain shadowy figures. It is only of the sporting brother among the members of the family that we become physically aware. But *Far Away and Long Ago* is reminiscence rather than autobiography, reminiscence that has been harmonized by a strong personality and, like *The Prelude*, so patterned as to reveal a passionate love of nature. Memory was more the artist with Hudson than with Muir or Burroughs or even Aksakoff, who was, at times, prone to become trivial in detail and repetitious. And the mystical element of his experience did not lead, as it did with Jefferies, to nebulousness. The casual manner in which scenes and characters and historical events, states of mind and of feeling, are presented shows the dexterous hand of the consummate essayist, as does the general texture of the writing. Despite its many striking details and its opaline variety, this uncannily evocative landscape of memory has the epic simplicity of the great Russian masters and the harmony of tone of an Old Crome.

Hudson was mistaken in thinking that *The Book of a Naturalist* (1919), which is as much a companion volume to *Adventures among Birds* as *The Naturalist in La Plata* to *Birds of La Plata*, was "quite as good as anything" he had done before. In the realm of the natural history of England, perhaps so, for, as the chapters on the earthworm, the mole, the bat, the dog and the serpent attest, it abounds in factual interest. But, as indicated in the title (which, taken "in sheer desperation" after finding his original phrase pre-empted, is his least happy one), the naturalist in him had somewhat elbowed aside the out-of-door essayist. Though several of the essays rank well as literature and one receives from them another dividend of wisdom, there is little lifting of the eyes, as in *Nature in Downland* and *The Land's End*, to gather in the beauty of the wider landscape, and, in the actual writing, little of that lyrical quality, the exaltation, characteristic of Hudson at his best. And, despite the grouping of some of the essays and the strong ending, *The Book of a Naturalist* is more of a collection of miscellaneous articles than a book.

The group of essays on the serpent, intended as chapters for the long-projected but never completed volume on this member of the reptile family, are of special value in explaining the strange fascination that serpents always had for him, a fascination inherited by Rima. He tries to exorcise man's irrational fear of snakes and, by exposing (as Browne and Waterton had done before him) its theological roots, to stop the persecution of them. Compared with the writings of Ditmars, these essays belong more within the world of art. The essay that undoubtedly attracted most attention in this volume was "The Great Dog-Superstition," an old magazine article that he was going to rule out "partly because it was somewhat polemical and touched on questions which are not natural history, pure and simple" but decided to put in "just for [the] fun" of waving a red flag before the many dog-devotees or canophilists, "a people weak in their intellectuals." No one acquainted with the writings of Hudson, particularly with *A Shepherd's Life*, can doubt his real admiration for the dog. But he felt that an excessive regard for it is unfair to other members of the animal kingdom likewise highly endowed (so he perhaps too optimistically thought) with affection, fidelity, good temper and intelligence, such as the squirrel, the fairy-like marmoset, the lemur, which is without "the monkey's pathetic old man's withered countenance," and the agouti, "a rodent moulded in the great Artist-Mother's happiest mood." There is also an interesting essay on that risky and strange experiment of Nature, the bat; and another on the earthworm, in which he has a vision of a time, eagerly looked forward to in *Birds in London*, when the brick and stone of cities will have sunk "beneath the surface" of the earth and been covered "with a deep rich mould and a mantle of ever-lasting verdure."

Although there is no essay in *The Book of a Naturalist*, unless it be "My Friend the Pig," that matches the best in other volumes, there are some episodes and moments of rapture, other than those in the essays already mentioned, that linger in one's memory: an old dog badger that, because his trotting over a flooded moor sounded like the cantering of a horse, was mistaken by a rural policeman for a ghost; a company of herons "lying and luxuriating in the tepid water" of Sowley Pond in the manner of "pigs, buffaloes, hippo-potamuses, and other water-loving mammalians"; the strange friend-ship of a cat for a rat, which was abruptly broken when the rat, wishing to give a downy lining to her nest, insisted on plucking out the fluffs from the cat's profuse side-whiskers (an episode that would especially have pleased Buckland); a crowded field of John-go-to-bed-at-noon, resplendent in their "dandelion orange-yellow, the most luminous colour in nature," and dancing in the wind on their tall, pliant stems; and a walk amongst a three-acre patch of fritillaries, on the level with the knees and as "thick as spikes in a ripe wheat-field," the dark "pendulous cups" sparkling with rain-drops and "trembling in the lightest wind."

A Traveller in Little Things (1921), with one of the most felicitous of titles, is mainly a gleaning and a diversion. Some of the essays were probably fashioned out of material that could not be worked into previous volumes: "The Two White Houses" and " 'Blood': A Story of Two Brothers," for example, will immediately be associated in one's mind with *Far Away and Long Ago*. There are essays on animals—wasps, chiffchaffs, a moorhen, a jackdaw and a dog; on villages, one of which, "A Wiltshire Village," is among his best; and on churchyards. In the main, however, this sheaf of essays belongs more within the sphere of human portraiture than that of the romance of natural history. There are many records of casual meetings with people, in the churchyard and the cottage or along the wayside, meetings from which Hudson was peculiarly fitted to extract what was most typical and significant. The frag-mentary quality of each experience was wisely preserved in the tell-ing, giving a suggestiveness to these essays or sketches that would largely have been lost had the attempt been made to shape them into short stories.

There is a goodly company of people in these pages: a girl persecuted by her blond family because she was Iberian; a travelling salesman whose sole fishing expedition not only secured a steady customer but quickened in him for at least once in his life the sense of beauty; and a rheumatic old codger in a tumble-down cottage, regarded by his fellows as a mean, grasping rascal, who warmed up to Hudson to the extent of bestowing upon him, with all due ceremony, a solitary walnut. One group of sketches is based on a theory of the author's that "beauty and goodness or 'inward perfections' are correlated," but since it deals more with the exceptions to what he regards as the rule, his theory receives but little support. Hudson's genius with children, already apparent in *The Purple Land, Birds in a Village, A Little Boy Lost,* and *Afoot in England,* is here given expression in a choice gallery of little boys and girls whom he had remembered over the years: Edmund and the boy actor, Freckles and Dimples, Dolly and Rose, grave Millicent and resolute Mab, and the flowerlike little girl with whom he watched the waves rush up Cromer Beach. Finest of all the portraits in *A Traveller in Little Things* is that of the samphire gatherer, a portrait comparable to Rembrandt's *Old Woman Cutting Her Nails.*

A sense of companionship is to be felt in all Hudson's volumes of essays, but it is, most frequently, that of being in his company as he ventures among animals or pauses to absorb the beauty of some scene. There was plenty of that other sort of companionship in him, that of a fellowly human being, capable of the deepest attachments. In *A Traveller in Little Things* this latter quality is particularly strong, and it receives poignant expression in "The Return of the Chiff-Chaff," a monody on all his dead friends, who came crowding about him "almost as in life" while he sought solitude by a pond half-covered with flowering bog-bean. Some solace for his "intolerable sadness" was found in the thought that they, by their very existence, had touched the visible world "with a new light, a tenderness and grace and beauty not its own." This essay is the chief expression of his attitude toward death, whose bourne he was soon to cross.

The greatest spread of Hudson's mind is reached in *A Hind in Richmond Park* (1922), a fitting epilogue to a long life of observation and thought. The sight of a deer in a London park sensitively adjusting one ear to catch every sound from a nearby woodland and the other to determine the meaning of Hudson's hunterlike whistle, starts him meditating. And in the process of comparing her delicately attuned senses with those of other animals, including man, Hudson is thronged with so many of the intriguing questions he had flushed in earlier essays and with so many memories that the book becomes a summing-up of his life as a field naturalist and, next to *Far Away and Long Ago*, the most profoundly self-revelatory of all his volumes. As art, however, it is not so good a book as, say, *Nature in Downland* or *A Shepherd's Life*, for it fails to capture so much of the beauty of the visible world. Though his mood remains that of the essayist, the emphasis on speculation may have clogged somewhat his lyrical spirit. Yet, altogether, *A Hind in Richmond Park* is, like Bridges' *Testament of Beauty*, a remarkable achievement, especially for a man in his eighties.

The movement of thought is leisurely. Since death claimed the author before the book was finished, the style, wanting in some of its usual cadence, is even more that of unstudied conversation than elsewhere in his writings. "It is," says Roberts, "as near his talk and way of moving through a world of ideas as book-words may get." Led by random thoughts and recollections, Hudson works his way slowly toward his main ideas: from the sense of smell, to which he devotes most of his pages, to sound and music, and then, spirally, to poetry and to art in general. One is gradually lured on by his interesting observations, his felicitous allusions and anecdotes, and the charm of his quiet voice, unsuspecting of the speculative treat in store. Casual though the arrangement seems to be, *A Hind in Richmond Park* is one of the most subtly integrated of all Hudson's books. It suggests the form of a loosely constructed fugue, the themes recurring again and again in a varied form.

With his vivid descriptions and illustrative anecdotes, many of them dating from his youth on the pampas, the psychology of smell and sound becomes fascinating reading. Convinced that there is "nothing in this dim spot which men call earth, perhaps nothing in the entire universe, more marvellous than the mind in its secret doings," he makes exploration into the great wilderness of the unconscious. Credence is given to telepathy, which he regards as, possibly, "a striking example of that vaguely conscious something, force or principle, in nature, which we sometimes roughly name 'unconscious intelligence,' a diffused mind in or behind nature which gives a sort of supernatural disguise to phenomena." Several chapters are devoted to the migratory impulse, which is to be found in many other creatures besides birds—even men. Always he keeps reminding us of the unity of all life, that we possess nothing that is not shared in some degree with beast and bird and insect.

Most self-revelatory are his discussions of poetry and music, and art in general. How much poetry meant to him is amply illustrated in all his writings, and here he tells us it is Chaucer's childlike spontaneity, his quick and loving sympathy, and his closeness to primitive man in the acuteness of the senses that make his poetry more attractive to him than even that of Shakespeare. In his conception of the origin and the effect of music Hudson is probably not entirely correct, but in describing his own reactions to it, especially in comparison with those to poetry, he speaks *de profundis*. Like Sir Thomas Browne and George Gissing, he was so sensitive to music that he might be "moved to tears by even the common and tavern sort." And in the presence of great music, he would "float away as in the dream called levitation and [be] in another realm far removed from earth, inhabited by beings who were once of the earth." In the uncompleted last chapter, Hudson speculates, as Jefferies had done in *The Story of My Heart*, upon the possibility of mankind evolving out of itself something superior to art as we now know it, something that will give fuller satisfaction to those "whose interest is in the whole of life."

What is most impressive in his discussion of art is the stressing of the deep-rootedness in all life of the sense of beauty, which is the origin of art. As early as *Birds of La Plata*, and again and again in many of the succeeding volumes, he had opposed the idea that all beauty is rooted in the sex feeling; rather, he reversed their relationship by claiming that this feeling is only "one of the many distinct elements contained in the root" of beauty. And he takes issue with Santayana, who held that the sense of the beautiful is a casual growth, limited to the mind of man, where it plays a very minor rôle. For it was one of the main articles of Hudson's faith that this sense is to be found in all the lesser "civilizations," those of beasts and birds and insects. "What we call spirituality [and the same may be said of the aesthetic faculty] is not ours by miracle;

it was inherent in us from the beginning: the seed germinated and the roots and early leaves were formed before man, as man, existed, and are ours by inheritance." Beauty is, indeed, "inherent in the granite itself," pervading it "like a subtle fire."

It was dramatically fitting that he who had experienced the beauty of the world so passionately and had made so much of it, in essay after essay, permanent against the invidiousness of Time, should have brought his life to a close on this exalted note. From his earliest days on the pampas, Hudson had felt an insatiable curiosity concerning the abounding diversity of the life all round him, a curiosity more protean than that of any of his predecessors in the out-of-door essay. Absorbing much of the earth's ageless beauty through his finely ramified roots, his being slowly unfolded into full leafage; and in the late summer of his life, the elements of the soil were transformed into the beauty of flowers. And he blossomed steadily into volume after volume until winter struck at his roots. *Far Away and Long Ago, A Shepherd's Life,* and arranged about them, *Idle Days in Patagonia, Nature in Downland, Hampshire Days, Adventures among Birds, A Hind in Richmond Park, Birds and Man, Afoot in England,* and *Birds in Town and Village*—what a well-blended florilegium to present to the Muses! If *The Compleat Angler* and *Selborne* have been enough to keep the names of Walton and White alive now for centuries, surely these shafts of bloom should keep Hudson's fragrant for a long time.

Artistry

I see, smell, taste, hear, feel, that everlasting Something to which we are allied, . . . the actual glory of the universe. . . .

—THOREAU

IF TO THE average person, the pageantry of nature makes at times a strong appeal, how powerful that appeal must be to the out-of-door essayist, with his unusually acute and urgent senses! "When removed from the sight" of grass, Hudson was "apt to fall," so he tells us, "into a languishing state, a dim and despondent mind, like one in prison or sick and fallen on the days 'which are at best . . . mere glimmerings and decays.'" "I must look at a leaf, or smell the sod, or touch a rough pebble, or hear some natural sound —if only the chirp of a cricket—or feel the sun or wind or rain on my face." And should such a one be fortunate enough to have his lot cast early in the midst of a romantically wild region, the natural world will ever be charged for him with an irresistible magic. What is learnt in the cradle, so goes the proverb, endures to the grave.

Exquisitely sensitized as Hudson was and with the pampas for his playground, it was inevitable that he would become entranced with nature in all its multifariousness. As a child, "the mere feel of a blade of grass made [him] happy"; and the keenness of the senses of animals was a continual source of admiration. His frequent remonstrances against the destruction of many forms of animal life were the result not only of a conviction of their educational value to mankind but of his own personal desire for the greatest possible diversity of sensuous experience. Even a spiderless world, such as Emerson and hosts of others have looked forward to with eagerness, would have scanted his "love of the beautiful, the grotesque, and the marvellous." Keen though his sight was, he never allowed it, as Ruskin did, to tyrannize over his other senses. For he yearned to envelop himself also in sounds and odors, flavors and textures—"to pierce and dwell in them as some tiny insect penetrates to the hollow chamber of a flower to feed at ease on its secret sweetness." Indeed, in the fullness of his sensory endowment and in his insatiable desire to absorb experience at every pore, he reminds one, among the poets, most of Keats.

The exercise of his senses never became an indulgence, as it sometimes did with Rousseau and Keats and Wolfe, for, learned in the psychology of the senses, he kept them constantly under the scrutiny of a critical intelligence. His training as a naturalist taught him the necessity for scrupulous accuracy and the value of objectivity. "A naturalist cannot exaggerate consciously; and if he be capable of unconscious exaggeration, then he is no naturalist." His sensuous impressionability, so disciplined, allowed him to gather many choice experiences for the out-of-door essay.

Sight, the highest of the senses and the chief messenger of the intellect, contributed, of course, most to this achievement. An impressive example of the naturalist's skill in visual observation is the account of the little tragedy wrought by a baby cuckoo in a robin's nest in a quiet nook of the New Forest. First we see the newly hatched bird lying at the bottom of the nest as "helpless as a piece of jelly with a little life in it." Within forty-eight hours, his bulk has doubled, and, irritated by the presence of an egg and a young robin in the nest with him, he moves, jerks, and wriggles "his lumpish body this way and that" continually. Hudson is careful to focus the attention upon the hollow ("a sort of false bottom") in the middle of the cuckoo's broad back, for it is the ultra-sensitivity of this hollow that is the cause of all the mischief. Whenever the cuckoo, by fidgetting, would force the egg onto his back,

a sudden change that was like a fit would seize the bird; he would stiffen, rise in the nest, his flabby muscles made rigid, and stand erect, his back in a horizontal position, the head hanging down, the little naked wings held up over the back. In that position he looked an ugly, lumpish negro mannikin, standing on thinnest dwarf legs, his back bent, and elbows stuck up above the hollow flat back.

Once up on his small stiffened legs he would move backwards, firmly grasping the hairs and hair-like fibres of the nest-lining, and never swerving, until the rim of the cup-like structure was reached; and then standing, with feet sometimes below and in some cases on the rim, he would jerk his body, throwing the egg off or causing it to roll off. After that he would fall back into the nest and lie quite exhausted for some time, his jelly-like body rising and falling with his breathing.

After the ejection of the egg, the struggle began with the young robin, who proved to be a more formidable antagonist.

It did not roll like the egg and settle in the middle of the back; it would fall partly on to the cuckoo's back and then slip off into the nest again. But success came at last, after many failures. The robin was lying partly across the cuckoo's neck, when, in moving its head, its little curved beak came down and rested on the very centre of that irritable hollow in the back of its foster-brother. Instantly the cuckoo pressed down into the nest, shrinking away as if hot needles had pricked him, as far as possible from the side where the robin was lying against him, and this movement of course brought the robin more and more over him, until he was thrown right upon the cuckoo's back.

Instantly the rigid fit came on, and up rose the cuckoo, as if the robin weighed no more than a feather on him; and away backwards he went, right up the nest, without a pause, and standing actually on the rim, jerked his body, causing the robin to fall off, clean away from the nest. . . .

After getting rid of his burden the cuckoo continued in the same position, perfectly rigid, for a space of five or six seconds, during which it again and again violently jerked its body, as if it had the feeling of the burden on it still. Then, the fit over, it fell back, exhausted as usual.

With what intensity the little, unconscious culprit plays his rôle! How well is the action mirrored in the patient, needle-sharp, dispassionate eyes of the spectator!

As has already been indicated and as we shall soon see at greater length, there are many equally graphic scenes in Hudson's essays. Such acuity of the eye, embedded as it was in a speculative matrix, enabled him to correct many scientists and philosophers as well as naturalists, even those of the stature of Darwin and Spencer and Santayana.

Hudson also had the eye of the painter in his feeling for line, composition, and color. What a sensitive, Chinese-like monochrome is his sketch of the one-sided, wind-warped hawthorns and blackthorns that have haphazardly sprung up from stray seeds on the Cornish coast!

They are like the trees and bushes on the most exposed coasts in Yorkshire and in other places, growing all one way, lying close to and sometimes actually on the ground, stretching out their branches and every twig towards the inland country. . . . Held by the feet in the grip of earth, the beaten bush strains to get away; it suggests the figure of a person crawling, or trying to crawl, the knee-like joints on the ground, the body-like trunk thrown forward, the long bare branches and terminal twigs, like the brown, thin naked arms and claw-like opened fingers of a starving scourged slave in the tropics, extended imploringly towards the land.

These trees are not mere pictorial grotesques, but living things, struggling like Laocoons to escape from the pitiless fangs of the wind. The broader, panoramic landscape, such as that of the maritime district of Sussex, Hudson can paint with a subtle sense of composition and perspective.

> It is not . . . from all points of view that the Chichester spire is of so much account in the landscape. The line of the downs must appear beyond it; and downs and spire look best from the green level land between the cathedral and the sea. In some states of the weather the spire has a singular beauty, as when sun-flushed, it appears white against a black cloud. Perhaps the most beautiful effect is an afternoon or evening one, when there are clouds, but in the east and north a pale clear sky, against which the grey spire and distant downs appear sharply outlined; the earth green, but the hills in shadow deepest indigo blue.

Whether it be a grasshopper or a hover-fly, a cuckoo or a red grouse, a hind or a human being, an immemorially quiet English village or the desert of Patagonia—all are within the scope of his artistry.

Many colors—the diverse garments of form—affected Hudson, as they did Ruskin and Hugo and Jefferies, like wine. At the sight of a patch of scarlet verbenas in full bloom, he was wont, as a boy, to throw himself from his pony "with a cry of joy to lie on the turf among them and feast [his] sight on their brilliant colour." In his penetration into the mysteries of the senses, he has much to say about the psychological effect of color—most notably, that of whiteness. Photography seemed to him to degrade open-air things, bringing them "down to one flat, monotonous, colourless shadow of things, weary to look at." Indeed, except for an occasional feeling that the continual presence of great masses of color might cloy his taste for the delicate touches of it, such as are to be found in scattered wayside flowers, there is something almost oriental in Hudson's response to color. The oriental preference for color to form is indicated in the remark that a certain stained-glass window without design had given him "more pleasure than any other window in any church or cathedral in England." A pampean landscape in a Buenos Aires gallery stirred in his youthful heart the ambition to become a painter, but he found himself wanting in dexterity. What a thick van-Gogh-like skin of pigment he would have applied to many of his canvases!

As shown in the Chichester sketch and in the "Secret of the Charm of Flowers," he had a firm command over his palette. Subtle is the choice of colors in the depiction of those "glassy flowers of [the] ocean," the jelly-fish ("great crystalline hemispheres, hyaline blue and delicate salmon-pink"), the belly of an extraordinary adder ("exquisite turquoise blue, . . . most like that of the forget-me-not, but being enamelled," suggestive rather of the blue "on some priceless piece of old Chinese pottery"), and the columbine ("albeit a true floral blue it is a blue of the earth, the material world we inhabit, not the divine [or human] blue of the blue geranium nor the more ethereal blue of the vernal squill on the sea-cliffs, and of the wild hyacinth seen in sheets of colour under the woodland trees . . . —the floral blues that bring heaven down to us"). A favorite subject was a beechen woods, either arrayed in the red-gold of October or winter-bare, like the one chanced upon during a walk over the Sussex downs:

> Innumerable white or pale columns standing on a floor of red and russet gold, and white columns and golden floor were all the more beautiful for being seen through the almost cloud-like tracery of innumerable purple and purplish-red or "murrey"-coloured branchlets. The rich colour of that temple and palace of nature—the golden floor and purple roof—made the wide band of the yew wood seem black by contrast; and above the black yews the smooth turf of the hill-top looked a pale green.

Missal-like is the picture in *Far Away and Long Ago* of the great old blossoming peach-trees seen against a lapis lazuli sky, with a large company of green parrakeets frolicking in the branches and sending down flurries of rose-pink petals.

Like Coleridge, Jefferies, Baudelaire, and others whose senses were extraordinarily alive, Hudson at times imaginatively translated the effects of one sense into those of another—most frequently that of color. Thus the singing of thousands of field finches in unison affected him like "the sight of flowing water or of rain when the multitudinous falling drops appear as silvery-grey lines on the vision"; the common bunting's "little outburst of confused or splintered notes," like "a handful of clear water thrown up and breaking into sparkling drops in the sunlight"; and the song of the skylark, like a fluid mosaic of many sober and brilliant colors, its acutest note ("a clear piercing sound like a cry several times repeated") resembling "a chance patch of most brilliant colour occurring at intervals" in the confused pattern. He can speak intelligibly of the yellow smell and the purple flavor. And to his childhood imagination, God assumed the form of a blue column, the blue varying in depth and intensity from sky-blue to "that of the morning-glory or wild geranium."

With a Monet-like sensitivity, he responded to many of the effects of the passing moment, placing his scenes in time and bathing them in atmosphere. The "deep rich mineral red" given to dead bracken by the rain is at its finest, he informs us, when the shower "is nearly over and the clouds are full of light." The bluish tint that invests juniper with "a rare, delicate, changeful beauty" is best seen "in the early mornings, when the level sunbeams strike on the bushes, wet with dew or melting hoar-frost." The higher hill-top groves on the downs impressed him most on hot, calm days,

> when the atmosphere near the surface appears as a silvery mist, or as thinnest white and crystalline flames, ascending, wavering, dancing, and producing an illusion of motion in all distant solid objects. . . . At a distance of a mile or two the tall columnar trunks of the pines, showing the light between, seem to have a wavering motion, and, with the high dense roof of branches, look absolutely black against the brilliant whiteness of the air and the pale hot sky beyond.

Much of the enchantment that certain villages had for him, such as the one described in "On Going Back," was the result, he knew, of "the mood, the season, [and] the magical hour." Impressionistic records like these, which he, unlike Constable and Ruskin, did not attempt to touch up, rival in exquisiteness of perception those of other major landscapists.

All the sounds of nature were as music to his ear: the crepitation of insects, the patter of rain on leaves, the many-toned chorales of the wind, the ceaseless moan of the waves along the shore, and the whole gamut of bird voices. The harsher sounds—the wailing of the curlew, the croak of the raven, and the screech of the jay—gave him scarcely less pleasure. Nor did he, like many other nature-listeners, draw the line at the braying of the ass. Although his imagination was probably no more quickened by sounds than Wordsworth's or Thoreau's, his ear was certainly more subtle and exact. Jefferies, too, had a delicately attuned ear of catholic range, but only occasionally, as in the description of the wind and of bird-song, does he approach his successor. In accuracy and suggestiveness of phrasing, especially as a critic of the songs of birds, Burroughs alone among the major out-of-door essayists is frequently his peer. Hudson's aural memory was, moreover, phenomenal: after twenty-six years he could still recall distinctly the language of a hundred and fifty-four of the hundred and ninety-two species of birds he had learned to know in South America, and of the hundred and ninety-two, there were only seven that completely eluded him.

In none of his writings is the keenness of his ear better attested than by his description of bird-song, from the brief characterization of the shrill chirp and long "sibilant and tremulous" note of the reed-bunting to the fuller passages on the strains of the skylark, the marsh-warbler, the willow- and the wood-wrens. To illustrate this gift, it might be well to turn, however, to the less well-known rendition of the performance of the leaf-locust.

> It has a sustained note, repeated several times with silent intervals of a second or less; then a longer interval of silence and the strain once more. It is a soft and silvery sound, and differs also from the music of other locusts and crickets in its *slowness*. For the locust sound is not one, but a series of sounds following so rapidly that they blend into one sustained chord of sound; whereas in this insect the points or drops of sound are heard distinctly as separate notes. . . . Thoreau called it "slumberous breathing," and Hawthorne more successfully describes it as "audible silence," and adds: "If moonlight could be heard it would sound like that."

> This is good, except that it omits a quality of the sound which is its principal charm—its *expression*. That is, its tenderness, a quality which we find in some bird music—our willow wren is an example—but do not find in other insect music. It is the most melancholy of all delicate sounds in nature; and because of its slow sadness and musicalness you might imagine it to be a human sound, although not a vocal one. Let us say, of a once human wood-haunting solitary minstrel, now faded and dwindled away to an almost unsubstantial entity, who no longer walks the earth but dwells in trees where he

has taken the colour and semi-transparence of the leaves he lives with; that at night time, when the moon sheds a misty silveriness on the dusky foliage, he wakes once more to memories of long-dead human affections, and with moth-like fingers sweeps the strings, drawing out those soft, low, yet clear penetrative sounds that make the silence deeper, and float down to us like the sound of tears.

A transcription of insect music such as this, at once scientifically accurate and suffused with emotion, would have appealed to both an Henri Fabre and a Lafcadio Hearn.

Excellence of sight and hearing one takes for granted in an out-of-door essayist, but Hudson's extreme sensibility to odors comes as something of a surprise. Little children, so he informs us, have almost as keen a sense of smell as the animals, and, "when they live with nature," it affords them as much "pleasure as sight or hearing"; but a good deal of it is lost during the process of growth, for man has long been contracting the olfactory lobe so that other areas of the brain might be further developed. Hudson, however, through the continual exercise of this sense, was able to retain most of its power to the very end. He was at times, he says, "as reluctant to pass" by a primrose without poking his nose into each of its blossoms "as the great Dr. Johnson was to pass a street-post without touching it with his hand." For certain flowering trees—orange, mimosa, acacia, the Pride of China—he cherished a love "almost like the love that some woman has inspired in us with her charm. . . ." And when a "smelling hunger" came upon him, he was wont to "spend entire days roaming about on boggy or marshy heaths" in order to "stand knee-deep" amidst golden withy or sweet gale and to rub his "hands and face with the crushed leaves and fill [his] pockets with them so as to wrap [him]self up in the delicious aroma." He even regretted that the modern Englishman, unlike the Elizabethan, regarded scents applied to one's own person as a sign of effeminacy and questionable morals, for it meant limiting himself to a sprinkle of cologne or lavender on his handkerchief.

In his study of the psychology of the senses, it was smell, about which little had been written, that became his favorite. He made an interesting distinction between what he called its lower and its higher nature: the one, as with the odors of spices and fruits, suggests flavors and is near the level of taste; the other is "more evanescent, yet more penetrating, touching the mind . . . to something more than a mere aesthetic satisfaction," and its effect is similar to the spiritual expression in certain flowers and bird sounds, in certain human faces and voices, and "in certain aspects of earth and sea and sky" during "rare atmospheric conditions." In the fragrance of the furze, for example, with its suggestion of the flavor of cocoanut and honey and its power of reviving events out of the past, the sensuous and the spiritual are combined; in that of frankincense, so valuable for religious ritual, there is nothing except the spiritual. Hudson's assertion that a scent, like a flavor, cannot be recalled, needs, so it seems to me, further qualification; on the other hand, his insistence that odors can affect the mind powerfully even when unconscious of them is quite convincing. Thus, to the explanation of some instances of "second sight," he brings forward the simple one of smell.

There are many odors in his pages: the unique one of bracken "when it first unrolls its broad fronds" (a strange combination of "castor-oil and the fish-and-cucumber odour of smelts"); the lilac-like aroma of willows in spring; the air on the downs in the evening of a hot spring day ("like the smell of a druggist's shop, blown abroad and rid of its grosser elements"); and, what must come as a shock to many, the carrion stench of the dog, "not the smell of carrion lying or drying in the sun, but of a dead animal lying and decomposing in a pool of water in hot weather." Upon landing in England, Hudson immediately detected in the air, so he amusingly tells us, a scent never encountered before: "an earth-born," thick, sweetish, warm smell, "half-flowery and half-savoury," "something like cookery and Russian leather, a happy, pleasant smell." Since he found at least whiffs of it almost everywhere he went during the following months, it became to his nasal imagination the Smell of England. One day, feeling himself more and more bathed in the scent while approaching "a big building from which issued clouds of steam and hot air from a dozen conduits," it dawned upon him that the Smell of England was that of the brewery!

To the sense of taste, closely allied as it is with that of smell, Hudson was also unusually responsive. Never hankering after the exotic, he preferred the simple and the familiar flavors. Every kind of berry along the wayside, except that of the elder, was savored, and many of the herbs, especially fennel and samphire. He can write suggestively of the purple taste (the family resemblance in the flavors of most purple fruits), and occasionally with some gusto of cooked foods. If during his intimacy with Gissing, the conversation ever turned to the culinary art, they must have found themselves in essential agreement. Yet flavors never stirred his imagination as they did that of Lamb or Keats or Proust; his descriptions of them do not tantalize one so much as those of Wolfe; and none of his essays matches Thoreau's on wild apples or Burroughs' on strawberries.

To a certain extent, all the senses are involved in that of touch. The drama of the cuckoo in an alien nest, the sketch of the writhen trees of Cornwall, and the essay on the "Charm of the Downs" are full of tactile and kinaesthetic impressions. One of the most recurrent of such impressions is his awareness of the resilience of the turf in downland, with its thick layer of interlaced fibers. The wind had an extraordinary effect on him, as on Wordsworth and Muir, blowing away, so it seemed, "some obstruction . . . to a perfect freedom of mind" and transforming him "into a new and different being, one as unlike [his] ordinary self as . . . a sparrow-hawk is unlike a barn-door fowl." Great winds occasionally brought telepathic communications. The most physically etherealizing of his experiences came on surpassingly brilliant days during the phenomenon called "visible heat," when he felt like "a bather standing breast-deep in a clear, green, warm tropical sea, so charged with salt that it lifts him up. . . ." Such a sensation was at times the prelude to a mystical experience.

Highly endowed as he thus was with the power of absorbing nature along all the highways and most of the byways of the cardinal senses—synthesizing their notations with emotion and evaluating them with thought—Hudson was able to give his panoramas of England and South America their chief sensory dimensions.

Hudson realized the difficulty of transcribing the impressions of his senses into words and the folly of competing with the phonograph, the camera, and the palette. In trying to convey the delicate, unearthly quality of the soft, silvery-blue haze that enveloped him as he stood on the sparkling sands of a Norfolk beach, he exclaims: "Do we not see that words fail as pigments do—that the effect is too coarse, since in describing it we put it before the mental eye as something distinctly visible, a thing of itself and separate. But it is not so in nature; the effect is of something almost invisible and is yet a part of all and makes all things—sky and sea and land— as unsubstantial as itself." To impart verbally a true impression of a hummingbird, "so unlike in its beauty [to] all other beautiful things," seemed to him "not more impossible than it would be to bottle up a supply of . . . 'living sunbeams' . . . and convey them across the Atlantic to scatter them in a sparkling shower over the face of England." The best a writer can do is to make a careful selection from the multitude of his sensory data and, like the sketcher or impressionistic painter, arrange them so as to quicken his readers to creativeness. The appeal should be made as much to the sensuous imagination as to the senses themselves.

The poet and not the naturalist, so Hudson believed, has the secret for revealing nature.

> It is because the poet does not see his subject apart from its surroundings, deprived of its atmosphere—a mere fragment of beggarly matter —does not use it too well, with all the details which become visible only after a minute and, therefore, cold examination, but as a part of the picture, a light that quivers and quickly passes, that we, through him, are able to see it too, and to experience the old mysterious sensations, restored by his magic touch.

The closest approximation to actual experience with nature is the poetic description of it, for the poet approaches reality through his perceptions and thus is at only one remove from it, whereas the scientific naturalist, striving to be impersonal and depending largely upon conceptual thought, is twice removed. The latter, in his search for knowledge and function, plumbs the depths of life, patiently tabulating many soundings and, through analysis, giving them intellectual value; the former, on the other hand, not unfamiliar with the findings of the naturalist but more concerned with the quality of his own perceptions, climbs to the heights on Jacob's ladder of the imagination and makes his appeal to man's sense of beauty. Hudson himself was neither pure poet nor pure scientist; rather, he was what he dubbed Thoreau, a poet-naturalist—a poet by temperament, possessing wings, and a naturalist by long habit, providing ballast.

Again and again in his writings, Hudson stressed, as did Wordsworth and Coleridge and Ruskin, the value of emotion over mere learning in the appreciation of nature.

The first sight of a thing, the shock of emotion, the vivid and ineffaceable image registered in the brain, is worth more than all the knowledge acquired by reading. . . .

Only when a scene is viewed emotionally, when it produces in us a shock of pleasure, does it become a permanent possession of the mind; in other words, it registers an image which, when called up before the inner eye, is capable of reproducing a measure of the original delight.

All the natural historians, from Aristotle downwards, in all they have said of the nightingale, are incapable of making it re-live in and flood my soul with melody as it is made to do in a couple of stanzas by George Meredith.

Thus it was that, like Thoreau, Fabre, and other out-of-door essayists, he disdained all naturalists with merely factual minds and atrophied hearts, especially the "necrologists," whose vision is conditioned by stuffed animals in show cases and circumscribed by the walls of a museum. His own keenness for birds had been whetted, so he tells us, not by "frigid ornithologists" but by the long succession of great poets. It was, indeed, the fullness and intensity of his emotional nature that gave him his phenomenal memory for sights and sounds, and aided in achieving in *Far Away and Long Ago* the power of total recall. Too much emotion, of course, blurs the lines of the etcher's plate or overloads the brush of the painter, as it does occasionally with Jefferies and Muir and Loti. So sure, however, was Hudson's sense of fact and so sane his whole attitude toward life that, no matter how rapturous his emotion, he never gives one the impression of being in danger of losing control over the instruments of his art.

The source of his emotional strength is to be found in what he calls the mythical faculty.

We may say that impressions are vivid and live vividly in the mind, even to the end of life, in those alone in whom something that is of the child survives in the adult—the measureless delight in all this visible world, . . . so rarely expressed in literature, as Traherne, let us say, expressed it; and, with the delight, the sense of wonder in all life, which is akin to, if not one with, the mythical faculty, and if experienced in a high degree is a sense of the supernatural in all natural things.

Anyone familiar with *The Golden Bough* needs no further evidence of the workings of this faculty in primitive peoples—peoples toward whom, it will be remembered, Hudson felt strongly attracted. Poets, above all, are able to feel and to preserve its power: Vaughan and Wordsworth, for example, were aware of an animateness similar to their own in the whole of nature, the one affirming that "each bush and oak doth know *I am*," and the other, that "every natural respires "with inward meaning." But, even in the most intellectual form, rock, fruit, or flower," lies "bedded in a quickening soul" and of men there are at least embers of the mythical faculty.

It is not sufficient to say that the sharper impression [Hudson is speaking of the effect the sudden view of three acres of fritillaries had on h.m] is due merely to the unusual appearance. I rather incline to believe that the source of the vivid interest excited is that faculty of the mind supposed to be obsolete, but which still faintly lives in all of us, though we may be unconscious of it—a faculty which [sees] a hidden meaning or spirit in all strange appearances in the natural world. It is the "sense of mystery," and is with us in sight of a magnificent and strange sunset, and of any unusual atmospheric strangeness, down to the smallest objects that engage our attention—an insect, a flower, even our chequered daffodil of the river-fields.

Not only did Hudson have the sense of immanence to a marked degree but he was strongly persuaded that Nature, informed as she is with at least unconscious intelligence and aestheticism, actually co-operates with one exercising the mythical faculty.

Our poets, . . . when they say that the sun rejoices in the sky and laughs at the storm, . . . speak not in metaphor. . . . In moments of excitement, when we revert to primitive conditions of mind, the earth and all nature is alive and intelligent, and feels as we feel.

I have sometimes thought that never does the world seem more alive and watchful of us than on a still, moonlight night in a solitary wood, when the dusky green foliage is silvered by the beams, and all visible objects and the white lights and black shadows in the intervening spaces seem instinct with spirit. But it is not so. If the conditions be favourable, if we go to our solitude as the crystal-gazer to his crystal, with a mind prepared, this faculty is capable of awaking and taking complete possession of us by day as well as by night.

All the most beautiful living things, from insect to man, like all the highest productions of human genius, produce in us a sense of the supernatural, . . . the sense of something outside of nature which shines on us through nature, even as the sun shines in the stained glass of a church window. . . .

Unless the soul goes out to meet what we see we do not see it; nothing do we see, not a beetle, not a blade of grass.[1]

And out of this co-operation—this *participation mystique*—comes profound experience and authentic art. Only when the soul reaches out and becomes interfused with the spirit of an object or the spirit that "rolls through all things" can it be said that one has seen with full comprehension. Such a person becomes thereby a confidant of Nature, and the records of their intimacies are the fruit of joint-authorship.

In Hudson, Nature found one to whom she could reveal much of her protean self. Many natural forms and phenomena besides flowers, serpents, trees, sunsets, moonlit nights, and the migratory flight of birds evoked in him, as in Shelley, Lawrence and many of the Chinese landscapists, the mythical faculty, even to the extent of giving him the impression of being in the presence of some supernatural power. Often he felt himself in communion with the spirit of some wild place, as with that of the plains of Patagonia. And at rare moments, the whole world became transfigured with spirit.

When walking [in the New Forest] one day, the loveliness of that green leafy world, its silence and its melody and the divine sunshine, so wrought on me that for a few precious moments it produced a mystical state, that rare condition of beautiful illusions when the feet are off the ground, when, on some occasions, we appear to be one with nature, unbodied like the poet's bird, floating, diffused in it. There are also other occasions when this transfigured aspect of nature produces the idea that we are in communion with or in the presence of unearthly entities.

The implication of supernaturalism may lead many to regard such experiences as a discredited part of nineteenth-century roman-

---

1 Note also passages quoted on pp. 21, 22.

ticism. The supernaturalism, however, is presented not as something real, but merely to help explain to the general reader a certain state of mind. As a matter of fact, the mythical faculty is deeply rooted, as we shall see, in one of the major philosophies, that of panpsychism, with its belief in myriad-spirited matter and an all-pervading Life-Force. And in the realm of art, this faculty is basic not only in the "organic principle" as enunciated by Schiller, Coleridge, and Emerson but also in the aesthetics of such naturalistic philosophers as Pepper and Dewey. Thus it is that "all the highest productions of human genius" beget in us "a sense of the supernatural."

It was the mythical faculty that enabled Hudson to penetrate to the very essence of an object or a locale and translate it into pure meaning. And, in a larger way, it provided him with the means of revealing Nature as well as describing her. In comparison with its power of perception, that of the analytical reason often seemed superfluous and even a hindrance, "like setting in motion a noisy engine" in the brain. When this faculty was working strongly within him and he could identify himself with the thing contemplated, his writing, like the sketches of Constable, becomes charged with intensity. What especially attracted him to poetry above all the other arts, even that of music, was the extent to which it gives expression to this primitive sensibility, which he likened to the ingredient in a salad that animates the whole. Indeed, it is the strength of the mythical faculty, permeating many of his best passages, that determines, more than any other quality, the character of his artistry.

The power of grasping things from within as well as from without allowed Hudson to enter intimately into their world and to present them as individuals, each with a personality and soul of its own. Though he occasionally resorted to the technique of the poet, setting imagination aglow with a word or phrase, his records are usually fuller and more diffuse, for the medium in which he worked is more detailed and discursive. He did not, however, fall into the error of piling up too much detail; instead, he knew how to quintessentialize his sense-impressions, choosing the most salient ones and in just sufficient number to bring a plant or an animal or a scene to life on the printed page.

His is one of the most transparent of styles for the presentation of the out-of-doors. Repelled by both the "tortured speech" of DeQuincey and the archaic simplicity of Morris, Hudson drew his vocabulary from the well of native English undefiled.[2] Since he thought the news of the open-air world of sufficient inherent interest to hold the attention of a reader, his pages do not glitter with curious embroideries of phrasing or with other contrived literary effects. There are, of course, a number of dull passages in his essays, particularly in those written for bread and cheese, but usually his phrasing has freshness enough to preserve the dew on the flowers and the sheen on chitin, fur and feathers, and his pages have wide margins of suggestiveness. As in the choice, so in the flow of words, he kept within the traditional idiom of English prose, that of Hooker, Defoe and Hazlitt, adding to it, however, something of the unconscious grace of the Spanish.[3] Painstakingly wrought though his style was, it gives the impression of complete artlessness, Conrad remarking that Hudson wrote as the grass grows. Such simplicity, absorbing many details in its broad, serene flow and dissolving the mere accidents of personality, allows the objects being described, even the most elusive ones, to shine through. In many of his descriptions it is as though flower and tree, bird and beast, man and the genii of many places, were speaking for themselves, using him only as their amanuensis. His words then come as near as words can to being things.

Together with the essential, intrinsic quality of objects, forces and scenes, he sought to present their "expressive" qualities: the aura acquired by them through old and close association with human beings. The associative factor in aesthetic experience, long recognized in the criticism of art, had been given a good deal of attention by eighteenth-century philosophers. Hence it figures prominently in the thought of Hazlitt and Wordsworth, and recurs again and again as a theme in the writings of Thoreau and Burroughs and Jefferies. As Hudson was aware, associations "may be untraceable: we may not be conscious and as a rule we are not conscious" that any such exist. And many of them, as romanticists generally do not seem to realize, are almost entirely subjective. Nevertheless, it is

---

2 Occasionally the bucket did bring up a few granules of sediment: such anti-quarianisms as *anent* and *albeit* and such scientific and literary jargon as *deglutition, glissading,* and *sustentation.*

3 As Cunninghame Graham has pointed out, the Spanish influence in his essays is most noticeable in *Far Away and Long Ago* and *A Hind in Richmond Park.* His bilingualism was the chief cause of an occasional lapse in idiom.

largely to the extent that they are felt that we are rewarded aestheti-
cally in our contacts with nature. For example, "there can be no . . .
'train of ideas' nor any vague sense of happiness due to association
caused by a bird's voice to one whose life or its early, most happy,
and impressive period has been spent apart from rural scenes. The
voice may be agreeable if the quality is good, but it is expressionless."

How well Hudson was able to capture the expressive quality of
a sound has already been amply illustrated in his description of the
recital of the leaf-locust. Extraordinarily sensitive, though perhaps
somewhat extravagant, is his analysis of this quality in flowers,
such as the association of the blue flower with blue eyes and the
clear blue of the sky. By means of metaphors and similes he frequently sought to increase the human associations around natural
objects, as with his likening of the baby cuckoo to a "lumpish
negro mannikin" and the wind-tormented trees of Cornwall to
starved, scourged slaves trying to crawl away from the lash of an
oppressor. Some coots, as they stood on floating weeds and preened
their plumage by the hour, reminded him of "mermaids for ever
combing out their locks," with "the clear stream for a mirror"; and
a doleful white owl, of "a feathered Dreyfus, Semitic features and
all, the head bowed, the weary eyes closed, the hooked nose just
visible amidst a wilderness of white whiskers." Thousands of such
humanizing touches are to be found in his essays, and never do
they falsify or sentimentalize the portraits. There was scarcely a
sight or sound in nature, whether it be of bindweed, wild garlic,
stag beetle, the call of the rhea, beechen woods or desert, but what
he could, when it had once arrested his attention, convert into a
human document. Often he reversed the process, describing human
beings in terms of animals, as when, unconscious of the offense it
might give, he likens a group of large blonde women, of slow,
deliberate manner, to "a herd of large beautiful white cows." Such
figures of speech, besides giving greater concreteness and color to
his style, enhance the expressive quality of nature and, as with
tendrils, bind man closer to her.

Because of the inevitable differences in our lives, many things
become peculiarly expressive to each of us, just as a morsel of cake
dipped in lime-flower tea became so to Marcel Proust. It is Hudson's
recording of his own personal associations that strengthens the
familiar-essay quality of his writings. Thus, while mentioning his

fondness for "the old, homely, cottage-garden blooms," he singles out the marigold as the "flower of flowers," because for him it "has an atmosphere, a sense or suggestion of something immeasurably remote and very beautiful—an event, a place, a dream perhaps, which has left no distinct image, but only this feeling unlike all others, imperishable, and not to be described except by the one word Marigold." Certain sights and sounds and, most subtly and profoundly of all (as others have noted), certain smells would suddenly open for him "cells where Memory slept." As an instance, he tells us that, though the sight of a Lombardy poplar and "the sound made by the wind in its summer foliage" brought many past scenes to mind, they were pictures only, until its fragrance touched "the nerve of smell, and then [they became] something more." In *A Hind in Richmond Park*, what flocks of memories are started, like game from thickets, during the discussion of the various senses!

It is in his search for the expression of a sight or a sound that this mythical faculty, blended with varying strengths of fancy, comes most spectacularly into play, inspiring him to fashion sentient creatures as embodiments of certain natural phenomena. The human quality in the slow, sad music of the leaf-locust leads to the creation of "a once human wood-haunting solitary minstrel." The evening primrose becomes a maiden originally intended to be the "most perfect type of grace and ethereal loveliness, . . . who soon outgrew her strength with all beauty of form, and . . . now wanders abroad, careless of appearances, in a faded flimsy garment, her fair yellow hair dishevelled, her mournful eyes fixed ever on the earth where she will shortly be." More dramatically, the strange, penetrating call of the wryneck is interpreted by the myth of an unusually sensitive boy metamorphosed into this shy bird as he recoils from the realization of the meaning of death; and the mechanistic principle of the universe is incarnated in the terrifying figure of a titan, with eyes gazing straight before him . . . like two immense round shields of grey ice" and having "no speculation in them." The Old Man of Kensington Gardens (in the poem of that title), the kakué near the end of "Marta Riquelme," the Lady of the Hills and other characters in *A Little Boy Lost* are also products of Hudson's mythopoeic imagination, as is, in part at least, Rima herself. Like the genii of *Prometheus Unbound* and the phantom Intelligences of *The Dynasts*, such creatures are, of course, not meant to be taken literally. Born out of a sense of the animateness of all things and a still deeper sense of mystery, they are meant only to titillate the fancy of his readers or to quicken their imagination. No more disturbing to one's sense of reality than the legends of Greece, Scandinavia or the Orient, these fresh personifications of the earth add color and flavor to his style. "To the full heart," as Thoreau has said, Nature "is all but a figure of speech."

Possessed as he thus was with acute, well-disciplined senses and a poetic temperament energized by the mythical faculty, Hudson became one of the best interpreters of nature. And with the presentation of both the intrinsic and expressive qualities of sights and sounds and smells—casting a searching light into the heart of things and weaving around them a garland of human associations—he was able to reap a rich harvest of experiences.

Most of this harvest was garnered in the form and with the spirit of the familiar essay. Though influenced by Thoreau, Burroughs and Jefferies, the form—"rambling, reminiscent, unsequential"—was, as we have seen, largely the result of self-discovery, the realization that it best captures the free rhythms and constantly changing aspects of nature as reflected in the mind and heart of a sensitive observer. After he had learnt how to let his senses and mythical faculty do much of the writing for him, his problem became primarily that of a Crome or a Constable or a Cox: to give just enough design to the copiousness of nature so as to keep it held within a frame of art. With Burroughs and Jefferies, the choice of this discursive medium gives one the impression at times of a certain want of artistry and a certain indolence of character or haste in composition. With Hudson, however, the choice seems to have come, as with Whitman and many of the vers-librists, from the desire to avoid interfering with his inspiration and to secure the effect of utter naturalness.

Marshalling the various items of his notebooks into companies and regiments, in the manner of the scientist or the scholar, and then leading them in serried ranks past a reviewing stand would have appeared to him too mechanical a performance, a violation against the ordinary procedure of the mind. For, except in rare instances, as with such philosophers as James and John Mill, the mind does not progress in the parade line of logic but darts hither and thither in the zigzag of scattered associations. Nor does Nature herself, so Hudson reminds us, arrange "her species in a line or row, or her genera in a chain." Moreover, the deployment of his notations in battle array would have done violence to the spirit of one who, with much of "the humility proper to an amateur," never sought to overwhelm an opponent, but rather, like Sir Thomas Browne, to express through the refinement of his senses and a rich vein of speculative thought his feeling of wonderment at the whole of life.

What he says of his "unmethodical method" in *A Hind in Richmond Park* is suggestive of the procedure in most of his essays: "We know from Butler, if not from our own feeble efforts at making poetry, that rhymes the rudders are of verses by which they often steer their courses;—a queer sort of rudder with a mind of its own to carry us into places which we had no intention of visiting! But it is quite true; and so with this rudder of mine which takes me where it will, and if it overshoots the mark and goes back I must go back with it." Extending his simile, one may liken the form of his essays to a leisurely cruise on a yacht. Quietly he slips from his anchorage, and, with his sails bellying to even the slightest breeze that blows and his own sweet will at the rudder, he tacks now this way and now that over the sea of sensory and meditative experience, his prow making a pleasant rippling music as it rides the waves. Rarely crowding the yards with canvas, he covers a comfortable distance and then slips, just as quietly, into some inviting estuary. It is, of course, the cruise itself that matters, with the passing glimpses of many wonders of the ocean of Being, but there are occasional ports of call where he unloads a light though precious cargo—emerald and golden days, sketches of many animals and men, and opaline memories of the far away and long ago.

A glance over the table of contents of a volume in which chapter outlines are given (as in *Hampshire Days, A Shepherd's Life*. and *A Hind in Richmond Park*) will indicate the truth of this analogy. The beginnings and endings of his essays are quietly impressive, and the variety of material that lies between is never amorphous, mere lengths of notes as often with even his chief contemporary rivals, but is presented as portraits, scenes, episodes and meditations, joined together by easy transitions, as though our guide and companion were pausing a while before one of the innumerable dramas of animal life continually taking place all around us, and then, at an easy gait, moving on to another. In a few of his essays, such as "Idle Days" and "Wind, Wave, and Spirit," the structure is indeed very loose, but usually some part of them, like the scene that brings the latter to a close, keeps their effects from becoming dissipated. When he limited himself to the portrayal of a particular animal or locale, or to the discussion of a definite idea, as in "Chanticleer," "Branscombe," and the "Secret of the Charm of Flowers," there was greater coherence or pattern, which he accomplished without sacrificing flexibility of structure—his very digressions often throwing light from various new angles upon his theme. In his discussions, as in "Guide Books: An Introduction," "On Going Back," and "Selborne" (to take three from one volume), he included, in familiar-essay fashion, many of his own personal experiences. And in still other essays, as in several of those of *A Traveller in Little Things*, he entered fully into the realm of the familiar essay, depending, in even larger measure, upon the charm of his personality and the engaging tone of his voice to hold his material together.

Within the essay itself, Hudson was adept at all the various techniques. As in the fugal sequences of *A Hind in Richmond Park*, he rarely allowed the large expository element of his writings keep him from preserving the natural flow of life and of thought. Prospecting for gold rather than for pyrites, he did not use, to the extent of many out-of-door essayists, the chronicle method of recording; instead, he preferred to group together as the subject-matter of his essays only the choice moments of his experiences. Such chapters as "Shepherd Isaac Brawcombe" and "The Ellerbys of Doveton" (in fact, the whole of the volume in which they appear) show his skill in threading his pages with narrative. For the anecdote, which can be a delight in itself as well as an effective means of clinching an idea, he had the touch of a master. Thus, in order to impress upon his readers the loneliness of the bleak and empty South Wiltshire Downs, he tells of a boy, hired as a bird-scarer, running hard a quarter of a mile just for a close view of a fellow-mortal. The many episodes taken directly from the lives of animals give a dramatic force to many of his accounts, and this quality is intensified when Hudson brings himself vividly into the scene. Now and then, there comes into his narrative, as when he was in search of a rare bird or insect, something of the thrill of a detective story. As pointed out in the discussion of *A Traveller in Little Things,* some of his experiences might readily have been fashioned into short stories; but, preferring to present them just as they occurred, he was satisfied with the form of the sketch. And though not so thoroughly bred to the idioms of English rustic speech as Jefferies and Williamson, he used it skilfully to vary the soliloquy of the essayist.

Since Hudson was well on into middle age before turning to the composition of essays and was, by nature, of a ruminative disposition, there is a certain gravity in his manner, even when humorous, and a certain deliberateness in his pace—that of a day in late summer or the flight of a heron. The tone of the voice is low-pitched but well-modulated, and its cadences are those of the spoken word. In order to secure this colloquial effect, he used a simple vocabulary and allowed his sentence structure to become at times fairly loose and elliptical. Never effusive, he did occasionally, however, give us long-breathed passages, which, in an unobtrusive way, add to the emotional perspective of his voice. Such a passage, which in order to call attention to its rhythm I have scanned in the manner of Saintsbury, is the one that follows, the emotional climax of *The Land's End*:

Thése | óld | mén ! cánnŏt sée | thĕ óbjĕcts | whĭch appéar | tŏ younger | eyes | —thĕ distánt | pássĭng | shíps, | and thĕ lánd— | thăt dím, | brókĕn | líne, | ăs ŏf ă lów ! clóud | ŏn thĕ hŏrízŏn, | ŏf thĕ íslănds: | théir síght | ĭs áltĕred | frŏm whăt ĭt wás, | yĕt ís, | pĕrháps, | nŏw áblĕ | tŏ discérn | thíngs | ĭnvísĭblĕ | tŏ ús— | óthĕr | íslănds, | ŭnchártĕd, | nót | thĕ Cássĭtérĭdes. | Whăt ăre théy, | thése óthĕr | íslănds, | ănd whăt | dŏ wĕ knów | ŏf thém? | Nóthĭng ăt áll; | ĭndeéd, | nóthĭng | căn bĕ knówn | tŏ thĕ | génĕrálĭty; | ónlý | thése | lífe-wéarý | áncĭents, | síttĭng | ŏn rócks | ănd gázĭng | ăt vácăncý, | míght | ĕnlíghtĕn ús | ĭf thĕy would. | Undoúbtĕdlý | thĕre ăre dífferĕncĕs | ŏf síght | ămong thém | whĭch woŭld máke | thĕir déscrĭptĭons | várý, | bŭt thĕy woŭld | próbăblý | áll ágrée | ĭn ăffírmĭng | thăt thĕ scéne | befóre thém | hăs nŏ resémblănce | tŏ thĕ éarlĭer | vísĭon. | Thís | gréy-fácĕd | vérý óld | mán | wĭth hĭs chín | ŏn hĭs hánds, | whŏ loóks | ăs if | he had not smiled | these | many | years, | would perhaps | smile | now, | if he were | to recall | that former | vision, | which came | by teaching | and served | well enough | during | his hot youth | and strenuous | middle age. | He does | not see | before him | a beautiful | blessed | land | bright | with fadeless | flowers, | nor a great | multitude | of people | in shining | garments | and garlands | who will come down | to the shore | to welcome | him | with sounds | of shouting | and singing | and playing | on instruments | of divers | forms, | and who will | lead him | in triumph | to the gardens | of everlasting | delight | and to mansions | of crystal | with emerald | and amethyst | colonnades | and opal | domes | and turrets | and pinnacles. | Those glories | and populous | realms | of joy | have quite | vanished: | he sees | now | only | what his heart | desires— | a silent | land | of rest. | No person | will greet | him | there; | he will land | and go up | alone | into that empty | and solitary | place, | a still | grey | wilderness | extending | inland | and upwards | hundreds | of leagues, | an immeasurable | distance, | into infinity, | and rising | to mountain | ridges | compared with which | the Himalayas | are but mole-hills. | The sky | in that | still land | is always | pale grey-blue | in colour, | and the earth, | too, | is grey | like the rocks, | and the trees | have a grey-green | foliage | —trees more ancient | in appearance | than the worn | granite | hills, | with gnarled | and buttressed | trunks | like vast | towers | and immense | horizontal | branches, | casting | a slight shade | over many | acres | of ground. | Onwards | and upwards, | with eyes | downcast, | he will slowly | take | his devious | way | to the interior, | feeling | the earth | with his staff, | in search | of a suitable | last | resting-place. | And when | he has travelled | many, | many | leagues | and has found it | —a spot | not | too sunny | nor too deeply | shaded, | where the old | fallen | dead leaves | and dry moss | have formed | a thick | soft | couch | to recline on | and a grey | exposed | root | winding | over the earth | offers | a rest | to his back— | there | at length | he will settle | himself. | There | he will remain | motionless | and contented | for ever | in that remote | desert land | where is no sound | of singing | bird | nor of running | .water | nor of rain | or wind | in the grey | ancient | trees: | waking | and sleeping | he will rest | there, | dreaming | little | and thinking | less, | while year by year | and age by age | the memory | of the world | of passion | and striving | of which he was | so unutterably | tired | grows | fainter | and fainter | in his mind. | And he will have | neither joy | nor sorrow, | nor love | nor hate, | nor wish to know | them | any more; | and when he remembers | his fellow-men | it will comfort | him | to think | that his peace | will never | be broken | by the sight | of human | face | or the sound | of human | speech, | since never | by any chance | will any wanderer | from the world | discover him | in that | illimitable | wilderness.

To keep the movement *largo expressivo*, fine use is made of long vowel sounds, short feet, and many monosyllables. Some of the sentences are deliberately long so as to give a more ample sweep to the rhythm, but most of these have Hudson's characteristically firm beginnings and endings. The sensitivity of his ear to consonance is well illustrated in the sentence that opens with "He does not see." The repetition of such words as *islands, nothing, vision, grey, smile, there* accentuates the rhythm as well as the psychological state of these old men. In order to prevent any monotony from so many monosyllables and, at the same time, to add more emotional chiaroscuro to his thought, he introduces some polysyllables: *immeasurable, unutterably, illimitable, Cassiterides,* and *Himalayas.* And, in spite of its insistent rhythm, he is careful to keep it from trespassing into the sphere of poetry.

As indicated earlier, most of Hudson's volumes are not, as is often the case with Burroughs and the later Jefferies, mere miscellanies. Though many of the essays were written to stand alone, they are so interrelated as to enhance each other's value as well as the effect of the volume as a whole. Such patterning, particularly if it is to preserve the casualness of the essay form, requires not only deftness in the use of anticipations, transitions, recapitulations, and the various other aids of articulation but also considerable architectonic skill. Since most of the volumes have, by this means, something of the vital relationships of a living organism, it is difficult to anthologize Hudson without showing him off to more than the usual disadvantage. And as has also been indicated, there is a singular unity throughout all his work, *A Hind in Richmond Park* being the coping-stone. Thus he found the familiar-essay form eminently suitable for almost the entire corpus of his experience.

"My credentials," says Hudson, "are those of a field naturalist who has observed men: all their actions and their mentality. But chiefly himself, for to know others a man must first know himself." In his presentation of men, he has of course little in common with the essayists of the eighteenth century, to whom the social life of the city, often trivial and artificial in quality, was the principal subject. Interested primarily in persons who harmonized well with the general life of a countryside, he chose to portray, rather, rural folk hardly affected by the passage of the centuries; and, biology being the dominant science of his age, he stressed their racial background and their close relationship with animals and with the natural forces of their environment. The large number of gauchos, cottagers, and casuals of the wayside sketched in his panoramas gives them a strong human flavor and him a place with the many portrait painters among the familiar essayists.

Emphasizing as the out-of-door essay does the observation of the natural world and the detachment of the observer, one must not expect to find in it quite the concentration of personality that there is in the work of Lamb or Hazlitt or Stevenson.[4] The personality that impregnates the pages of Hudson is, however, sufficiently varied and profound to assure him a place among the major figures not only of the tradition that White and Thoreau inaugurated but also in the larger one of Montaigne. Having been brought up in the midst of wild nature and having found his chief pleasure in the pursuits of a field naturalist, he approached life by a route other than that of most familiar essayists, who draw heavily upon the multifarious activities of towns and cities; but different though much

---

[4] Probably in defense of himself as much as in criticism of Thoreau, Burroughs even maintained that a strong personality may actually deprive a person of intimacy with nature. Hudson was somewhat of the same mind when he says, in his discussion of Bloomfield, "The lower kind of inspiration is . . . often better suited" to the "mere descriptions of rural scenes," in which nature is shown "by the common light of day" rather than "by a succession of lightning flashes" (*Afoot in England*, p. 275).

of his material was, he wrote scarcely less apropros of himself. Passages that cling just as tenaciously to the memory as the portraits of animals, men, and locales are those in which he is the anatomist of his own personality, telling us of the peculiar "expression" certain objects have for him and what wisdom he has been able to distil from his observations of life in the fields and the woods. The soulscapes become, in the end, quite as important to us as the landscapes.

As is characteristic of the familiar essayist, Hudson continually reveals his personal idiosyncrasies and incidents from "the days of other years," and these give many vivifying touches to his selfportrait and draw us closer to him in companionship. He tells us, for example, how he equipped himself when in search of birds, the sort of beverages he most liked, what was good for his weak digestion when it took a turn for the worse, and even his peculiar manner of sneezing. Often in his volumes there is a welling-up of memories —most insistent of all, those of his youth, when dangers and joys were more elemental and intense. This reminiscent mood, stirring a deep range of emotions, is more frequent and pervasive in him than in the other out-of-door essayists and evokes more of the artist. Thus it is that in our mind's eye we see him silhouetted against the primitive and exotic backgrounds of the pampas of La Plata and the plains of Patagonia as well as against that of southern England.

What completes one's delight in Hudson's companionship is his wide-ranging, luminously reflective mind. "I take it," he remarks, "that the only persons capable of seeing things as they are in their right relations and proportions are those who have no profession and no vocation or calling, which, when followed with enthusiasm, absorbs their attention. . . . To specialize is to lose your soul. To speculate is to love your own soul." Though he once desired nothing better than to wander about in search of rare birds, he was in time content "to see very many things with vision a little clearer than the ordinary, rather than to see a very few things with preternatural clearness and miss all the rest." Greater as an impressionist and observer than as a thinker, he nevertheless sought to encompass all his experience with speculation. "If we need to build," he declares, "and there is any wind or cloud to build on, 'tis best to go on bravely with the building business. Who cares if the structure is all to tumble down again?" His acquaintance with the literature of science undoubtedly helped to cross-fertilize the thoughts that grew out of his various observations of nature; yet, in the main, even the more obvious ones have about them the freshness of discoveries. And since he presented these thoughts as though meditating aloud or talking casually to a friend, the pleasure one receives from listening to him—a pleasure characteristic of the familiar essay—is not merely in the thoughts themselves but in the easy, sinuously flowing way in which his mind progresses.

"I have not . . . gone beyond . . . the modest ambition of a field naturalist to see the things that lie on the surface," says Hudson in a self-deprecatory summing-up, reminiscent of those of Newton and Fabre. "It is for the biologist to seek for pearls in the deep waters; for me to keep to the safe shallows where the children paddle, and the wet sands at low tide where I can gather my little harvest—my ribbons of sea-weed and a few painted shells." Like Herrick and Davies, who sang of how roses first came red and when bats take wing, he included in his pages many curious little inquiries, such as those into the supernatural reputation of the owl and the raven, the rarity of the pure green iris in the human eye, the effect of the bicycle on women, and why "well-nigh all that is best in our poetic literature has been produced by southerners—by Englishmen in the southern half of the country." But these little matters—these ribbons of sea-weed and painted shells—bring in their train larger issues, just as a hind's sensitive adjustment of her ears in opposite directions led on, in the last of his books, to the discussion of poetry and music and the future of all art. So after a while, one has the feeling that he is in the presence of that rare creature, a wise man, who is seeking also for pearls in deep waters.

Hudson was not without a quiet sense of humor, especially noticeable when humanizing his animal portraits and reminding man of his various shortcomings. But when his depths were sounded, his writing usually gives forth a certain penetrating melancholy tone. The encroachment of industrial civilization upon the wild places of the earth and the wanton destruction of the multitudinous folk of these places by "the Caliban in man," such as had occurred in the Argentine within his own life-span, gave him the feeling that "the beautiful . . . cannot be preserved in our age. . . ." This sadness was intensified by his essentially tragic vision of the destiny of human life. Yet what impresses one more in Hudson is the plenitude of enjoyment he found in the adventure of life—an enjoyment that at times becomes rapture. The pied beauty of the floral and animal world attracted him most, and by recording that beauty and by calling attention to its values, he thought he might help to lead men back to the wellsprings of joy. He was, indeed, a true saunterer, seeking only, as Thoreau has strikingly put it, to restore this Holy Land, our common dwelling-place, to rightful worship.

Thus it was that Hudson became the most successful of the out-of-door essayists in the fusing of natural history with the familiar essay. A better naturalist than Thoreau and Jefferies and even Burroughs, he was not overwhelmed by his observations as was Thoreau; he did not indulge in the mere piling up of details, on the one hand, and the extreme subjectivism, on the other, of Jefferies; nor did the scientist displace the poet and artist in him as befell Burroughs. It is true that he conceived no *Walden*, for he could not bring to bear upon his experience quite the humanism and originality of a Thoreau, nor, dependent as he was upon the larger units of expression, the essay and the volume as a whole, did he possess Thoreau's aphoristic power. But of the four, he was the surest in artistry, blending the beauty of nature with his own passion and giving it through the written page a persistent life against the flux of change; and beside *Walden* he was able to place a half dozen lesser masterpieces. Burroughs, with all his charm, and Jefferies, with all his intensity, can lay no such claim upon immortality. And though without the knowledge of the world of men of a Montaigne or a Bacon or a Hazlitt, he is, more than any other out-of-door essayist, except Thoreau, of their lineage in the wider essay tradition.

Landscapes and Figures

I believe a leaf of grass is no less than the journey-work
of the stars,
And the pismire is equally perfect, and a grain of sand,
and the egg of the wren,
And the tree-toad is a chef-d'oeuvre for the highest,
And the running blackberry would adorn the parlors of heaven, . . .
And the cow crunching with depress'd head surpasses any
statue,
And a mouse is miracle enough to stagger sextillions of
infidels.

—WHITMAN

How could such beauty walk the common way?

—SACKVILLE-WEST

ENDOWED TO A high degree with the artist's feeling for nature—a
sense of line, mass, color and composition, a Pissarro-like response
to the implications of the fugitive moment, and an essentially poetic
perception, keen in its penetration into the innermost beings of
birds, beasts, and men and in its summoning of the genii from
their most secret haunts—Hudson was able to embody in his essays much of its pageantry. The pampas of La Plata, the plains
of Patagonia, the countryside of southern England, with their characteristic flora and fauna, are so fully and freshly depicted that
they become new realities in the realm of human experience, analogous to the re-creation of Selborne, Walden Pond and the Catskills
by White, Thoreau and Burroughs; Dorset and Devon by Hardy,
Llewelyn Powys and Williamson; Morocco and the Arabian Desert
by Loti, Cunninghame Graham and Doughty; the Alps, the Sierra
Nevadas and the Himalayas by Ruskin, Muir and Younghusband;
and the Arctic and Antarctic by Stefansson and Byrd.

Although Hudson did not make the weather or the procession
of the months so frequently a theme in his pages as Burroughs had
done, there is in them much of the ritual of nature, her changing
vestments of the day and the seasons. The recording of bird-song
and the delight in flowers often have for their setting frescoes of
spring, and there are also such larger vernal scenes as the ancient
peach orchard of *Las Acacias* in bloom, the giant beeches of Savernake showing a dusky-red and purple life in their twigs, and the
promontory of Land's End during a biting nor'easter. The autumnal
landscapes, though wanting in the richness and variety of those
of Thoreau and Burroughs, both of whom were accustomed to more
gorgeous foliage, are among the most impressive, being often
suffused with one of his profoundest moods, that of melancholy.
Many of them can be found in *Adventures among Birds, Nature in
Downland, Afoot in England,* and *The Land's End*—among them,
the view along the road from Kingsclere to Wolverton against a
changing sky: elms in deep yellow, oaks in tawny gold, beeches in
red- and russet-gold, and, scattered amongst dark pines, larches in
lemon yellow. Winter, laying bare the earth's anatomy, also had a
strong appeal. "Is there anything in rural England," Hudson once
exclaimed, "more gratifying to the eye than a winter prospect" in
the "green diversified country" of the Sussex Downs, "with leafless

beechen woods spread over slopes and summits, and gathered like
darkest purple clouds within the combes and hollows of the great
round hills!" And in *Nature in Downland* and *The Land's End*
there are wintry scenes aplenty.

Yet, reared as he was under the intense blue skies of the pampas
and ever seeking life at its fullest, the season that suited him best
was summer, the high noon of the year. *Birds in a Village,* the first
recording of his English impressions, opens on a brilliant day in
mid-May and closes on an equally radiant one in early July. In the
New Forest, for long his favorite haunt in England and the chief
setting of *Hampshire Days,* he found "the richest, fullest time of
the year" to be "when June is wearing to an end." The Sussex
Downs, both in their cultivated and uncultivated parts, seemed to
him "most enjoyable during the eight or ten hottest weeks of the
year." And though there are in his pages many evening and some
nocturnal landscapes—that of the locust trees of *Las Acacias* bathed
in an eerie *clair de lune,* and the Turneresque one of the Rio Negro,
with the sky above in conflagration and the gale-roughened waters
quivering and flashing like flames—most of them are done in the
full light of day, and he was especially fond of the transfiguring
effects of visible heat, which lent a glittering, silvery quality to distant objects on the pampas, the downs, and the sands of the sea,
and sometimes gave him the feeling of a disembodied spirit.

Unlike Chateaubriand and Turner and Pierre Loti, Hudson never
lusted for the picturesque and the spectacular. After tasting southern England and assimilating it to the bone, he felt no special urge
to behold the classics of European topography—the Roman Cam-
pagna, the Rhineland, and the Alps—not even those readily accessible to one with a light purse, the Lake District and the Trossacks.
Like Old Crome, whom among the English painters he most resem-
bles, this "traveller in little things" had the power of universalizing
the humbler scenes and was content if they yielded what he most
sought.

For pure landscape never attracted him so much as it did the
early romanticists[1] and such out-of-door essayists as Muir and Mary

---

[1] Some members of this group, to be sure, preferred landscapes in which there
were human figures. But few even of these, of whom Wordsworth and Keats are
representative, would have accepted, as did Hudson, insects and birds and beasts
as adequate substitutes.

Austin. "This visible world," he declares, "is to me but a sad and empty place without wonderful life and the varied forms of life, which are in harmony with it, and give it a meaning, a grace and beauty and splendour not its own." Thus he looked upon the downs less as aesthetic elements in a landscape than as "small islands of animal life, . . . scattered over the sea-like smooth green waste, vacant as the sea." It was because of the greater abundance and variety of its wild life that he preferred the southern to the more picturesque northern part of Hampshire. The coasts of Cornwall and Norfolk would have lost much of their appeal but for the gulls and gannets and geese ranging there. And in his nocturnes there is far less regard for the star-strewn sky, of all sights the one most evocative of sublimity, than for glow-worms, stag beetles, death's-head moths, bats, owls (whose call "seems . . . to make the gloom deeper"), and for those lesser Milky Ways, the myriads of fireflies along some river bottoms. Perhaps, like Socrates, Hudson recognized the danger of becoming too deeply absorbed in cosmic awe. So, focussing his attention on the worlds within this globe rather than on those without, he filled his landscapes with the shapes and colors, the movements and sounds, of many insects, beasts, and birds.

It was largely because of feeling himself drawn toward those places where there were the greatest abundance and variety of wild life that he was led at times to doubt the wisdom of his ever having left his native shores. Yet what he lost in quantity, he gained in perspective. For familiarity with two such contrasting environments as the epically wild La Plata, with its many populous nations of animals and its full orchestra of bird voices, and the sweetly humanized English countryside, with its sparse fauna and its modest woodwind ensemble, enabled him to see the one intensified against the background of the other. Through his reading and also, as he would have insisted, through the exercise of his ancestral memory, Hudson had a good sense of English fields and hedgerows before landing at Southampton. But since he did not actually see the face of England until his thirty-third year, when fully mature as an observer, he could look upon it with something of the detachment of an outsider. His search for the old, traditional England, the England of Bloomfield and White and Walton, kept him in the south, where it has lingered the longest; and his love of the wild, nourished on the pampas, took him to many out-of-the-way places unsung by native writers. England, in turn, proved a good vantage ground from which to evaluate his experiences in La Plata and Patagonia and to achieve the proper aesthetic distance.

In spite of the attention given to the minutiae of landscape—insects, flowers, birds—Hudson (as has already been noted) did not attempt to rival the needle of the etcher or the brush of the realistic painter. The out-of-door essay militates against the set, detailed landscapes that Ruskin, for example, was wont to paint. Instead, its effects are mainly those of sketches and of water-colors, with their economy and intimacy, or of impressionistic paintings—a scene being suggested by a number of little touches scattered throughout an essay or a panorama achieved by the arrangement in a volume of a group of such scenes. With its greater appeal to both the sense of actuality and to the imagination, this medium seems to reveal more profound aspects of nature than the set description. Although the medium of painting has the greater advantage, many passages of Hudson open upon prospects as impressive in one's memory as Crome's *Mousehold Heath*, Turner's *Chichester Canal*, Constable's *Old Sarum*, and many of the Sung dynasty paintings of the environs of Hang-chou.

LANDSCAPE BACKGROUNDS

City parks and country estates are occasionally to be glimpsed in Hudson's essays, rarely though because of the art of a gardener, for, like Arthur Eden in *Fan*, he found their frequent prettinesses cloying, their cultivated blooms meretricious, their rhododendrons dreary, and their trimmed and brushed lawns wearisome. "An acre or so of green linoleum or drugget, drawn evenly and smoothly over the ground surrounding a large house, would probably have as good an effect as a perfectly smooth grass lawn." Enchanted as he had been during his youth on the pampas by a nature little marred by man and still possessed of the grace and spirit that wildness gives to all things, what he sought after most in landscape were "the unconquered provinces of Nature's dominions." For him as for Thoreau, the wilderness blossomed as the rose, and he did much to make the appreciation of it a part of Western culture.

Nature did not, however, speak to him, as she has to many of her lovers, most entrancingly through the mountain crag, the cataract, and the ocean. Though conceding that the enjoyment derived from mountain scenery may, because of the greater novelty, seem fuller and keener than that from walking or riding through a countryside with striking prospects, he maintained, as did the eighteenth-century writers on the picturesque, that the sense of a "sudden glory" and of the freedom got from surveying a wide expanse from the modest height of the greater downs is as strong as from a mountaintop. "We can no more get a new sensation or a larger measure of the quickly-vanishing pleasure we have enjoyed by transporting ourselves to the highest summits on the globe," this son of the plains speciously argues, "than we can change a Skye terrier into an eagle by taking it three or four miles up in a balloon and throwing it out of the car." Surely, the actual experience, if not a reliance upon the testimony of Ruskin or Muir or a deeply spiritual Hindu, would have cured him of this delusion. But Roberts, with all his persuasive powers, was unable to get Hudson to spend a summer amongst even the gentle mountains of the Lake District.

The sight of the eternally restless ocean and the cadence of its surf, especially "after a long absence," always gave him a "shock of recognition and wonder and joy, as if [he] had been suffering from loss of memory and it had . . . suddenly come back." And, like Jefferies, he was wont to greet Poseidon with an eloquent gesture: cupping the salty water in his hands, he would drink as in some mystic rite. But the sea, particularly in its ordinary aspects, could not hold him long. The contemporary craze for it he regarded as a symptom of disease, "the result of a life too confined and artificial in close dirty overcrowded cities." In retrospect, a holiday spent at the seashore was usually looked upon as "a somewhat vacant time compared to one spent in wandering from village to village." For unless one has the access to them of a Beebe—if not with a bathysphere, then at least with a diving helmet or aqualung —the creatures of the deep cannot be readily chronicled in out-of-door-essay fashion.

Thus there is little of the sea in the Hudsonian landscape, nothing at all comparable to what one finds in Belloc and Beebe and Tomlinson. Though there are seascapes in several of his volumes, it is in *The Land's End* that we are made most aware of the ocean: large purple patches of water near the Cornish cliffs contrasting with the brilliant green of the deeper parts ("as if hundreds of hogsheads of claret or Burgundy had been emptied into it"), and the general effect of a Mediterranean blue; billows, harried by the wind, crashing against the rude promontories and granite cliffs and booming in the half-drowned caverns beneath. Characteristically, these scenes are often but the settings for the activities of the creatures of the mainland: the aerial maneuvers of gulls and gannets and the comings and goings of the fishing fleet.

Obeying a strong human impulse, Hudson found much pleasure in following a stream, the loveliest form that water takes: "There is no more fascinating pastime than to keep company with a river from its source to the sea." Included in his volumes are sketches of pampean streams, with their sedges and bulrushes, their flowers and their bird-life, and of the Rio de la Plata, with its brick-red waters and its broad *sayus*-swamps. Most hauntingly evoked of all the South American river scenes are those of the Rio Negro, whose waters flow like silver or polished steel through a valley featured with high, crimson-flowered and crimson-fruited cacti, profusely berried piquillins, and graceful little chañar trees, with their grey-green mimosa foliage. On its surface glide flocks of black-necked swans, "their white plumage shining like foam in the sunlight"; just above the river shuttle purple martins that nest in the overhanging cliffs; and high overhead soar grey eagles, black vultures, and the condor. Little wonder, then, that most other large streams, in comparison, seemed to him so commonplace as to have "no higher purpose than to water man and beast, and to serve, like canals, as a means of transport."

Among England's baby rivers, the Somerset Exe, the Test, the Itchen, and the Wylye flow most memorably through his landscapes—swift, crystal-clear, cool streams, all of them, toying with the swaying, hairlike poa grass rooted in their pebbly beds as they meander between rough moors and velvety-flanked downs, across wide meadowland, or among softly weathered cottages clustering round some ancient church. The essay in *Afoot in England* through which the Exe flows contains a graphic picture of this "silvery serpent" as it sluices from Exford to Dulverton, "singing aloud, foamflecked, between high hills clothed to their summits in oak woods." But as an unfoldment of a succession of scenes through which a river may pass, the essay is not so expressive as Belloc's "On Streams and Rivers" or, to cite a poem, Wordsworth's *River Duddon*. The

Test and the Itchen, on the other hand, are intimately portrayed, the reader being made fully aware of the pageantry along their margins.

> Twin rivers they may be called, flowing at no great distance apart through the same kind of country, and closely alike in their general features: land and water intermixed—greenest water-meadows and crystal currents that divide and subdivide and join again, and again separate, forming many a miniature island and long slip of wet meadow with streams on either side. At all times refreshing to the sight and pleasant to dwell by, they are best

> When it is summer and the green is deep.

> Greens of darkest bulrushes, tipped with bright brown panicles, growing in masses where the water is wide and shallowest; of grey-green graceful reeds, and of tallest reed-mace with dark velvety brown spikes; behind them all, bushes and trees—silvery-leafed willow and poplar, and dark alder, and old thorns and brambles in tangled masses; and always in the foreground lighter and brighter sedges, glaucous green flags, mixed with great hemp agrimony, with flesh-coloured, white-powdered flowers, and big-leafed comfrey, and scores of other water and moisture-loving plants.

There is a sensitive rendering of the rich articulations and shapes of trees, as might be expected of the one to whom, in his youth, they had been especially numinous. Prominent in Hudson's topography is one of the chief creations of seventeenth-century England and in turn a strong influence on the psychology of her people, the hedgerow,

> that wild disordered tangle of all the most beautiful plants in these islands—black and white thorn; privet with its small grape-like clusters; yew and holly and ivy with late, honeyed blossoms for bees and wasps and hornets; and briar and sweet-briar, bramble and bryony; also poisonous black bryony and traveller's-joy, a green and silver tapestry; and wayfaring tree, spindlewood and cornel, with scarlet, purple and orange-coloured berries; and dark deadly-nightshade, pushing its slender stems up through the interlaced branches—all massed together for common protection like a packed herd of wild swine on their defence in some savage solitude, displaying bristling backs and bared gnashing tushes to a hostile world.

So much did trees continue to be a necessity to him that when he asked his friend W. B. Thomas to help find a cottage in the country, his one stipulation was that there be a tree in the garden, "a real tree with a columnar trunk and satisfactory branches." Like Old Crome in the painting of *The Poringland Oak* and like Thoreau and Muir, he will pause to individualize a tree, such as the aged Farringdon yew, the wonderfully fragrant one of his birthplace—known as *el árbol* in that part of La Plata—and the wild clematis tree on the edge of the woods overhanging the Chilgrove vale in Sussex. And he realized as fully as Ruisdael, Cowper and Thompson, the grandeur of large trees gaunt and hoary with age.

Of groves and woods, Hudson has given us many pictures, some done in a few strokes and others in detail: the trees grouped around his two homes on the pampas, the one with its long stately row of century-old ombús, a species that he has firmly planted in the imagination of English-speaking peoples, and the other with its fragrant acacias and Lombardy poplars, its feathery trees of paradise, its red willows, and its large and varied orchard; the richly variegated woodland scenery of southwest Hampshire, especially the sun-filtered mansions of the wide-spreading oaks along the Exe; many beech groves nestling in the coombes of the downs or crowning them like temples; the forest of incredibly old yews at Kingly Bottom, with their cathedral gloom; and that metropolis of jays and daws, Savernake Forest, beloved also by Jefferies for its deep seclusion. Some of the interior woodland effects that particularly delighted him were masses of briar rose spangling "the rough green tangle with its rosy stars," undergrowths of holly amidst oaks, and dark-red pine columns rising from a sea of fresh bracken. The mysterious voice of the wind-swept forest found in him, as in Sibelius, a good interpreter:

It speaks to us, and somehow the life it expresses seems nearer, more intimate than that of the sea. Doubtless because we are ourselves terrestrial and woodland in our origin; also because the sound is infinitely more varied as well as more human in character. There are sighings and moanings, the wails and shrieks, and wind-blown murmurings, like the distant confused talking of a vast multitude. A high wind in an extensive wood always produces this effect of numbers. The sea-like sounds and rhythmic volleyings, when the gale is at its loudest, die away, and in the succeeding lull there are only low, mysterious, agitated whisperings; but they are multitudinous; the suggestion is ever of a vast concourse—crowds and congregations, tumultuous or orderly, but all swayed by one absorbing impulse, solemn or passionate. But not always moved simultaneously. Through the near whisperings a deeper, louder sound comes from a distance. It rumbles like thunder, falling and rising as it rolls onwards; it is antiphonal, but changes as it travels nearer. Then there is no longer demand and response; the smitten trees are all bent one way, and their innumerable voices are as one voice, expressing we know not what, but always something not wholly strange to us—lament, entreaty, denunciation.

"To go out into some open place," so Hudson declares, is "an old ineradicable instinct in us. . . . It seems enough that it is open, where the wind blows free, and there is nothing between us and the sun." Strengthened as this instinct was by his early surroundings, the woods and forests, with all their "green everlasting gladness," never had so strong an effect on him as vistas opening upon wide, untilled and unenclosed country: downs standing bare under a cloud-patterned sky and stretching away "in fluctuation fixed" to the far horizon and, what impressed him even more, featureless flat wastelands—long strips of sea-saltings, broad and desolate marshes and heaths, the barren grey plains of Patagonia, and the grassy ocean of the pampas. These spacious, whale-backed hills and harsh wildernesses, with their beckoning to the imagination as well as to the eyes and feet, always gave him, particularly when experienced in solitude, a deep sense of freedom. On the downs, in addition to the increased sense of power that comes with height, he felt his mind becoming "more aerial, less conscious of gravity and a too solid body," until he almost realized the sensation of being other than he was: a creature who might "lift great heron-like wings" and soar into the skies. In all these vast places, wherever there was plenty of wing-space, his psyche felt something of the same rapture: "If a man be capable of an exalted mood, of a sense of absolute freedom, so that he is no longer flesh and spirit but both in one, and one with nature, it comes to him like some miraculous gift on a hill or down or wide open heath."

The sight of large birds high over such places, reducing the drifting clouds to a mere background, always quickened his sense of sublimity, a quality in landscape upon which he set considerable store.

The great soaring bird . . . —eagle, or vulture, or buzzard, or kite, or harrier, floating at ease on broad vans, or rising heavenwards in vast and ever vaster circles—that is the one object in nature which has the effect of widening the prospect, just as if the spectator had himself been miraculously raised to a greater altitude, while at the same time the blue dome of the sky appears to be lifted to an immeasurable height above him. The soaring figure reveals to sight and mind the immensity and glory of the visible world. Without it the blue sky can never seem sublime.

La Plata, with its many large, high-flying birds, frequently evoked in him this exalting emotion. In England, on the other hand, even though herons and ravens, gannets and gulls, gave some height to the upper air, this source of sublimity was all but denied him. "The great soaring bird is nowhere in our lonely skies. . . . " Only through his historical imagination could he recapture the grandeur that once was characteristic of English heavens. It is largely these two elements—broad, open places and skies of great height—that endow Hudson's canvases with one of their chief insignia, a sense of immense space.

Another quality of landscape upon which he set high value, though not of course to the extent of a Lorraine or a Poussin, was its human associations, "some sign or token of some eldest nation" making a "strange land not so strange." "Is it not," he asks, "the absence of human life or remains rather than the illimitable wastes of thick-ribbed ice and snow which daunts us at the thought of Arctic and Antarctic regions?" The discovery of some Indian relics near his home in La Plata and occasional encounters with those whose ancestors originally possessed the land helped to humanize his experiences while wandering over this vast wilderness of grass. One of the things that drew him to Patagonia, it will be remembered, was the opportunity to investigate the remains of the Stone Age. The richness of English landscape in human links with the immemorial past compensated, in large measure, for its want of sublimity. One of the main appeals of the downs was the hieroglyphics that primitive man had scored upon their surfaces. The exercise of his historical sense along old Roman roads or amidst ruins, such as those at Silchester, the site of Roman Calleva Atrebatum, gave him a "peculiar sense of satisfaction, of restfulness, of peace." Land's End, not so intrinsically imposing as other headlands along the Cornish coast, was because of its patina of ancient associations invested "with a sublimity and fascination not its own." And many particular localities of England were spiritualized for him by the unseen presence of their eloquent portrayers.[2]

With such a sensitivity, it is not surprising that the choicest of Hudson's landscapes are those of places lying open to the twelve-winded sky. How skilful was his portrayal of the South Sussex Downs—with their humble-bees and little blue butterflies, their moles and adders and oxen, their stonechats, whitethroats and skylarks, and their sheep- and cloud-flecked slopes—has already been pointed out in the discussion of *Nature in Downland*. Especially engaging is the prospect upon which the book opens: a thistle-filled August day from the top of Kingston Hill, the "innumerable faintly-seen silvery stars moving athwart the immeasurable blue expanse of Heaven" and dappling the turf with patches of lustrous white. His panorama of the South Wiltshire Downs, though suffering somewhat from being a composite one (many parts of it appear in volumes other than *A Shepherd's Life*) likewise cuts deep into the memory. These hills are not so noble as those of Sussex and their silence deeper; but there are lovely valleys—the Bourne, the Avon, the Nadder, the Ebble, and, especially, the Wylye—and the prehistoric temple of Stonehenge and the spire of Salisbury, soaring larklike into the heavens, give it a certain physical and spiritual unity.

Of uplands, the next in prominence are those of West Cornwall, which, with their outcroppings of boulders, slope down to the castle-like cliffs along the coast. Lichen-stained and moss-cushioned stone fences, often gemmed with colt's-foot and wild hyacinth, separate the meager, rock-strewn fields of this vast moorland; and, particularly in the wilder and more desolate parts, there are such luxuriating effects as scattered "thickets of hawthorn and blackthorn, with tangles and trails of ivy, bryony, traveller's joy and honeysuckle," and acres and miles and leagues of furze, interspersed here and there with bracken in its vivid green. Other uplands well rendered are the desolate moor of Axe Edge, "covered with a dense

---

2 Yet, on one occasion, Hudson did say, "To my mind there is nothing in life so delightful as that feeling of relief, of escape, and absolute freedom which one experiences in a vast solitude, where man has perhaps never been, and has, at any rate, left no trace of his existence" (*Idle Days in Patagonia*, p. 7).

growth of heather, bilberry, and coarse bog grasses" and overlooking the most unhomelike of farms, with "scabby or leprous-looking hills" for their background; Nore Hill, beloved also by White, with its view of a diversified countryside, in which hangers irregularly lift "their steep, bank-like fronts—splendid masses of red and russet gold against the soft grey-blue autumnal sky"; the heath near "Deadman's Plack," where large patches of false brome grass shine emerald-green amidst great masses of purple ling; and Brean Down, looking like "a hippopotamus standing on the flat margin of an African lake, its breast and mouth touching the water, and all its body belly-deep in the mud."

In panoramas such as these, many vignettes—in the richness and variety of which English landscape is pre-eminent—not only enhance the general effect but are satisfying in themselves. Often they are of wild flowers, for Hudson was as susceptible as Dorothy Wordsworth, Ruskin, and Maeterlinck to their infinite patterns and colors—dreams of fair flowers meaning as much to him, so he said, as the dreams of fair women to "the Tennysons and Swinburnes who write poetry." Two of these vignettes or *morceaux*, chosen from the many that crowd for inclusion, are of bird's-foot trefoil and furze, the one along a road stretching over a high down near Stonehenge and the other on the slopes of the Cornish moors.

On one side of the road, where the turf had been cut by the spade in a sharp line, the plant had found a rare opportunity to get space and light and had thrust out such a multitude of flowering sprays, projecting them beyond the turf, as to form a close band or rope of orange-yellow, which divided the white road from the green turf, and at one spot extended unbroken for upwards of a mile. The effect was so singular and pretty that I had haunted this road for days for the pleasure of seeing that flower border made by nature.

I like to come upon a furze-patch growing on a slope, to sit below it and look up over its surface, thrown into more or less rounded forms, broken and roughened into sprays at the top, as of a sea churned by winds and cross-currents to lumpy waves, all splashed and crowned as it were with flame-coloured froth. With a clear blue sky beyond I do not know in all nature a spectacle to excel it in beauty. It is beautiful, perhaps above all things, just because the blossoming furze is not the "sheet of gold" it is often described, but gold of a flame-like brilliance sprinkled on a ground of darkest,

harshest green. . . . In some places where the moorland has been
reclaimed and parcelled out into grass fields the furze flourishes
on the stone hedges: the effect is here singular as well as magnificent,
when, standing on a high stone wall, you survey the surrounding
country with innumerable furze-clothed hedges dividing the green
fields around you in every direction, and appearing like stupendous
ropes of shining golden bloom. Hedge beyond hedge they stretch
away for miles to grey distant hills and the pale blue sky beyond. On
some hedges the plant grows evenly, as if it had been cultivated and
trimmed, forming a smooth rope of bloom and black prickles. In
other and indeed most instances, the rounded big luxuriant bushes
occur at intervals, like huge bosses, on the rope.

Of his panoramas of flat lands unrolling to the far horizon, the
two most arresting are those of the pampas of La Plata and the
barrens of northern Patagonia—lands so spacious as to seem empty.
The former, parts of which are pictured elsewhere than in *The
Naturalist in La Plata* and *Far Away and Long Ago,* is, if not a
greater artistic achievement than that of the Sussex downs, surely
his most haunting evocation of landscape. Hudson knew this illimitable sea of wild, fertile lands as on the morning of its creation,
before ploughshares, fences, and the lines of many houses had
marred its charming disorder and before some of its most beautiful
wild life had vanished, to return no more. And no one else so
privileged—no native writing in his own tongue, not even Cunninghame Graham, master of landscape though he is—has succeeded
so well in making this great pastoral land a part of the spiritual
geography of the world. The plains undulating around *Los Veinte-
cinco Ombúes* are, of course, an important element in this panorama, but the broader, marshy ones of Chascomús, where the
horizon makes a perfect circle, dominate the canvas.

The various seasonal aspects of the pampas, all deeply bitten
into the soul of Hudson, are graphically set forth: mid-summer
days, when the quivering heat creates on the parched earth the
illusion of pools of water, each shining like molten silver in the
sun, and when bleating flocks and whinnying or bellowing herds,
half-mad with thirst, kick up great clouds of dust; late summer
days, when glistening thistledown fills the air and collects in the
swales in such masses as to frighten horses as they gallop through;
a "thistle year," when cardoons, reaching the height of ten feet and

growing "as thick as sedges and bulrushes," become more a menace than a boon; and the furious *pampero*, with its "blended uproar of thunder and wind," its torrents of rain, and its deadly hail-stones. And over these plains blows the wind with its "endless variety of sorrowful sounds, from the sharp fitful sibilations of the dry wiry grasses on the barren places," to "the long mysterious moans that swell and die in the tall polished rushes of the marsh," the most fascinating of aeolian sounds to Hudson.

In spite of the appearance of emptiness, many colorful touches catch the eye: patches of white and scarlet verbenas and viper's bugloss amidst the silver-panicled grass; luminously yellow cama-lotes along the watercourses and the marshes; as well as the groves of trees around the ranchos, looking like islands washed by a grassy sea. The animals are extraordinarily varied and picturesque: viz-cachas gossiping in their clay-colored villages, which break the flatness of the landscape; flocks of rheas, with their quaint grace and majesty; innumerable birds calling and singing in the trees of the estancias and among the reeds and sedges and bulrushes along the streams and in the lagoons: flamingoes and great rails and téru-térus, herons and egrets and swans, tinamous with their tender fluting notes, black tyrants and ovenbirds and firewood-gatherers, bank-parrots and green parrakeets, short-eared owls wheeling about trees in the evening "like so many moths about a candle," yellow-shouldered troupials with their plaintively sweet cadence, and crested screamers emitting their jubilant cries, "the loudest animal-sound of the pampas." High in the skies, lending it sublimity, caranchos, chimangos, hen-harriers, peregrine falcons, and grey eagles wheel on their ominous fringed wings.

Strangely stirring is the panorama of the desert of Patagonia, stretching away in broad, irregular undulations, leagues upon leagues, beyond the narrow confines of the valley of the Rio Negro, its grey gravelly surface scantily clothed with barren flora (scattered tufts of wiry bitter-grass, a few woody herbs, dark undeciduous bushes, thorny dwarf trees, and, especially near the coast, evening primroses, with their fragrant pale-yellow stars) and visited by only a few animals (the hare-like dolichotis, troops of little singing and trilling birds, the grey-plumaged rhea, the graceful guanaco, the orange-chested hobby, the red-backed buzzard) and by roaming bands of Indians. The melancholy of these wastes, deeper than that of the pampas, was consonant with one of his fundamental moods. In "The Plains of Patagonia," there is a brilliant analysis of the spell that this time-forgotten, brooding solitude casts over susceptible souls, drawing them close to the fiery core of life.

Although among the Hudsonian landscapes of England's open spaces the upland scenes are decidedly the better, there are many good ones of flat lowlands: heaths, such as the one extending, with its fragrant furze and ling, its bog asphodel and myrtle, its golden withy and snow-white cotton grass, from Beaulieu to Southampton Water; the grasslands along the Somerset coast, whose ancient glory he delighted to recreate in his imagination; the soggy countryside along the west Sussex coast, its verdure relieved by the browns and purples of elms and the red-tiled and yellow-thatched roofs of farmhouses; and the autumnal Norfolk coast spreading out from redbricked Wells, with its wide, rust-brown marsh, its vast stretch of smooth and ribbed beach beyond, desolate except for a troop of gulls and, crow-high in the distance, a few scattered men and boys digging for bait.

In the depiction of the more obviously beautiful parts of the English countryside—ecstatically green fat pasturage, rose- and honeysuckle-bordered lanes, and orchards ablow with cherry and with apple—Hudson is not so pre-eminent as Walton and Jefferies and Edward Thomas. But with arcadian villages, which are often the center of such landscapes, he had been peculiarly fitted by temperament and circumstances to excel. Like Clare and Cobbett and Barnes, he was, as he put it, "a villager with the village mind." To seek out, after months of confinement in the reflexological formicary that London seemed to be, one of these haunts of ancient peace brought him a feeling of joyful liberation. The very sight of one of these sanctuaries in its green setting would almost move him to tears, and so great was his aversion to Londoners, with their antlike scurryings and their crowd mind, "the formic acid of the spirits," that on beholding villagers he felt like embracing them all —collectively. In the end, nearly two hundred of these villages became enshrined in his memory, places among which his thoughts loved to loiter, "revisiting cottages and conversing with old people and children."

Besides the sense of freedom, there were other elements in this joy. He shared with Ruskin a delight in old, grey-stoned, thatched or tile-roofed cottages so weather-stained and richly dappled with lichen and moss and so naturally grouped along the roadside as to appear as indigenous in their settings as the ancient oaks and elms that shade them. And in their gardens were blooms

so old that they have entered the soul . . . —fragrant gillyflower and pink and clove-smelling carnation; wallflower, abundant periwinkle, sweet-william, larkspur, love-in-a-mist, and love-lies-bleeding, old-woman's nightcap, and kiss-me-John-at-the-garden-gate, sometimes called pansy; . . . hollyhocks and peonies and crystalline white lilies with powdery gold inside, and the common sunflower; . . . evening primrose, long naturalised in our hearts, . . . goldenrod, grandly beautiful in its great, yellow, plume-like tufts; . . . and best of all and in greatest profusion, . . . the marigold.

Wide-spreading trees and the mellowing influence of centuries have made the village church, with its low square tower or grey-shingled spire, as much a part of its surroundings as the hedgerow. It is in it, "of all houses made with hands, that one can know that perfect rest and contentment, the peace which passeth understanding, experienced in our communings with nature, where nature has not been marred by man." Like Cunninghame Graham, he was a haunter of churchyards, not only because he found there companionship with birds and with many generations of villagers, but because the ivy-covered mounds, the lichen- and moss-embroidered stones, and the "British dragon trees," the funereal yews, made him at times, as the nightingale did Keats, almost enamored of death.

The intimacy of village with countryside, of its inhabitants with other of Nature's children, the many rural sights and sounds and smells—horses, oxen, and cows being led along shady streets, birds sporting above the commons, even the super-flylike humming of the threshing machine in a distant field—gave the quality of naturalness to human life, the feeling that it was not too preoccupied with itself, but more a "part of nature's life, unstrenuous, slow and sweet." Like Gaskell and Eliot and John Moore, he applauded the sympathy and the solidarity of temper and of mind that held the various households of these communities together—the unanimism characteristic also of primitive groups, the lack of which amongst the larger units of contemporary society has been deplored by many besides Jules Romains. The many tales of "the frustrate life, the glorious promise which was not fulfilled, the broken hearts and broken fortunes, and passion, crime, remorse, retribution" told of villagers, as in the pages of Crabbe, T. F. Powys and O'Flaherty, Hudson believed "would really form only one brief chapter in the long, long history of the village life with its thousand chapters." Usually indifferent to the moves on the world's chessboard, he often took a keen interest in village affairs, and like Hardy, Massingham and Williamson, relished the traditions and customs that give a sense of continuity and permanence to rural life. He regretted the disappearance of the village idiot, for "God's Fool" was not solely "a perpetual source of amusement" but, as Wordsworth likewise held, a nourisher of "compassion and sweet beneficent instinct, or soul growths." And he even lamented the dying out of so anachronistic a custom, in these democratic days of ours, as curtseying, which reminded him of the "pretty drooping motion of the nightingale, the kitty wren, and wheatear." Thus many villages became for him not merely physically inviting places but large, kind human hearts hidden amidst wooded hills and along shaded valleys.

This attitude of Hudson toward villages invests his sketches of them with an arcadian quality. Even in that of "A Wiltshire Village," a group of straggling cottages which had little that was picturesque and which he knew only during the leanest of seasons, late winter, there is this quality. At the same time, one is never conscious of any distortion or glossing over of facts, any use of rose-colored spectacles. He was familiar enough with the ugliness of some villages and with villagers who, through their possession of "all the tribal relationship without any of its feeling," could lead so country-loving a man as Jefferies to prefer, instead, the hum of the most crowded city; but, shedding their dust as quickly as possible, he rarely paused to include them in his landscapes, and when he did, as with the one in "Her Own Village," it was to give point to an idea. His panorama of southern England may seem, as a result, to contain too large a proportion of idyllic villages, but those depicted are true to actuality. Although he put no particular village so memorably upon the map as did White and Jefferies and Warde Fowler, his skill in capturing the spirit of these hamlets, often by means of some unusual experience, is as deft as elsewhere in his landscape art.

Some of the villages, such as Farringdon, Churt, South Harting, and Coombe (in Hampshire), are individualized with only a few suggestive particulars. More fully sketched are Selborne, Burbage, Cookham Dean, Abbotsbury, Branscombe, and "Winterbourne Bishop." Selborne, already a Mecca for pilgrims, did not long give him a sense of complete satisfaction, but shining ever in his mind was his first visit there, when its every feature took on a heightened significance because of "the thought of one whose memory was interwoven with living forms and sounds." Salient in the sketch of Burbage is the long, sheltered road, deeply sunken by centuries of wear from "hoof and wheel and human feet," with whitewashed and pale-brick cottages grouped desultorily along its green banks, and stretching across the neutral-toned, late winter landscape "like a many-coloured serpent lying at rest, extended at full length upon the ground." Cookham Dean, though never mentioned by name (Hudson was usually chary of revealing the name of a village, particularly if the record of his experience there was of a personal sort), is the setting for "Birds in a Village." Gradually, as one reads along, it assumes shape: a stragglement of cottages in a coombe, most of them with old orchards of cherry, apple and walnut trees; rows and groups of great elms; an extensive common, with a large, rush-bottomed pond; and, nearby, cornfields, woods and the Thames—a paradise for birds!

Most arcadian of the fuller sketches are those of Abbotsbury and Branscombe, each the subject of an excellent essay: Abbotsbury, with its old thatched cottages arranged in a double row along a narrow crooked street, "like a procession of cows with a few laggards scattered behind the main body," its remains of a once great religious house, its flowery and reedy water-meadows, where swans breed and innumerable starlings foregather in winter, its intensely red road winding over the neighboring hill, and the nearby sea, with the great Chesil Bank, "one of the seven wonders of Britain"; Branscombe, with its gurgling, swift-flowing streamlet, its lampless roads, making the night profound and "infinitely refreshing," its friendliness to visitors, and its grand setting: the "hills beyond hills of malachite," the "long leagues of red sea-wall," in the niches of which nesting gulls appear like sculptured figures on the façade of a cathedral, and the wide expanse of ocean. Least arcadian, and yet the most intriguing and original, is that of "Winterbourne Bishop," the setting of *A Shepherd's Life* and recently identified as Martin, which lies almost on the border of Wilts and Hampshire. Its grey and reddish-brown cottages had few flowers in their gardens; except in the churchyard, there were few trees to afford shade in summer and to serve as windbreaks in winter; the brook that ran along its one, long, winding street dried up in summer, the bed becoming littered with rubbish and clogged with dock and nettle; and the encompassing downs, stretching bleakly away fold on fold to infinitude, made it appear insignificant and intensely lonely. But, seen through the eyes of Caleb Bawcombe and Hudson, it becomes singularly impressive.

A hater of cities, "inflamed or festering pimples" on the body of the earth, he gave them little attention in his topography. As though reflected in the wondering eyes of a boy is the picture of Buenos Aires, with its narrow, medieval streets and fiendish-looking beggars, its many churches and picturesque festivals, its gabbling *lavanderas* along the waterfront, and its great, gory slaughtering grounds and walls of skulls. In *Birds in London* there are good descriptions of some of the oases of that brick wilderness, such as those of St. James's Park on a rough, wild morning in January and Kensington Gardens before the axe had been put to its venerable, daw- and rook-haunted grove. Elsewhere in his volumes there is an occasional inviting vignette, as the one in *Birds in Town and Village* of gulls floating in a faint haze over the Thames in mid-winter. Hudson was, however, no Canaletto or Utrillo, or even a Wordsworth awe-struck upon Westminster Bridge in the early morning sunlight. Market-day and fairs gave interest to country towns, but few are his sketches of them. The drunkenness and the cruelty toward birds blinded him to the picturesqueness of what Eric Gill calls the "truly noble town" of Chichester, except that of its cathedral; commonplace Penzeance, which was frequently visited during later years, meant little more to him than a convenient headquarters for saunterings upon the Cornish uplands. On the other hand, the ancient quarter of St. Ives, with its houses "like a crowd of big rough men pushing and elbowing one another for room," attracted the artist in him, and York, Winchester, and Exeter were appreciated for more than their cathedrals.

Of the few towns or cities for which he cared, Bath and Wells are the best depicted: Bath, with its "wide, clean ways," its solid white stone houses of dignified aspect, its great abbey church, as uplifting to the spirit as any cathedral, and the "considerable amount of nature in its composition"—trees and streams and rocks and verdant hills; village-like Wells, "breath[ed] upon" and "caressingly" touched on every side by nature, which flows "through it like the waters that gave it its name in olden days, [and] that still gush with noise and foam from the everlasting rock, to send their crystal currents along the streets," and graced with a cathedral whose west front, "in spite of the strange defeatures Time has written on it," is "beautiful beyond all others."

Thus a richly variegated landscape unfolds in Hudson's pages: southern England, with its sweetnesses as well as its asperities, the primeval pampas of La Plata and the inviolable desert of Patagonia. Hampshire, the Sussex and South Wiltshire Downs, and West Cornwall had had their interpreters, but Hudson, with his greater artistry and his more profound personality, was able to stamp their lineaments more indelibly upon the consciousness of England and, indeed, of Western civilization. What is more important, he was one of the first to make the vast provinces of La Plata and Patagonia a part of the creative literature of the world. No other out-of-door essayist— not Thoreau or Burroughs or Jefferies or Muir or Beebe—has given us greater beauty of landscape, and though Ruskin surpasses him in exuberance and in bravura, and Loti, in the picturesque and the exotic, he is of their royal company.

Yet, as already indicated, he was not primarily concerned with landscape. The movements and sounds of insects, birds, beasts, and men in their various environments absorbed him more deeply.

BIOLOGICAL PRINCIPLES

Before Darwin, man was not generally aware that animals are indeed his kith and kin. It is true that some earlier naturalists, in spite of laboring under the belief that the adaptation of animals to their various environments is the result of aptitudes specially bestowed upon them, made many a shrewd interpretation at least indicating such a relationship. And, as reflected in the humanitarian movement of the late eighteenth and early nineteenth centuries, there was (as we have seen) a growing sense, not merely of compassion toward creatures of fur and feather but of comradeship. It is significant, however, that even in the romantic re-discovery of nature, communion was sought mostly with such insensate elements

of landscape as the ocean, the mountains, and "the light of the setting sun"—elements inviting the fullest expansion of the ego—and
only rarely with the folk of the wild. And that communion usually
led, as Belinda's with the looking-glass, to a further idealization of
what was regarded as peculiarly human.

The theory of evolution, with its aeon-long perspective of the
ascent of man from a few primordial forms to the throne of life,
focussed the attention, rather, upon the mysteries pregnant in mere
protoplasm. Man became thereby more imaginatively sympathetic
toward the various creatures who, by playing rôles in this unfolding
drama, contributed to the phylum of progress.

> Striving to be man, the worm
> Mounts through all the spires of form.

With the bridging of the great gulf between human and animal
life, man came to feel more and more an essential solidarity with
the other children of life, sharers as he felt them to be in his own
destiny. Later, the bond between man and animals, established by
biology, was strengthened by anthropology, comparative sociology,
and Freudian psychology.

The theory of evolution gave pattern to Hudson's innate "animism" or panpsychism, and one of the leitmotifs of his writings
became the unity of all life—"this flame of life [is] one. . . ." All
the manifold creations of Nature are strands quivering in an un-
imaginably intricate web, and the removal of any one of them will
not only alter the pattern but may lead to the disintegration of the
fabric. Although he did not stress the nexus that exists between
fauna and flora and between the organic and the inorganic,[3] it would
not have surprised him to learn that chlorophyl and hemoglobin, the
quintessence of the green and red bloods of the world, have been
found to be closely related chemically, and that all matter has been
reduced to three particles: protons, neutrons, and electrons. What
he stressed, as did most of the immediate followers of Darwin, was
the functional and psychological unity of all living creatures, whether
they wear chitin or scales or feathers or fur or clothes.

---

[3] Scientists are still in dispute as to whether a certain slime belongs to botany
or to zoology. In at least some of his ascriptions of humanlike qualities to flowers,
Maeterlinck has the support of several distinguished botanists. All atoms may
indeed possess, as Samuel Butler suggested, a modicum of awareness and volition.

Of the many qualities attesting that unity, those given most emphasis were intelligence and the sense of beauty. Concerning the permeation of intelligence in all animal life, Hudson observes:

> A life-long intimacy with animals has got me out of the common notion that they are automata with a slight infusion of intelligence in their composition. The mind in beast and bird, as in man, is the main thing. Man has progressed mentally so far that, looking back at the other creatures, they appear practically mindless to him. . . . The simple truth of the matter is that our instincts have been more modified and obscured, as instincts, in us than in the lower animals. But though the instincts of animals are less modified and obscured, they are also interwoven and shot through or saturated with intelligence. In what do the ordinary occupations of hunting, fishing, shelter-building, rearing and protecting the young, and so on, differ in the animal and the savage or primitive man?

While he did not explicitly make such nice distinctions between the percipient, the perceptive, and the reflective levels of intelligence as did, say, Lloyd Morgan, there can be little doubt that he was using the word in conformity with most of its general meanings.[4] For later in the same volume he says, "Little by little the knowledge comes" to the psychologists who are digging to get at the roots of man's higher faculties "that, notwithstanding the enormous difference between man and animals, mentally it is one of degree only, that all that is in our minds is also in theirs."

Although the minds of beasts and birds seemed comparatively open to Hudson—probably to few more open—those of insects were often baffling. Yet he had no doubt that some trace of intelligence resided also in them. And, as the following passage indicates, this faculty was not confused with their marvellous social instinct.

> The question of insect intelligence—naturalists are agreed that insects do possess intelligence—is an extremely difficult one. . . . We regard the order Hymenoptera as the most intelligent because most of the social insects are included in it; but it has not yet been proved, probably never will be proved, that the social instincts resulted from intelligence which has "lapsed." Whether ants and bees were more intelligent than other insects during the early stages of their organic

---

[4] See *British Birds*, p. 403, and *Dead Man's Plack, An Old Thorn, & Miscellanea*, pp. 352, 358.

societies or not, it will hardly be disputed by any naturalist who has observed insects for long that many solitary species display more intelligence in their actions than those that live in communities.

Fabre, always remembering his experience with the processionary caterpillars, was surely not among the naturalists referred to, but Huber and Morgan and Hingston, as well as many more recent entomologists, have uncovered sufficient evidence to be convinced that insects possess at least enough intelligence to profit by experience and to alter their habits in order to cope with new conditions. Certain acts of insects—ants growing funguses in subterranean galleries, herding aphids like cows for milk, and performing elaborate operations with the precise teamwork that Beebe witnessed in Pit #5 of the Guiana jungle—bespeak some aspects of intelligence that were indeed late in achieving expression in *Homo sapiens.*

There are, of course, many who, in spite of such a qualifying phrase as "the enormous difference between man and animals," will object to the extent to which Hudson stressed the prevalence of intelligence throughout the animal world. Burroughs, for example, though he himself did much to enhance that world imaginatively, lent the main weight of his influence in the opposite direction. "Animals," he asserted, "take the first step in knowledge—they perceive things and discriminate between them; but they do not take the second step—combine them, analyze them, and form concepts and judgments." Yet he exposes the weakness of his argument by making exception of the dog and the ape. More recently, Julian Huxley, maintaining that man, through his achievement of an accumulative tradition, itself the product of conceptual thought, can aid materially in guiding his own evolution, has been underscoring the uniqueness of man.

The chief weight of contemporary opinion appears, however, to be on the side of Hudson. Few will grant to animals any considerable capacity for reflection or disinterested generalization—the kind of thinking men seem to do in the mind alone—since the higher forms of intelligence depend largely on the development of the neocortex. But what we call "the wisdom of the wild"—foxes doubling on their tracks, coyotes shifting their defenses to meet a new attack, a flock of penguins roughening a slippery thoroughfare with their beaks in order to make a safe passage to the sea—has for some of its components insight, foresight, adaptation of means to ends, sustained teamwork, transference of ideas, and a good deal of the subconscious, if not actually the conscious, mind, the elementary mind-stuff from which intelligence was elicited. As one descends the organic scale, with its ever-greater structural and neural differences, it becomes increasingly difficult to interpret the animal in terms of human thought-patterns. "We do not and never can know," says Hudson, "what an insect knows or feel what it feels." Yet so distinguished a naturalist as Arthur Thomson has discovered in that little pin-point of jelly, the amoeba, tenacity of purpose and the ability to choose alternatives. Thus, even to one who believes in "emergent evolution," there are grounds for thinking that intelligence is inherent in all animals, and, mind and matter being so deeply interfused, potential in all protoplasm.

Many of the arguments denying intelligence to animals could disconcertingly be turned against man himself, whose reactions often seem hardly less blind and stereotyped. Perhaps as frequently in the human as in the insect world, actions that spring from the social instinct are accredited to the intellect. As is now generally recognized, it was largely the development of tools by the use of the opposable thumb and the establishment of a method of transmitting culture through the medium of words—both synchronized with the development of the brain—that raised man far above animals in intelligence. Without corresponding tools, such an extension of the animal's reflective power would be, as Hudson pointed out, a hindrance to him and might lead to disaster, for much thinking would but "dim that bright perception on which his safety depends." Be all this as it may, Hudson, trying like most naturalists to bring animals closer to the business and bosoms of men, kept stressing the bond of intelligence between them.

Stressed, too, more than by most out-of-door essayists, were some of the other highly prized qualities that animals share with man.

We in our early years are little wild animals, and the wild animals are little children.

Our best and highest qualities have their small beginnings in these lowlier beings. That union or feeling of preference and attachment of an individual towards another of its own or of a different species, which I first began to observe in horses during my boyhood, is, like play, unconcerned with the satisfaction of bodily wants and the business of self-preservation and the continuance of the race. It is a manifestation of something higher in the mind, which shows that the lower animals are not wholly immersed in the struggle for existence, that they are capable in a small way, as we are in a large way, of escaping from and rising above it.

Besides a delight in sheer fun[5] and disinterested friendship, there are to be found occasionally in animals a sense of right and wrong, gratitude, a humanlike love, and self-sacrifice—a "fiery spirit" that, as observed by Maeterlinck in the swarming of bees and by Muir when a Canadian honker came back to strike him for wounding one of its flock, "makes them forget their own safety." Even what we call spirituality, the most beautiful offshoot of the mind, "is not ours by miracle; it was inherent in us from the beginning: the seed germinated and the roots and early leaves were formed before man, as man, existed, and are ours by inheritance." And "it is sometimes borne in on us," as Hudson reminds his readers now and then, that in some ways "man is a little lower than the brutes." Perhaps man's only true dignity, as Santayana (also a strong influence in the recognition of our kinship with animals) has remarked, lies in his capacity to despise himself.

The aesthetic faculty was as much emphasized as intelligence. All healthy creatures rise at times above mere self-preservation and the perpetuation of the species, and revel in the possession of their senses and in the world about them. And this zest, when combined with the impulse to impart the emotion to others, leads to artistic expression. "Even the small ants," so Hudson was persuaded, "have their aesthetic sense and have developed a stridulating instrument; albeit the sounds they draw from it for their own pleasure are inaudible to us." And all dipterous insects, though "they have not evolved any such set performances" as those of the robber-fly, "yet in their freer way do find the chief pleasure of their brief lives in aerial exercises with the accompaniment of music." Many animals in whom the "voice is greatly developed"—asses, cats, dogs, foxes, and the loquacious rodents—"join in noisy concerts and choruses;

---

5   The practical benefits derived from play, which Karl Groos makes much of, Hudson regarded as incidental to the instinct rather than its *raison d'être*.

. . . and in the howling monkeys this kind of performance rises to the sublime uproar of the tropical forest at eventide."

The chief evidences of this faculty presented by Hudson come from his observation of birds, which are more subject to the "universal joyous instinct than mammals. . . . As they are so much freer, . . . more buoyant and graceful in action, more loquacious, and have voices so much finer, their gladness shows itself in a greater variety of ways, with more regular and beautiful motions, and with melody." This *joie de vivre* is often expressed in beauty of form and of plumage—the sun-bittern's strangely painted wings, the cock-of-the-rock's flame-colored mantle, the peacock's crest and ocellated train—and in grace of flight. The weaving of nests, which at times shows a finer architectural sense than that of some primitive peoples, brings with it the joy of the artist. Under the guidance of the aesthetic faculty, the sportive spirit has found expression in a variety of dance forms, and dancing itself can produce a reflex action "strong enough to mark [a] bird's whole character—language, bearing, and habits being coloured by it, and even the domestic relations interfered with." It is, however, in song that birds find their fullest and most exquisite aesthetic expression. Many ornithologists have corroborated these observations: Beebe, for example, concluding that one of the dances of the albatross is inexplicable except in terms of sheer exuberance; Seton, that the leapings, boundings, and stampings of the grouse are instinctive and not dependent upon the sexual urge; and Eckstein, that the canary in its singing comes "very near to man's own high conception of art for art's sake, song for song's sake, the creation of impersonal beauty."

It was in large measure his belief in the deep-rootedness of the aesthetic impulse that led Hudson to be critical of the extent to which Darwin, in his theory of sexual selection, subordinated the sense of beauty to biological necessity. He was, to be sure, fully aware of how powerful a force sex is in the evolution of life, so powerful indeed in man that, as one gathers from a reading of *A Crystal Age*, it is now one of the chief drawbacks to his further progress. And he would not have denied that there is a certain affinity between the aesthetic and the sexual emotions, both often functioning together, the one frequently intensifying the other. Aesthetic taste has aided in the choice of mates, and sexual feeling, in the choreography of dance and the tuning of song. Although he may not have given the problem all the attention it requires, Hudson was not unaware that some aesthetic activities that now seem to have no sexual significance whatever, were once a part of the courtship pattern, just as Greek and English tragic drama was once integral with religion. But that does not mean that their ultimate source is sex, for the aesthetic sense is just as radical in the structure of life.[6] The beauty of butterfly wings and of bird-song, as well as that of the robber-fly's dance, is not gyved to the perpetuation of the species.

"In a vast majority of species," says Hudson in further criticism of the theory of sexual selection, there is very little selection of any sort, the female merely accepting the first male that seeks her out.[7] Of the grasshopper who, with growing impatience, was awaiting the outcome of the rivalry of her two serenaders, he remarks: "That she distinguishes one singer above others, or exercises 'selection' in the Darwinian sense, seems unlikely: it strikes one, on the contrary, that having so long suffered neglect she is only too willing to be claimed by any one of them." The female bird, according to Eliot Howard, accepts the male because she favors his particular territory, bird-song being more for the claiming of such territory than for the wooing of a mate. Among the mammals, as is well known, there is little courtship or deliberate selection; even the female of the subhuman primates, as Earnest Hooton has pointed out, remains "passive, acquiescent, and devoid of aesthetic perception. She does not choose, but only stands and waits." It was perhaps the influence of the society in which he moved that led Darwin to read preferential mating so thoroughly into his theory of evolution.

There is still another important reason why Hudson was "never wholly satisfied" with the theory of natural selection, of which sexual selection is a part, "as the only and sufficient explanation of the change in the forms of life." Like Lamarck and Butler, he underscored the integration of organisms with their surroundings.

6　"Proficiency in all kinds of dancing-antics, aerial and terrestrial," and the highest perfection in melody occurs, it is true, "at the season of courtship," but this season is also that in which "the conditions of life are most favourable [and] vitality is at its maximum" (*The Naturalist in La Plata*, p. 281).

7　Wallace, Morgan, Spencer, and others were of the same opinion.

There is a sense of the *thing itself*—of the tree or wood, the rock, river, sea, mountain, the soil, clay or gravel, or sand or chalk, the cloud, the rain, and what not—something, let us say, penetrative, special, individual, as if the quality of the thing itself had entered into us, changing us, affecting body and mind.

It is possible that something of this feeling was in the mind, or at the back of it, of Willughby . . . when he suggested that the white colour in birds and beasts in the Arctic regions was due to the constant intuition of snow, and the force of the imagination. . . . Who at this day [1922] can believe that the winter snow-white fur and feathers of hare, weasel, grouse and other arctic species, the sand-colouring of animals which is almost universal in sandy deserts, and the green plumage of many hundreds of species of birds in tropical forests, have been brought about by means of the Darwinian principle —the gradual accumulation and inheritance of a long series of small individual variations favourable to the individual itself and its descendants in the struggle for life? The insurmountable objection is and always will be that such variations are of the individual.

We ourselves are the living sepulchres of a dead past. . . . What has truly entered our soul and become psychical is our environment—that wild nature in which and to which we were born at an inconceivably remote period, and which made us what we are.

The unity of life encompasses the whole environment, or, as an outstanding physiologist has put it, "We cannot separate organic from environmental structure, any more than we can separate the action of the environment from the reaction of the organism." [8] Darwin himself, whose theory does not include an explanation of the causes of variations but limits itself to pointing out how the useful ones are transmitted and the useless discarded, was actually more of a Lamarckian than he was aware of or would admit.

Like Butler and Bergson, Hudson rejected the idea, so popular among nineteenth-century biologists, of the mechanical adaptation of organisms to their changing environment. Rather, most is accomplished through a super-abundance of vital energy, an urge to realize one's potentialities, and, particularly among the more advanced forms of life, the guidance of the intelligence. He was convinced, for example, that with birds, intelligence is, in most instances, the directing "principle of life, supplementing and modi-

---

[8] J. S. Haldane, *The Philosophical Basis of Biology* (New York, 1931), p. 14.

fying habits to bring them into closer harmony with the environment, and enlivening every day with countless little acts which result from judgment and experience, and form no part of the inherited complex instincts." All faculties and forms acquired through the co-ordination of inner with outer forces are, after careful winnowing, transmitted by the various agencies of inheritance to the generations that follow, occasionally changing or evolving them into new organic forms, with new patterns of behavior.[9] In some such manner, through vast stretches of time, the amoeba has spiraled to man, and the aesthetic propensities of insects, birds, and beasts have blossomed into the arts of our civilization.

Science, however, never "barred" against Hudson "the gate that lets in dreams": poet that he was, the exquisite correspondence between organism and environment, "the plasticity and intelligence for the readjustment of the vital machinery" to meet all contingencies and thus perpetuate a form for millions of years, and man's kinship with life "in all its appearances, in all organic shapes, however different from the human," impressed him less than "the wonderfulness and eternal mystery of life itself; this formative, informing energy—this flame that burns in and shines through the case, the habit, which in lighting another dies, and albeit dying yet endures for ever." One may observe many individual players and become familiar with a few of them, but the drama in which they perform their brief rôles extends with ever-shifting scenery into eternity. *Omnia exeunt in mysterium.*

ANIMAL PORTRAITURE

There is no Bambi or Red Fox or Lobo the wolf or Ku-Ma the jaguar or Salar the salmon in Hudson's volumes. In this type of portraiture—which, for its method, owes much to the novel and the half-fictionalized animal stories and biographies popular since the eighteenth century, and, for its material, to the studies in animal psychology by field naturalists and scientists—the scattered observations of a whole species are strung on a narrative thread in order to present a single individual. Concerning this technique, Hudson remarks:

---

9 Hudson has nothing to say about the changes or mutations in the germ plasm that come suddenly and are the result of mere accident.

We think a great deal of Professor Owen's feat in re-constructing the entire framework of the gigantic Dinornis, long extinct, from the fragment of a single bone. It is nothing compared to that of the new naturalists, who build you up the entire psychology, and whole life from the cradle to the grave, so to speak, of fox, and caribou, and bobcat, and chipmunk, and forty others from a few isolated facts concerning the habits of those animals.

[Such] writers . . . are not exactly naturalists, nor yet mere fictionists. . . . To a considerable knowledge of animal psychology and extraordinary sympathy with all wildness, [they] unite an imaginative insight which reveals to them much of the inner, the mind life of brutes.

The world is seen through the eyes of a composite creature, and usually the author, like the omniscient novelist, absents himself from the scene. The consistency such portraiture aims at is of a more imaginative sort than truth to fact: namely, truth to character and to ensemble; and what is lost in verisimilitude is gained in sustained emotion and in heightened drama. Created in America by Charles Roberts and Ernest Thompson Seton, this genre soon achieved a considerable vogue. It gave encouragement, on the one hand, to admittedly fabular portraits, like those of *The Jungle Book* and *Anaconda*, in which animals feel and think on the level of men, and even speak their language; and, on the other, to spurious hodgepodges, in which the folk of the wild are exploited to yield the sentimental ardors of popular fiction.

Almost all the writings of this school were branded by Burroughs as "nature faking." Hudson was also conscious of their defects: the heightening of some details beyond the warrant of actuality; the theatricality of some of the situations; and the reading of human emotions and thoughts too facilely and explicitly into birds and beasts, making them a much "more intelligent and nice-minded people than, say, the African pigmies or other low-down savages." There was always the danger, too, of these stories being taken by the masses as gospel truth. Yet, since they acquainted many persons with the lore of the wild and awakened a sympathy for the brute creation, and since Hudson himself knew on what plane of reality to accept them, he spoke well of the best of this genre, saying of Roberts, who is at once more truly imaginative and more objective than most of his fellows:

All that the orthodox naturalists, and hunters, and trappers, know of the wild animals, he knows; and to his knowledge he adds a keen sympathy with wild life, and, above all, he possesses imagination and invention. The result is a book [*Red Fox*] which, purely as a story, is as delightful to read as the unforgettable adventures of Brer Rabbit and Brer Fox. At the same time, the author infuses his own into the animal mind with so nice a judgment and so much restraint that we do not regard his life of a fox, or any other animal, as mere romance, but it does produce the right illusion, and knowing that it was founded on truth, that there is so much truth intermixed with it, we are pleased to take it as all true.

In the out-of-door essay, where the main intent is to preserve the casualness and the wholeness of actual experience, the portrait of an animal, sketched impressionistically in the manner of observation, is rarely enlivened with more than one incident; and it is usually presented so as to blend with the rest of the complex life of its locale. Such portraiture, Hudson well knew, would never capture the popular fancy as does that of the fictional school, for the general public prefers full-length and detailed paintings to sketches and vignettes—the heroic canvases of Potter or Rubens to the intimate drawings of Il Pisanello—and the melodramatic devices that give to the biography of an animal the climaxes of a romance. Yet the out-of-door essay is not without its own romance—the sense of wonder at the beauty, the variety and the mystery of the unfolding scene, the thrill of adventure amongst the furtive creatures of the wild—and mingled with the romance is the companionship of one who has become a part of all that he has observed. It was certainly well that Hudson chose to remain within this genre, with its deeper and more truly poetic sense of reality.

In laying bare the springs of action, his portraiture is remarkably sure. "Even for one who is a good observer, whose mind is ever on the watch secretly, and who in this way takes in knowledge unconsciously as he inhales the air," long experience is necessary in order to know animals well enough to insinuate himself into their mentality. Any creature chanced upon in field or hedgerow Hudson was careful to place beside the genetic image of it always present in his mind. And he was curious not only in regard to the larger issues of biology and psychology, but to the lesser ones, such as the reason squirrels bite off twigs and leaves, the reaction of serpents to the color scarlet, pre-natal suggestion, the effect of albinism on others, the sense of direction, and receptivity to telepathic communications.

Although he was lenient toward the fictionists and continually emphasized the intelligence and aesthetic sensitivity of animals, Hudson was careful to guard against any indulgence on his part in the pathetic fallacy. Once when fancy suggested that were he a gull a larger sense of sublimity would be his, he reminded himself that "this is a delusion, seeing that we possess such a sense only because we are bound to earth, because vast cliffs overhanging the sea and other altitudes are in some degree dangerous." If the pathetic fallacy appeared in any work that was avowedly natural history, Hudson could be as severely critical as Burroughs. Thus he even said he could not read Maeterlinck's *Life of the Bee*, which, in spite of a tendency toward anthropopsychism, adheres for the most part to the main facts and is impregnated with the quintessence of the outdoors. What little coloring is lent to his own portraiture by this fallacy—and there is some, even though he was thoroughly capable of humanizing his "sitters" without sentimental distortion—is so obviously the play of his fancy, like the grace notes of a melody, that it never puts the reader under any illusion.

Acceptance of "the fierce, sane cruelty of life," the pain involved in the struggle for survival, aided in giving his profound sympathy for all life, as it has most of the contemporary writers on the outdoors, the requisite toughness. The sight of a spider killing a grasshopper led to this comment: "He who walks out of doors with Nature, who sees life and death as sunlight and shadow, on witnessing such an incident wishes the captor a good appetite, and, passing on, thinks no more about it." The "spectacle of a Pierre Loti going about the world with a pocket-handkerchief to his eyes, sobbing at the thought of the sad destiny in store for all the lower animals . . . encountered in his wanderings" seemed to Hudson a "pitiable" one, since the dangers that continually threaten the life of any wild creature tend to keep its muscles and its faculties at full stretch, and death, when it strikes, usually strikes with the leap of a puma, mercifully swift.

Let us have no *Book of Pity and Death* on our list, no mawkish weepings and ravings of disordered minds, however beautiful the writing may be. Let us rather make haste to burn all such literature so as to escape infection; and always bear in mind that the children of life are the children of joy, that the lower animals are only unhappy when made so by man; that man alone, of all the creatures, has "found out many inventions," the chief of which appears to be the art of making himself miserable, and of seeing all nature stained with that dark and hateful colour.

Far better than the sentimentality of a Landseer is the savage vigor of a Géricault or a Barye!

Man's insentience to the suffering he wantonly inflicts upon the brute creation moved Hudson to fierce anger.[10] "The man who can needlessly set his foot on a worm is as strange to my soul as De Quincey's imaginary Malay, or even his 'damned crocodile.' " In his own experience, "abstention from killing," even for the purposes of science, had made him, because of "the new or different feeling towards animal life which it had engendered," a happier person as well as a better observer. But toward the animal kingdom as such he wished to preserve a "benevolent neutrality; a keen and kindly interest in every form of life, with indifference as to its ultimate destiny; the softness which does no wrong with the hardness that sees no wrong done." And he emblazoned upon his escutcheon, it will be remembered, not only "Persecute nothing!" but also "Pet nothing!" It is this godlike impartiality that, in large measure, gives to even his most touching portraits the quality of detachment.

Although his general approach was conditioned by his scientific training, it was not primarily as a naturalist that Hudson looked upon animals—but, rather, as an artist. In addition to the genetic portraits he carried in his mind, there were also, as with birds, "one or two or several, in some cases as many as fifty, images of the same species . . . as it appeared at some exceptionally favourable moment and was viewed with peculiar interest and pleasure." Seeing in animals beauty of ultimate value and admiring them for their personalities—the highest compliment that can be paid another—he pre-

---

10 Probably under the stress of war, he gave his approval to fox-hunting, for "without this glorious sport," he reasoned, "we should want horses for our cavalry, and men of the right kind on their backs, to face the Huns who would destroy us" (*The Book of a Naturalist*, p. 52). In the present age of tanks and atomic bombs, such an argument, as Hudson would have been the first to recognize, is no longer valid.

sented them as one would human beings, each with his own distinctive lineaments and traits. Thus, besides imparting information to his readers, he stirred their emotions and imaginations.

How well equipped he was as an artist—the acuteness and harmony of his senses, his mastery of the essay technique, his empathy with all creatures and intuition for essences—has already been discussed. Sketches though his records usually are, they give one the impression that the nuances of form and character have been grasped with absolute fidelity. His narrative skill enabled him to present, with the simplicity and directness of a Defoe and often with an intimacy especially charming to children, many episodes in the wild chronicle of Nature—most of them of common occurrence (the hardest to present), but some quite sensational. His figures are never paraded in a herd before us, as they are in most scientific volumes; they are casually grouped within the spaciousness of his essays as though by Nature herself, each giving dramatic palpitation to some part of the panoramas of the pampas of La Plata, the barrens of Patagonia, or the countryside of southern England. His poetic insight, made more sure by his knowledge of psychology, aided him in seizing, as an eagle its prey, *la vérité vraie* of an insect, beast, or bird—revealing its very soul. And often the intrinsic interest of his records, as in most great portraiture, is considerably enhanced by the emotional chiaroscuro of the artist himself.

There are many animals in Hudson's portfolio of sketches, from pumas and horses and deer and rheas to such miniatures as moles and toads and pipits and spiders—some merely glimpsed and quickly drawn in a few telling strokes; others, as though sitting for their portraits, observed leisurely and painted with precise particularity. So complete was his sense of oneness with all life, so catholic his taste, that, as with Browne and Hodgson, all the creatures sired by evolution, if living the free life of the wild untouched by disease, were beautiful in his sight—if in no other way, then, like the chameleon and grasshopper and flittermouse, as grotesques. Probably more than any other major out-of-door essayist, Hudson realized that the design and color and function of every living creature form an artistic unity. Though birds were his favorites, he sought to achieve something of the aesthetic impartiality of Nature toward all her broods. "It is a consolation to think," he remarks in regard to some dogs that had disturbed him during one of his observations, that they are not my pets; that I shall not grieve, like their mistress, when their brief barking period is over; that I care just so much and no more for them than for any other living creature, not excepting the *fer-de-lance,* "quoiled in the path like rope in a ship," or the broad-winged vulture "scaling the heavens by invisible stairs." None are out of place where Nature placed them, nor unbeautiful; none are unlovable, since their various qualities—the rage of the one and the gentleness of the other—are but harmonious lights and shades in the ever-changing living picture that is so perfect.

THE GREEN MYRIADS IN THE PEOPLED GRASS

The inclusion of many insects, more than appear in the pages of his chief English and American predecessors in the out-of-door essay, gives a sense of intimacy and completeness to Hudson's landscapes, particularly those of the Sussex Downs, the New Forest, and La Plata. Without the company of these innumerable atomies "moving swiftly or slowly" about him, each deep in his day's employ, "their multitudinous small voices united into one deep continuous Aeolian sound," it would have seemed to Hudson, especially in lonely, shelterless places, "as if some mysterious malady or sadness had come upon nature." So interested did he become at times in these fantastically articulated creatures that he exclaims:

If the power to attain to all that De Quincey craved, or pretended that he craved for, were mine, I should not value it; I should give it all to be able to transform myself for the space of a summer's day into one of these little creatures on the South Downs; then to return to my own form and place in nature with a clear recollection of the wonderland in which I had been. And if, in the first place, I were permitted to select my own insect, I should carefully consider them all, since they differ as greatly from each other as bird from serpent, and fish from mammal. I should pass in review the slow beetle, heavily armoured, and the fantastic fly, a miracle of inconsequence; the esteemed humble-bee, and the wasp, that very fine insect gentleman in his mood of devilish cheerfulness; the diligent ant, absorbed in his minute business; the grasshopper, with his small stringed instrument and long grave countenance; and the dragon-fly, with those two great gem-like orbs that reflect a nature of an unimaginable aspect. And after all I should make choice of the little blue butterfly, despite his smallness and frivolity, to house myself in.

The knowledge of that strange fairy world it inhabits would be incommunicable, like the vision vouchsafed to some religionist of which he has been forbidden to speak; but the memory of it would be a secret perennial joy.

As various chapters of *The Naturalist in La Plata* and many passages throughout his essays indicate, Hudson might well have become, had he abandoned himself to entomology, one of the company of Lubbock, Fabre, Forel, and Wheeler. Such an impulse, it will be remembered, did occasionally spring up in him, but he chose, rather, to keep his presentation of insects in proportion to the other major divisions of animal life and to the other objects in a landscape as they affect a sensitive observer—that is, as "shining gems in nature's embroidery." And if there are no portraits or episodes in his volumes quite so memorable as some in those of Bates and Belt and Beebe, and if they do not become quite the symbols they are at times with Fabre—as in the seven-day march of the processionary caterpillars round and round the narrow, fifty-three-inch rim of a vase—many of them have a reality just as insistent and are painted in pigments no less durable.

When he was young, so Hudson tells us, wasps attracted him beyond all other insects because of "their singular and brilliant coloration"—yellow, golden brown, black and gold, metallic blue, deep purplish blue, blue and crimson—and "their formidable character." The practice wasps have of paralyzing, rather than killing outright, other insects in order that their "grubs can vivisect them at leisure"—an observation dramatically reinforced upon his attention when, as the Hudson family were seated at dinner, a wasps' nest "detached itself from the ceiling and fell with a crash on to the table, where it was shattered to pieces, scattering a shower of green half-living spiders round it"—was an abomination in his sight and raised in his youthful mind, as it has in others, disquieting thoughts concerning the governance of the universe. Of the later experiences with these redoubtable creatures, one of the most amusing is that in which a few wasps, greedily sopping up an over-ripe pear, kept some forty blue-bottle flies, which were jostling each other on the rim of the ever-deepening cavern of nectar, from getting even a single sip. If a more venturesome fly "would put out his proboscis and begin sucking at the edge," one of the wasps

"would turn quickly round to face the presumptuous [fellow], lifting his wings in a threatening manner. . . . "

> Occasionally hunger would overcome their fear; a general movement
> of the flies would take place, and several would begin sucking at the
> same time; then the wasp, seeming to think that more than a mere
> menacing look or gesture was required in such a case, would start up
> with an angry buzz, and away the whole crowd of flies would go to
> whirl round and round in a little blue cloud with a loud, excited hum,
> only to settle again in a few moments on the big yellow pear and
> begin crowding round the pit as before.

Toward spiders Hudson felt peculiarly sympathetic, observing
and admiring them, as he did no other species, always in an essentially "non-scientific spirit." Besides ministering to his aesthetic feelings, they touched the sense of compassion, for Nature has laid
upon these arachnids, as in the cruel treatment accorded them by
wasps, too heavy an affliction "in compensation for [their] paltry
drop of venom." Something of this sympathy is shown in the excellent analysis of their endowments with which the essay on them in
The Naturalist in La Plata closes. Of individualized portraits and
graphic episodes, the ones that stand out are those of the little white
spider (*Thomisus citreus*) gyrating fantastically around his inamorata throned on a cluster of bell-heath flowers, loving her "for her
beautiful white body," but fearing her "on account of those poison
fangs which he could probably see every time she smiled" encouragement—good choreography for a Roussel; the mortal combat between "two envenomed little duellists" over the possession of a
web, each trying to entangle the other in some "cunningly thrown
snare," one of them finally catching the other and wrapping him
"in a silvery cocoon, which, unlike the cocoon the caterpillar weaves,
. . . was also [his] winding-sheet"; and the huge, venomous *Lycosa*,
king of pampean spiders, who gave chase to Hudson even though
he was on horseback and leaped upon his outthrust whip in order to
carry the attack home. There is also a scene reminiscent of ones
from Jonathan Edwards and White: myriads of gossamer spiders
(the "most spiritual of living things"), some, like fairy aeronauts,
"floating unseen" on their tiny, silken parachutes, "like an ethereal
vital dust in the atmosphere," and others, "so numerous that they
continually baulked one another in their efforts to rise in the air,"
weaving a gauzy veil over the pampas, and best viewed when, like

moonlight across water, the declining sun flings a broad, silvery causeway to one's very feet.

Equally impressive are the pampean storms of dragonflies, when countless multitudes of these brightly-hued, sinister-eyed, scaly serpents of the air flee, panic-stricken, on their rustling parchment wings, before the *pampero*, or, finding a shelter in one of the widely scattered groves, cling to the trees in such masses as to give many of them the appearance of being "hung with curtains of some brown glistening material, too thick to show the green leaves beneath." Not so impressive, but likewise rare, is the vista of the vivid green fronds of a half acre of bracken in a Hampshire woods stippled evenly with a host of turquoise-blue dragonflies, each three to six inches apart, "their heads to the wind, their long bodies all pointing the same way."

Many moths and butterflies lend their erratic beauty to Hudson's landscapes: hundreds of ghost-moths dimly seen in their whiteness swinging their quaint, rhythmic love-dance over a twilit meadow along the Wiltshire Avon; thousands upon thousands of butterflies —white, yellow, orange, red, and black—hovering over a field of blossoming alfalfa in the midst of the pampas; and most of all, those fairies among these winged flowers, the little pale-blue ones of the downs, whose hue, that of the sky and the atmosphere, seems to have entered their very souls, making them "more aerial in habits, more light-hearted and playful in disposition than [their] other-coloured relations." Among the butterfly incidents, one remembers the attack made by a meadow-pipit, one of the littlest and most timid of birds, upon a great hawk-moth, the blows of whose strong wings failed to relax the vulture-like grip of its furious assailant. And there is that delightful picture of Hudson covered with "shivering, fluttering, squeaking or creaking" death's-head moths, which had literally been showered upon him by a whimsical hostess. It made him feel, he says, as if he had been "standing in some wilderness never trodden by human foot, [him]self an unhuman solitary, and merely by willing it . . . had drawn those beautiful beings of the dark to [him], charming them as with a flowery fragrance from their secret hiding-places in a dim world of leaves to gather upon and cover [him] over with their downy, trembling, mottled grey and rich yellow velvet wings."

The soft, will-o'-the-wisp light of the glow-worm seemed most beautiful when beheld a foot or so above the earth "in a tangle of bramble and bracken, [and] other plants with slender stems and deep-cut leaves," for then its exquisite golden green "looks as if enclosed within an invisible globe, which may be as much as fifteen inches in diameter, and within its circle the minutest details of the scene are clear to the vision, even to the finest veining of the leaves, the leaves shining a pure translucent green, while outside the mystic globe of light all is in deep shadow and in blackness." The tiny flashlight of the firefly did not appear quite so lovely or so satisfying, for in watching its sudden gleams and zigzags of fire, often surprising one like the explosions of rockets in a dark sky, "there is an element of impatience which interferes with the pleasure." Fireflies are indeed at their best "in multitudes, sparkling everywhere in the darkness, so that no regard is paid to any individual light, but they are seen as we see snowflakes." Then, as in the following nocturne, they give the impression of a galaxy of stars:

> Riding on the pampas one dark evening an hour after sunset, and passing from high ground overgrown with giant thistles to a low plain covered with long grass, bordering a stream of water, I found it all ablaze with myriads of fireflies. I noticed that all the insects gave out an exceptionally large, brilliant light, which shone almost steadily. The long grass was thickly studded with them, while they literally swarmed in the air, all moving up the valley with a singularly slow and languid flight. When I galloped down into this river of phosphorescent fire, my horse plunged and snorted with alarm. I succeeded at length in quieting him, and then rode slowly through, compelled to keep my mouth and eyes closed, so thickly did the insects rain on to my face. The air was laden with the sickening phosphorus-smell they emit, but when I had once got free of the broad fiery zone, stretching away on either hand for miles along the moist valley, I stood still and gazed back for some time on a scene the most wonderful and enchanting I have ever witnessed.

There are a number of other sketches of insects before which one should like to pause: among them, a colony of leaf-cutting ants, "more populous than London," thousands of whom tumbled pell-mell in the deep pit Hudson scooped across their line of march; a maze of jet-black, crimson-banded flies "performing a sort of complicated dance" upon some purple patches of thyme on a down, "all agitating and waving their glistening wings, as if that bath of sweetness had made them mad with delight"; two flies, an *Asilus* and a *Tipula*, locked in mortal combat, the one plunging his rostrum, again and again, into the soft part of his victim's body, as a man would his dagger; a hornet, strong man among all insects with his golden-red armature, keeping a timid bank vole from feeding on some sap that had oozed into a deep cleft of an elm's rough bark; portly, opal-eyed "Lady Greensleeves," the grasshopper who, on her crimson throne of a cluster of guelder-rose berries, banquetted for sixteen days at Hudson's table; and three rival grasshoppers, perched high on thin stalks of "good-for-nothing" grass in Harewood Forest, looking in the sunlight like verdigris—one of them, with half his vocal organs torn off in a fight, trying desperately but unsuccessfully to strum a serenade, and the other two, so engrossed in their minstrelsy as to forget the object of it, their lady-love.

The music of insects, superior to that of beasts, has come to mean much to many persons and even to some nations, for around its intrinsic beauties have gathered richly "expressive" ones. The steady, pulsing undersong of the vast insect choir—one sound, yet "diffused and flowing like water over the surface" of the earth, "under the trees, and the rough bushy tangle[s]"—was to Hudson the soul of the summer made audible. Of the individual voices, that of the chief pampean cicada (surely not the Greek *tettix*), with its persistent whir, like "the sound of sawing through an iron bar," he found too rasping and brain-piercing. The fiddling of field crickets, when softened and etherealized by distance, was much to his liking, sounding "like a subtle music without rise or fall or change; or like a continuous, diffused, silvery-bright, musical hum, which surround[s] one like an atmosphere, and at the same time pervade[s] and tremble[s] through one like a vibration." The best of his transcriptions are the performances of the delicate green leaf-locust of the pampas (already quoted) and the great green grasshopper—to him, supreme among English insect musicians and, next to the glow-worm, the most poetic.

It is a sustained sound, a current of brightest, finest, bell-like strokes or beats, lasting from three or four to ten or fifteen seconds, to be renewed again and again after short intervals; but when the musician is greatly excited, the pauses last only for a moment—about half a second, and the strain may go on for ten minutes or longer

before a break of any length. But the quality is the chief thing;
and here we find individual differences, and that some have a lower,
weaker note, in which may be detected a buzz, or sibilation, as
in the field-grasshopper; but, as a rule, it is of a shrillness and
musicalness which is without parallel. The squealings of bats, shrews,
and young mice are excessively sharp, and are aptly described as
"needles of sound," but they are not musical. The only bird I know
which has a note comparable to the *viridissima* is the lesser white-
throat. . . . It is this musical sharpness which pleases in the insect,
and makes it so unlike all other sounds in a world so full of sound.
Its incisiveness produces a curious effect: sitting still and listening
for some time at a spot where several insects are stridulating, certain
nerves throb with the sound until it seems that it is in the brain,
and is like that disagreeable condition called "ringing in the ears"
made pleasant. Almost too fine and sharp to be described as metallic,
perhaps it comes nearer to the familiar sound described by Henley:

> Of ice and glass the tinkle,
> Pellucid, crystal-shrill.

Crystal beads dropped in a stream down a crystal stair would produce
a sound somewhat like the insect's song, but duller.

One of the most moving spectacles of insects, so it seemed to Hudson, takes place "where an ancient or large ivy grows in some well-
sheltered spot . . . and flowers profusely, and when on a warm
bright day" in autumn, all those "not wholly dead"—flies of all
sizes and colors, bees, wasps, butterflies, and especially large female
hornets, for whom the weaker species quickly make room—"revive
for a season, and are drawn by the ivy's sweetness from all around
to that one spot." Crowded together on the clustered blossoms or
swarming in the air around, this throng produces a humming sound
that "may be heard fifty yards away like a high wind." They "are
anything but melancholy," for "their life has been a short and a
merry one," full of feasting and revelry. But to a sensitive observer,
particularly on a grey day in late autumn, when these merrymakers,
along with hosts of others from summertime, flash upon the inward
eye, there comes a profound melancholy, a sense of the "tremendous
tragedy of the passing year." And in a passage of much beauty,
Hudson intones a dirge over their evanishment:

> On . . . a day of silence and desolation a remembrance of the late
> summer has come back suddenly like a lightning-flash to my mind,

with such startling vividness as to affect me powerfully. A vision of the vanished insect life that a little while ago covered these green flowering hills. I moved and had my being amid that life as in a golden mist spread over the earth; my ears were full of the noise of innumerable fine small voices blending into one voice; wheresoever I looked their minute swift-moving bodies appeared as thin dark lines on the air and over the green surface. Forms so infinitely varied, yet so wonderfully fashioned, each aglow with its complete separate life, and all in harmony with all life and all nature, responsive in a million secret springs to each and every external influence; so well balanced in their numerous parts and perfect in their equipment, so intense in their lives as to seem fitted to endure for ever. And now in so short a time, in a single day and night as it seems, it is all over, the feast and fairy-dance of life; the myriads of shining gem-like bodies turned to dead dust, the countless multitude of brilliant little individual souls dissipated into thin air and blown whithersoever the wind blows!

MAN'S NEAREST OF KIN

Being ourselves mammalians, wingless treaders of the ground, we have a more fellowly feeling toward beasts: the pathways of their behavior are more accessible to us than those of insects, and the charm of some of them, if not so suggestive to the imagination as that of birds, is more intimate and more enduring.[11] Hudson admired them not only for their physical beauty and the evidences in them of man's higher attributes, but for their unawareness of self, which allows them to become completely absorbed in the passing moment, and for the keener, fiercer grain of their flesh: the exquisiteness of their senses—the nose of a dog or horse, the wing-membranes of a bat, the ear of a hind—and an intensity that can convert the passing moment into ecstasy. Indeed, with a greater camaraderie than that of Whitman he could "turn and live" with them.

Had Hudson devoted his life to the study of the four-footed along with the six-footed, he would, in all likelihood, have achieved lasting fame as a zoologist, a career that was well inaugurated by

---

[11] It is quite possible, though, that in the near future we shall feel a generally closer relationship with birds than with beasts, for, like us and unlike the other mammals, they make far greater use of sight than smell and thus have created more analogous patterns of behavior.

such observations as those on the death-feigning instinct of the jaguar, the opossum, and the fox; the violent excitement of cattle at the smell of blood or the sight of something scarlet; the persecution of a weakly member of a herd or one in extreme distress; imitation and protective resemblances in snakes; and, especially, in that excellent essay, not yet superseded, on the vizcacha. But, as has already been said, he came to prefer the way of life of the out-of-door essayist, presenting the full context of his experience with nature.

Acre-broad vizcacha villages so studded the pampas that a person on horseback could view almost a hundred of them at the same time. Now and again, we are given glimpses of their neat furry inhabitants, each "jealous of any intrusion into his particular burrow," gossiping incessantly like prairie-dogs or rushing off to seek out friends in the neighboring *vizcacheras*; and, at the discharge of a gun or the sound of a thunderclap, we hear, as though from the whole surrounding plain, the uproar of their blended cries, from the deepest booming bass to the shrillest shrieks and squeals. There are several equally exotic sketches of armadillos, those contemporaries of the giant glyptodonts, and of graceful guanacos: an armadillo mangling a venomous serpent with the serrated edges of his armature and then eating it tail-first; another drabbling the boy Hudson with mould as he dug his way, in spite of the grip on his tail, to safety from the fumigation visited upon the rats in the fosse surrounding *Las Acacias*; a guanaco with a very un-Johnsonian passion for white linen, who made off, at the very last moment, with a shirt laid out for a party, the only clean one in the rancho, and thus led his master, his nakedness covered with a towel, a merry chase before the swallowing of all but the starched bosom rendered further pursuit useless. And haunting to the memory, however faulty in psychology, is the imaginative sketch Hudson provides for an enterprising painter of one of these wild cameloids who, having felt his fate upon him and having withdrawn from the herd, has painfully reached the ancient burial-ground of his tribe in southern Patagonia, there to deposit his bones among those of countless ancestors.

The grey wilderness of dwarf thorn trees, aged and grotesque and scantly-leaved, nourished for a thousand years on the bones that whiten the stony ground at their roots; the interior lit faintly with the rays of the departing sun, chill and grey, and silent and motion-less—the huanacos' Golgotha. In the long centuries, stretching back into a dim immeasurable past, so many of this race have journeyed hither from the mountain and the plain to suffer the sharp pang of death, that, to the imagination, something of it all seems to have passed into that hushed and mournful nature. And now one more, the latest pilgrim, has come, all his little strength spent in his struggle to penetrate the close thicket; looking old and gaunt and ghostly in the twilight; with long ragged hair; staring into the gloom out of death-dimmed sunken eyes.

Of all the distinctly American beasts in Hudson's volumes, the one that has attracted most attention is the puma, conqueror of the deadly jaguar. Though his ascription of the unwillingness of this preternaturally cunning beast to defend himself against man, even when attacked with only a knife, to a disarming feeling of friend-liness toward human beings has been strongly challenged, some of the episodes with which he illustrated his defense linger in the memory: that of an audacious puma who, detected in the act of killing sheep in the high enclosure of an estancia near El Carmen, leaped over the head of Hudson as he stood at the gate trying to penetrate into the gloom; and that of one who sat throughout the night near the body of a broken-legged hunter, guarding him, at least so Hudson thought (was not the puma, rather, using the man as a decoy?), against their common enemy, a jaguar.

Of beasts common to both the Argentine and England, most is said about the deer, the horse, the cow, the dog, the fox, and the cat. A wide-antlered stag, "encountered in some incult place where it is absolutely free and wild, moves us," so he observes, "to a strange joy—an inherited memory and a vision of a savage, pre-historic land of which we are truer natives than we can ever be of this smooth sophisticated England." The sight of palish-yellow deer standing motionless among the cardoon bushes of the pampas, gaz-ing at him and then, with a whistling cry, bounding away in long arcs, was a frequent experience in his youth. On one occasion, he was so fortunate as to see two bucks in an open space amidst a waste of grey-green thistles, their horns interlocked and their noses almost touching the ground, pushing furiously back and forth, side to side, and round and round, intently watched by a number of does, who, in their excitement, kept continually circling about them.

In contrast to this violent Barye-like scene, which only death brought to an end, one likes to recall the reposeful, Pisanello-like portraits of two hinds: the one, lying in a grassy hollow of Savernake Forest, enjoying the dainty attentions of a jackdaw to her face, she continually turning her head, like a man being shaved, so that a thorough job could be done; and the other (whom we have already met) lying under an oak tree in Richmond Park, chewing her cud and delighting in the memory-provoking little sounds that issued from the nearby woods—like "the man who, after dining well, smokes his cigar in his easy-chair and amuses his mind at the same time with . . . a fascinating story . . . of old unhappy things and battles long ago."

Born as Hudson was on one of the most far-flung galloping-grounds of the world, where man was almost a centaur, it is appropriate that the patient, gentle-eyed horse should occupy a prominent place in his pages. We are given a good general characterization of the Barbary-blooded pampean species: not so dashing or showy as the English hunter, carrying "his head low and almost grazing the ground with his hoofs" in order not to waste "his energies in vain parade," he is no less courageous, for in spite of his terror at the smell of Indians, which his almost preternatural sense can pick up from a great distance, he "will when 'maintained by a man,' readily charge into a whole host of yelling savages." Though no such master of equine portraiture as Will James or Cunninghame Graham, Hudson has left us an interesting group of sketches: among them, lean, old Zango, who, after having spent most of his life under a guerrilla officer in the Banda Oriental, provided the Hudson children with their first riding-lessons; iron-grey Moro, who, during spells of bad weather, could not resist the home-call from a distant estancia and who, though high-spirited and hostile toward strangers, refrained from injuring a little boy using his tail for a swing; and fawn-colored Cristiano, brown in one eye and pale blue-grey in the other, who, never relaxing the vigilance of the wild life to which he had been born, always trumpeted an alarm at the outcry of a lapwing or the sight of a horseman on the horizon.

For the much maligned *Equus asinus*, who, in spite of a heart never "recreant to the wild," has had a heavy burden to bear through the centuries, Hudson always had a generous and affectionate word. More than horses and cows, the kinsfolk of Modestine, in their "dirty or dusty coat[s] of dull indeterminate greys and earthy and heather-like browns," harmonized with one of his favorite haunts, the boulder-strewn hills and wide, rough moors of Cornwall. They usually responded to his greeting with their hinder parts, "as much as to say that they [had] enough of human beings in the village" and here "prefer[red] to be left alone," but the lure of an apple often brought them nuzzling around him. Their "long-drawn reiterated droning and whistling cry"—horrible or sickening to Cowper, Wordsworth, and Chesterton (none of whom, in all probability, heard it under the proper conditions: from a distance of half a mile in some desolate, silent place)—impressed Hudson's more catholic ears as "the highest musical performance in the mammalian order," more electrifying and more provocative to the mind than the "neighing of wild horses" or "the trumpeting of wild swans."

[It] is not a mere call or cry like the shrill neigh of the horse and wrathful mutterings and prolonged clear *crescendo* lowing of the bull; it is uttered by the animal for its own sake when he is in the mood, and is therefore as truly a set song as the liquid warbling of the woodlark. . . . A song no doubt evolved from various ancient equine cries and calls—a resounding trumpet blast, followed by measured hee-haws, and concluding with a series of prolonged stertorous and sibilant sounds, diminishing in power till they cease. . . .

The effect of the sound is enhanced when you catch sight of the animal, standing at ease in a group, grey amidst the tall grey-green plumed grasses [of the pampas], their great ears erect or pointing forward, and alarm in their faces—a noble animal, horse-shaped but with a distinction of its own, an element of strangeness in its beauty.

For the gentle, broad-browed, pensively gazing cow, "sweeter of breath than the rosiest virgin," Hudson, like Cuyp and Jefferies and Bonheur, had a great fondness, and he steadily refused to partake of her flesh. The morning and evening lowing of a herd, particularly as experienced on the pampas, where the new-born calves were not immediately snatched from their mothers, meant more to him "than any other natural sound—the melody of birds, the springing and dying gales of the pines, the wash of waves on the long shingled beach." The sight of three pairs of long-horned, shaggy black oxen drawing a wagon of golden wheat through a downland valley, attended by five laborers in rough grey garments, appealed as strongly to his imagination as to that of Virgil, Burne-Jones and Yeats, and made him wish to become the owner of one of the great chalk hills of southern England so that the scene might be commemorated by some Gutzon Borglum in "gigantic blocks of granite and marble—red, black, grey, and yellow"—and thus become a joy forever.

To the bovine sketch already included in these pages there should be added that of the frivolous young thing, unsobered as yet with a calf of her own, whose furious charges, first against a rook and then against three gulls, made her appear as ludicrous as "a rhinoceros charging a ball of thistledown or a soap-bubble, and causing it to float away with the wind it created"; the infuriated cow whose sharp horns impaled a puma when she surprised it devouring her newly dropped calf; a herd of three hundred horned cattle frantically mulling around the blood-stained spot on the pampas where one of their number had been slain. And there is that still more harrowing one of a bullock being slaughtered by gauchos, as fascinating in its violence, despite the smallness of scope, as anything by Goya or Kipling or Zuloaga. After the beast had been drawn up close to the house,

one of the two or three mounted men engaged in the operation would throw his lasso over the horns, and, galloping off, pull the rope taut; a second man would then drop from his horse, and running up to the animal behind, pluck out his big knife and with two lightning-quick blows sever the tendons of both hind legs. Instantly the beast would go down on his haunches, and the same man, knife in hand, would flit round to its front or side, and, watching his opportunity, presently thrust the long blade into its throat just above the chest, driving it in to the hilt and working it round; then when it was withdrawn a great torrent of blood would pour out from the tortured beast, still standing on his fore-legs, bellowing all the time with agony. At this point the slaughterer would often leap lightly on to its back, stick his spurs in its sides, and, using the flat of his long knife as a whip, pretend to be riding a race, yelling with fiendish glee. The bellowing would subside into deep, awful, sob-like sounds and chokings; then the rider, seeing the animal about to collapse, would fling himself nimbly off. The beast down, they would all run to it, and throwing themselves on its quivering side as on a couch, begin making and lighting their cigarettes. . . .

The crimson torrents of blood, the deep, human-like cries, made the beast appear like some huge, powerful man caught in a snare by small, weak, but cunning adversaries, who tortured him for their delight and mocked him in his agony.

Of those living lawn-mowers, the ever-nibbling sheep, so much a part of the landscape of both La Plata and southern England, there is surprisingly little in Hudson's pages. In *A Shepherd's Life*, one finds, it is true, a pleasant recording of the music of browsing-bells, which varies from flock to flock according to the number of bells and the proportion of big and little ones. Though one would have liked, along with more of the actual ritual of sheep-herding, a few individualized figures, this book at least gives one a continual sense of their many-toned tremulous bleatings. In *Nature in Downland*, however, in spite of all that is said about shepherds, the sense of the presence of sheep is vague and intermittent. The reason, perhaps, that they did not evoke the artist in Hudson is their want of individuality and dignity, the result of being compelled to live submissively in crowds and of being extremely susceptible to the taint of domesticity. Best of his few sketches is that of Libby, his sister Mary's lamb, who, finding the society of dogs thoroughly congenial, was pleased not only to provide them with a comfortable pillow while they slept but to join them "in the siege and assault of a vizcacha village, . . . frisking about from burrow to burrow, now taking a flying leap over the pit-like mouth, then diving down to see how things were progressing inside. . . ."

One of the most treasurable of Hudson's portraits, sketched with light strokes and a playful humor, is that of the Wiltshire pig with a cultivated taste for elderberry *hors d'oeuvres*. Appreciating the intelligence and the "natural, pleasant, camerados-all or hail-fellow-well-met air" of the porcine tribe and pitying this particular pig because of the filthiness of his sty, Hudson, while going toward the fields from the cottage where he was staying, was accustomed to pause and scratch the pig's back, which would make him "wriggle his body and wink and blink and smile delightedly all over his face," and to place an apple in his trough, for which he would say "something like 'Thank you' in a series of gentle grunts."

But he never ate it greedily: he appeared more inclined to talk than to eat, until by degrees I came to understand what he was saying. What he said was that he appreciated my kind intentions in giving him apples. But, he went on, to tell the real truth, it is not a fruit I am particularly fond of. I am familiar with its taste as they sometimes give me apples, usually the small unripe or bad ones that fall from the trees. However, I don't actually dislike them. I get skim milk and am rather fond of it; then a bucket of mash, which is good enough for hunger; but what I enjoy most is a cabbage, only I don't get one very often now. I sometimes think that if they would let me out of this muddy pen to ramble like the sheep and other beasts in the field or on the downs I should be able to pick up a number of morsels which would taste better than anything they give me.

The presence of large clusters of elderberries nearby gave Hudson an inspiration. Plucking the finest of them, "as big round as [his] cap," he invited the pig to taste it.

He sniffed at it a little doubtfully, and looked at me and made a remark or two, then nibbled at the edge of the cluster, taking a few berries into his mouth, and holding them some time before he ventured to crush them. At length he did venture, then looked at me again and made more remarks, "Queer fruit this! Never tasted anything quite like it before, but I really can't say yet whether I like it or not."

Then he took another bite, then more bites, looking up at me and saying something between the bites, till, little by little, he had consumed the whole bunch; then turning round, he went back to his bed with a little grunt to say that I was now at liberty to go on to the cows and horses.

Thus, for several weeks, Hudson made glad the heart of his friend, feeding him two or three times a day with huge clusters. Then, on one fateful day, a dealer came along, and, binding him "hand and foot," carried him away to his doom, squealing indignantly.

In his estimation of dogs, those prime favorites among beasts, Hudson had (as has already been noted) his reservations, which have led to some misinterpretation, even by so sympathetic a critic as Massingham. Unlike Warde Fowler, who usually had his carefully-trained terrier Billy at his side, he rarely desired the companionship of a dog on his field trips, for the continual dashing and crashing and splashing of this outcast of the wild would have spread only panic in his wonderland, sending all creatures scuttling to their hiding-places and leaving for the naturalist almost a blank day. For the pampered pet-dog of lonely women and of the fashionable, degraded as it has been into a mere toy, there was only compassion. On the other hand, for those that perform some of the work of the world, the true servants and friends of man, he had all respect—chief among them being the rough-haired, eloquent-eyed sheep-dog, whose training is lingered over delightedly in *A Shepherd's Life*.

As companion-pieces to gaunt old Caesar and the many dogs seen through the memory of Caleb Bawcombe, one remembers patient Pechicho, with the "profoundly wise baboon-like expression" on his extraordinarily long, "spectacled" face, who came limping from nowhere to help drive home laggard sheep and who later, even though he seemed to enjoy being teased and mauled around "most unmercifully" by the Hudson children, vanished just as mysteriously; the great, lumbering, and obedient dog who, when he reached spraying range of a skunk after much goading, dropped down as if shot dead and, as soon as he could move again, made a bee-line over the vast plain to the nearest mud-bank; the little, long-haired red bitch who, dragging her drowned pups from a shallow pool, buried them, and until their bodies were furtively removed, keened nightly over their graves; and that further justification of Bacon's encomium, the dog who refused to leave the body of his slain master and for two days, until overtaken by exhaustion, kept sallying forth against the besieging vultures. Of fuller sketches, comparable to those of the blind old retriever and boundlessly energetic Jack, there is that of the little red dog of Regent Street, who, by barking a false alarm, succeeded in stealing a large bone from a starving lurcher, and the amusing one of big, shaggy, good-natured Dandy, who, finding it difficult to navigate his way home after quenching his thirst from the basin under a leaky beer keg, "would emit a low growl and show his teeth" whenever mockingly offered a sip of this beverage.

In comparison with "the good honest dog," the feline-minded fox is "like the picturesque and predatory gipsy to the respectable member of the community. He is a rascal, if you like, but a handsome red rascal, with a sharp, clever face and a bushy tail, and good to meet in any green place." Here is the handsome fellow Hudson chanced upon in a glade of Savernake Forest:

Standing on that carpet of vivid green spring grass, with the clear morning sunlight full on him, his red colour took an intensity and richness never previously seen. In form he appeared no less distinguished than in colour. His sharp, subtle face, large, leaf-shaped pointed ears, black without and white within, and graceful bushy tail, gave him the appearance of a dog idealised and made beautiful; and he was to the rough brown or red common dog what the finest human type—a model for a Phidias or a Praxiteles—is to a Connemara peasant or a Greenlander.

Besides the vulpine sketches already pointed out, there is that of two sets of cubs playing with half-grown rabbits in the moonlight while their mothers were away, pursuing one another round and round, a rabbit often turning abruptly and leaping over its pursuer; a fox who lost his leg in a trap but lived to a rare old age on the cliffs of Devon; and another, iron-grey and tawny colored, standing on his hind legs, his ears at the keyhole of a hut on the western border of the Argentine, listening to the dulcet sounds of a flute played by a lonely sheep-rancher.

The incorruptible cat, subtle in intelligence and impenetrable of soul, with something in it still of the tiger burning bright, always intrigued Hudson beyond the other "lower animals that live with or near us," and its comparative want of sociability, like that of "the human hunter in the wilderness or the angler by the brook," was attributed to its solitary way of life. To the one already glimpsed might be added, though none of them so interesting as Rrou or Calvin or Basta, Caleb's otter-spirited tabby, who met his death on a railroad track, hypnotized by the long parallel stretch of shining steel and the sight of an oncoming train; the mother who, never quite satisfied with her kittens' quarters, applied to her dog-friend again and again to help transfer them to a still more cozy nook of the house; and Warder, who, upon learning telepathically that his strange-acting mother was being chloroformed in a distant room, "jumped up and rushed to the door, uttering a series of unearthly cries, . . . then furiously clawed at the door to get out, and finally collapsed in a forlorn heap on the floor."

Hudson was not an angler, nor a patient listener to the tales of anglers, for it seemed to him that the person who "catches, or tries to catch a fish, must tell you something to astonish and fill you with envy and admiration." So, unlike most of the out-of-door essayists, he gives us but few episodes out of that strange, remote world, the piscatorial, and no individualized portraits. Of marine mammals, there are a few, largely seen, however, through the eyes of another: an exciting duel in the bay of St. Ives between an eight-foot conger and a seal, the eel with his teeth fastened tenaciously in the head of his adversary and constantly wriggling his black body out of reach, whilst the seal kept crying savagely; a lonely baby seal, lost from his mother, who came to look upon the friendly ferryman, whose boat he followed like a spaniel, "as a sort of companion—perhaps as a seal of curious habits, which looked a little like an adult seal, but progressed in a somewhat different manner, keeping always to the surface of the water and swimming with the aid of two long wing-like fins"—and who, before his friend could intervene, had his brains wantonly "scattered on the water" by a sportsman passenger.

There are a number of sketches of smaller beasts before which one should like to linger: a mole who, while using his twitching muscles to throw off dirt after a swim in the ground, looked like "a black ball spinning round so rapidly as to give . . . the misty appearance of a revolving wheel or the wings of a hovering hawkmoth"; and a pampean mouse, who, with some trepidation (for Hudson kept standing by), removed her squeaking, blind and naked offspring, one by one, to a completely hidden spot in the nearby stubble. The graceful friskings and scamperings of that bright-eyed, dynamic little rodent, the squirrel, "blithe-hearted" as a bird "and as volatile in disposition," usually brought Hudson to a halt; and a fight between two of them, with all its "amazingly quick" doublings, "feints, attack, flight, and chase," seemed to him one of the prettiest of spectacles amidst the greenwood trees. The most interesting portrait is that of the squirrel who, like the discontented one of childhood memory, sought for a happier hunting-ground down the coast of Norfolk, only to find himself marooned in the middle of a swirling current on the outermost channel-pole of the harbor of Wells-next-the-Sea. The sensitivity Hudson ascribed to the wing-membranes of the bat belongs, as we now know, to the use of supersonic squeaks in radar fashion. But there remains in the memory the picture of him standing in a deep Selborne lane, spinning his pliable cane above his head in order to ascertain whether a pair of these eldrich creatures, shuttling over him in their broken-bone way, would continue to make vicious little swoops at his objectionably striped cap.

For that inveterate enemy of rodents, the malignant-eyed weasel, as well as for its larger cousin, the stoat, he had a considerate word.

> Even as the jungle tiger . . . and the roaring lion strike with panic the wild cattle and antelopes and herds of swine, so does this miniature carnivore, this fairy tiger of English homesteads and hedges, fill with trepidation the small deer he hunts and slays with his needle teeth—Nature's scourge sent out among her too prolific small rodents; her little blood-letter who relieves her and restores the balance. And therefore he, too, with his flat serpent head and fiery killing soul, is a "dear" creature, being, like the poet's web-footed beasts of an earlier epoch, "part of a general plan."

We see one of these fairy tigers despatching a terrified field vole with his sharp teeth and, upon being momentarily deprived of his conquest, uttering such sorrowful and softly musical sounds as to make the interloper as ashamed of himself as if he "had teased a pretty bright-eyed little child by keeping his cake or apple until [he] had made him cry"; another, in the process of hypnotizing some susceptible birds in a woods near Boldre, "wriggling and spinning round with such velocity that his shape became indistinguishable"; and a whole troop of pampean weasels, in appearance much like little friars in black robes and grey cowls, performing as intricate a dance over the burrows of a vizcacha village as that of water-beetles on the surface of a pool.

For convenience' sake, it may be well to pause a moment to view a cluster of sketches of batrachians and reptiles before continuing on to the collection of birds: a burly, pampean wrestling frog who so surprised Hudson with the suddenness and violence of his grip that he was able to effect an escape; a toad half-way up a down on Salisbury Plain—very dark amidst eye-bright and daisies and milkwort—who, after being set upon Hudson's knee and fed with flies, looked as if he were "carved out of a piece of black stone" with two shining topazes for eyes; and another, "painfully crawling a few inches" along a hot, dusty road near Silchester and then "sitting up and gazing with his yellow eyes over the forty yards of that weary *via dolorosa* which still had to be got over before he could bathe and make himself young for ever in [the] river of life."

The most arresting of this cluster—none of them, though, so spectacular as some of Crèvecoeur and Waterton and Ditmars—are those of serpents, the graceful beauty of whose lines had been somewhat neglected by Hudson's major predecessors in the out-of-door essay. Western man's hostility toward the entire ophidian race had its origin, so he thought, not only in our remembrance of the melancholy event that took place in Eden but also in "our ignorance concerning serpents and the amount of injury they are able to do us" and in "our superstitious dread of swift and unexpected death." And this hostility is maintained in us primarily through early training. Even Hudson in his boyhood rambles was struck with horror at the sight of a serpent. But, upon further acquaintance, horror changed into "a sense of a mysterious being, dangerous on occasion as when attacked or insulted, and able in some cases to inflict death with a sudden blow, but harmless and even friendly or beneficent towards those who [regard] it with kindly and reverent feelings." And with this deeper sense came an appreciation of its strange and singular beauty. Usually when he speaks of these "lords of life," there come into his expression a certain tenderness and intensity, as if there survived in him, as in D. H. Lawrence and many Hindus, something of the veneration and love of serpents characteristic of primitive peoples.

In addition to the dreaded *vivora de la cruz* that had been his bed-fellow as he lay wounded in a rude cabin in the Patagonian wilderness and the many colubrine snakes that hibernated under the flooring of *Las Acacias* and kept up a hissing conversation of considerable variety throughout the night, there should be mentioned, to round out this group in the Hudsonian procession of animals, the long, mysterious serpent in the barren weedy ground near the edge of the moat of *Las Acacias* that slowly flowed across the instep of the terrified young Hudson like a coal-black current of quicksilver; a pair of adders at bask in a sequestered spot in the New Forest, their broad, zigzag bands an inky black against the straw-colored bed of dry fern, undisturbed by the pieces of scarlet cloth being dropped upon them. And, finally, there is that panoramic picture of colubrines which, because of a drought, had gathered in vast numbers in the swales of the pampas, "all lying motionless, stretched out full length, and looking like dark yellow or tan-coloured ribbons, thrown" on vivid green grass. When Hudson dismounted and approached any one of the dozen that were constantly in sight, he was greeted with a fine display of rage, for these harmless serpents have, as a means of protection, the gift of mimicking "the fierce, threatening gestures and actions" of the gangsters of their race.

ETHEREAL MINSTRELS, PILGRIMS OF THE SKY

Before we begin to note some of the innumerable avian figures animating Hudson's panoramas—as memorable in their way as those painted by Audubon and Thorburn—it would be well to pause and consider why birds mean a great deal to many of us, lending, as they do, more beauty and luster to the natural world than any other form of animal life and becoming in our imagination, as in the Egyptian representation of the sun, the Greek of the soul, and the Christian of the Holy Ghost, "the symbol . . . of all that is highest in the spiritual world." Why is it that a goodly proportion of us earthbound creatures, when asked what form we should prefer if our own were denied us, choose that of a bird? How could a man like Lord Grey of Fallodon, for long one of the chief players on the political stage of Europe, say that "the pleasure of seeing and listening" to birds is "purer and more lasting than any pleasures of excitement, and, in the long run, 'happier than personal success' "? More particularly, how came Hudson to declare that it had always been his "ambition and principal delight to see and hear every bird at its best" and that, had it been within his power, he would have chosen to seek out wild birds as Ulysses did knowledge, following them like sinking stars until he became "a name for always wandering with a hungry heart"?

One of the reasons for the popularity of birds is their accessibility: more than beasts, they bring the wild into our daily lives. Sparrows and, in many places, pigeons and starlings are, like the poor, with us always. But, given the least encouragement, many of the less common species will gather round our dwelling-places, even our most urban ones, and suspend their procreant cradles from every coign of vantage in shrubbery or on barn and house. It is only on Stupidity Street, where the people do not even realize what valuable allies they can be in our incessant and dubious struggle against weeds and vast armies of destructive insects, that the boughs are empty and no birds sing. So many-specied and so widely distributed are these allies that most of us need wander but a short distance from our doorsteps to gather a varied flock of them into the aviary of our memory. Certainly it was, for the most part, their presence on the pampas in vast and multifarious numbers that determined Hudson's absorption in them.

South America can well be called the great bird continent, and I do not believe that any other large area on it so abounded with bird life as this very one where I was born and reared and saw, and heard, so much of birds from my childhood that they became to me the most interesting things in the world. Thus, the number of species known to me personally, even as a youth, exceeded that of all the species in the British Islands, including the sea or pelagic species that visit our coasts in summer. . . .[12]

It was not only the number of species known to me, but rather the incalculable, the incredible numbers in which some of the commonest kinds appeared, especially when migrating.

The autumnal migration . . . began in February when the weather was still hot, and continued for three long months, . . . [during which] the sight and sound of passage birds was a thing of every day, of every hour, so long as the light lasted, and after dark from time to time the cries of the night-travellers came to us from the sky. . . .

I can almost say that when I first opened my eyes it was to the light of heaven and to the phenomenon of bird migration—the sight of it and the sound of it.

The bird is, moreover, one of the loveliest and most varied of living forms—to Hudson, supreme in beauty. Though some are better proportioned than others—the thrushes coming perhaps nearest to perfection among the smaller birds and the peregrine falcon among the larger—all their lines, from the dainty ones of the hummingbird to the fantastic or noble ones of the lyre-bird and the eagle, flow gracefully. Their carriage—geese with their high chests, penguins like pygmies in evening dress—is more vertical than that

---

[12]   There are at least 350 species of the tyrant-bird and about 250 of the wood-hewers. Thus these two families alone "outnumber all the species of birds in Europe from the Eagle to the Wren" (*Birds of La Plata,* p. 163). Change *thus these two families* to *songsters,* and the statement will be almost as accurate.

of beasts and thus more suggestive of the human posture, and by raising their wings while standing still, they assume "the angel pose." All are harmoniously colored: some, like the starling and the pigeon, in modest black and blues and greys touched with iridescence, and others, like the sacred quetzal and the crested cock-of-the-rock, in greens and oranges and scarlets "that far outshine an eastern king's array." And often their eyes, from the "drop of pity [that's] a wren's eye" to the smouldering fires of the eagle-owl, have in them the lights of gems. The desire to feast his eyes upon these volant creatures as one can on a flower became "so insistent and so intense" in Hudson as a boy that he trapped and for a short time kept them in a large cage.

Unlike flowers and gems, birds have the gift of flight, the most unearthly and wonderful quality of their beauty. And the expression of their winged bodies across the wide fields of the sky is amazingly diverse: goldfinches and flickers rising and dipping as though flying low over a rolling sea; gulls flapping slowly in the dawn, "shedding white rings of tumult"; thousands of geese or starlings cleaving the air in formations so precise that no two of them seem ever to touch wings; terns, kestrels, and peregrine falcons hovering in concentrated might over their prey; skylarks and crested screamers climbing the air to cloudy heights; and, most marvellous of all solo performances—indeed, of all methods of locomotion—that of the eagle, the condor, or the albatross soaring athwart the blue depths of the empyrean with scarcely a quiver in its great, broad pinions. So marked is the variety of wing-expression within even certain common species that it never stales. Thus, after gazing upon the flight of gulls and jackdaws along the Cornish coast, Hudson exclaims:

> I watch and am never tired of watching their play. They rise and fall and circle, and swerve to this side and to that, and are like sportive flies in a room which has the wind-roughened ocean for a floor, and the granite cliffs for walls, and the vast void sky for ceiling. The air is their element: they float on it and are borne by it, abandoned to it, effortless, even as a ball of thistledown is borne; and then, merely by willing it, without any putting forth of strength, without a pulsation, to rise vertically a thousand feet, to dwell again and float upon an upper current, to survey the world from a greater altitude and rejoice in a vaster horizon. To fly like

that! To do it all unconsciously, merely by bringing this or that
set of ten thousand flight muscles into play, as we will to rise, to
float, to fall, to go this way or that—to let the wind do it all
for us, as it were, while the sight is occupied in seeing and the
mind is wholly free! The balloons and other wretched machines to
which men tie themselves to mount above the earth serve only to
make the birds' lot more enviable.[13]

Many another, as far back as Archytas and Icarus, has yearned for
the same power: to open his arms wide and launch himself into
immensity!

The mating of birds and their attachment to home, both of
which are more humanlike than with beasts, bring them close to us
emotionally. Although there is probably less actual courtship and
surely less exercise of the sense of beauty in the selection of a mate
than is ascribed to them by popular fancy, the delicate suit the cock
pays the hen, unlike the indiscriminate rutting characteristic of the
rest of the animal kingdom, suggests a romantic attitude toward
love. The sight of a male making advances with a suggestive bit
of nesting material in his beak and, later, feeding his mate as she
sits on the nest is a very pretty and eloquent one. So also is the
solicitude for the young, which occasionally leads to daring and
self-sacrificial deeds. "Witness the pewit—the mother bird, when
you have discovered or come near her downy little one," exclaims
Hudson; "could any human mother, torn with the fear of losing her
babe, show her unquiet and disturbed state in a plainer, more under-
standable way!" [14] Human, rather than beastlike, too, is the bird's
maintenance of the marital ties—almost all species, including the
parasitic cowbird and the highly gregarious starling, being monoga-
mous and many of them pairing for life. The sexual motive is thus

---

13 Warde Fowler gives similar testimony: "I may well watch [the wood-wren]
for half an hour, and feel as much indebted to the sight of his delicate form and
harmonious motion as I should to the contemplation of the gracefullest of Greek
vases or the purest melody of Mozart" (*Summer Studies of Birds and Books,*
London, 1895, p. 62).

14 Some ornithologists would demur at this statement. Louis Halle, for example,
says, "I cannot imagine avian anguish [at the loss of fledglings]. The valor with
which birds defend their young seems more an unfeeling response to the practical
impulses which nature has imposed on them than a matter of deep parental devotion. To the end of racial survival, and no other, birds are the most practical
creatures imaginable" (*Birds against Men,* New York, 1938, p. 54).

often transcended by the enjoyment the pair find in each other's companionship.

Helping to maintain these ties is, as with human beings, the mutual love of home. Birds will cling tenaciously to their bailiwick even when robbed year after year of eggs and young, and when, through exploitation by man, it has lost its original charm. And since for most of them home means two widely separated and dissimilar spots, their birthplace and their winter resort, the home-call seems to be ideally combined with the longing for some far-off place. In order to satisfy this *Sehnsucht*, which twice a year reaches the intensity of a passion, they make epic flights across vast stretches of continent and ocean, the little arctic tern, for instance, performing the sublime flight between the Arctic and the Antarctic via Canada and Europe and the west coast of Africa. No other spectacle of animal life on this globe has the grandeur of this cyclic oscillation of millions upon millions of birds, "wailing their way from cloud to cloud," and it is so unlike all the others "as to give it among natural things something of the supernatural." Spring is not spring to many of us until those that left us in the autumn have returned and, one species following another, put upon it their official seal.

The mastery of the air that birds enjoy, and the limitlessness of their domain, have done much to heighten man's own sense of freedom and joy. The spirit of no other creature seems so free, and with freedom, as Michelet found especially in the swallow and Shelley in the skylark, comes a corresponding degree of "clear keen joyance." This "free, joyous, joy-giving" quality, which is greater in birds than in mammals and shows itself in more diverse ways, Hudson regarded as the "best thing" in the winged world, and, though at times giving man a sense of apartness from them as from "the fairies or angels," it has beautifully liberated his imagination, not only in potent symbols of religion and of nationality, but in the creations of many individual artists, from Aristophanes and Hsü Hsi to Shelley and Meredith and Respighi.

Most intimate of all the bonds between men and birds is that of music, their calls and songs being the most varied and exquisite of outdoor sounds and, along with flight, the most vivid expression of their joy. In our "images of bird life at its best," so Hudson reminds us, sight and sound, more intertwined "than in any other order of beings," can hardly be dissociated: the voice, whether "loud or low, is aerial too, in harmony with the form." Being denied some of the other means of expression, birds have concentrated on the vocal art, and as a result "their voices exceed those of all other creatures, human or animal, in power and brilliance and purity and all lovely qualities, if we except the sounds which are lovelier to us because of their [associations], or, in other words, because they are human and ours." The annual spring *Meistersingenfest*, the daily matins and vespers, the impromptu recitals throughout the day and the year, the infinite variety of the calls and cries—especially when they seem to have as their burden some human intimations or become interfused with our deeper experiences—can be profoundly moving. Thus the song of the skylark pierced the hearts of Shelley and Aksakoff, and the sweet, plaintive strains of the songsparrow "often brought tears" to the eyes of John Muir. "Whenever a man hears" the wood thrush, says Thoreau, "he is young" once again, "and Nature is in her spring. Wherever he hears it, it is a new world and a free country, and the gates of heaven are not shut against him."

For these and various other reasons—the deft craftsmanship of their nests, the pied beauty of their eggs, the intensity and yet fragility of their lives, the large element of the mysterious in them —birds are to many of us Nature's most eloquent expression. The study of them, appealing strongly to the detective in us all, has been aptly described as the most scientific of the sports and the most sporting of the sciences. "The bird-watcher's life is an endless succession of surprises. Almost every day he appears fated to witness some habit, some action, which he had never seen or heard of before, and will perhaps never see again." Thus it was that birds came to be central in Hudson's experience, the most provocative stimulus to his imagination; and to them he devoted a third of his writings.

In the strict sense of the term, he never became a great ornithologist. Although the two volumes of *Argentine Ornithology*, his chief claim to such a title, are still, after sixty years, the standard work in their field, the more purely scientific parts, it must be remembered, were not of his composition. Many of the virtues of the scientific mind were his, particularly, as exemplified in his studies of the parasitic instinct of the Argentine and the screaming cowbirds, carefulness and detachment of observation, freshness and

richness of speculation. And, living out his early life in a region
where the cataloguing of the wild life was not complete, he was
able to achieve one of the supreme ambitions of an ornithologist,
the discovery of species new to science—a spine-tail (*Synalloaxis
hudsoni*) and the black tyrant (*Cnipolegus hudsoni*). (By only a
few months did he miss having another bird, the screaming cowbird, likewise distinguished by his name.) But his want of any great
skill in morphology, as indicated in his dependence upon another
for the writing of the scientific introduction to *British Birds*, and
also his failure to master all the pertinent scientific knowledge then
available—the outcome of certain deficiencies in early training and
of a deep distrust of the museum ornithologist in particular and the
purely scientific or abstract mind in general—would have kept him
from becoming a Seebohm, a Saunders, a Chapman, or a Murphy.

In the realm of bird-psychology, however, Hudson must be
acclaimed a great pioneer. Having mastered, through long and intimate acquaintance, the language of birds—a language of sound and
motion—he was able to eradicate many a deep-rooted misconcep-
tion of their habits and mental characteristics and to reveal many
of their secrets. Yet even here, though certain traits are occasionally
used to hold an essay together, he rarely presents his findings in the
scientific manner of, say, Edmund Selous, Eliot Howard or Edward
Armstrong, among his most distinguished successors in this realm.
Instead, wishing to keep his ornithology subordinate to aesthetic
appreciation, he usually scatters his observations on avian folkways,
as on those of insects and beasts, here and there among many other
matters. In this manner, he was able to bring birds home to the
hearts of men as only a few others have succeeded in doing—St.
Francis, Audubon, Michelet, and Burroughs.

The intelligence of birds was rated by him far above that of
their position in the scale of being,[15] and this trait serves as a convenient theme for the grouping of a number of his portraits and
episodes. We see yellow-breasted marsh-troupials taking turns on a
thistle-top to act as sentries for the feeding flock, and a wise gander,
who had been caught in a trap and readily tamed, assuming the

---

[15] The tendency among contemporary observers, such as Howard and Huxley,
is to depreciate avian intelligence, placing much of it on the instinctive level of
insects.

guardianship over a heterogeneous flock of barnyard fowl, particularly seeing to it that they were all cooped at night against the foray of a fox. And, against a grey fresco of autumn, we see a flock of geese immediately shedding all fear during their daily visits to a certain protected marsh on the Norfolk coast, sitting or standing there in every attitude of repose. It was indeed largely the intelligence of the wild goose that made the shooting of them seem to Hudson like "shooting at a human being."

The sportive spirit, present in even that mere ghost of a bird, the solemn heron, is richly illustrated. At times it expresses itself in aerial frolics, the highest form of athleticism, as when the lapwing rises high in the sky, only to hurl himself "downwards in the approved suicidally insane manner, with sudden doublings this way and that, and other violent eccentric motions designed to make him lose his head; and finally to come at fullest speed within an inch, or as much less than an inch as he can, of dashing himself into a pulp on the ground below." At other times, the love of play expresses itself in mischief, a primitive sort of humor (of which man is not, as has often been claimed, the sole possessor), as with the magpie who pilfered the coin upon which a family depended for its weekly provisioning and hid it edgewise between the wooden floor and the side of his cage. And, yet again, as with kittens and children, it assumes the form of a mock-attack: a ringed dotterel alighting on the back of a companion, almost upsetting him, and then folding his wings and standing nonchalantly by as if nothing had happened; a chimango hawk, after terrifying a squadron of coots with a sudden swoop, merely eyeing them for a while and then flying quietly away; a pet jay dashing from his perch and just brushing Hudson's head with his wings whenever no eyes were on him, and also enjoying the game of catching shillings tossed in the air and arranging them in a neat pile.

Frequently with birds, play takes the more aesthetic form of dance. Among the sketches not already singled out are those of a pet trumpeter making its matutinal rounds of the bedrooms of a rancho, saluting each person upon awakening "by dancing about the floor, bowing its head and dropping its wings and tail, continuing the performance until its presence was noticed and it was spoken to"; a dozen jacanas "forming a close cluster," and, to the accompaniment of "short, excited, rapidly repeated notes," displaying, like

loosely grouped flags, their satiny, greenish-golden wings—some
holding them up vertically and motionless, and others, either vibrating them rapidly half-open or waving them up and down in the
slow, measured manner of a butterfly; and, seen against the arching
sky, a flock of a hundred white-faced ibis, one moment spreading
out in a long straight line, and in another, after suddenly throwing
themselves together like a cloud of starlings, continuing their journey by re-forming like a regiment, now in the figure of a phalanx,
and later in that of a half-moon or triangle.

How such intricate evolutions as those of the ibis or, to take a
more familiar performance, the wheelings and whirlings of the
starling, can be so smoothly executed—a whole flock appearing to
be moved by one mind or impulse—Hudson attributed, not, as
Selous does, to thought-transference, but rather to the almost instantaneous heeding of the leader's signal and to the assistance that a
delicate sense of touch gives to eye and ear.

> It is a sensation of repulsion informing each member of the flock
> of the nearness to it of others, and prevents them from touching
> or striking against and impeding one another. When the flock turns
> or changes its formation, it may be observed that while numbers
> of birds are streaming away to this or that side with accelerated
> speed, others, at points where confusion would seem inevitable,
> suspend their flight, and remain almost motionless at equal distances
> apart until the moment comes for them to join in the swift movement.

Another trait that serves as a theme holding together a large
number of sketches is the pleasure some birds find in the presence
of members of other species—a pleasure that varies from symbiosis
or cupboard love to disinterested friendship. Among no English vertebrates is the symbiotic relationship so strong as that between the
spur-wing plover and the African crocodile, but, of a less pronounced sort, we are presented with several illustrations, such as
that of the jackdaw (reminiscent of the one in the hind sketch)
probing for parasites around the ribs of a donkey lying stretched
out on a bed of moss in the midst of a Cornish furze-thicket, while
two other donkeys stand by, "gazing at the busy bird and probably
envying their comrade his good luck." Perhaps, as Hudson thought,
the main reason the robin, of all English birds, seems the friendliest
toward man—especially noticeable when a person is active in his

garden—is that he finds in him, as the swallows do in the horses galloping over the pampas, a good flusher of quarry.

Of disinterested friendship, in which the chief pleasure is that experienced in the mere presence of another, there are also some sketches: a sandpiper and a blue bittern living together like two friendly hermits, the dainty piping of the one, when disturbed, contrasting wonderfully with the harsh, grating scream of the other; a pheasant waiting to be joined at their trysting-place by a blackbird before proceeding with his evening meal; and a swan buffeting a fisherman "with the greatest fury" for hooking his solitary companion, a large trout, with whom he had, in spite of the ancient enmity of their tribes, moved about the lake and rested "like one being." Some of the friendships are with human beings (an unforgettable experience for any one of us) : a pheasant who cherished an affection for a woman, attending her on walks and putting himself forward as her guardian; and a jackdaw that attached himself, not to his rescuer and provider, but to another boy in the neighborhood, and so eager was he to be with his chosen companion that he "had to be caught and confined every day during school and church hours." And frequently, as with the tits, wrens, chaffinches, yellowhammers, dunnocks, thrushes, and blackbirds Hudson saw congregated at the foot of a crumbling wall of ancient Calleva, a fraternal feeling will hold together flocks of diverse species for hours at a time and even for whole days.

The great vernal and autumnal drama of migration, carrying the imagination to the dark backward and abysm of time, continually fascinated him. Though never conveying so consolatory a cosmic message as it did to those with the grace of faith, from Job to Bryant, it provoked in him, more than any other event in the animal world, a sense of the marvellousness and the mystery of life. Rejecting inherited memory, popular with the leaders of his day, as the prime cause, Hudson held to the explanation that suggested itself during his youth, before he had access to much scientific knowledge: the inciting force of this timeless drama is the sense of polarity, "the pull of the north." Other solutions have been advanced more recently: accidental wanderings becoming habitual and, through age-long repetition, instinctive; the effect of waxing and waning daylight upon the gonads; and, one of the latest, the hunger for a certain vitamin found in the north especially conducive to breeding.

Hudson's theory, limited in scope though it is, has at least this advantage: it helps explain the uncanny sense of direction that guides birds over wide wastes of desert and ocean, a sense that, though dependent also upon the Coriolis force, owes much to a susceptibility to terrestrial magnetism.

The way in which the passion of migration comes upon birds, manifesting itself in a growing unrest and wildness, and bears flock after flock of them unresistingly aloft upon long, perilous journeys, reminded him of "globes of thistledown, resting in still weather on the grass, trembling at the first faint movement of the air, and finally lifted and carried away by the increasing wind." If for any reason they are held back from taking off on their flyways, as the swifts in *Afoot in England* were by the necessity of feeding late broods or as many are by the love of home (an explanation that Hudson does not sufficiently stress), their torment gives them the appearance of "those doomed wretches in the halls of Eblis whose hearts were in a blaze of unquenchable fire, and who, every one with hands pressed to his breast, went spinning round in an everlasting agonised dance."

Many are the scenes in Hudson's portfolio of this spectacular drama: purple swallows from the cliffs overhanging the Rio Negro at their autumnal muster, first hovering above the tall Lombardy poplars along the banks or wheeling wildly about in the blustery wind, and, "as occasion offered, dropping down, a few at a time, to cling, like roosting locusts, to the thin vertical branches, clustering thicker and thicker until the high trees looked black with them"; buff-breasted sandpipers, on an early lap of their prodigious flight to arctic nesting-grounds, wave after wave of them passing in disciplined order for days at ten-minute intervals over a spot two miles from the Hudson rancho; glossy ibis, in flocks of fifty to a hundred, passing in rapid succession for hours, "now soaring high in the air, . . . then descending with a graceful curve towards the earth," and invariably, "on coming to water, dropping down and sweeping low over the surface as [though] wanting to alight and refresh themselves, but unable to overcome the impulse urging them to the north." *Hampshire Days* ends with several pictures of immense numbers of migrants, looking at a distance like black confetti being blown along by gusts of wind.

The sight and sound of birds in large numbers seemed to Hudson, at least for many days thereafter, "above all the delights this spectacular world can afford."

> It is not merely that the pleasure in the single bird is intensified, or doubled or increased a hundred-fold. . . . There is a new element in it which makes it different in character. The sight dwells with pleasure on a pleasant landscape; but if we then ascend a hill and look upon the scene from that higher standpoint a quite different feeling is experienced; the wider horizon is a revelation of vastness, of a greatness which is practically new, since the mind had previously become attuned to earth as viewed from the lower level. Now we get the element of sublimity. So, in the case of a large bird seen in flocks and vast numbers—seen and heard; it is a sudden revelation of wild life in its nobler aspect—of its glorious freedom and power and majesty.

Many experiences of this sort, other than those with migrants, are vividly recorded: an immense swarm of sparrows in an abandoned Cornish tin-mine, so numerous that when alarmed they poured out of the pit like a column of smoke; golden plovers so dense on the marshy ground near *Las Acacias* as to resemble a living, moving floor, and the tangle of their thousands of voices like the wind blowing on many "tight-drawn wires of varying thicknesses"; and an army of military starlings, beaks and scarlet breasts all pointed one way, probing the turf of the pampas, the hindmost constantly flying forward to alight in advance of those in the front line, the total effect being that of a huge, elongated mass rolling slowly over the ground.

Even more exhilarating was the spectacle of immense concourses of large birds. Crested screamers, "in size like a swan, in shape like a lapwing," afforded Hudson a number of such experiences, in one of which many flocks of them, each composed of about five hundred, were grouped around a lake on the pampas, awaiting their turn to sing. "Presently one flock near [him] began singing, and continued their powerful chant for three or four minutes; when they ceased the next flock took up the strains, and after it the next, and so on until the notes of the flocks on the opposite shore came floating strong and clear across the water—then passed away, growing fainter and fainter, until once more the sound approached [him] travelling round to [his] side again." In England, the most thrilling

experiences of this sort were with the wild geese over the marshe
near Wells in Norfolk, in one of which four thousand of then
were stretched across the cloudless, late afternoon sky in three skein
of immense length until they reached their roosting-place on the
flat sands, above which they remained stationary or slowly circled
around at the same height, the skeins and interspersed phalanxe
merging into one vast cloud, and then descended, "a few at a time
detaching themselves from the throng and sweeping obliquely down
wards, while others, singly or in small parties, with half-closed
wings appeared to hurl themselves towards earth with extraordinary
violence."

The great variety of birds already gathered in these pages indi
cates the remarkable catholicity of Hudson's taste. Taking the
"auspices" in two contrasting regions created in his memory twin
aviaries, and the continual comparison of one with the other helped
him, as it did in the presentation of landscape, to a just appraisal
of each. At times, especially when the sight of a certain bird o
group of birds has him enthralled, he may speak deprecatingly of
other species, for, like the Shakespearean scholar who always said
that the play then being read was the bard's best, Hudson had his
rook and wild geese and sparrowhawk days as well as those fo
"the little dicky-birds," the starling, the pipit, the swallow, the
marsh-warbler, and the willow-wren.

> Just as nature as a whole has "special moments" that have "special
> grace," so it is with bird life; and with the individual bird, if seen
> at its best in certain conditions and in harmony wth its surroundings,
> then, whether it be the jacana . . . or the floating swan, as Ruskin
> saw it, glorified by the setting sun, . . . that particular one will
> strike the beholder as the most perfect—as possessing a charm
> above the others, and as the living central gem of which all visible
> nature forms for the moment only the appropriate setting.

If a bird is slighted in one passage, he usually makes generous
amends in another.

Hudson's liking for the larger and, so he insisted, the nobler
birds—the "huge ones," as Warde Fowler playfully put it, that said
"solemnly over your head" and vanish "over the hill while you
adjust your glass"—seemed somewhat *outré* to many English bird
lovers. But it was he—brought up in a land where the "huge,'

najestic birds had not been banished or destroyed by collectors,
portsmen, and pheasant-breeders—who had the normal and more
ealthy attitude. As much as he too liked the birds that can be
bserved more intimately—those that "twitter and warble, and flit
ither and thither, flirting their feathers, and with their dainty grace-
ulness and airy, fairy ways wind themselves" round one's heart—
e felt less of a gulf between his mind and those of "the larger,
nore mammal-like, and therefore more human-like" birds, the
ninds, for example, of the various members of the sagacious cor-
ine family. Alone on the traditional desert isle, he would have
referred owls, who above all other species fostered in him a sense
f the mysterious, rather than Fowler's wagtails for companions.

Especially reprehensible to most of these critics was his spring-
ng admiration for the raptorial order, the natural enemies of the
ighly-prized songsters.

When pursued by a Hawk the Heron performs with marvelous
ease and grace an aerial feat unequalled by any other bird, namely
that of rising vertically to an amazing height in the air. The swift
vertical flight with which the pursued ascends until it becomes a
mere speck in the blue zenith, the hurried zig-zag flight of the
pursuer, rising every minute above its prey, only to be left below
again by a single flap of the Heron's wings, forms a sight of such
grace, beauty, and power as to fill the mind of the spectator with
delight and astonishment.

[It] is one of the sights of bird life which makes me envy the
sportsmen of the old time when falconry was followed and the
peregrine was flown, not at skulking magpies, as the way is with
our Hawking Club, but at noble heron.

lthough Hudson was careful to assure his readers that he was not
lvocating a return to falconry, passages such as these were taken
 indicate a certain want of humanity. Yet, it should be remem-
:red that not only did Hudson, like Audubon, hail from a country
here birds of prey were rampant (throughout a large portion of
)uth America the chimango hawk is the commonest bird known)
it it was one of the chief articles of his creed to persecute nothing.
nd in addition to giving height to the sky, "the sight of them and
e sound of their shrill reiterated cries completed and intensified
e effect of Nature's wildness and majesty."

This attitude of Hudson, it is interesting to note, chords wel
with a dominant note in contemporary verse. Nature does not appea
quite so red in tooth and claw to the present generation as she di
to that of Tennyson. The sight of a hawk in an aerial duel o
pouncing upon its prey will, of course, awaken in the poet sympath
for the intended victim—a sympathy qualified, however, by the reali
zation that it owes much of the brightness of its faculties and th
intensity of its experiences to the existence of its assailant—but i
will also arouse an admiration for the courage, the swiftness, an
the fierce beauty of the feathered wildcat. Both, after all, are onl
comporting themselves within the domain of their instincts an
thus fulfilling their lives. One of our leading poets, perceiving in
carnate in these creatures, as did the Egyptians, some of the chie
attributes of God, says he would "sooner, except the penalties, ki
a man than a hawk."

A large number of aerial corsairs, "fledged with desire of trans
gression," hurtle and soar and swoop in Hudson's landscapes:
carancho turning upon a lapwing tormenter, and, even though h
victim tried to lose itself amongst three hundred hovering an
screaming companions, seeking it out and bearing it away in it
talons, unopposed; a peregrine falcon, speed demon of the airway
flying up from her perch on Hudson's favorite red willow, circlin
high above the dovecote, and, when the terrified pigeons had reache
the proper height, striking down her chosen victim of the day wit
a blow of her claws, and, after a moment's pause in mid-air, dro
ping down for the pigeon and catching it in her talons before
touched the tree-tops; and a wood owl, who was the village p
until his spectral habit of "gliding about unseen in the darkness o
downy silent wings" and suddenly alighting with "demon claws
on anybody's shoulder terrorized the villagers, and who, after bein
struck down and severely injured by one of them and thus losin
"confidence in his human fellow-creatures," flew away to rejoin h
kindred of the wild.

The prize of this group is the sketch of the Magellanic eagl
owl, who, wounded by Hudson, was stung to such fury as to l
transformed into a monster of terrifying aspect, with the flame-li
eyes of a dragon.

Each particular feather stood out on end, the tawny barred tail spread out like a fan, the immense tiger-coloured wings wide open and rigid, so that as the bird, that had clutched the grass with his great feathered claws, swayed his body slowly from side to side— just as a snake about to strike sways his head, or as an angry watchful cat moves its tail—first the top of one, then of the other wing touched the ground. The black horns stood erect, while in the centre of the wheel-shaped head the beak snapped incessantly, producing a sound resembling the clicking of a sewing machine. This was a suitable setting for the pair of magnificent furious eyes, on which I gazed with a kind of fascination, not unmixed with fear when I remembered the agony of pain suffered on former occasions from sharp, crooked talons driven into me to the bone. The irides were of a bright orange colour, but every time I attempted to approach the bird they kindled into great globes of quivering yellow flame, the black pupils being surrounded by a scintillating crimson light which threw out minute yellow sparks into the air.

Among the other large or medium-sized birds in Hudson's landscapes, the corvine family, in which there is likewise something of the freebooter, figures prominently. The jackdaw, with his black cassock, grey hood, and mischievous little grey eyes, was to him a perennial source of entertainment, especially when frolicking about the spire of Salisbury and the façades of the Abbey church at Bath and of Wells Cathedral. In addition to the daws we have already seen de-ticking the hides of donkey, cow and deer, and struggling for places on the rims of the chimney-pots of St. Ives, there is the impudent fellow whom only a stunning rap on the head with a walking stick could cure of his persistence in pulling the buttons off the shoes of his little mistress; the daw so enamored of a parrot as to allow him to pluck out most of her feathers; and the colony of 'Bishop's Jacks" nest-building in their crude, blundering way among the sculptured potentates on the west front of Wells Cathedral.

There are vignetted many adventures with crows, which Hudson considered second only to ravens in "power, courage, and sagacity" but which never were to him the favorites they became to Burroughs and Archibald MacLeish: one, croaking with rage, vainly attempting to drive home a blow upon an insolent kestrel; a flock of them flying constantly around a house where death impended and "alighting on the roof, uttering their raucous cries and apparently in a great state of excitement"; and "a queer gaunt unfinished hobbledehoy-looking" fledgling, "with a head much too big for his body, a beak that resembled a huge nose, and a very monstrous mouth," emitting "his harsh, throaty hunger-call" to every passer-by—wagtail and rook and even Hudson himself!

One of the most impressive spectacles of English birdlife to him was the approach of a large company of rooks, each following the other "with slow deliberate motion at long intervals" and with appropriate solemn sounds, as though "in a funeral procession." The goings-on in rookeries fascinated him as they have many another bird-watcher from Virgil to Cobbett and Jefferies, and he gives us an intimate account of one of their social crises, in which one pair filched some sticks from the nest of another and, upon detection, seemed to consider themselves fortunate in not being summarily expelled from the colony. And in another sketch, hundreds of them are to be seen "circling like a black cloud" around a big tree from which a skinned horse had been hung by its hind legs, "clinging like a swarm of bees to the carcass, all fighting with one another for a place, screaming with excitement and tearing at the flesh . . . until nothing but the suspended skeleton remained." And of ravens, with their harsh, savage croak and "loud, angry bark, as if a deep-chested man" were baying "like a bloodhound," there are also several good sketches: a pair in the Mendips who, like Poe's messenger of doom, "invariably when a light was seen burning at a late hour in any cottage . . . would come and tap at the window"; and another of these long-lived creatures, in "sublime conflict" with a falcon above a cliff in Somerset, both mounting higher and higher into the sky, and occasionally, when locked together in close fighting, falling headlong for a great distance "like one bird"—a conflict similar to that witnessed by Williamson over the Needles on the Isle of Wight.

To this sedately colored, if not sedately mannered, corvine group there should be added the fifteen magpies, "like preternaturally shrewd and mischief-loving little boys," enjoying a game of romps amidst quietly feeding partridges and wood-pigeons in a yellow stubble field of a Sussex down, one magpie, unwilling to suffer a tamed creature in his presence, persistently keeping a domestic pigeon from associating with its wild kindred; and the uproarious spring convocation in Savernake Forest of the even more restless and chattering jays, summoned by a cry "louder, sharper, [and] more prolonged" than that of the carrion crow during its mating season—convocations that reminded Hudson of Wallace's description of the bird-of-paradise assemblies in the Malayan region.

Sea-fowl, as well as a delight in primeval places, drew him to inland marshes, the sedgy banks of streams, and the varying shores of the ocean. The impressiveness of sea-fronting granite cliffs is considerably enhanced by birds perching on their ledges, tier above tier, or flying to and fro athwart their faces—those along the highest ledge, seen from below, looking like mere varicolored specks. And their aerial maneuvers—gulls floating and wheeling slowly and exquisitely in a blue sky, "pouring out their insistent loud angry anxious cries," gannets sailing by "in an everlasting succession of beautiful curves and wave-like risings and fallings," geese spread in loose, clanging chains across the "day's enormous dome," egrets cleaving the air with measured beat like enormous white butterflies, herons and clarion-voiced crested screamers towering into the zenith (magnified as all of them frequently are by a strong sunlight)—give romance and sublimity to any coastal scene. Although there are not, proportionately, as many sea- as land-birds in Hudson's essays, a goodly number and variety can be seen winging their way across his sea- and shore-scapes.

In those of the west coast of Cornwall, most hauntingly depicted are the gulls, "flying about in an aimless way, dropping down at intervals as if to exchange remarks with those on the water," and then, like whitecaps taking wing, "wandering off again." Picturesque old St. Ives afforded these "wave-gleaners" not only a frequent largess but also an effective setting for their graceful movements. And Hudson has sketched them there "as a white cloud hanging over the harbour" and as a whirlwind of innumerable white forms enveloping the returning fishing fleet, scrambling madly for the small fishes and waste-matter cast overboard—each bird as it rises with a fish in its beak being "instantly swooped down upon and chased by others," all emitting a "tempest of hard, piercing, and grinding metallic noises." Along the same coast, we also see cormorants, of "an ugly reptilian look when fishing in the sea," but, when "standing erect and motionless, airing their spread wings," resembling birds in heraldry; and gannets, which, "when the sky is black with tempests and the tumbling ocean is all grey and white with whirling spindrift," appear like fragments of "wave and spray

and wind and cloud . . . torn away by the blast, into which guiding
spirit[s] or intelligent . . . particle[s have] been blown to make
[them] cohere and give [them] form and weight and indestruc-
tibility."

Of more individualized portraits and episodes of these three
sea-birds, there are the pair of cormorants expressing their nuptial
joy "by rubbing their snaky necks together, crossing and see-sawing
them, first on one side then the other, like knife and steel in the
butcher's hands," and, a few days later, the cock, with a devotion
rare with him, bringing the nesting-hen "twenty times an hour . . .
a bit of seaweed or a stick," which she ceremoniously accepts and,
bowing this way and that and putting it down and taking it up
again, gives back with a gesture bespeaking, "Dear, you must not be
so generous!"; the large flock of gannets fishing near the shore of
Sennen's Cove during a severe windstorm who, unable to lift themselves from the heavy sea when the gale suddenly ended in a perfect
calm, were flung by the enormous waves upon the beach, where
men and boys, waiting with sticks and iron bars, slaughtered them
"without mercy, even as shipwrecked men on this dreadful coast
in the ancient days had been slaughtered," and soon "the sands
were covered with their carcasses"; and the herring gull who broke
one of its wings against a rope or spar of a St. Ives boat as it
swooped for a discarded fish. The bird could not understand what
had happened to it:

> it made frantic efforts to rise, but the whole force exerted being
> in one wing merely caused it to spin rapidly round and round.
> These struggles eventually caused the shattered bone to break through
> the skin; the blood began to flow and redden the plumage on one
> side. This was again and again washed off in the succeeding struggles
> to rise, but every time a pause came the feathers were reddened
> afresh. At length the poor thing became convinced that it could no
> longer fly, that it could only swim, and at once ceasing to struggle
> it swam away from the boats and out towards the open bay. Hardly
> had it gone a dozen yards from the boat-side where it had fallen
> before some of the gulls flying near observed it for the first time,
> and dropping to within three or four yards of the surface hovered
> over it. Then a strange thing happened. Instantly, as if a shot
> had been fired to silence them, the uproar in the harbour ceased;
> the hundreds of gulls fighting on the water rose up simultaneously
> to join the cloud of birds above, and the whole concourse moved

silently away in one direction, forming a dense crowd above the wounded bird. In this formation, suspended at a height of about thirty yards over and moving with him, they travelled slowly out into the middle of the bay.

There are interesting groups of various members of the plover and duck families (which, in spite of the comparative smallness of some of them, are best included here): a spur-wing plover pecking sharply at the nose and hanging from the ear of a sheep lying almost upon her nest, until the sheep "fairly beaten, struggled to [its] feet, throwing the bird off, and lazily walked away, shaking [its] head repeatedly"; a mother coot drubbing her piggish brat, who, after gorging for twenty minutes straight (like "a hungry Italian greedily sucking down macaroni") on the many succulent stems of water-crocus fed him, refused to make way for his brother, and actually snatched from her a morsel meant for the other; and a flock of sheldrakes on the coast of Somerset, each cock, with his "curious sign-language," ceremoniously informing his mate when it was time for her to "go to her burrow to lay her egg," and never losing his temper when she displayed reluctance to enter the dark, narrow tunnel of an abandoned rabbit-burrow.

Geese, both wild and domestic, thoroughly endeared themselves to Hudson. "Only those who have lost their souls," he declares, "will fail to understand" why "a certain distinguished man of letters and church dignitary" lived "in the loneliest village on the dreary east coast . . . because it was the only spot in England in which, sitting in his own room, he could listen to the cry of the pink-footed goose." Among the sketches that would have delighted Ts'ui Po, Lü Chi, Ma Fên and other Chinese painters, who regarded this noble creature as the bird of *Yang*, the symbol of light and masculinity in Nature, are those of the white goose, motionless on a deep, glittering snowdrift, neatly side-stepping a man who, as the last move of an elaborate ruse, suddenly hurled himself at her; two upland geese saluting a friendly spectator in St. James's Park, "advancing with a quiet dignity" and uttering "a few soft low sounds, accompanied with certain graceful gestures," thereupon turning and leaving—not abruptly, but, like courtiers, half-pausing at intervals to turn "first to one side then the other, inclining their heads as they went"; a gander in high dudgeon because the garden-gate had been rudely closed against him and all but three of the flock he

had just led back from their forest feeding-grounds; and a pair on
their long journey across the pampas to their antarctic breeding
haunts, the goose, with one wing broken, "walking steadily on in a
southerly direction," while her mate,

> greatly excited, and calling loudly from time to time walked at a
> distance ahead, and constantly turned back to see and call to his mate,
> and at intervals of a few minutes he would rise up and fly, screaming,
> to a distance of some hundreds of yards; then finding that he had
> not been followed, he would return and alight at a distance of forty
> or fifty yards in advance of the other bird, and begin walking on as
> before. The female, . . . unable to fly, had set out on her long journey
> to the Magellanic Islands on her feet; and her mate, though called to
> by that mysterious imperative voice in his breast [the migratory im-
> pulse], yet would not forsake her; but flying a little distance to show
> her the way, and returning again and again, and calling to her with
> his wildest and most piercing cries, urged her still to spread her
> wings and fly with him to their distant home.

Among the birds of the Argentine, his favorite was the crested
screamer, as intelligent and as lofty in spirit as the goose and,
though without the elegance of the swan and the peacock, more
truly beautiful. After raising itself laboriously from the ground, this
heavy bird climbs the sky in the manner of the vulture and the
eagle, "sweeping round as it ascends" and "describing each succeeding circle with increasing grace," until its dark form appears like a
floating speck in the blue sky or vanishes from sight altogether into
the empyrean. And as though exulting "in its sublime power and
freedom," like the skylark it sings while it soars, its resounding notes
becoming "wonderfully etherealized by distance to a soft silvery
sound." Throughout the night, enormous flocks of them, all singing as with one powerful voice, "count the hours," making the plains
echo for miles around with sounds as of "thousands and tens of
thousands of great chiming bells." To the sketches of crested
screamers already pointed out there should be added the one of the
tame cock moving majestically about the chicken yard of an estancia,
tenderly mothering "forty little animated balls of yellow cotton"
entrusted to his care, and threatening with his wings a swarthy and
beardless peon, who was probably associated in his mind with the
savages responsible for the destruction of his early home; and that
of a pair of them rushing from the ground to welcome a fast

approaching storm and, after an enormous spiral upward, disappearing in the masses of black cloud lit by flashes of lightning—all the time, above the muttering thunder, jubilantly pouring out their loud and clear song.

Three other species should be included among these larger birds before turning to the smaller ones: the parrot, whose mimicking of human speech was deemed not "so wonderful as the imitative faculty of some mockingbirds" or the marsh-warbler; chanticleer, whose far-heard lusty proclamation in the dim silent hour of the dawn always seemed to Hudson "like a resurrection in which [he] had a part"; and that unbirdlike survival of an age when giants stalked among avians as well as mammals, the rhea, which, next to the tinamou in the feathered world, is best adapted to the grassy ocean of the pampas—its "commanding stature" and periscope-like neck giving it "a wide horizon," and its "dim, pale, bluish-grey" plumage, the color of cardoons, rendering it invisible in the haze of the distance. Of individualized figures, there are those of a very old and ragged Mexican parrot, "long fallen into the period of irregular or imperfect moult" in a Wiltshire inn, who violently rejected Hudson's blandishments of food and head-scratching but was utterly captivated by his Spanish, spoken as it was in the "caressing falsetto" of a native girl, which probably evoked in his bosom "some vague memory of a vanished time"; a cochin cockerel, "in the hobbledehoy stage of that ugliest and most ungraceful variety," dashing savagely at a bevy of martins as they kept dropping lightly down on the margin of a puddle to gather pellets of clay for their nests—the cochin looking like a Dogberry closing in on a flock of fairies; and a rhea running fleetly before a band of gauchos charging with twirling *bolas*, "one wing raised vertically, like a great sail—a veritable 'ship of the wilderness' "—and then, when hard pressed, suddenly doubling at right angles.

If Hudson had his geese and jackdaw and hawk days, he also had his days—indeed, more of them—for the "jocund lyttel fowles" of the fields and hedges: swallow, thrush, pipit, finch, robin, and even "the little bottle-tit whose minute body, stript of its feathers, may be put in a lady's thimble." More accessible for intimate acquaintance, more numerous and more varied, and, above all, gifted with the miracle of song, they endeared themselves as much to him as to Warde Fowler or any other English bird-lover.

The first sight of a hummingbird, particularly if seen suspended sprite-like on misty wings before one's face, the iridescence of its scale-like feathers changing prismatically, comes to one "like a revelation." But the mechanical quality of its actions, the product of an insectlike intelligence, makes this opalescent creature less interesting to the psychologist than almost any other species, and one can, after a while, so it seemed to Hudson, even grow "tired of seeing the feathered fairies perpetually weaving their aerial ballet-dance about the flowers." Several of the experiences with hummers are well vignetted: thousands of them in their glittering green mantles revelling in the fragrant sweetness of the acacia trees on the Hudson estancia, and many other thousands in a glade of a marshy forest near the Rio de la Plata poised about their favorite flower, the viper's bugloss, each bird sucking honey for a minute or two and then, like a tiny rocket, darting back into the shadow of the trees.

Never wearying were the martins, swifts, and swallows—especially, as with Michelet and Jefferies and Williamson, the swallows, which, from the moment of their arrival in spring "overflowing with gladness" until their departure in autumn, skate across the sky and twitter their primitive music. Thousands of sand-martins we see streaming down the valley of the Itchen "in the shelter of the woods, their pale plumage and wavering flight making them look in the distance like great white flies against the wall of black-green trees and gloomy sky beyond"; swifts holding for an hour their shrill evening revels over Selborne, scattering and floating above the church for a few moments, then closing and rushing down across the Plestor and along the village street for a distance of forty or fifty yards, after which they rise again to some height in the sky and repeat the performance; and swallows wheeling over a Sussex village, so numerous that, when seen from a high window, they resembled "a multitude of bees . . . flying about over a hive." There are a number of individual likenesses: a pair of martins securing a Poe-esque revenge on sparrows that had dispossessed them, by building their new nest so close to the old one as to entomb the hen sparrow; a swift who, after pursuing his mate on her mad flights away from the nest four times, finally succeeded in making her "stay put," and then went off with his cronies to enjoy his "supposed night out" by rushing and sailing about in the upper air until early morning;

and a swallow who, while hawking over the Hampshire Exe, would occasionally drop down to dip and wet his under-plumage in the water, and, as a result, almost got caught in the jaws of a large pike.

Starlings, "splendid in [their] spangled glossy dress of metallic purple, green, and bronze," are scattered, here and there, in almost all Hudson's volumes of the English countryside.[16] We see them plodding the ground in their rooklike manner and foregathering by the tens of thousands at their favorite roosting-place for their beloved evening games, during which they appear like a large dark cloud in the sky, "now extending to an immense length across the sky, like a long bar of vapour, and now gathered into a huge oval or oblong black mass," until after wheeling about for some time the cloud pours back into the trees. Most vocal of birds, their perpetual, ever-varying chatter amused Hudson—"a sort of bird-Yiddish," he calls it, in which a few fragments of borrowed melodies, poorly rendered, are interspersed with much gurgling, jarring, clicking, tinkling, squealing, hissing, kissing, and whistling. A small company of them is described worrying a kestrel out of their territory by dropping upon his back, half a dozen at a time, whenever he started to hover, and a larger company, at the appearance of a sparrowhawk, "flying at furious speed towards the nearest flock of sheep," falling down amongst them "like a shower of stones and instantly" vanishing "from sight."

Of the statuesque, musically-gifted thrush family, one remembers the courageous storm-cock who, taking advantage of the insecure hold a sparrowhawk had on a telegraph wire, unperched him by plummeting like a stone upon his back; the group of them that, by disgorging yewberries, kept studding the green turf of Kingly Bottom with bright pinky-red blobs; and an orphaned blackbird who, after being nursed from sure death by Hudson, would welcome him back from a saunter along the Itchen by "bounding over the lawn with long hops, looking like a miniature very dark-coloured kangaroo" and who soon got to know, by noting the eating habits of the household, just when he might expect the next snack. Emboldened by his example, other birds came to join "Blackie" at mealtime,

---

[16] The volumes on the Argentine might be included in this statement, if one were to consider under starlings their cousins in the new world: the military starling, the various cowbirds, and the yellow- and crimson-breasted troupials.

and, eager to absorb all their lore of the wild, he began to consort with them more and more, without, however, giving up "his acquaintance with and confidence in us."

The chief attraction of the pipits was in their calls and songs: the melody of the tree-pipit creating in one "a soft delicious languor, a wish to lie perfectly still and drink of the same sweetness again and again in larger measure"; the strain of the rock-pipit being unique to the seashore, for he is the only songster inhabiting that region exclusively; and the thin but penetrative little complaint of the meadow-pipit, "the most anxious sound uttered by any small bird" in England, infecting the mind not only with its sadness but with its mystery. One can gather from Hudson's portfolio a dainty cluster of pipit-sketches: a tree-pipit festooning an elm with his honeysuckle-sweet song by flying from branch to ground and back again; a rock-pipit being whirled into the midst of a flock of gulls by a sudden gust of wind as he paused over his nest in a chink of the Cornish cliffs, and being swooped upon by their irascible leader a "white flying image of wrath"; and a meadow-pipit, under the impression that a passing cuckoo was in very truth "the big greedy son" whom she had fed and warmed with her breast, and who had gone away, "goodness knows where," arising and flying after him "just to accompany him . . . a little distance on his way," and perhaps "to tell him of her undying love and pride in his bigness and fine feathers and loud voice."

Even for that "wingèd Arab of the streets," the ubiquitous sparrow, Hudson had a good word. Though distracting to one's enjoyment of the country, where, in relation to other birds, it has the status of an unskilled laborer, in the city this pert gamin, "the chimney-sweep" among birds, is "with all his faults . . . a pleasant merry little fellow," who can be even pretty and graceful when begging for and deftly catching small scraps of bread, and whose barrel-organ of chirrupings comes, amidst the din of the streets and "the muffled thunders of the Underground," like "a sound of subdued and happy laughter." Some of the other members of the finch family to be met with are the bullfinch Hudson rescued from a dirty cage in a hot kitchen and set free in the Abbey Garden at Lewes enjoying ecstatically the first moments of liberty; a presumptuous chaffinch driving away from a mixed company a blackbird bedraggled and listless from moulting and, a short time later, being himself furiously buffeted and made to flee wildly for his very life by the same blackbird, whom brooding had kindled to anger, and anger had made strong; and the linnet Hudson bought at the Saturday evening market in London in order to save from further torture, which died before it could be released to join the flock flying over Cissbury Hill.

Many other small birds catch one's eyes among the details of Hudson's far-spreading landscapes, but there is only space enough here to single out a few more: a scissor-tail tyrant-bird, "one of the most courageous of that hawk-hating, violent-tempered" family, sallying out from his nest on the top of a red willow near the Hudson rancho to attack "in mid-air with amazing fury" a marauding chimango, and pursuing it with scythe-whetting cries; the color of a pair of kingfishers turning to a splendid sea-green as like arrows they darted low across a broad meadow gleaming with buttercups; and, like Winslow Homer's water-color of red-winged blackbirds amidst wild rice, a small company of delicate long-tailed tits "drifting, in their usual desultory way," along the banks of the Avon near Bath, and pausing in the very bush Hudson was admiring.

The long deep-red pendent catkins and the little pale birdlings among them in their grey and rose-coloured plumage, with long graceful tails and minute round, parroty heads; some quietly perched just above the water, others moving about here and there, occasionally suspending themselves back downwards from the slender terminal twigs— the whole mirrored below. That magical effect of water and sunlight gave to the scene a somewhat fairy-like, an almost illusory, character.

The chief glory of many of these "smale foules" is their songs, and for them (as already indicated) Hudson had the discriminating ear of an impresario. As he discovered from his own ineffectual efforts at acquiring, while still in the Argentine, some just notion of the music of English songsters, it is not an easy matter to convey to another, through the medium of words, one's impression of bird sounds. Although the spelling out of songs and call-notes into articulate speech does have some significance to the person who has heard the birds at firsthand, and such onomatopoeic names as chickadee, phoebe, and bob-white are undoubtedly of some use in identification, it is only a "fancy and a delusion," so he maintained, to think, for example, that such expressions as "sweet—sweet—sweet— very merry cheer" or "little-bit-of-bread-and-no-cheese" or any other group of words or syllables represents the lyrics of the song-sparrow and the yellowhammer to an uninitiated reader. The same song may actually, at different times, be translated by the very same person into totally different words.

Nor is there much gained by transcribing (or taming, as it were) bird-song into our musical symbols, for though many birds, like the cuckoo, keep time accurately and a few, like the song-thrush, occasionally utter a perfect musical phrase, most avian music is beyond the laws of our artificial diatonic and chromatic scales.

> We have not yet invented any system of arbitrary signs to present bird sounds, nor are we likely to invent such a system, because . . . we do not properly know the sounds, and, owing to their numbers and character, cannot properly know more than a very few of them; and . . . because they are different in each species; . . . just as our human notation represents solely our human specific sounds, so a notation of one bird's language, that of the skylark, let us say, would not apply to the language of another species, the nightingale, say, on account of the difference in quality and *timbre* of the two.

Even the finest recordings of Schuyler Mathews, which are scored upon the Scotch or folk-song scale, are of little assistance (except perhaps to the technically trained and highly imaginative musician) in the communication of bird-song, for there is always the further difficulty of reproducing the aerial quality of the notes, the quality "which tells you, even in a deep wood, . . . that the new and strange sound is uttered by a bird. The clanging anvil is in the clouds; the tinkling bell is somewhere in the air, suspended on nothing. . . . " [17]

---

[17] After focussing much technical knowledge upon the problem, Warde Fowler came to the conclusion that "to write the song of Robin on a musical stave is . . . not only to translate him but to traduce him. . . . If [the songs of birds] are to be compared with anything human, it should rather be with that rude music of primitive man out of which our own has gradually been evolved—with the cries of victory, the wailing of women, the weird chant of the prophetess. . . . Where these have assumed a stereotyped form, as in . . . the Greek Paean or Linus-chant, they may perhaps be considered analogous to the songs of such birds as have developed a fixed phrase by which to express their emotions. . . . As far as I can judge, there is in the music of the birds neither time nor rhythm nor scale; and these are the essential and primal elements out of which, together with tonality, our human music has been developed" (*Summer Studies,* pp. 131, 133-4). And Burroughs remarks, "Bird-songs are not music, properly speaking, but only suggestions of music. . . . There is something elusive, indefinite, neutral, about bird-songs that makes them strike obliquely, as it were, upon the ear" (*Ways of Nature,* Riverby Edition, pp. 29, 30).

Though eschewing such techniques, Hudson was yet able, in the tradition of Nuttall, Jefferies and Burroughs, to communicate well—probably no essayist better—the charm of bird-song: its intrinsic beauty and its enhancement through association with certain places and with certain human experiences. Many of the individual notes, sometimes as beautiful in their way as the ecstatic cries of Madame Butterfly in *Un bel di vedremo* and Isolde over the body of Tristan, receive separate attention, such as the exquisite note of the linnet, "the equal of which for purest melody and tender expression is not to be found among our feathered vocalists." The timbre of a note or phrase or song is generally indicated: its resonance, its brightness, its mellowness, its sweetness, and its clarity. Comparison with some other well-known sounds—those of inanimate nature, insects, beasts, human beings (both vocal and instrumental), and those of other birds, usually of closely related species—often aids in establishing the tonal color. Thus the singing of a company of sedge-warblers scattered about in the rushes of an island is likened to the performance of "small fantastic human minstrels . . . on a variety of instruments, some unknown, others recognisable—bones and castanets, tiny hurdy-gurdies, piccolos, banjos, tabours, and Pandean pipes—a strange medley!" And, rather frequently, as has been previously stressed, the sounds are imaginatively translated into visual impressions.

Even though rarely resorting to actual musical notation, he was usually careful to give us the register, strength, and carrying power of the various voices, and some general idea of the shape of the songs: the linking of the phrases, the variations in pitch, the tempo, the proportion of recitative to cantabile. Some songs are heard better as solos and others chorally: the sedge-warbler, for instance, is at his best with a "wide margin of silence" around him, and the meadow-pipit, with a dozen or more widely-scattered fellow-choristers. At times, the shape is that of a set song, the score being adhered to closely, as with that little automaton, the chaffinch, or, more often the case, rendered with some liberty, as with the tree-pipit and the yellowhammer. And then again, the shape may be that of an impromptu, each individual singer, as with the throstle and the blackbird, being his own composer. When there are borrowings from other vocalists, Hudson was concerned not only with the extent of the borrowing but with the manner in which it is treated. Thus he

tells us that the mockingbird, "when imitating the small or weak
voiced songsters," subdues or smalls his voice, the notes, however
gaining "in power and penetration" because of "his larger organ."
All the variations in the repertoire of a particular species, all the
interpolations of originality were always keenly appreciated, and
when Hudson chanced upon a singer of genius, he became a
enraptured as an inveterate opera-goer listening to a new inter
pretation of an old rôle by a Caruso or a Patti.

The effect of atmosphere and of distance upon bird-song is als
sensitively indicated. The tender silveriness in the sunlit air after
copious shower gives to sounds a purer, brighter, and more resonan
quality. The strains of the marsh-warbler, so we are informed, "ca
only be properly appreciated when the listener stands or sits on
level with the reeds within a very few yards of the singer." As the
distance is increased between a bird and its audience, the lower
guttural, and harsh notes are successively sifted out, leaving in the
ears the higher, more shrill ones. Thus, heard from afar, some song
lose their essential character: that of the furze-wren, for example
may under such conditions be confused with the stonechat's or the
linnet's or even the pipit's. The rapture of the skylark is considerabl
improved by distance, for the unpleasant throaty notes die awa
and the high reiterated trills, their shrillness softened, live on.

Also, the personal presence of the songster, the various move
ments of the body that accompany the delivery of the notes, is often
as with the stonechat and the lark, an integral part of the charm o
the song, and, more than most recorders, Hudson was eager tha
we visualize every characteristic gesture. The starling (he tells us)
"especially when emitting his favourite saw-filing or milking-a-cow
in-a-tin-pail sounds, . . . trembles on his perch—shivers as wit
cold—his feathers puffed out, his wings hanging as if broken, hi
beak wide open, and the long pointed feathers of his swollen throa
projected like a ragged beard." On the other hand, the white-bande
mockingbird, with an "abandon and joyousness resembling, bu
greatly exceeding, that of the skylark,"

passes from bush to bush, sometimes delaying a few moments on,
and at others just touching the summits, and at times sinking out of
sight in the foliage: then, in an excess of rapture, soaring vertically to a
height of a hundred feet, with measured wing-beats, like those of a
heron: or mounting suddenly in a wild, hurried zigzag, then slowly

circling downwards, to sit at last with tail outspread fanwise, and vans, glistening white in the sunshine, expanded and vibrating, or waved languidly up and down, with a motion like that of some broad-winged butterfly at rest on a flower.

The intrinsic beauty of bird calls and melodies is considerably nhanced when one associates them with certain aspects of the day nd of the season and with certain landscapes; and to this sort of xpressiveness Hudson was extraordinarily sensitive. The twittering f swallows far up in the early crepuscular sky, softer and more rolonged than later in the day, seemed to him peculiarly in har- nony with the shadowy morning twilight over the pampas. The hiffchaff is best heard in March, piping the reveillé of spring; the obin in autumn (hence his title, "yellow autumn's nightingale") nd the missel-thrush amidst mid-winter gloom and tempest. The harm of the powerful whistle of the ring-ouzel is "mainly due to he place you hear it in, the wildness and solitude of the rocky lens or the mountain side," and the bell-like tinkle of the meadow- ipit accords well with wide moors and other lonely waste places— he notes of both songs, like those of many others, seemingly induced y their habitual settings. The throstle is heard much better from he tree-tops in woods, lanes, and fields than on the spacious, velvety- anked downs. As David Cox also perceived, most in tune with that pen sunny world, giving tongue, as it were, to the wind and the oating clouds, the blue sky and the sunshine, is the soaring song f the lark.

Close though many avian sounds are, in their oboe- and flute-like uality, to those of the human voice, to speak of them in terms of uman emotions, describing them as tender or plaintive or joyous, is, s Hudson well knew, only a rough expedient and often fallacious. or example, the nightingale was a bird of sorrow and despair to the ireeks and to most Elizabethans, influenced as they were by the hilomela legend, whereas to many subsequent artists—Coleridge, .eats, Kingsley, Meredith, Bridges—it has been a bird of joy and ope. To Hudson, however, its warble, though approaching the uman voice in its rich prelusive throb and in " 'one low piping ote,' . . . four times repeated in a wonderfully beautiful crescendo," as in it "no *human* feeling. Feeling of some un-human kind there erhaps [is], but not gladness, such as we imagine in the skylark's ong, and certainly not sorrow, nor anything sad." Nonetheless, whether the songs of birds actually express or only seem to express human emotions, they are most delightful to man, as Burroughs likewise felt, in proportion as they suggest "refined, bright, and highly-musical human voices, . . . expressive of various beautiful qualities—sympathy, tenderness, innocent mirth, and overflowing gladness of heart." "Just as Carlotta Patti . . . rose to the birds in her miraculous flights, so do some of the birds come down to and resemble us in their songs," and among English birds, the human note is strongest, he thought, in the linnet, the swallow, the pied wagtail, the dove, the tree-pipit, the blackcap, and, most of all, in the willow-wren and the blackbird.

Furthermore, bird-song becomes still more expressive as it reverberates through the labyrinth of memory. The slightest bird sounds could work magic on Hudson, because almost from the cradle they had intrigued him and come to be associated with many of his happiest moments. And since his imagination had long been fired by what the poets had said of the charm of British birds, he listened to them, from the very beginning, not "as an English naturalist would to those of, let us say, Queensland, or Burma, or Canada, or Patagonia, but with an intense interest"—the feeling that "these were the birds which [his] forbears had known and listened to all their lives long" and which had inspired many of the greatest artists.

If for no other reason than that birds vary in expressiveness to each of us according to the differences of our personalities and experiences, there can be no unanimity in regard to Hudson's evaluation of the songs he transcribed. One may disagree, for instance, with his admiration for the song of the greenfinch, even though he has Wordsworth and Jefferies on his side. There may be an occasional inaccuracy, as when, in *Birds in a Village*, the woodpigeon is called a "dismal croaker"—an epithet he was later careful to delete. But, by and large, his transcriptions stand as models of sureness and subtlety of perception. His corrections of previous renditions by poet and ornithologist, as in his analysis of the call of the jackdaw and the song of the ring-ouzel, show the refinement of his ear. And there is that quality in many of his passages that allies them to poetry—the quality of imagination.

The major singers of the Argentine and of England are all heard in Hudson's panoramas, but the ones best presented are the mockingbird, the blackbird, the skylark, and the bird that he did much to establish in this group, the marsh-warbler. The short, energetic strains of the blackcap, the wide repertoire of the throstle, the varied melodic spurts of the robin redbreast, and the superb artistry of the nightingale, the purity of some of its notes, "the exquisite phrasing, the beautiful contrasts"—all were, to be sure, greatly admired; but little is said of the first three, and thinking perhaps that the fervent nocturne of the nightingale had already been sufficiently immortalized, he limited his analysis of it largely to annotations upon the renditions of others.

The white-banded mockingbird's "own divine song," which accomplishes the "seeming impossibility" of providing "beautiful contrasts and harmonious lights and shades" without following any definite pattern, "delights the soul," so Hudson was convinced, "beyond all other bird-music. . . ." Among the English mastersingers, he preferred the serenely artless blackbird, whose soft, flute-like tones suggest those of "an exquisitely pure and beautiful contralto," and whose delivery has the leisureliness of a person "at peace and supremely happy, . . . talking sweetly and mingling talk with snatches of song." And he tells of a virtuoso among blackbirds chanced upon in the New Forest, who "sang differently each time, or varied the strain so greatly as to make it appear like a new melody on each repetition, yet every one of its strains could have been set down in musical notation."

The song of the marsh-warbler had been well described by the man who discovered the bird to be a regular visitor to English shores—Warde Fowler. It seemed to Hudson's ear, despite its small volume and poor carrying-power, as sweet as that of any other mastersinger, and, interspersed as it is with the melodies of others, to excel all but that of the mockingbird in variety. In his own rendition of the song, the number of the borrowings is emphasized and the fine artistry with which they are treated. Unlike the starling, the marsh-warbler never attempts to reproduce sounds outside its own register, and, by subduing harsh and guttural notes and by harmonizing phrases and songs to its own native tones, imparts to many of them a silvery sweetness.

Above all others, the song that the lark rains down from the sky typified for him, as it has for many, "the exuberant life and joy of nature to the soul." It is "a continuous torrent of contrasted guttural and clear shrill sounds and trills, so rapidly emitted that the notes, so different in character, yet seem to interpenetrate or to over-lap each other," and the impression given is that of dazzling light.

> To say of a sound that it is bright is to use a too common metaphor; this sound shines above all others, and the multitude of voices made one by distance is an effulgence and a glory. I have listened to it by the hour, never wearying nor ceasing to wonder at that mysterious beautiful music which could not be called crystalline nor silvery, but was like the heavenly sunshine translated into sound; subtle, insistent, filling the world and the soul, yet always at a vast distance, falling, falling like a lucid rain.

Since their highest notes can be heard three miles away, the effect of larks singing above the downs is that "of an innumerable com-pany of invisible beings, forming an unbroken circle as wide as the horizon, chanting an everlasting melody in one shrill, unchanging tone."

The exultant outburst of the missel-thrush, though not that of a major singer, is almost as impressively one of overflowing glad-ness because of the bird's custom of rejoicing most passionately in weather that silences all others—when "the south-west raves all day and all night" in mid-winter and "there is no gleam of light any-where and no change in [the] darkness of immense ever-moving cloud above." It was this habit of flinging its soul upon the encircling gloom that led Hardy to detect trembling through

> His happy good-night air
> Some blessed Hope, whereof he knew
> And I was unaware.

And in Hudson's interpretation, which was published at almost the same time, there is something of the same perception:

> If you observe him in rough or gloomy weather, perched on an elm-top, swayed about this way and that by the gusts, singing his best, you must believe that this dark aspect of things delights him; that his pleasure in life, expressed with such sounds and in such circum-stances, must greatly exceed in degree the contentment and bliss that is ours, even when we are most free from pain or care, and our whole beings most perfectly in tune with nature.

Yet, as Hudson reminds us, "the dulcet strains of a few of the most highly-esteemed songsters contribute only a part, by no means the largest part, of the pleasure we receive from the bird sounds of any district." Indeed, some minor songsters, like certain of the figures in the realm of human art, may move us more intimately, and, in the end, become more precious. Thus the cooing of the stock-dove meant more to Wordsworth than the fiery aria of the night-ingale, and it was the hurry-scurry, defiant lyric of the chaffinch, more than any other sound, that led Browning to exclaim, "Oh, to be in England now that April's there!" In the transcription of bird-song, Hudson did his most valuable service by drawing attention to the lesser voices of the English wood-wind ensemble and the Argen-tine orchestra—those that, like the violet or forget-me-not beside the flaunting poppy and dahlia, go almost unheeded amongst the operatic and more familiar loud ones, and those rarely heard, either because the bird itself is rare or the song seldom performed.

In addition to the birds already noticed—the starling, the yellow-hammer, the reed-bunting, the greenfinch, the various pipits, the ring-ouzel, the yellow-shouldered troupial—many others sing in his two aviaries: the cuckoo, with its fluty, far-reaching, bounteous twin notes; the shy redstart, whose song collapses into a "curious little farrago of gurgling and squeaking" tones after a brief prelude of two charming sounds, "the bright pure gushing robin-like note, and the more tender expressive" one of the swallow; the sedge-warbler, whose harsh, scolding notes, enunciated with extraordinary rapidity, seem to overlap and mingle in a continuous stream with the melodi-ous ones, giving the effect of water gurgling and prattling in a shallow pebbly channel; the cirl-bunting, who pours out its notes so quickly "that, heard at a distance," its lyric "acquires almost the character of a long trill" and so penetratively that they sound distinct above a peal of bells; the harlequin-feathered stonechat, best of the songsters of the furze on the downs, whose delicate song, rising and falling rhythmically, is also a dance; and its less con-spicuously garbed relative, the whinchat, whose fugitive warble of half a dozen low, tender notes, almost as short as that of the red-start, is "a mere drop of sound, yet to all other bird sounds" on silent heaths and furze-grown, brambly hillsides "like the drop of dew or rain among many other crystal, colourless drops, which catches the light at the right angle and shines with loveliest colour."

Of the lesser songsters of the Argentine, we hear the plaintive evensong of the rufous tinamou, "perhaps the sweetest bird-music heard on the pampas," with its "five modulated notes, flute-like in character, very expressive, and uttered by many individuals answering each other as they sit far apart concealed in the grass"; the delicate melody of the chingolo song-sparrow, sung from the disc of a thistle-flower, "the multitudinous notes not mingling but floating away, as it were, detached and scattered, mere gossamer webs of sound"; the duet of red ovenbirds, "the first bird, on the appearance of its mate flying to join it, [beginning] to emit loud, measured notes, and sometimes a continuous trill, somewhat metallic in sound" but changing to rapid triplets, "strongly accented on the first note, in a *tempo vivace*" as soon as the other bird strikes in with "loud single notes in the same time"; the post-mating strains of the yellow field-finch, progressing gradually from the somewhat throaty notes uttered as it soars upward, to the clearer and brighter but excessively attenuated ones at the ending, "the finest threads of sound and faintest tinklings, as from a cithern touched by fairy fingers"; and the silvery, bell-like voice of the little scarlet tyrant, "so low [it] can scarcely be heard twenty paces off, and somewhat resembling the sound of water running from a narrow-necked flask, but more musical and infinitely more rapid."

Among the best transcriptions are those of the willow-wren, the furze-wren, and (Hudson's prime favorite among all the smaller birds) the wood-wren. The secret of the charm of the willow-wren, who had come into his own with the accurate description of Fowler and the praise of Burroughs, was traced to the humanlike quality of his voice, which gives the impression "of a fairy-like child with an exquisitely pure, bright, spiritual voice laughingly speaking in some green place." The furze-wren has the peculiarity of singing while he chides and chiding while he sings, and his "buzzing stream of sound, . . . interspersed with small, fine, bright, clear notes, both shrill and mellow," gives one the impression of "a close-woven . . . black or grey cord, set and sparkling with loose thread-ends of silver, gold and scarlet." Except occasionally, when singing a prelude to his song in the air—his "long sharp wings [beating] time to the clear measured notes"—the wood-wren is not a particularly attractive performer. And he does not compare well with other melodists, including some of the minor ones, in many of the qualities most highly esteemed in bird-song. What then is "the mysterious something" in his music, Hudson asks, "that makes it to some of us even better than the best"?

It is more harmonious, or in more perfect accord with the nature amid which it is heard; it is the truer woodland voice.

The chaffinch as a rule sings in open woods and orchards and groves when there is light and life and movement; but sometimes in the heart of a deep wood the silence is broken by its sudden loud lyric: it is unexpected and sounds unfamiliar in such a scene; the wonderfully joyous ringing notes are like a sudden flood of sunshine in a shady place. The sound is intensely distinct and individual, in sharp contrast to the low forest tones: its effect on the ear is similar to that produced on the sight by a vivid contrast in colours, as by a splendid scarlet or shining yellow flower blooming solitary where all else is green. The effect produced by the wood wren is totally different; the strain does not contrast with, but is complementary to, the "tremulous cadence low" of inanimate nature in the high woods, of wind-swayed branches and pattering of rain and lisping and murmuring of innumerable leaves—the elemental sounds out of which it has been fashioned. In a sense it may be called a trivial and a monotonous song—the strain that is like a long tremulous cry, repeated again and again without variation; but it is really beyond criticism—one would have to begin by depreciating the music of the wind. It is a voice of the beechen woods in summer, of the far-up cloud of green, translucent leaves, with open spaces full of green shifting sunlight and shadow. Though resonant and far-reaching it does not strike you as loud, but rather as the diffused sound of the wind in the foliage concentrated and made clear—a voice that has light and shade, rising and passing like the wind, changing as it flows, and quivering like a wind-fluttered leaf. . . .

As the lark in its soaring song is of the sky, so the wood wren is of the wood.

Scarcely less delightful than the songs themselves are the many calls and cries, and Hudson's skies are full of their wildness: the caw-cawing of daws and crows and rooks; the brain-piercing screams of jays, "the startled solitary's outburst of uncontrolled rage at the abhorred sight of a fellow-being in his woodland haunt"; the melancholy outcries of ringed dotterels; the moaning of doves; the short, clacking notes of wheatears, as of "two pieces of stone struck smartly together"; the high-pitched nasal laughter of wrynecks; the drumming of woodpeckers; the prolonged fluty call of wood owls and the sepulchral, sibilant cry of their cousins, the white owls, reminding one of the shrieking of the night wind "in the roof of some old haunted house"; the reeling of nightjars; the long, querulous sounds of chimangos feeding on carcasses, "resembling the piteous whines of a shivering puppy"; the weird, humanlike shrieks of ypecaha rail; the protracted lament of courlans; the catlike wailing of lapwings; the shrill, piercing pipe of redshanks; the singularly clear, far-reaching, two-noted tolling of curlews; the harsh booming of bitterns; the aerial bleating of snipe, as of "invisible kids wandering lost on invisible mountains"; the gruntings of woodcock, "followed by a burst of sibilant sound, shrill as the scream of a bat or the piercing squeak of a frightened shrew-mouse"; the long metallic trill of teal; the shrill, confused whistling of tree duck; the short, rapidly reiterated call of blue ibis, "as of hammerstrokes on an anvil"; the stentorian trumpeting of Coscoroba swans; the powerful and prolonged screams of great heron; the plaintive yelpings of sea gulls. As memorable as any of the calls and cries described by Hudson is that of Magellanic geese:

Listening to [them] when, during migration, on a still frosty night, they flew low, following the course of some river, flock succeeding flock all night long; or heard from a herdsman's hut on the pampas, when thousands of the birds had encamped for the night on the plain hard by, the effect of their many voices (like that of their appearance when seen flying) was singular, as well as beautiful, on account of the striking contrasts in the various sounds they uttered. On clear frosty nights they are most loquacious, and their voices may be heard by the hour, rising and falling, now few, and now many taking part in the endless confabulation—a talkee-talkee and concert in one: a chatter as of many magpies; the solemn, deep, *honk-honk*, the long, grave note changing to a shuddering sound; and, most wonderful, the fine silvery whistle of the male, steady or tremulous, now long and now short, modulated a hundred ways—wilder and more beautiful than the night-cry of the widgeon, brighter than the voice of any shore bird, or any warbler, thrush or wren, or the sound of any wind instrument.

ADAM'S RACE

If birds were the first and most distinctive inspiration, human beings attracted Hudson no less vitally, and his sketches of them are hardly less impressive. How "various" and how "infinitely rich," he exclaims, "is this world of humanity in which we exist, half-knowing before we die some few score of our fellow-men, while all the others, the thousand million, are strangers yet!" To fix an arresting face in his memory, he made a point of conversing with the person, and in his eagerness to introduce his readers to the unusual men and women who had crossed his path he could not at times resist the impulse to insert sketches of them even when aware, as in his anecdote in *The Land's End* illustrating the rarity of naturalists among countrymen, they would in no way advance the presentation of his thought. There are hundreds of persons in his essays—more than appear in those of his chief predecessors and in most of his successors.

Gifted though he was as a teller of tales, Hudson never in this sort of writing tampered with the actual experience by trying to make more out of it than the facts warranted. The very slightness of many of his sketches is, indeed, a sign of their genuineness as well as a measure of his power. And though capable of profound insights into human nature and astute generalizations on certain ethnological and social groups, he rarely attempted to make detailed psychological analyses of the persons presented. "I class myself," he says, "somewhere between the two extremes: not satisfied with the mere semblance or appearance of things, seeing men as trees and rocks, or as works of art, I am nevertheless not teased—'tormented,' De Quincey would have written—with that restless desire to pry into and minutely examine the secret colour and texture of the mind of every person I meet." The usual effect, like that of Hogarth's *Shrimp Girl*, is one of a quick, shrewd summing-up by the intuition of the most salient characteristics of an acquaintance. Slight though they are, these sketches have in them nonetheless the insistency of reality.

The angle of vision from which he delineated mankind is essentially the same as the one used for insects, birds, and beasts— the detached scrutiny of the field naturalist. In order to keep man in the proper perspective, he continually placed him against the rest of the animal kingdom and, as the anthropologist does, against his immediate progenitor, primitive man. In certain fundamental respects, he occasionally reminds us, man is not the paragon of animals: "Even as the lower animals . . . excel us in physical power and speed and endurance, so do they surpass us in beauty of form and colouring, grace of motion, and in melody." In his endeavor to escape from too restrictive a viewpoint, as in his desire to maintain a godlike impartiality toward all the children of life, there may come into his portraiture, as in that of Thoreau and the Chinese land-scapists, a certain impersonal, unhuman note. But this note is never the result of a want of the milk of human kindness or of an essential loyalty to humanity.

The persons Hudson preferred were, of course, those who, like the creatures of the wild, are in contact with the great natural forces and in harmony with the countryside in which their lot has been cast. People of the pavement, who, having signed over their birth-rights to that great neuter, the Dynamo, are degenerating biologi-cally and fast becoming the psychotic robots of cheap commodity manufacture, seemed to him mere interlopers on this globe and thus outside the range of his sympathy and of his art.

> The townsman, town born and bred, . . . is, in spite of all the time I have spent in his company, a comparative stranger to me—the one living creature on the earth who does not greatly interest me. Some over-populated planet in our system discovered a way to relieve itself by discharging its superfluous millions on our globe—a pale people with hurrying feet and eager, restless minds, who live apart in monstrous, crowded camps, like wood ants that go not out to forage for themselves—six millions of them crowded together in one camp alone! I have lived in these colonies, years and years, never losing the sense of captivity, of exile, ever conscious of my burden, taking no interest in the doings of that innumerable multitude, its manifold interests, its ideals and philosophy, its arts and pleasures.

The main villains in his pages are the persecutors of animals: birdcatchers, like the pigeon-hating ones of "Birds in a Village" and the huge, gross Yorkshireman who sold linnets for sixpence in the London Saturday evening market; gamekeepers, brutalized by possession of the gun, well indicted in "The Sacred Bird" for their systematic depredations; sportsmen who kill for killing's sake, like the wanton slaughterers of the inquisitive little titlark and the or-phaned seal; and that special "curse of rural England," the chief persecutors of rare birds, collectors, unforgettably pilloried in "Some-thing Pretty in a Glass Case." The sight of aigrettes on a woman's hat always put Hudson in a rage; "he would have seen no beauty in Aphrodite," so Roberts has phrased it, "if she had worn birds' feathers, though she had come nude to him." Nor was there any less repugnance for the imprisoners of birds, such as the owners of the bullfinch he released in the Abbey Garden at Lewes and the white owl scanted in an uncovered cage in the kitchen of a Chichester inn, where a big fire and several gas jets stabbed his ultra-sensitive eye-balls every night until twelve.

Indians, with their birdlike cries, their barbaric pigments, and their primitive way of life, harmonize well with any wild landscape, and though Hudson (except in his fiction) gives us few individualized portraits of them, one has a recurring sense of their presence in the panoramas of La Plata and Patagonia. The people that lend the most wildness to the English countryside are their psychological brethren, the gypsies—aliens, "yet more native than any Englishman in the land." When one of them spoke of "his life, spent in roaming about the country, of his very perfect health, and of his hatred of houses, the very atmosphere of any indoor place producing a suffocating and sickening effect on him," he made Hudson feel that "his was the wild, the real life, and . . . there was no other worth living." Admiration for robustness and the vagrant open-air life did not, however, blind Hudson to the defects of the Romany folk in southern England, evidently of a different strain from that of the gypsies one meets in *Lavengro* and *The Romany Rye* or else in a period of moral decadence. In their brains was discerned the cunning of the wild animal, plus "a small, an infinitesimal, dose of something else which eludes us."

But that something else is not of a spiritual nature. . . . It is still the animal's cunning, a special, a sublimated cunning, the fine flower of his whole nature, and . . . it has nothing mysterious in it. He is a parasite, but free and well able to exist free as the fox or jackal; but the parasitism pays him well, and he has followed it so long in his intercourse with social man that it has come to be like an instinct, or secret knowledge, and is nothing more than a marvellously keen penetration which reveals to him the character and degree of credulity and other mental weaknesses of his subject.

It is not so much the wind on the heath, brother, as the fascination of lawlessness, which makes his life an everlasting joy to him; to pit himself against gamekeepers, farmer, policeman, and everybody else, and defeat them all, to flourish like the parasitic fly on the honey in the hive and escape the wrath of the bees.

Being without the sympathy toward them of a Borrow or an Augustus John, he makes as little of them in his essays as do Walton and White and Jefferies.

The gauchos of the Argentine and the cottagers of southern England form the bulk of his sketches of human figures. Simple in their manner of living, at one with the beasts they herd and the soil they till, and in rhythm with the changing seasons, they blend well, as in the paintings of Breughel, Crome and Millet, with any pastoral landscape. The cottagers in particular, flourishing and dying like trees in the places where they first took root and absorbing much of their wisdom directly from nature, are, as Cobbett, Whitman, Manzoni and Tolstoy also realized, the strongest fiber of the social fabric. In the presence of both gauchos and cottars—born and reared as he had been to their rhythms—Hudson was able to shed much of his aloofness. It is in this spirit—not unmindful, however, of the brutalizing effect of some tasks and of excessive toil—that they are presented.

Among the most romantic figures that the modern world has created are the semi-barbarous gauchos, with their baggy pantaloons, ponchos and heavy spurs, their *facones, boleadoras* and guitars, their waddling gait, turbulent passions, wild melancholy songs, and basically democratic way of life; and, like the Tartars, Mordvinians and Bashkirs in the pages of Aksakoff and the various Bedouin tribes in those of Doughty and Freya Stark, they enliven Hudson's Argentine landscapes with their flaunting colors. At their best, as in certain landowners of aristocratic descent, they appear like figures out of the Old Testament; at their worst, when revelling in cruelty, they remind one, as they do Molina Campos, of Nature in some of her more savage moods. Toward such half-wild horsemen, it was well that he adopted the amoral attitude of Nature herself; to have assumed the rôle of moralist would have betrayed too anthropomorphic a viewpoint. Some of their portraits, particularly those in *Far Away and Long Ago*, are among the best Hudson ever drew, whether in essay, tale or novel, and they vie with those of Cunninghame Graham.

Among the many gauchos that might well be placed beside those met earlier are: the old codger who, until spectacles were placed before his own failing eyes, thought the wearing of them by an English settler a mere affectation; black-bearded, eagle-eyed Barboza and that other master of the *facón* with one eye dark-blue and the other black;[18] Bruno Lopez, gambler, fighter, and once a fugitive from justice, who was so affected by the evensong of the tinamou as to feel like casting himself face down upon the ground and crying; the foster-brothers, Ambrose and Cyril de la Rose, who, though of very different origin and character—the one a gentleman to the bone and the other with plebeian features and a certain vulgarity in his gay manner—had an extraordinary affection for each other; the dignified, silvery haired and bearded Alcade, usually astride a big black horse in a costume profuse with silver ornaments, including ponderous silver spurs and heavy silver whip-handle, who, in order to save his daughters, had to refuse protection to a cousin, an officer fleeing from mutinous men. And there is the most bizarre hermit who ever came a-begging to anyone's door, in comparison with whom other beggars are dandies.

He had a small, sun-parched face, and silvery long hair; but his features were fine, his teeth white and even, his eyes clear grey and keen as a falcon's. There was always a set expression of deep mental anguish on his face, intensified with perhaps a touch of insanity, which made it painful to look at him. As he never accepted money or anything but food, he of course made his own garments—and what garments they were! . . . He wore a pair of gigantic shoes, about a foot broad at the toes, made of thick cow-hide with the hair on; and on his head was a tall rimless cow-hide hat shaped like an inverted flower-pot. His bodily covering was, however, the most extraordinary: the outer garment, if garment it can be called, resembled a very large mattress in size and shape, with the ticking made of innumerable pieces of raw hide sewn together. It was about a foot in thickness and stuffed with sticks, stones, hard lumps of clay, rams' horns, bleached bones, and other hard heavy objects; it was fastened round him with straps of hide, and reached nearly to the ground. . . .

It was commonly reported that he had at one period of his life committed some terrible crime, and that, pursued by the phantoms of remorse, he had fled to this distant region, where he would never be met and denounced by any former companion, and had adopted his singular mode of life by way of penance. . . . When closely ques-

---

18 It is possible that these two portraits are of the same man. Compare pp. 141-50 of *Far Away* with pp. 150-1 of *Idle Days*.

tioned or otherwise interfered with, then old Con-stair Lo-vair [the name given him by the Hudsons from certain oft-recurring sounds in his recitations] would show that his long cruel penance had not yet banished the devil from his heart. A terrible wrath would disfigure his countenance and kindle his eyes with demoniac fire; and in sharp ringing tones, that wounded like strokes, he would pour forth a torrent of words in his unknown language, doubtless invoking every imaginable curse on his tormentor.

One glimpse is given us, through the awed eyes of the six-year-old Hudson, of an historical figure: Don Eusebio, the court jester of Rosas, marching along a street in Buenos Aires "with tremendous dignity" in a general's uniform—it being "one of the Dictator's little jokes to make his fool a general—all scarlet, with a big scarlet three-cornered hat surmounted by an immense aigrette of scarlet plumes" and accompanied by a bodyguard of twelve soldiers, "also in scarlet, . . . walking six on each side of him with drawn swords in their hands."

Acting somewhat as foils to these picturesque figures are the various members of the Hudson family and the scattered English and Scotch settlers who, though engaged in the same sort of activities as the gaucho, clung to many of their native customs. To those already presented there should be added the tall, slim girl of Cannon House who fell into a wasting illness after her superhuman feat of saving her sister from a bolting horse; Jack the Killer, who fought not, as the gaucho does, by slashing and cutting his adversary into submission but rather by maneuvering for the right opening and then plunging for the heart; and the Gilmours, whose son was kidnapped at the age of five by a discharged gaucho and was found only after having lived for thirty years the life of a gaucho and a soldier. The second nature he had acquired during his long absence his mother, like the singer of the "Song at the Feast of Brougham Castle," thought

was nothing but a colour, a garment, which would wear thinner and thinner, and by-and-by reveal the old deeper ineradicable nature beneath. So she imagined, and would take him out to walk to be with him, to have him all to herself, to caress him, and they would walk, she with an arm round his neck or waist; and when she released him or whenever he could make his escape from the house, he would go off to the quarters of the hired cattlemen and converse with them.

They were his people, and [like the real heir of *Pudd'nhead Wilson*]
he was one of them in soul in spite of his blue eyes. . . .

There are hundreds of portraits of English cottagers. One of
Hudson's chief compensations for walking and cycling about the
countryside was that he could become more intimate with them.
"They were mostly poor people" in out-of-the-way villages or on
remote farms; and he and his wife were also "poor, often footsore,
in need of their ministrations, and nearer to them" for that very
reason. Responding to his innate courtesy and simplicity of manner,
many of these humble folk came to regard him as "one of them,
of their very kin, and though rarely seen and perhaps regarded as
the vagabond of the family, not less well loved on that account."
And they revealed to him, as they did to Wordsworth and Jefferies,
Hewlett and Williamson and Frost, what was withheld from others:
their most intimate experiences and what was most fundamental
and permanent in their characters. It was probably his delight in
the feeling of oneness with them, as well as gratitude for their
many kindnesses and love of their surroundings, that caused him to
sentimentalize their portraits somewhat—to read something of himself into their characters.

Very conscious was Hudson of the differences between the cottagers of the various counties of southern England. Noted earlier
in these pages were his differentiation of the four racial types of
Hampshire peasantry, his admiration for the hardihood and indi-
vidualism of the Saxon of the Sussex Downs, his preference for
those with the Iberian strain, and, most valuable of all despite a
certain want of sympathy, his trenchant analysis of the Cornish
character. The people most loved were those of Somerset.

> They are never wildly enthusiastic like the Lancastrians about any-
> thing, but they are sweeter, more engaging in temper and manner,
> whether on account of their softer climate or the larger infusion of
> Celtic blood in their Anglo-Saxon veins I know not. They are perhaps
> a perfect amalgam, like their Welsh neighbours on the other side
> of the Severn with the harsh lines of the Welsh features subdued,
> and like their Saxon neighbours on the east side without their stolid-
> ity. Moreover, they are not without a spark of that spirit which is in
> the northerner—the romance, the inner bright life which is not
> wholly concerned with material things.

Especially attractive were the women of this county, with their lithe
figures, their regular features, smiling grey-blue eyes and mobile
mouths, their delicate light-brown skin tinged with rose, their graceful manners and air of refinement above those of their sisters of
southern England.

There pervades his scenes of cottars in their inglenooked homes
the sweet humanity to be found in the paintings of Israels and
Lhermitte, the poems of Gibson and Masefield, and the novels
of Eliot and Hardy. Enlivened as they usually are by the skilful
insertion of some of the cottager's own words, one finds oneself
remarking, "How natural it all seems! How utterly true!" As companion-pieces to the interiors already pointed out, one recalls the
salvationists—an inarticulate giant of a man, his classically featured
sister, his gentle comely wife, and their two small children—rearing
a lamb as an offering at the next encampment of their Army; the
outraged mother who had run away from her husband when he
threatened to board out their son so that she might increase her
earnings as a dressmaker; the couple profoundly saddened by the
death of their daughter, who, like Wordsworth's Lucy, had preferred the flowers on the heath to toys and dolls; gaunt, white-
bearded Flowerdew, fast becoming engulfed in poverty, relating to
his young family his experiences at a market-town fourteen miles
away with as much zest as "if he had just returned from Central
Africa or from Thibet"; and two gentle sisters, at the insistence
of their sporting brother, preparing a heron for the table—a roast
that became something more than "a piece of resistance."

As in his description of pub-ridden Chichester, Hudson depre-
cated the public-houses for their brutalizing effect upon the peasantry, but, tired wanderer that he often was, with an interest in
his fellowmen and a taste for wine, his steps would lead him now
and again into some wayside inn. These experiences yielded him
interiors of a different, more racy sort: rustics in solemn discussion
over their beer and pipes or, reminiscent of paintings by Brouwer
and van Ostade, in hilarious spirits. One remembers the oppressive
silence that greeted Hudson in the inn of Cookham Dean when,
after some introductory talk concerning the wildlife round about,
he innocently asked (not knowing that the opprobrious epithet had
been given these villagers by their neighbors), "And what about
badgers?" In another scene, this time an East Dean pub, we over-

hear six men, "a long time busy with their blue mugs," discussing the difficulty of turning out of bed early enough to get to work, one of them denouncing beer as "the curse of the country" and yet, after accidentally upsetting his tall mug with the most eloquent of gestures, ordering it refilled. Best of all these interiors is that in which "The Story of a Jackdaw" takes shape: the cozy bar-parlor of a Wiltshire inn, where fifteen to twenty representative men of the village have foregathered for an evening of good-fellowship. It was only after some chaffing by his fellows and after his throat had been primed by Hudson that the sweep proceeded to relate how he acquired his remarkable pet.

There are a number of tales in his volumes such as may be heard, *mutatis mutandis*, in village inn or cottage the world over— tales of smuggling and poaching, of sheep-stealing and its dire consequences, clashes between peasants and landlords over the abolition of ancient privileges or the introduction of labor-saving machinery, miscarriages of justice, the working-out of curses, broken fortunes and broken hearts, bastardy and unburied corpses. Among the South American tales there are those of how a gaucho scout, encamped on the Rio Colorado, became aware of the great Mendoza earthquake by observing the leaves of the red willows trembling during a dead calm, how the great tree Caligdawa, whose topmost branches reached up to heaven, was felled, and how a quarrel over a parrot led to the Guarani Indians settling in Paraguay. Among the English ones, other than the many in *A Shepherd's Life*, there are those of a young woman suddenly dropping dead a few days after hearing in broad daylight an owl hooting in the great horse-chestnut near her cottage, a Hampshire farmer sending only the words "As a tree falls so shall it lie" to a dying daughter because she had married against his will, the erection of the gibbet on the hill above Coombe and the reason for its preservation.

Among the peasantry, the class receiving most attention is that of the shepherds, the Abrahams and Isaacs and Jacobs of the downs. One of these picturesque figures standing motionless against the sky on a high curve of a down, crook in hand, rough-haired dog by his side, in the midst of a cloudlike flock of quietly feeding sheep was to Hudson, as to Cox, "of those rare human forms in [England], which do not ever seem out of place in the landscape." There are good analyses of the shepherd in *Nature in Downland*

and *A Shepherd's Life*, and in the latter, along with many sketches of those whom his life touched, is the full-length portrait of Caleb Bawcombe—the most skilfully modelled figure (except, of course, that of the artist himself) in Hudson's portfolio. Among the other shepherds that should be included in this group is the one who enlightened Hudson as to how moles exist on the top of waterless downs; the young shepherd with a face such "as the old Greek sculptors have left to the world," who, jolly after a few glasses of beer, jauntily trolled out a song while swinging along a street in Salisbury; and that other broad-shouldered, deep-chested Apollo of a Hampshire down, with light-brown hair, rosy-brown, rough-hewn face, and piercingly blue eyes—one who, "washed clean and clothed becomingly in white flannels" and strolling about "in some great gathering" would have been regarded "with a kind of worship— an impulse to kneel before him." And there are many young Davids of the downs, the most picturesque being the shy, ruddy-faced one standing knee-deep amidst tall grass and the rose-red spikes of sain- foin on a steep down, and wearing in his peakless cap a big woolly thistle blossom. In consequence of Hudson's feeling for shepherds, almost as impressive a group of solitaries can be gathered from his essays as from the poems of Wordsworth.

Many other cottagers, not previously mentioned, press for recog- nition, but there is room here to single out only a few: the woman who discovered a dunnock's nest in a furze bush and, in order to protect the fledglings, allowed herself to be blackmailed by her rough sons until the birds were ready to fly; the dissenter who yielded to the vicar's demand that his wife curtsey to the vicaress— with the proviso, however, that the vicaress return the salutation; the aged woman in Wolmer Forest, daughter of the hornblower to the starving "Selborne mob" of 1820, cudgelling her old brains to recapture for Hudson some of her mother's reminiscences of White; another Hampshire woman who, under the impression that her parents would be eager for the latest village news, made it a point to visit their graves once a week; and the powerfully built and eloquent laborer, "a sort of Walt Whitman both in appearance and temper of mind," who at the age of sixty-five had retired so that he might devote himself to the raising of his class to a higher level not only of economic but of moral and intellectual life.

As regards clergymen, Hudson had mixed feelings. It was disillusioning to find many of them, though preaching a gospel of mercy, insensate to the cruelty of man toward such fellow-creatures as beasts and birds. Thus one is not surprised to find among his portraits those of a young curate who, in order "to wash out the Sunday taste with blood," went a-shooting every Monday, and the lepidopterist who demonstrated how any insect might be caught, no matter how wild or swift. "I cannot imagine him," says Hudson, "in white raiment, with a golden harp in his hand" in that "beautiful country of the Future," for "if here, in *this* country, he could see nothing in a humming-bird hawk-moth among the flowers in the sunshine but an object to be collected, what in the name of wonder will he have to harp about!" And there is humor as well as satire in the sketch of three clergymen who, after killing a wasp, rocked "in their chairs with laughter until they could laugh no more for exhaustion" because Hudson, after exclaiming "And you call yourself religious men!" proceeded to expatiate, tongue in cheek, upon the existence of a Society for the Protection of Wasps. Yet, over against these likenesses, there are those of the vicar who sided with the laborers against the landowners during an agricultural crisis and who kept his church open at all times as a shelter for the poor and the "tall, handsome, white-haired" octogenarian who, instead of the usual blooms, chose to grow "fennel, goat's-beard, henbane, and common hound's-tongue" in his garden, and when speaking of them would stroke "their leaves and stems caressingly."

The manor house appears in an unfavorable light in some of the sketches, for Hudson felt that much of the drabness of village life could be attributed to caste feeling and that in the long shadow of even the best-intentioned squire ("a giant among pigmies") the "moral weeds" of servility, hypocrisy, and parasitism "spring up and flourish." With the establishment of the pheasant as the sacred bird of England and with the gamekeeper as its overzealous protector, the manor also had a baneful effect upon the wild life of the surrounding countryside. Hence there is much of the satirist in the portraiture of squires, as in that of the one who, with the bribe of a hall, expected the villagers to surrender their ancient right-of-way through his beechen woods; short, fat, red-apple-faced Sir Ranulph Damarell, worshipper of the great god Belly, who "exploded in a half-suppressed sniggering laugh" when Hudson

commended some villagers for having kept the birds from starvation during a prolonged frost; and the squire of Abbotsbury, who,
with a duck-gun, shot starlings out of their roosting-place amid
reed and osier beds until even he, "a very monarch" among sportsmen, was sickened at the sight of the dead and wounded falling
like rain into the water. There is, on the other hand, a real bond
of sympathy between the cottager and the true aristocrat, and whenever Hudson came upon one among the landed proprietors, like
the squire of "Norton," it warmed the cockles of his heart.

Children were attractive largely because of their naive, animal-
like charm, in which there is a sense of wonderment at even the
littlest things of life and a spontaneity often revealing the depths
of unconscious being, and because of their "nearness to or oneness
with Nature, resulting from [their] mythical faculty." His belief
that they absorb wisdom from nature intuitively is of course somewhat romantic, but Hudson, unlike many of the early nineteenth-
century romanticists, did not trace that wisdom to any transcendental
source. Attractive also were the integration of the personalties of
children and, as one might expect of the creator of Rima and of
him who preferred the strains of the willow-wren and wood-wren
to the passionate arias of the nightingale, their essential innocence.
Because of this feeling toward children—intensified as it was in
Swinburne and Francis Thompson by his own childlessness—and
his utter naturalness of manner, he could draw very close to them.
For denaturalized ones, however, the little ladies and little Fauntle-
roys of the drawing-room, he had no real interest. "I prefer [the
boy] raw, and would rather have the street-Arab, if in town, and
the unkempt, rough and tough cottage boy in the country."

The feminine mind, so Hudson held with Lewis Carroll, reaches
its perfection in childhood and is not actually fascinating again until
much later, after it has passed the self-conscious stage and become
fused with a strong character. The fairy-like bevy of little girls in
A Traveller in Little Things were in his memory like a bouquet
of rare blossoms: among them, Rose, strangely knowing at the age
of three and amused at being taken for a baby; exquisite Dolly,
whose death called forth his most poignant poem; Millicent, who,
in her almost startlingly distinct voice, gravely declared that even
though her uncle regarded Hudson as a common tramp she would
never forget the way he had once taken her up in his arms and

kissed her; and Mab, of indomitable will, who looked upon the world of grown-ups in the same light as other children look upon dolls and Teddy-bears: "an endless complicated game, which varied from day to day according to the weather and time of year, and had many beautiful surprises." At least five more girls from other volumes should be arranged with this bouquet: Hudson's first love, the grave little Anjelita, with her white, cameo-like face, the girls that begin and end "Birds in a Village," and the two dark sprites of "Wind, Wave, and Spirit," who, with their black hair streaming behind them, raced along the edge of the surf like little dark maenads. Tender and deep though the emotion is in these delicate sketches, it is nicely—perhaps some would say, too severely—restrained by the detachment of the connoisseur who, after watching the brief blossoming of a little charmer and fixing her image indelibly in his memory, continues in his pursuit of beauty forever wandering on her way.

Occasionally the boy, like the bright little fellow who offered Hudson a sprig of southernwood, blossoms as precociously as the girl. But, for the most part, the boy's world is a coarser one, and even though he becomes in the end a fuller human being, his growth is comparatively slow. Boys are quite as numerous as girls in these essays: the little actor in a queer get-up, with a tired expression on his quaint, small face; the weary, tattered, part-gypsy lad who watched with Hudson the wooing antics of the white spider and beside whose sleeping form was placed a penny; the small chap fearlessly treading the dark and lonely path from the village school to the cottage where he was being boarded, who would divulge nothing more about his father's desertion of his mother than that it was the result of an "upset"; and the bashful choir-boy who, while his cows were grazing on the heath, passed his time singing most sweetly. Since boys rarely reveal their innermost feelings, one appreciates them mainly through their activities or hobbies; and, as one might expect, those most interesting to Hudson were the nature-enthusiasts, those who, if their senses remained keen and their memories retentive, would mature into village naturalists, well versed in the lore of the wild. Among these promising lads, many of them shepherds, is the queer little fellow who had been kept from school to save his soul from standardization and whose "impetuous torrent of words in a high shrill voice" reminded Hudson of "a lark in a cage"; the vole-faced, shifty-eyed bird-scarer who from his own observation had discovered that swifts "be up flying about all night and come back in the marning"; and the shepherd-boy who grieved over the death of several two-day-old ring-doves he had discovered in a beech tree and was eager to watch grow up.

The final group of portraits in the pageantry of Hudson's fifteen volumes of essays, and one worth pausing before, is that of the wayfarers he encountered along the highways and byways of southern England. The open road beckoned as invitingly to him as it did to Borrow, Whitman and Davies, and with his skill of capturing a likeness in a few bold strokes and gathering "the minds of men out of their brains," he was able to animate his landscapes with many of them: a gentle-mannered blind man whose inner eye—the picture of the countryside that remained in the memory after an explosion had taken away his sight—guided him over a long route for the retailing of tea; a laborer's wife, with "sun-parched eager face, . . . questioning eyes and friendly smile," who was visiting her native village after a long absence in order to show it off to her fourteen-year-old daughter and who flared up when Hudson called it squalid; a tramp, encountered in a Goring lane, who startled him with his Jefferies-like face; two old women, both visitors to their native village, who met for the first time in their lives in the graveyard and were getting along nicely with each other, becoming even confidential, until the subject arose as to whether a son or a daughter was the better support for a mother in her old age; a very ordinary-looking, middle-aged Australian who was made inexpressibly happy when he recognized the ancestral Hampshire farm, which was last beheld at the age of three; and a clover-seed salesman, looking like "an Oxford undergraduate on a holiday" though thirty and married, whose freshness and bloom was attributed to his close association with clover, the beauty and fragrance of which had entered into his soul and impregnated his whole being.

The quality that impressed Hudson most in his observation of all the multifarious children of life—beasts and birds and insects, as well as men—was the mystery that encompasses and is a part of them, a mystery as unfathomable as life itself. And with his essentially tragic interpretation of that mystery, together with the realization of man's failure to grasp in full measure the joy that nature has placed within his reach, there inevitably came into his portraiture of human beings a note of melancholy, an undertone of the still sad music of humanity. It is well, therefore, that the last two portraits before which we shall linger—the best of these casuals of the way-side—should be those of a solitary old woman, "lightly moving or flitting moth-like or ghost-like over [a] low flat salting" in search of samphire, and several aged pilgrims to Land's End, muffled in their great-coats, too feeble to venture down upon the rough, wind-swept promontory, sitting in dejected postures on the high rocks, twenty to thirty yards apart, each absorbed in his own mournful thoughts but all with the same expression of infinite weariness gazing steadily out on the troubled, cold, grey sea—the first portrait, a companion-piece to Wordsworth's leech-gatherer; the second, to Hewlett's gypsies in Fifield Ashes; and both of them, subjects that would have tempted the brush of a Rembrandt or a K'un-ts'an. In the unsmiling, unchanging eyes of the crone, which "were like those of a captive bird or animal, that [are fixed on] us, yet seem not to see us but to look through and beyond," Hudson thought there could be discerned "a shadowy something which sadness had left in them, when all pleasure and all interest in life forsook her, with all affections, and she no longer cherished either memories or hopes." And these forlorn-looking pilgrims, having reached the Ultima Thule of their life-long dreams—what were their dim sad eyes try-ing to descry in the distance, far beyond the waste of waters upon which they would soon have to embark on that greatest of adven-tures? Was it the blessed isles of their youthful anticipations, "bright with fadeless flowers," where "a great multitude of people in shining garments" would "come down to the shore to welcome" them? Or was it only a silent, empty land of complete rest?[19]

These old men cannot see the objects which appear to younger eyes —the distant passing ships, and the land—that dim, broken line, as of a low cloud on the horizon, of the islands: their sight is altered from what it was, yet is, perhaps, now able to discern things invisible to us—other islands, uncharted, not the Cassiterides. What are they, these other islands, and what do we know of them? Nothing at all; indeed, nothing can be known to the generality; only these life-weary ancients, sitting on rocks and gazing at vacancy, might enlighten us if they would.

---

[19] There is a curious resemblance between the description of this land and that of Patagonia.

Internal Landscapes

> Let the spirit dive
> Deep in self's sea, until the deeps unlock
> The depths and sunken gold of being alive. . . .
>
> —MASEFIELD

> I found in myself, and still find, an instinct to-
> ward a higher, or, as it is named, spiritual life, as
> do most men, and another toward a primitive
> rank and savage one, and I reverence them both.
>
> —THOREAU

AS WITH MOST familiar essayists (and with Rembrandt), the most prominent figure in the Hudsonian landscape is Hudson himself. Reticence, along with a sense of the limitations of his medium, kept him, it is true, from revealing all the facets of his personality. (In his last volume, for instance, we find him apologizing several times for having to illustrate the psychology of the senses with incidents out of his own life.) Yet he did not hesitate to present the boy Hudson at full length and with many intimate details; and though there are but few glimpses of him as a young man, the many of his middle and later years, adding stroke upon stroke to the composite self-portrait, give one the impression of a completely coherent and well-rounded personality. Much of the interest, as well as the unity, of his pageantry of La Plata, Patagonia, and southern England comes from a sense of the author's presence, and it is the purpose of this chapter and the one on his philosophy, to discuss those qualities of personality that have not already been dwelt upon.

As might be expected of one whose senses absorbed so large a part of the natural world and who believed that the sense of the beautiful was God's greatest gift to mankind, there was in Hudson, more than in Wordsworth or Thoreau, a large pagan acceptance of the sensuous beauty of life for its own sake. To him, the most substantial and unequivocal pleasure during the brief span between birth and death is the immediate enjoyment of all natural beauty wherever found. In Christianity he would have preferred a larger element of pagan worship, such as that of the sun-god by the ancient Persians. On a fine day in June or October, when "drinking in the pure air like a draught of eternal life," who can believe in original sin, with all its dire consequences? And one of the best faculties of the brain seemed to Hudson that of storing for long years within ourselves, like the "gladness of old sunshine," memories of vanished impressions.

His appetite for sights, sounds, tastes, scents, and textures being so enormous, he felt, when taking stock of himself just before passing over the threshold into manhood, that he should be quite content if only he could continue to live in his paradise of sense impressions:

To rise each morning and look out on the sky and the grassy dew-wet earth from day to day, from year to year. To watch every June and July for spring, to feel the same old sweet surprise and delight at the appearance of each familiar flower, every new-born insect, every bird returned once more from the north. To listen in a trance of delight to the wild notes of the golden plover coming once more to the great plain, flying, flying south, flock succeeding flock the whole day long. . . . To climb trees and put my hand down in the deep hot nest of the Bien-te-veo and feel the hot eggs—the five long pointed cream-coloured eggs with chocolate spots and splashes at the larger end. To lie on a grassy bank with the blue water between me and beds of tall bulrushes, listening to the mysterious sounds of the wind and of hidden rails and coots and courlans conversing together in strange human-like tones; to let my sight dwell and feast on the *camaloté* flower amid its floating masses of moist vivid green leaves. . . . To ride at noon on the hottest days, when the whole earth is a-glitter with illusory water, and see the cattle and horses in thousands, covering the plain at their watering-places, to visit some haunt of large birds at that still, hot hour and see storks, ibises, grey herons, egrets of a dazzling whiteness, and rose-coloured spoonbills and flamingoes, standing in the shallow water in which their motionless forms are reflected.

Even though the arrangement of his impressions into essays must have brought the pleasure of lingering over them and viewing them in a better perspective, he was wont to complain that it kept him from new experiences with "living, breathing, palpitating nature." With senses continually refreshed by the feeling of wonder, he could keep on returning to nature again and again, without satiety.

As indicated in such scenes as the opening one of *Nature in Downland* and the closing one of "Wind, Wave and Spirit," Hudson had the gift of being able to surrender himself completely to the passing moment. Though he was at times acutely aware of the evanescence of these sensations—the "tragic dividing of forces on their way"—and the fragility of his own health, there is none of that feverishness in his enjoyment characteristic of the later Jefferies. The speculations of a field naturalist frequently enriched particular moments, but such was the vividness of his senses and the strength of his aesthetic faculty that many of these moments were sufficient unto themselves.

Thought was not; in enjoyment it expired.

Few others have ever felt richer "in the simple worship of a day."

In a paradise of sense impressions, there always lurks the danger of a loss of emotional as well as intellectual perspective. The last sensation, though of less intrinsic value, may seem the supreme one simply because it is the last: the mere focussing of one's consciousness on what is still palpitating may leave far more significant sensations in a penumbra. Thus, when Hudson was seated amidst his notebooks busy on an essay or volume, it often occurred to him that some recent sight—a squirrel frisking fantastically or a black redstart just arrived from Holland—was worth "a hundred times [more] than" those recorded a year earlier; and the wooing of a spider once made him feel, for a time at least, that spiders generally are "the most interesting beings in nature—the proper study of mankind, in fact." Yet, despite the great number of his sensuous experiences, there is no promiscuity in the appreciation of them. His sensibilia, unlike those of Rousseau, Whitman and many other romanticists, never break into a Dionysian rout. Pater himself and his followers of the 'nineties, even though their search usually led them toward the realm of art, did not seek the perfect moment, when appetite becomes distilled into passion, with a more gemlike flame. And the record of these moments, small as well as great, always gives one a feeling of an organic whole, for they are seen against the background of his entire experience and that of a large part of mankind.

Leading this natural aesthete to many of his best landscape moments were his fine instincts as a wayfarer. It was, for example, his custom never to consult a guidebook until he had first formed his own impression of a place, for whilst a Baedeker may direct the attention to more items of interest, it weakens reliance upon one's own perceptions and eliminates that element of experience which, like certain chemicals used in dyes, imprints them indelibly upon the memory—the joy of discovery. Continually lured on by the charm of the unknown, Hudson relied most upon first impressions. "In a majority of instances," he remarks, "the more familiar a place becomes to us the less well we know it. At all events we have ceased to know it in the same way; we no longer vividly, consciously see it in its distinctive character." Whenever he felt himself growing too attached to any one spot—that his "vegetative nerves" were fastening themselves "like tendrils to every object and 'every grass' " —he would become alarmed and hasten to break all tethers in order to become once more, what he most wanted to be, "a wanderer with no ties." And knowing how difficult it is to beget a golden time again, he rarely revisited a place that some moment of rapture had enshrined in his memory.

Many of his experiences, it is true, began and ended in the senses. But when under the influence of the mythical faculty, he was able to perceive "the powers behind the veil of sense"—not only those within many natural objects and creatures and those abroad in many places but also (it will be remembered) "something far more deeply interfused," the spirit of nature as a whole. Thus, even though yearning for a life of sensations, he came to value most, as did Keats, Thoreau and Rilke, those that revealed the inner rhythm of each several object and the fugal pattern of Nature's plastic stress.

A large number of these moments, both the purely sensuous and the sensuous-mystical, we have already shared with Hudson in these pages. Some of them were spectacular ones, which, had they come to us directly, would in all probability have compelled attention. What is, however, equally impressive, and in some ways more so, is his appreciation of the humble growths of mother-earth and the simple everyday immediacies of life, which most of us, with our various preoccupations, pass by unnoticed. These things can loom large in our lives, many of them, particularly in childhood and old age, reaching somewhat the same level of importance as the larger ones.

The big things pass, the little things remain.

It is, indeed, chiefly because Turner trafficked too much with grandeur and did not record enough of the common, unrhymed poetry of rural life that he has never been so close to the hearts of the English as Constable.

Like many of the romantic writers and painters, Hudson had the power of looking upon the seemingly inconsequential things of ordinary experience with imagination. Perhaps in no way is his essential creativeness and artistry more apparent than in his ability to make the slightest things ponderable and the commonest com-

monplace take on beauty. This was accomplished not only by an
affectionate intimacy and fine selectivity of detail but by weaving
around each object a wealth of associations and by the intensity of
his emotion. Indeed, in the changing of the water of everyday life
into wine, Hudson belongs with Crome and Constable and Cox,
Ruskin and Thoreau and Morris, Herrick and Wordsworth and
de la Mare.

Many little or familiar things—ivy, the evening primrose and
the camalote, geese and hawks, shepherds and little girls, spiders
and snakes and donkeys—have become more precious to us because
of his canticle of them, as simple as a folk air and with its occasional poignancy. How much, in *Adventures among Birds*, is made
out of the caged cardinal of his youth and his meeting with a weary
redwing on the sand dunes of Norfolk! Once in that same county
he came upon a pool of rain water in the middle of a pale-green
pasture, upon which floated several ducks; and as the result of "the
sudden magic of the sunlight," lending to the wind-ruffled water
the deep blue of the sapphire and to the plumage of the birds a
surpassing whiteness, he could not but exclaim to himself, "I have
never seen a more beautiful thing!" And fuller though the detail is
and different the emotional response, his little sketch gives to the
imagination something of the same release as Snaith's "Moorhen"
and Allingham's "Four Ducks on a Pond." Even fresh cow-dung,
when covered with a dense mass of great, yellow Asilus flies, took
on for him the aspect of "an embossed mound" of barbaric gold—
a response difficult to those not of Hindu sensibility.

Not only through his search for the perfect moment and through
the strength of his mythical faculty was Hudson's hedonism saved
from superficiality and amorphousness but likewise through his
capacity for thought—thought that kept touching life on many
sides and often embraced the largest concepts. Though the pages
of great thinkers provided valuable assistance, he preferred to forge
his own mind rather than merely furnish it with the ideas of others.
As much as Wordsworth and Whitman, he recognized the value
of wise passiveness. Many a thought sprang up in his mind, as
though spontaneously, while he galloped over "the green floor of
the world" and along the Rio Negro or sauntered over the uplands
of Sussex, Wiltshire, and Cornwall. It is this quality—the deter-
mination to understand the world and himself in himself rather

than in Darwin, Spencer, Butler, William James, and others—that gives his thinking a strong individual flavor. If one is merely eager to gain information—to gulp down facts and figures—there are (except of course in the realm of Argentine ornithology) many more amply furnished minds to consult than Hudson's. What turns one to him, apart from aesthetic enjoyment, is a certain quiet, permeating wisdom—knowledge long saturated in experience.

Most of his thoughts on landscape, biology and animal psychology, as well as a few on human beings, have already been presented. Among these, as is to be expected of a traveller in little things, are many concerning the "small unpainful riddles" of life, such as the secret of the charm of flowers, birds, and little girls. If Hudson, like Herrick, had written an extended "argument" to his collected works, there might well have been included such further ones as: why the Devil's name is associated with many singular features of landscape; the effect of muzzling upon the temper of dogs; the depth to which earthworms burrow; why some persons find they must sleep in a north-south position in order to get a proper night's rest; the disturbing effect of the surreptitious gaze of one creature upon another; and why old peasants do not survive their mates for long.

Though more occupied with the non-human world, Hudson's mind kept reaching out also to other major concerns of mankind: the value of art, the elements of a good life, the problems of society, and the nature of the force behind life. Since he rarely gathered his thoughts on any of these subjects into a single essay and had little of the power to make an *obiter dictum* memorable by its very phrasing, one must not expect to find among his writings anything so well focussed as Montaigne's "Of Books" and "Of Custom, and How a Received Law Should Not Easily Be Changed," Hazlitt's "On Wit and Humour" and "On the Difference between Writing and Speaking," or, to turn to a fellow out-of-door essayist, Thoreau's "Life without Principle" and "Civil Disobedience." The very way in which his thoughts are scattered through his volumes adds, however, to their suggestiveness.

Of man's aesthetic faculty and its manifold creations, Hudson had much to say. Though the origin of a thing does not determine its value, he did art good yeoman's service by contesting Darwin's assertion (later supported by Freud) that all beauty is a by-product

of the sex impulse, and Santayana's, that all its various manifestations, in comparison with the realities of man's existence on this
globe, are like the wild strawberry springing from the crevices of a
granite mountain—mere casual and superficial growths. Yet some
of the uses to which this faculty has been put during the history of
mankind disturbed him. "To be a great, an *exquisite*, artist," so he
declares, "is not the greatest thing. A great artist . . . is a quite
small being compared to a great man." For the great man, never
losing wholeness of vision, responds to the full complexity of life,
whereas many artists, unable to create well in more than one field,
warp their general outlook on life by concentrating too closely on
a limited area of experience and starve many of their emotions by
overfeeding one. The result is specialization and elaboration, which
in turn lead to abnormality and degeneration—"at all events, [to]
something wholly out of proportion to and out of harmony with
things as they exist." Unless art comes as naturally as fruit to the
tree or, as to many Renaissance artists, along with other activities—
so Keats and Thoreau and Morris likewise felt—it had better not
come at all. Certainly this has been the secret of much of the
strength, if also some of the weakness, of English art.

Then, too, like the grasshopper suitors in Harewood Forest who
were more interested in their own musical rivalry than in their
inamorata, some artists, Hudson thought, become so absorbed in
their artistry as to forget one of art's prime functions—to serve the
whole of life. As was increasingly noticeable in his day, they withdraw into their private worlds, where they are wont to employ an
esoteric language not readily comprehensible except to a small
coterie, and, dissociating form from substance, arrogantly exalt art
above life. Such "pure" or orchidaceous artists are without the
breadth possessed, say, by many-sided Morris: the ability to "despise
perfection in art as . . . a thing [not] great enough for man" and
to refuse to seek out "beauty [as the] sole object" of art. In spite
of the formal values involved, their belles-lettres or *beaux-arts*
impressed Hudson much as Poe's verse did Emerson—a "mere
by-product of the mind, a beautiful excrescence, which is of no
importance to the race, and without which most of us are just as
rich and happy in our lives."

Such art may actually commit the greatest injury of which it is
capable—leading life astray. But even in the best art, the art that

haunted elms in Kensington Gardens—just though that anger was—
he gratuitously attacks the government's purchase of the Blenheim
paintings for the National Gallery—"half a dozen dreary canvases,
. . . dust and ashes for the hungry and thirsty!"

There is, however, a more intimate connection between art and
nature than Hudson was aware of. He had, it is true, a sense of the
harmony that exists between certain works of art and their milieu: an
English church or cottage with the surrounding countryside and
Wagner's music with the landscape of primeval Europe—harmonies
similar to those between Frank Wright's homes and the American
landscape or between the music of Williams and Fabini and the fen
country of England and the plains of Uruguay. And he felt deeply
how certain places, like Selborne, the Lake District and Walden,
have become spiritualized, acquiring a glory not altogether their
own, through association in our minds with the writings of the
men who loved them. Knowing how much our attitude toward
nature as a whole has been influenced by the reading of Wordsworth, Thoreau and Meredith, he also recognized, in some measure,
what truth there is in the Whistlerian dictum about Nature imitating
art. But his remark that "when we go back to Nature" after looking
at the paintings of Constable and Turner "we are only too glad to
forget all about" them, indicates that he was not to the same degree
aware of the power of the other arts to awaken our consciousness to
certain aspects of nature. How many of the qualities revealed by
Chinese or Cézanne landscape, for instance, would elude us as we
tramp among hills and mountains, if we have not been trained to
alertness!

As has already been pointed out, Hudson was aware at times,
in his own writing, of a certain co-operation on the part of Nature—
a *participation mystique*. But what he failed to realize sufficiently,
else the artificiality of art would not have been stressed so much,
was that the same sort of co-operation is to be found, in varying
degrees, in all forms of art. In fact, every artistic creation that is
deeply intuited and shaped under continuous inspiration from Nature possesses many of the qualities of a living organism—a principle suggestively stated by Coleridge, profoundly influential in the
thinking of Thoreau and Whitman, and ably defended in our own
day by Bergson and Herbert Read. In order to clarify his vision,

the artist makes a selection from the diffuse abundance of nature, and, to project it, intensifies some of the elements chosen; but during the whole process, he is obeying inner laws with which Nature herself has endowed him. The principle of proportion known as dynamic symmetry is based, for example, upon the laws of the logarithmic or "constant angle" spiral, one of the most wide-spread forms of life. Because the Chinese landscapists, especially those of the tenth century, attempted to follow the procedure of Nature and create from within—conceiving a form of their own to express their ideas of the inner reality of Nature rather than merely copying a particular scene—they were able to depict more profoundly than our Occidental artists the great elemental forces of Nature and man's relationship to them. Indeed, it is through the development of the artistic instinct in man that Nature has reached her clearest and highest expression.

To some extent, Hudson was aware of the Promethean rôle art has played in the development and enrichment of culture. It was of course one of the chief means by which Nature brought man to self-expression and thus to his present high level in the animal world. But, except perhaps among the early primitive peoples, he did not fully appreciate the excellent way in which art summarizes the various stages in the development of a particular culture. Nor did he sufficiently realize, as the following passage indicates, that certain works of art and certain periods of civilization possess final values in themselves.

What a wail there would be in the world if a sudden destruction were to fall on the accumulated art-treasures of the National Gallery, and the marbles in the British Museum, and the contents of the King's Library—the old prints and mediaeval illuminations! And these are only the work of human hands and brains—impressions of individual genius on perishable material, immortal only in the sense that the silken cocoon of the dead moth is so, because they continue to exist and shine when the artist's hands and brain are dust; and man has the long day of life before him in which to do again things like these, and better than these, if there is any truth in evolution.[4] But the forms of life in the two higher vertebrate

---

[4] The fallacy in this argument was pointed out long ago by Hazlitt in his "Why the Arts Are Not Progressive." One cannot improve upon the pyramid of Khufru or *Hamlet* or Bach's *Passacaglia in C Minor,* if for no other reason than that it is impossible to reproduce the conditions of which they are perfect expressions.

classes are Nature's most perfect work; and the life of even a single species is of incalculably greater value to mankind, for what it teaches and would continue to teach, than all the chiselled marbles and painted canvases the world contains. . . .

How much of a whole culture is epitomized in the Parthenon, the *Divine Comedy*, the paintings of Leonardo and the sculptures of Michelangelo, *Faust* and *The Magic Mountain* and *Ulysses*! Great artists and past cultures have discovered fine harmonies between the shifting phenomenal world and the "Unseen Spirit"; and even though Hudson was looking forward to a more permanent adjustment between man and Nature, those past achievements are beautiful and significant in themselves—manifestations of the highest workings of that Spirit and bulwarks against the tides and shifting currents of the centuries. It was primarily because of his failure to lay so full a claim upon his cultural patrimony as the great Romantics of a century earlier that he was kept from becoming more than a man large against the background of nature—a man, Goethe-like, grand also against the background of humanity's entire creativeness.

Despite these deficiencies in his general attitude toward art, Hudson made considerable use of its various creations in the enrichment of his own life, and the generous inclusion of them in his essays and letters gives fuller relief to the self-portrait. Since his acquaintance with aesthetic theories was slight, one must not expect much technical criticism, though, as a craftsman of poetry, essays and fiction, he could speak from the vantage-point of intimate experience. Nor, except in the province of nature writing, will one find his historical knowledge of any of the arts extensive, for even in poetry, where his appreciation was wide and deep and in some periods extraordinarily minute, his background was that of an amateur. When he touches upon a work of art, therefore, his comments are rarely those of a specially trained sensibility; they arise, rather, out of broad natural feelings and knowledge, and are primarily concerned with the texture and value of the experience presented and the quality of the personality behind the work. Though tending, particularly in the graphic arts, to place observed fact above reason and sometimes above imagination, he insisted that reality be depicted with a glow, and, since mystery is latent in all reality, with an element of strangeness. This general human approach to the various arts is appropriate to the familiar and, even more so, to the out-of-door essayist; for however wanting the comments may be in critical value, they at least shed considerable light upon their author.

When buildings are included in his essays the emphasis is usually on how well they harmonize with the landscape and the extent to which nature has been at work upon them. The palatial red-brick pleasure domes of the mighty Kubla Khans of the business world and the naked, granite, boxlike conventicles of the Methodists are not only ugly in themselves but an affront to Nature. Because the spire of Chichester pulls the surrounding countryside together more effectively than the nobler and more lyrical one of Salisbury, it was held in higher regard. Of considerable aesthetic value to any building are the natural floral embellishments.

> The way . . . in which the colours are distributed [over Salisbury Cathedral] is an example of Nature's most perfect artistry; on the lower, heavier buttressed parts, where the darkest hues should be, we find the browns and rust-reds of the minute aerial alga, mixed with the greys of lichen, these darker stainings extending upwards to a height of fifty or sixty feet, in places higher, then giving place to more delicate hues, the pale tender greens and greenish greys, in places tinged with yellow, the colours always appearing brightest on the smooth surface between the windows and sculptured parts. The effect depends a good deal on atmosphere and weather: on a day of flying clouds and a blue sky, with a brilliant sunshine on the vast building after a shower, the colouring is most beautiful. It varies more than in the case of colour in the material itself or of pigments, because it is a "living" colour. . . .

Since birds, with their aerial evolutions, make us lift up our eyes, they add much to our appreciation of architecture; and of these the most valuable are the daws, with their conspicuous black plumage, their loquacity, and their everlasting restlessness. "The noblest cathedral without any jackdaws soaring and gambolling about its towers is apt to seem," so Hudson provocatively puts it, "little more than a great barn, or a Dissenting chapel on a gigantic scale."

Buildings deeply scarred by time or almost completely taken over by nature attracted him profoundly. Roman Calleva (now Silchester), with its many relics and its vast walls overgrown with ivy, bramble and thorn, and providing anchorage for many trees, was a favorite haunt. Glastonbury Abbey seemed the "loveliest" of English ruins, even though it had been somewhat desecrated by the hand of the restorer. "Fifty years of sun and rain will prepare the fresh, hard surfaces for the vegetation that makes a ruin beautiful—valerian, ivy-toadflax, wall-flower, and grey and green lichens and mosses." [5] As might be expected of one who felt consanguineous in spirit to the generations of the barrows, the grey, rough-hewn guardians of the necropolis that is Stonehenge seemed to surpass, particularly on an early summer morning, any other building erected by man, enjoying pure fame.

As indicated earlier, rose-and-creeper-covered cottages, weather-stained village churches and cathedrals appear with some frequency in Hudson's landscapes. He took issue with White on the proper size of a village church:

> [The] smallness, or "meanness" as he expresses it, of the Hampshire churches is, to my mind, one of their greatest merits. The Hampshire village would not possess that charm which we find in it—its sweet rusticity and homeliness, and its harmonious appearance in the midst of a nature green and soft and beautiful—but for that essential feature and part of it, the church which does not tower vast and conspicuous as a gigantic asylum or manufactory from among lowly cottages dwarfed by its proximity to the appearance of pigmy-built huts in the Aruwhimi forest. These immense churches which in recent years have lifted their tall spires and towers amidst lowly surroundings in many rural places, are, as a rule, the work of some zealot who has seared his sense of beauty with a hot iron, or else of a new over-rich lord of the manor, who must have all things new, including a big new church to worship a new God in—his own peculiar Stock Exchange God, who is a respecter of wealthy persons.

As with Ruskin, a special virtue of English cathedrals is that many of them, being the expression "of many minds and many periods, . . . are imperfect even as Nature is in her rocks and trees. . . ." The

---

[5] One need only look at the ruins depicted in Poussin's paintings to see that there is another way of appreciating them.

fault with Salisbury Cathedral,[6] so he argued, is that "it came complete from its maker's brain, like a coin from the mint, and being all in one symmetrical plan, . . . has the trim, neat appearance of a toy cathedral carved out of wood and set on a green-painted square."

The tender, mystical twilight of church interiors, often enriched by rare stained glass, various stone sculptures, and by brasses and old wooden carvings, moved him deeply. The inscriptions on the walls, looking at times "like the pages of an old black-letter volume without margins," provided him, as did those on gravestones, with material for an occasional essay. He was not unmindful of certain structural defects in even the greatest of these interiors—"a Wells divided, a ponderous Ely, a vacant and cold Canterbury," and an Exeter spoilt by a monstrous organ in the wrong place. That of Salisbury seemed "too light and airy," but after a while he made the discovery that he "could go oftener and spend more hours" there "without a sense of fatigue or depression than in any other," for he experienced no such

instantaneous change, as of a curtain being drawn excluding the light and air of day and of being shut in, which [one does] on entering other religious houses. This is due, first, to the vast size of the interior, the immense length of the nave, and the unobstructed view . . . owing to the removal by the "vandal" Wyatt of the old ponderous stone screen—an act for which I bless while all others curse his memory; secondly, to the comparatively small amount of stained glass there is to intercept the light. So graceful and beautiful is the interior that it can bear the light, and light suits it best, just as a twilight best suits Exeter and Winchester and other cathedrals with heavy sculptured roofs. One marvels at a building so vast in size which yet produces the effect of a palace in fairyland, or of a cathedral not built with hands but brought into existence by a miracle.

Unlike Jefferies, who had a real passion for Greek and Roman marbles, Hudson was seldom attracted to sculpture. More sensitive to color than to form, as are most of those who put emotion above reason, he shows a greater knowledge and appreciation of painting. A landscape of the pampas, "with a pool and reeds and rushes,

---

6 It was only after many visits that Hudson sufficiently warmed up to this cathedral to call it "a marvel of beauty in its entirety" (*Afoot in England*, p. 228). Those of Exeter and Wells were more to his liking, but there is less about them in his essays.

and a group of wild horses on its edge in the foreground" so enchanted him as a youth that he felt "life without the power which such art confers on its followers [would] hardly [be] life at all." Had the skill been commensurate to the will, this lover of the wilderness would probably have painted in the tradition of Moran and Bierstadt and Keith, for, even had he been of a later generation, he could scarcely have brought himself to the more abstract approach of, say, Paul Nash or John Marin. As to his appreciation of paintings, his eye was occasionally held by an animal portrait, those of Altamira and Meidum as well as of Swan and Landseer, and by landscapes, most of all those of Turner, whose audacity at least he thought splendid. In the portraiture of human beings, as Rothenstein was made to realize, he insisted upon a close likeness—"a sense or an illusion of being in the presence of a living person with whom [he was] engaged in a wordless conversation, and who is revealing his inmost soul" to him. Drawings and water-colors should have held him most, for in them there is greater immediacy of experience and closeness to inspiration, but even here his demand seems to have been more for a transcript of reality than a translation.

Chinese pottery, Roman mosaics, Persian and Turkish carpets always regaled his eyes, but to most household furnishings he remained indifferent, in large measure because that part of his sensitivity—his background and pursuits being what they were—had never been cultivated. Except for binoculars and bicycles and the cinema, the products of the machine meant little to him, and, though taking great interest in the handicrafts of early primitive peoples— their arrowheads, flint knives and scrapers, their mortars and pestles, their pottery and precious-stone ornaments[7]—and some in those of the gauchos, he seems to have given little attention to the small rural arts of England. As a result, one misses in his writings of that countryside what one enjoys, say, in Massingham and Williamson, a generous inclusion not only of rural crafts but of folk songs and folk ballads.

Hudson's taste for literature was more catholic than his principles would seem to allow. Since purely artistic values were not of prime value to him, he generally disapproved of the "literary man's writer[s]"—DeQuincey, Landor, Peacock, Wilde, George Moore—

---

[7] Some of those he gathered are now in the Pitt-Rivers Museum.

deeming most of them insincere. "When I read C[hesterton]," he says, "I am inclined to exclaim with the young fellow after witnessing the old man's feat of balancing an eel on his nose—'What made you so wonderfully clever?' " And as much as he admired Tennyson and Swinburne, he was somewhat repelled by their frequent absorption in their artistry. With what has been called "red brick literature"—that dealing with deracinated, over-urbanized lives (whether of a Limehouse or a Mayfair) and suffering greatly when read *alfresco*—he had little affinity. But, moving as he occasionally did amongst the authors of such books and having been, for some strange reason, induced to write one himself, he was not unacquainted with even this sort of literature.

In the realms of natural history, travel literature, and the out-of-door essay he was, as has already been noted at some length, very familiar. A listing of books he knew in these as well as other realms of prose literature would be impressive.[8] Those in which animal psychology is used to explain some extraordinary human reaction, as in Keats's *Lamia* and Holmes's *Elsie Venner*, always intrigued him, and, on such occasions, his comments, like the ones passed by a sailor on the seamanship of a Kipling or a Masefield, have the value of a specialist's. Any book was welcomed that, like those of Warde Fowler, Alfred Williams, John Halsham, Edward Thomas, H. J. Massingham, Olive Schreiner, Henry Forbes, Morley Roberts, Hilaire Belloc, and Charles Doughty (to name only some of his contemporaries), took him beyond his experience as a field naturalist or added another portion of the earth to his mental geography. He had a special fondness for the sketches of Cunninghame Graham, detecting in them "the rare union of two qualities—intense individuality, and detachment, which enables [him] to identify [him]self even with those who are most unlike us." Landor's *Imaginary Conversations* was too sculpturesque ("one gets tired of being long at that elevation, sitting on a column as it were") and *The Private Papers of Henry Ryecroft* (perhaps because of knowing Gissing personally) wanting in "all that was most interesting" in the author's life. A man after his own heart was Sir Thomas Browne,

---

8 A partial list is to be found in Herbert F. West's *W. H. Hudson's Reading* (Milwaukee, 1947). One can indeed relive much of the literary history of his times by going through his letters.

who "could afford to give himself away freely, simply because he could do it in words of such charm, and with so godlike a gesture, that the sophisticated and the simple both feared to laugh at him lest their laugh should be taken for that of fools." Because of their strong human flavor, he found much pleasure in such biographies and journals as those of Hunt, DeQuincey, Trelawny, Borrow, Bashkirtseff, Blunt, Strindberg, and Strachey. Of Samuel Johnson, particularly as the author of *The Lives of the Poets* and the hero of Boswell's *Life*, he "never . . . tired." [9]

Of all the arts, those that receive the most attention are music and poetry, "born of one mother . . . [and] nourished at the same savage breasts." As a boy, he discovered "that half a dozen lines charged with poetic feeling about nature often gave . . . more satisfaction than a whole volume of prose" on the same subject, and, with an ear previously attuned only to the music of the voice and the guitar, that of the cathedral orchestra of Buenos Aires on a great saint's day came as a revelation, making him tremble "with an excess of delight" and haunting him for weeks afterward. As we have seen, he continually sought expression in verse; and without much exaggeration it might be said that he married a voice. In comparison with his technical knowledge of poetry, that in music was decidedly limited, nor was his taste so sure, but he kept fairly well abreast of the latest developments in both mediums, reading Yeats and Pound and listening to the atonalities and polytonalities of the concert halls.

In the course of his speculations on music, which are largely from the point of view of a naturalist, he has some suggestive things to say about its relationship to poetry. It seemed incredible to him that any composer should have attempted to set such great poems as "They Are All Gone into a World of Light," "Ode to the West Wind," "Ululume," and "Itylus" to music, for these sister arts "are furthest apart when at their greatest. . . ." Their relationship is sometimes suggested in the poetry "in which the thought, however lofty, is felt and expressed with passion, when thought and passion are welded into one"—but never in music. Indeed, the occasion upon which these "two distinct supreme arts . . . actually meet and become

---

[9] His reading in the novel, which was extensive, will be considered in the next chapter.

one," so Hudson argues, "is when both (as arts) are at their lowest, when the music is nearest to primitive music, and the poetry is the lowliest, the simplest, the nearest to emotional speech." The finest example of such a union seemed to him to be the ballad of "Auld Robin Gray." "Perhaps the only song of the nineteenth century to be mentioned in the same breath" is "Swanee River."

Two other theories of Hudson in regard to music are not so convincing. He is probably correct in tracing the beginnings of human music further back than did Diderot and Spencer—to "emotional sounds emitted by the human and semi-human species of the Pliocene before articulate speech was invented." And he is certainly right in opposing the latter's assertion that all music is vocal in origin and has for its chief function the improvement of speech. But very questionable is his argument that "the faculty or invention of speech but served to develop the original animal music to our higher music. Rhythm, which is rare in animal and is essential in human music, is an outcome of emotional speech. . . . " For, as Edmund Gurney pointed out long ago,[10] the cadences of speech, particularly of impassioned speech, are innumerable and without definiteness, and some of them, such as the gliding transitions and the ungraduated pitch, would be inimical to the creation of melody. Merely because one of the instruments of music, the larynx, happens to be the same as that of speech is no proof that speech has vitally affected its general structure. Some musical forms, it is true, have been conditioned somewhat by their association with words, but, essentially, all of them are of unique inception.

Also questionable, for he does not refer only to his personal responses, is the contention that music makes its appeal entirely to the emotions: "Music is wholly emotion—emotion recollected in tranquillity—passion purified from pain, sublimated, beautified, glorified, but always passion, passion, passion and nothing else." He was careful, however, not to narrow its expressiveness to the recollection of specific emotional experiences—"the passions that have swayed the soul on particular occasions and long-past states of happiness and misery." Rather, it is the purest sort of emotion—the feeling that "all these events and passions have left in the mind, even after the actual facts, the cause of the associations, have been for-

10   *The Power of Sound* (London, 1880).

gotten." Such a contention is, of course, given strong support by
the great bulk of music, of which the symphonies of Tschaikowsky,
Sibelius and Shostakovitch are among the highest examples, though
even here the appeal is, to a certain extent, an intellectual one, especially to the trained musician. But when music is most music, as in
some of the compositions of Bach and Mozart, it is essentially
untranslatable in terms of the sensuous imagination, the intellect,
or the usual varieties of emotion, no matter how thoroughly purified
or glorified. Such absolute music makes its appeal primarily to the
musical imagination, which has nothing to do with anything except
music, and it brings tidings to us of a world just as authentic and
as wonderful as those brought by any of the other arts.

Much as he enjoyed natural sounds, Hudson was too aware of
the peculiar genius of music, the art least dependent upon the outside world, to wish them imitated in it: "The least touch of what
may be called realism in music is fatal to its charm and its mystery."
With his interest in the human overtones in the world of sounds,
he took great delight in the songs of simple people, the arias from
the older operas, the songs from Handel's oratorios, and the music
dramas of Wagner. When speaking about the various effects of
music upon him, he could be profoundly self-revelatory. The music
that engaged his deepest emotions seems to have been scored in the
key of melancholy; and, as might be expected of one who felt
especially close to primitive man, that melancholy was often part
of the pathos of distance:

> It is essentially the "Passion of the Past"—not of mine only, my
> own little emotional experiences, but that of the race, the inherited
> remembrances or associations of its passionate life, back to a period
> so remote that it cannot be measured by years. A dreadful past, but
> at so great a distance that it is like the giant terrifying mountain, the
> heart-breaking stony wilderness with winter everlasting for its crown,
> seen afar off, softened and glorified with rose and purple colour, at
> eventide.

In his discussion of orchestral music, in which Tschaikowsky
seems to have been a favorite, he stressed its human associations by
pointing out that the evolution of many instruments has been
toward a stronger human expression and that the most skilful blending of their sounds is "like an echo of vocal music." It was because
of there being much less of this quality in the piano than in the

violin, the 'cello, the flute and the oboe, that he did not care much for it as a solo instrument. Yet, despite the stressing of human associations (of which he makes too much), it was probably the interfusion of a large element of the non-human with the human that made him declare that orchestral music "is, in our species, the better half of music." "We are far more powerfully affected by" such sounds, he says, "than by vocal, because singing is wholly, purely human and is ours, but instrumental music is not ours in the same way: it is ours, . . . but clarified, beautified, spiritualised beyond the range of the human voice, and the expression is consequently intensified." Though "reminiscent of the earth and our earthly lives," it seems to come "from otherwhere."

Since poetry is more immediate to experience than prose and more explicit than music, it is not surprising that it should have provided Hudson with what was, "apart from nature," his "chief pleasure . . . in life." And that pleasure is communicated—by paraphrase, quotation, or comment—on almost every page of his essays. His own experience in writing verse undoubtedly helped to develop a greater sensitivity to its formal values, and he was sufficiently alive to intellectual poetry to suggest that it would have been better had Wordsworth included thought along with emotion to be recollected in tranquillity. But what he insisted upon most in poets, as in other writers, was that they speak from full personal experience: "To me they are no good even if they write like angels if they do not write from the heart." His characteristic emphasis upon content—particularly the sort of material that interested him—occasionally led him astray, as when he calls the decidedly artificial "Music's Duel" of Crashaw "perhaps the finest bird poem in our literature" and the ingenious but poetically unimpressive *Paradise of Birds* by Courthope "the finest [apologue] written in this century, perhaps in any century since man invented the art of imparting lessons of wisdom by fable and allegory." But, even though he depended too much upon personal taste as a divining-rod, his was, in the main, remarkably sound and sure.

An ingratiating quality in his essays is the space given the *petits maîtres* among poets. In large measure, this appreciation was the result not only (as already noted) of a sense of kinship and a feeling that they, with their "lower kind of inspiration," could better reveal rural life but also a sense of obligation because of the pleasure they

In such moments we sometimes feel a kinship with, and are strangely drawn to, the dead, who were not as these; the long, long dead, the men who knew not life in towns, and felt no strangeness in sun and wind and rain. . . .

I look at them [the unsubstantial multitude that his imagination has summoned out of a barrow near Beaulieu into the twilight]—their dark, pale, furious faces—and think that if they could be visible thus in the daylight, all who came to that spot or passed near it would turn and fly with a terrifying image in their mind which would last to the end of life. But they do not resent my presence, and would not resent it were I permitted to come at last to dwell with them for ever. Perhaps they know me for one of their tribe—know that what they feel I feel, would hate what they hate.

What Hudson most admired in primitive man, making him seem superior to the generality of those who now possess the earth, were the keenness of his senses and directness of his emotions, which allowed him to lead a more zestful life; the integration of his personality, in which the aesthetic sense, well commemorated not only in the cave paintings of Montignac and Altamira but in the relics that could be picked up along the Rio Negro, was closely linked with his other faculties; and, in spite of the supernatural impurities, his worship of the earth, in which, through the power of his animistic feeling, all nature appeared to be alive and intelligent, and to feel as he felt. When modern man is most profoundly moved, when life seems to hold its finest savor—as many other contemporary artists have come to realize—it is his older, deeper, primitive self stirring within him. "The noisy burn, the roar of the waterfall, and thunder of long waves on the shore, and the sound of rain and whispering winds in the multitudinous leaves, bring . . . a memory of the ancient time"; and the slumbering "old bones" of the greatest antiquity "rejoice and dance in their sepulchre." By allowing this still-persistent self to become more and more deeply buried beneath the appurtenances of society, man was losing, so Hudson believed, more than has been gained through civilization. Thus, to some extent, it was that he delighted in surprising the minds of his fellowmen in their "secret doings," for what is now the unconscious was once part of the waking mind of emergent man. And when seeking human companionship outside his immediate circle of friends, he found it most, as have many romanticists, in the presence of children, "the psychological representative[s] of primitive man," and of peasants, who have weathered the centuries little changed.

As is to be expected of one with such affinities, there is some idealization in Hudson's estimate, for in spite of primitive man's brilliant accomplishment in the domestication of plants and animals, the conquest of fire, and the creation of language and art—triumphs comparable to the harnessing of rivers and the liberation of nuclear energy—he had but little capacity for abstract thought; and his response to nature, if more vital and wholesome, was unquestionably less aesthetic than that of the generations whose taste has been cultivated by Wordsworth and Thoreau and by Hudson himself. Yet if this attitude places Hudson in the tradition ennobling the savage, it does so with a decided difference. Certainly his was a more realistic appreciation than that of most of his predecessors, for not only did he, to a degree, know primitive man firsthand in the American Indian and, because of his background and training, have a surer intuition of what a child of the ancient earth must have felt, but he kept modifying his conceptions according to the latest developments in anthropology. Thus, as indicated in his response to music and Abel's to the killing of Rima, he was not unmindful of the defects of primitive man and his world. But, being by temperament a primitive (he did not, like Thoreau, Jefferies and Whitman, have to struggle to become one) and missing keenly the embodiment of many of the primitive virtues in the highly industrialized society with which he had, in middle age, cast his lot, he could not help looking back nostalgically upon peoples in whom they were ingrained.

It was from his feeling toward both the historic and the immemorial past that he received—what most of us do from the major religions and a few from art—his chief sense of continuity and permanency in life, and hence could appropriately refer to it as a "sacred passion." The individual life-span, when seen against the background of history, and the whole of history, when seen against aeons of simple barbarism and terrestrial time, appear pitifully brief.

> Last week in Babylon,
> Last night in Rome,

Morning, and in the crush
Under Paul's dome. . . . 12

But dwelling imaginatively upon all the "generations of deciduous man" stretching back, *in saecula saeculorum,* to the Bronze and Stone Ages brought Hudson a sense of the persistence of the human race despite all mutations, "its undying vigour, its everlastingness"; and with these meditations came a feeling of "sweetness and peace," even the peace which passeth all understanding. At times, it made death itself, the strongest of all our fears, seem to be merely an illusion:

The knowledge that my individual life is but a span, a breath; that in a little while I too must wither and mingle like one of those fallen yellow leaves with the mould, does not grieve me. I know it and yet disbelieve it; for am I not here [at Calleva Atrebatum] alive, where men have inhabited for thousands of years, feeling what I now feel—their oneness with everlasting nature and the undying human family? The very soil and wet carpet of moss on which their feet were set, the standing trees and leaves, green or yellow, the rain-drops, the air they breathed, the sunshine in their eyes and hearts, was part of them, not a garment, but of their very substance and spirit. Feeling this, death becomes an illusion; and the illusion that the continuous life of the species (its immortality) and the individual life are one and the same is the reality and truth. . . . And this very [illusion] which our reason can prove to be the most childish, the absurdest of all, is yet the greatest, the most fruitful of good for the race. To those who have discarded supernatural religion, it may be a religion, or at all events the foundation to build one on.

With the vastness of its perspective, this passion for the past was, in some measure, an aid to Hudson in the evaluation of con-temporary civilization. But, combined as it was with an engrossing love for nature and with certain idiosyncrasies, it kept him, though not to the extent that it did Doughty, from giving much attention to many of the more immediate, as well as to some of the basic, problems of society. His friend Roberts, by pointing out (probably in the manner of Spencer or Bagehot) that "politicians and parlia-ment [represent], however feebly, the organ by which society

12 Ralph Hodgson, "Time, You Old Gipsy Man" (*Poems,* New York, 1927). Used by permission of the publisher, The Macmillan Co.

[adapts] itself to a changed environment," tried to stimulate in him more of an interest in politics, but even this biological approach met with only momentary success. All governments, primarily because of the imperfections inherent in human nature, continued to seem bad,[13] and politicians as such were interesting to him only as instruments for the passing of laws to protect bird life. Typical is his remark that when forced to listen to "the ridiculous hubbub" of politics during its periodic invasion of a village, he "was like one who hears a military band with loud braying of brass instruments and rub-a-dub of drums, but is at the same time giving an attentive ear to some small sound issuing from some leafy hiding-place in the vicinity—the delicate small warble of a willow-wren, . . . [that is], the real heart of the people, not all this imported artificial noise in the air." The first World War did, however, impinge upon him sharply, provoking some trenchant observations on the function of war in Nature's economy, but by then he was in his mid-seventies and, rather than orient himself thoroughly to the general political situation, thought it better, in the few years that remained, to devote his full attention to the completion of his own work. "The world is a shambles, but I wasn't born to set it right."

Had he either been born an Englishman or felt sympathetic toward certain contemporary trends, Hudson might well have concerned himself more with the economic and social landscape about him. But industrialism, a spendthrift of the earth's irreplaceable resources, was leaving in its wake the ugliest of centuries. True, it had brought with it astonishing mechanical progress and, though poorly distributed, material prosperity, but, in doing so, had exploited and deformed the great mass of humanity. It had drawn in men from the countryside, where, despite the dawn-to-dark labor, their natural powers had at least remained uncorrupted, and herded them into drab, conglomerate cities, in which, to their physical and psychological harm, they became mere cellules or scales in or upon a monstrous organism. With the mechanization of even their leisure, they were losing, more and more, all vertebrateness of mind and

---

13 Cunninghame Graham must have been amused at Hudson's description of a visit to Parliament: "The 'six-hundred gentlemen' look somewhat monotonous, like a vast flock of sheep, with two rams facing each other in the centre, each with his dozen or twenty capones grouped round him" (letter to Cunninghame Graham of July 27, 1893).

spirit, and becoming an easy prey for demagogues. To see the future of civilization at the mercy of the urban proletariat, filled Hudson, as it has many another, with profound misgivings.

Because of his ready sympathy for rural folk, who, through their contact with the soil, would never become altogether helots in soul, he did concern himself with some of their immediate problems. At the time of his arrival in England in 1874, agriculture was in a state of depression. There had been a series of bad harvests, and, for the first time since the repeal of the Corn Laws, British farms were feeling the strong competition of the American prairies, which were being converted into corn and wheat fields. Moreover, to make matters worse, the very system by which they were operated—the attempt on the part of the landlord "to get the highest possible rent for his land" and on the part of the tenant "to get his labour at the lowest possible rate"—was, so Hudson maintained, a "hideous" one, "a compact between landlord and tenant aimed against the labourer," the "most patient and submissive of men." Since little was done to correct these conditions, many cottagers, usually those of the better sort, were obliged to abandon their way of life (for agriculture is more than a means to a livelihood) either by emigrating to another country or by submitting to the tyranny of the Dynamo and becoming broken to its alien routines. Yet, much as his sympathies were engaged on the side of the laborers and much as he disliked the way "God's footstool has been parcelled out among private persons," he feared the effect the "wild and whirling words" of the socialists was having upon them and allied himself politically with the tenant farmer. There is, however, perhaps more of old age than of conservatism in the avowal made late in life: "I want things as they are because they may be worse."

Opposed as he was to what seemed the fundamental aim of the school system—to "fabricate the souls of children much in the way in which shoddy is manufactured"—Hudson thought it egregiously stupid to stuff down the throats of country children a diet that had been specially concocted for little urbanites. Information and knowledge unrelated to their daily lives would, like green apples, lie heavy upon their stomachs and quickly be disgorged. The very act of shutting up children "during all the best hours of the day" keeps them, as Wordsworth and Halsham also maintained, not only "from learning the things" that are of more moment, but from enjoying the most precious period of their lives. Even the lonely bird-scarer who ran a good distance over ploughed ground just to see one of his own species cycle by seemed better off than the majority of "his fellows poring over miserable books in school." This attitude of Hudson's was largely determined by the memory of his own un-constrained childhood, but it was also a reasoned one, for he knew a good deal at firsthand about country schools and children. Of much the same mind (to name only three literary figures who looked upon the peasantry sympathetically) were Rousseau, Cobbett, and Jefferies; and at the present time the curriculum in village class-rooms is being modified more and more to accord with rural sensi-bilities and preserve local traditions.

The sort of society that appealed most to his imagination, when untrammeled by immediate problems and the cautiousness that comes with advancing years, was the one that insured for both the individual and the group their fullest natural flowering. Believing in the essential soundness of human nature—one of the chief tenets of nineteenth-century romanticism—and, theoretically at least, not far from the anarchism of Thoreau, he held that the individual should be granted the freest play of his instincts and faculties com-patible with the preservation of his own biological vigor, the family unit, and the most vital social groups to which he belongs. And the group, which, even in its larger organizations, is, as it were, merely an insignificant outpost in a jungle, should keep itself receptive not only to the laws of its own organic development (such as those formulated by Kidd and Spencer) but also to the elusive influences that keep impregnating it from the vast reaches of encompassing nature. (It was because of the static condition of the society of *A Crystal Age*, its inability to take the world arriving, that led Hudson to repudiate it.) Looking upon industrial civilization, with its pro-liferation of creature comforts at the expense of mental and spiritual nourishment, as a force that is uprooting mankind, he thought that even such countries as those known to him in his youth, La Plata and the Banda Oriental, with all their slovenly ways, their poverty, their social crudities, and their political instability—were better places in which a human being might realize and enjoy himself and in which society, in the long run, might achieve its most desirable expression.[14] For in countries like these, where there are scarcely any of the mere complexities of highly industrialized life and little or none of its hectic bustle, the individual might live amidst clearer realities more intuitively and society (like that of the United States until the end of the nineteenth century) remain close to the formative processes of Nature.

Few have appreciated more than Hudson the value of the primitive in man—its great dynamic power. And though he never felt the glamour of the South Sea islanders as did Melville and Loti and Gauguin—for the primitivism of these tribes is a "soft" one and their development, in an arrested state—few would have welcomed more, both for what light they shed upon earlier peoples and what they have to teach contemporary men, the many fine studies that have recently been made of them by field anthropologists.[15] He did not, however, wish man to renew his worship of the darker gods, as did Lawrence, or to revert to any period of primitive civilization. Since mankind is now, so he believed, on the wrong path and in danger of becoming irretrievably lost, it will be necessary to retrace, as many of our artists are helping us to do imaginatively, some of its steps so as to reabsorb the primitive virtues, but mankind should always maintain an "erect posture of mind" and seek "the upward and not the downward truth."

In order to make England thoroughly receptive to the more vital influences of nature once again and Englishmen a "happy breed," much machinery would have to be destroyed, as Morris likewise thought, and what was retained, widely distributed. Though this meant her becoming, as of old, a little England, Hudson, like Hewlett and Blunt, would have liked to see her essentially a nation of handicraftsmen, fishermen, shepherds and farmers, each with his own small tenancy or freehold and all gathered together in villages, finding pleasure in their work and enjoying their dances and songs

---

14 Though there are few signs as yet, it is not impossible that, as Keyserling and Waldo Frank have prophesied, South America will have a great cultural rôle to play in the future of all mankind.

15 Hudson's criticism of Frazer was that, even after writing "a cart-load of books about [the] folklore, legends and old religious beliefs" of "the lower races of mankind," he still did not let "us see and know them as they are, and how they compare with civilised Europeans in their faculties and instincts" (*A Hind in Richmond Park*, pp. 98-9).

and the various other arts. In such a society, possessing an *esprit de corps* even stronger than that met with in many of the villages he visited, there would be little caste feeling (one of the blights on present-day England and on civilization as a whole), each individual being valued according to his real worth, and the larger groups, in their relationship with each other, occasionally submitting themselves to the authority of a wise ruler.[16] (As is becoming more and more obvious to many of us, the village—Branscombe, "Tatarsk," Dinkels-bühl, Barbizon, Concord, "Winterbourne Bishop"—speaks a more universal language than Moscow and Berlin, Paris and Washington and London; and so, in a civilization made up of groups of villages, there would be fewer provocations for war, that other great curse upon humanity.) Indeed, with the qualities of villagers, so he felt, mankind might be set upon a more promising path through the jungle.

This social philosophy of Hudson's, strongly influenced as it was by his pampean background, gets to some of the roots of our ills; but, wanting in implementation and overlooking certain fundamental conditions of the contemporary world, it is of little pragmatic value. The cataclysm that is the prelude to *A Crystal Age* and to Jefferies' *After London*—the destruction of our technological civilization—may be almost upon us. But until such a cataclysm actually occurs (it hardly seems likely that, as Butler envisioned in *Erewhon*, there will be a spontaneous uprising against the machine), it is the part of wisdom to accept the more essential technical inventions and learn, as Geddes and Chase and Mumford have been teaching us, to control them in the best interests of humanity. If the natural powers of the individual, especially the imaginative and spiritual ones, can be preserved and the creative minority in a culture be given ample scope, we need not develop into the terrifying creatures predicted in Capek's *R. U. R.*, Huxley's *Brave New World*, and Orwell's

---

16 Hudson was never explicit as to just what are the qualifications of a wise ruler or how he is to be chosen—questions that many besides Plato have found extremely difficult to answer. We can be sure, however, as the following quotation indicates, that it was not a totalitarian one he had in mind: "The Inca system of government was founded on that most iniquitous and disastrous doctrine that the individual bears the same relation to the state as a child to its parent, that its life from the cradle to the grave must be regulated for it by a power it is taught to regard as omniscient—a power practically omnipresent and almighty" (*The Purple Land,* p. 346).

Nineteen Eighty-Four. And if the various cultures of the world can be reconciled and the state expanded to embrace all mankind, we shall at least not be guilty of a self-inflicted catastrophe. Yet, whatever our goals (those just mentioned are, of course, arduous ones), it is imperative, as Hudson should have realized more fully, that they be achieved within the context of contemporary civilization.

As the result of his failure to comprehend the extent of man's capabilities as a tool-using animal—how far indeed Nature transcends the natural world—he tended to interpret too narrowly some of the creative forces that are shaping humanity. Throughout the development of civilization, man has endeavored to direct the processes of Nature to his own purposes, and, in so doing, has been able not only to improve upon them in some ways, as in personal ethics and in art, but even to reach a certain degree of independence from them. In the last few generations, with the invention of the machine and the harnessing of the atom, and with his considerable knowledge of the process of evolution, man's opportunity to further his own development, and thus, in larger measure, to control his destiny, has been enormously increased. Although scientific achievement has been outstripping the sense of social responsibility, there is no reason why the machine and the atom cannot ultimately be converted wholly into instruments of life. Since the aesthetic sense is so deeply embedded, it is quite possible that man will be able to create with the machine objects as satisfying to his artistic feelings as Greek vases and Gobelin tapestries. And if contemporary civilization often seems irresponsible—like a bus speeding recklessly along a causeway snaking through the Everglades—we should remember that, despite its thousands of years of existence, humanity is as yet only in its adolescence.

As stressed by Darwin and many subsequent thinkers, the more varied the environment, the more complex are individual consciousness and social relationships. And such a consciousness, in turn, continually demands a more and more highly civilized milieu, in which it might develop still further. In the course of time, cities, with their libraries and universities, their research laboratories, their symphony halls and theaters and art galleries, have come to be the centers of learning and of the arts and the chief proving-grounds for new ideas; and though long, continuous residence in them is usually harmful even to those who can best utilize their facilities (engendering in some minds, as Hudson puts it, "the phantasma-gorical ideal"), they have aided materially in producing many extra-ordinarily keen minds that have pursued truth far in innumerable directions, and many vivid and rich personalities. Johnson, Lamb and Dickens, for example, were so largely products of the city that they felt at a great loss anywhere else; and in our own day, urban life has done much to develop such fine minds and personalities as those of Freud and Dewey and Toynbee, Eliot and Berdyaev and Santayana. Some city dwellers have in fact been among the most appreciative of nature, even at its wildest. Because of these limita-tions, which, like those in his attitude toward art, involve the sur-render of some of the larger privileges of humanity, Hudson's plan for a civilization, like Lawrence's, would probably result in one resembling much more the Creto-Mycenean or the Etruscan than that of Periclean Athens, Renaissance Italy, or Elizabethan England.

Yet it should always be remembered that any disregard for the laws of Nature, any overweening transcendence of our environment, invites disaster: certain traits of character, however beautiful in themselves, may have no survival value and lead only to a frangible super-civilization; the neuroses and psychoses concomitant with ad-vanced stages of industrialization may reach epidemic proportions; and, if the machine is not kept under better control, man may devolve into a mere worker, tending a machine a few hours a week and spending the rest of his time indulging a corrupted taste. Hav-ing seen enough to confirm her worst fears, Nature may then scrap the human experiment as suddenly as she did the Pleistocene fauna, and continue imperturbably on with her everlasting enterprise. Un-questionably, at the present time, mankind is in a precarious position, for (among other things) the masses have remained intellectually and socially stagnant throughout the great technological (and demo-cratic) advances of the past two centuries. Therefore, even if our angle of vision does not entirely coincide with that of Hudson, it behooves us to give heed to his warnings, particularly those corrobo-rated by the major critics of the machine age. It is indeed well for the individual that he accommodate himself to the best of both the world of nature and the world of man—his roots deep in the sub-soil of his own racial past and in the earth, and his flowering twigs reaching continually upward for the light. And it is well for society to make such a way of life available to all.

Novels and Tales

The brain-stuff of fiction is internal history.

—MEREDITH

To snatch in a moment of courage, from the remorseless rush of time, a passing phase of life, is only the beginning of the task. The task approached in tenderness and faith is to hold up unquestioningly, without choice and without fear, the rescued fragment before all eyes in the light of a sincere mood.

—CONRAD

NO MATTER HOW wide our personal experience with the world may be, it will remain circumscribed unless we have recourse to books; and among the many Hudson was acquainted with were a large number of short stories and novels, which, more than all other forms of art, give "a picture of this complex and vari-coloured life we see about us," and thus broaden and deepen our understanding and knowledge of our fellowmen. The leading figures in English fiction, both past and contemporaneous, were known to him, and among Americans, especially attractive were Hawthorne, with his "sombre . . . genius," and Melville, whose greatness he was one of the first to recognize. The Russians, however, came to mean most to him, particularly Tolstoy, with his elemental simplicity, the extraordinary fullness of his portrayal of man's life, his admiration for the children of nature, and "his almost supernatural power of displaying his own intense spirituality in many of the characters he created." "I am so fond of truth, of sincerity, in a novel," he declared, "I can hardly enjoy one unless it is by some Russian." [1]

The novel and the short story also inspired him creatively. The human drama of the pampas, as it was pictured in his memory, called insistently for recording; and to the recording, he was able to bring an unusual sensitivity. Its exotic coloring, its primitiveness, and its remoteness—intensified by long residence in England—appealed strongly to his romantic temperament. And yet, born of a different race and nurtured in a different tradition, he could look upon it with a detachment rare among South American writers. The drama of English life called to him hardly at all for expression in fiction, for long observation is necessary in order to grasp any way of life imaginatively, and, by the time he might have been ready, another genre absorbed most of his creative energy. An episode out of England's distant past did however intrigue his historical imagination; and, gifted with the power of travelling with ease in the realm of fantasy, he transported himself to the remote future and to

---

1 He was aware, however, of the "strain of insanity which appears instinctive or ingrained, not only in D[ostoevsky], . . . but in all Russians" (letter to Garnett of November 25, 1917). As to whether they exerted any literary influence upon him, there is little evidence, even in *Far Away and Long Ago* and the short stories.

the Venezuelan jungles, where his temperament could be thoroughly indulged.

Though appreciative of the technique of others, as his criticism of *The Voyage Out* and *Rachel Marr* indicates, he took no passionate interest in it. To do so would have seemed to him, as it has to most of his English and Russian confrères, to run the risk of artificiality. Thus we do not find in his fiction, as we do, say, in Conrad and James, any considerable appeal to our sense of form. Yet, within the various conventional patterns adopted, he was at least competent. The angle of vision is usually well-chosen; the narrative flows along, at varying speeds, naturally, the illusion never broken by personal intrusion. Though weak in complicated plotting, he was strong in the illuminating episode and, as with the announcement of Edgar's death to Elfrida and the discovery of Nuflo's hideout, its disposition for the sake of contrast. If one may judge from *Fan*, he was not skilful in the purely dramatic scene, but the retrospective manner in which most of his stories are told somewhat conceals this shortcoming.

The creation of character seemed to Hudson, as it has to many, of far greater importance than the handling of plot. His comments upon the novels of others (*Roderick Hudson, One Ash,* and *Sons and Lovers,* for example) were chiefly concerned with the closeness of their men and women to the people he knew in the flesh. In the projection of his own characters, he was always careful, by means of gesture as well as the rendering of outer features, to have them seen in space, interacting one with another. More concerned with the effects than the causes of behavior, he kept (unlike the contemporary novelist) to the broader outlines of psychological analysis; but they are firmly drawn and at times deeply revealing. (Of Dorothy Richardson's Miriam, he remarked, "*I* don't want to see all of a person's inside[,] unless it is a more interesting inside" than hers; and he remained critical of any large dependence, as in the early work of May Sinclair, upon the new psychology.) Wanting in sympathy for townspeople, he did not altogether succeed in his portrayal of the English middle-class, but with those who draw their strength from the soil—peasants and Indians and gauchos—he was always convincing. Of some moment in the history of fiction are his portraits of gauchos and their households, which not only introduced a picturesque people to English readers but deserve a place alongside

those of Sarmiento, Güiraldes, the poet Hernández, and the drama-
tist Sánchez. And with Rima, he was able to create memorably with
only the eye of the imagination.

Among some of his characters there is a striking resemblance.
Herne and Smith, as well as the two men of the negligible "Tom
Rainger," have in them much of the conventional Englishman in
foreign lands. In order to make Richard Lamb and Abel Guevez de
Argensola more substantial, Hudson seems to have found it necessary—certainly a limitation in his creative power—to pour in much of
himself: Abel, for example, shares both his dislike for sports and
politics and his great love for poetry, the creatures of the wild, and
nature as a whole. All these men are possessed with a romantic concept of love, the feeling (as Herne expresses it) that God "shines
brightest in some woman" one has "had the unutterable happiness to
know [—] some divine woman." There are anticipations of Rima,
that quintessence of romantic love, in several of his earlier heroines:
in Lettice, who, when adorned with passion flowers, looked "like
some immortal nymph of the woods"; Voletta, who found intense joy
treading "on the grass," feeling "sun and wind on [her] face,"
seeing "the earth and sky and animals"; and, most of all, Transita,
who "had caught the spirit of the wind and sunshine and was all
freedom, motion, fire—a being half-human, half-angelic." Unfortunately, there is also a certain Leightonesque quality in several of
his feminine portraits.

In the revelation of character through speech, Hudson was not
always successful. His English middle-class figures speak at times as
though out of a conventional novel or from the boards of the Victorian stage, the worst offender being Mary Starbrow, who often
tears her passion to tatters in the manner of melodrama. It is largely
this inadequacy that reduces the effectiveness of his more dramatic
scenes, especially those between lovers. The formality of their diction
may, to some extent, have been due to his early dependence upon
literature for the idiom of his emotions in English and to the infre-
quency with which he, a reticent man, gave expression to love in his
own life. On the other hand, his art is triumphant in the portrayal
of gauchos with deft strokes of dialogue—a difficult thing to do in
English.

His settings, particularly those of nature, excite in the reader, as
the novels of Hardy and Conrad did in him, an unusual pleasure.

As in the best use of local color, they are of value in explaining some of the general traits of his characters and in establishing their various moods; thus an autumn gale intensifies Smith's dejection over Voletta's inability to reciprocate his love, and the more menacing aspects of the jungle are perceived by Abel only after the death of Rima. Some of the characters are closely identified with their backgrounds, Marta with the mountain glooms of Jujuy, Elfrida with the river Test, and Rima with her "wild paradise." And occasionally, as in "El Ombú," "An Old Thorn," and, most explicitly, *A Little Boy Lost*, the setting itself takes an active rôle in determining the destiny of a human being. It is always painted within the register of the particular narrator, and never for its own sake. "I might fill dozens of pages with descriptions of pretty bits of country I passed that day," says Richard Lamb, "but must plead guilty of an unconquerable aversion to this kind of writing. . . . Anyone who cares for these things, and knows how evanescent are the impressions left by word pictures on the mind, can sail the seas and gallop round the world to see them all for himself." *Green Mansions*, where setting is more a part of the story, has a different man for narrator, with a different experience.

There is considerable variety in the tone of Hudson's style, from the informality, ironic humor, and ebullience of *The Purple Land* to the studied elaborateness of *A Crystal Age*, the richly-wrought, wistful poetry of *Green Mansions*, and the noble simplicity and gravity of most of the short stories. For the purposes of the novel, in which "a certain roughness and carelessness" (as Northcott remarks in *Fan*) seems actually to be preferred by most readers, it is a style of rare distinction, with something of the texture of a Hawthorne or a Turgenev. It can absorb a considerable amount of detail without halting the movement of the story, and rise to lyrical intensity. It is impregnated throughout with the personality of a man looking at life freshly. The naturalist is in evidence elsewhere than in the painting of landscape frescoes: the thin, tremulous voice of crazed old Peralta, when raised to "a reedy shriek," is likened to "the long, shrill cry of some water-fowl heard at night in the desolate marshes," and the swimming and diving of the Crystallites, to "the unconventional freedom and grace of a company of grebes." Other aspects of personality already presented are also in evidence, but one is most impressed with the insight into certain situations and characters, the warm sympathy for struggling humanity, and the profound sense of the cruelty of things.

Ralph Herne, a good part of which Hudson himself deemed "rather tedious and even twaddly," was written, like "Tom Rainger," for the young. Though picturesquely set against the background of the English colony of Buenos Aires, the story itself—that of a man "saved and purified" by a woman's love—is conventional. There is some awkwardness in the structure: the "Preamble," for instance, leads one to expect that the narrator is a participant in the story— an angle of vision that might well have been maintained—but what follows is presented from the point of view of an omniscient observer. Despite the crudity of the brushstroking, the portrait of Herne is built up with a certain life-like solidity. Of a warm emotional nature, which in its exuberance makes him appear more Latin than English, he is liable to folly, which plunges him quickly into the slough of despond; but, devoted to the highest ideals of the medical profession, he can, when put to the acid test, act nobly, particularly if given the least word of encouragement by his beloved. It is, of course, the background of a pestilence-stricken city, depicted with something of the effectiveness of a Munthe or a Defoe, that gives the portrait its impressiveness. Herne, in an exhausted condition, groping his way through the intense darkness of "Black Day" to the bedside of Lettice, his beloved—almost stepping into a freshet that overflowed a gully-like street and then wrenching himself loose from the grip of a desperate woman—is a scene of some power.

The Purple Land, which takes its reader galloping across the Banda Oriéntal as it appeared in the time of Hudson's youth, may best be classed as a tale of adventure. The far-flung pampas and widely scattered ranchos possess the appeal of distance and of frontier wildness; the natives are children of nature—the men, impulsive and picturesque, the women, mostly gracious and beautiful; and the hero frequently encounters not only the eager eye of discontented wives and lovelorn maidens, but, beset as his route was by revolutionary bands, the bright face of danger. The various adventures, amatory and otherwise, are presented with a broad humanity, an arch humor, and great gusto—a gusto wanting in most of Hudson's writings. Though the author disclaimed identity with his hero, he does not succeed in persuading all of us that Richard Lamb is not, to a certain degree, an imaginative projection of his youthful self—the self that so alertly and ardently looks out from the Smithsonian portrait.

The weakness of the beginning and, more pronounced, of the ending (the circumstances of Lamb's elopement and the extent of the penalty imposed are sensational enough to demand fuller treatment) results from the book's being originally part of a larger whole. The looseness of its structure, which at first glance gives one the impression of a series of character-sketches separated by an occasional story, may lead some, as it did Swinnerton, to deny *The Purple Land* sufficient design or meaning. But this very looseness, which is indeed not so great as that of the picaresque novel and is characteristic of the autobiographic technique, gives to the narrative a sense of naturalness that accounts for much of its charm. The personality of the hero is strong enough to hold the various sketches and stories together, and by the time one reaches the end, so fully has the locale been viewed in emotional and intellectual perspective, they take on meaning. Thus *The Purple Land* moves along on a thematic as well as on a story level.

The portrait of Lamb is painted in the virile, fluent manner of a Sorolla. General Coloma summarizes him well: "You are brave to rashness, abhor restraint, love women, and have a light heart. . . ." Since the "Oriental world is . . . an oyster only a sharp sword will serve to open," we even exult with him over the slaying of the cut-throat Gandara. His roaming eye, scarcely restrained by the thought of his wife waiting for him in Montevideo, marks him as a man more for amourettes than any grand passion; but, handsome and eloquent and daring, he is not altogether to blame for being irresistible to feminine hearts. "Love cometh up as a flower," he says in self-justification, "and men and charming women naturally flirt when brought together." His joining the hopeless rebel cause in order to redeem his pledge to Dolores and his rescuing of Demetria from the sinister Don Hilario do much to keep him in our good graces. To what extent the youthful Hudson shared these attributes, if not the adventures themselves, we cannot be sure. But the love of freedom, which had much to do with bringing Lamb into complete sympathy with the natives of the Banda Oriental, he did almost entirely share. The understanding and love of children, notable in the sketch of that forlorn little shepherdess, Anita, and the fanciful story of Alma and the white mist of Yí, is also Hudson's own, as is, of course, the accurate knowledge and panpsychic love of nature. "While the last rich flood of sunshine came over the earth from that red everlasting urn resting on the far horizon, I could," declares Lamb, "had I been alone, have cast myself upon the ground to adore the great God of Nature. . . ."

The large number of minor figures, most of them probably drawn directly from life and with the striking individuality that a wild country nurtures, gives *The Purple Land* a strong, racy flavor. Though not so skilfully done as in *Far Away and Long Ago*, many of them are brought to life with a few strokes, and the idioms and rhythms of gaucho talk are well suggested. Among the men, there is Uncle Anselmo, with his massive silver trappings and his delicious Shandean rigmarole about Manuel and Pascuala, a story worthy of the pen of Chaucer or Hardy; "Eyebrows," singing amorous ballads in a whining falsetto to the accompaniment of a cracked guitar; Santa Coloma, of the many disguises, with his absorbing love for his lost sweetheart and for his native land; fierce old Peralta, rendered insane by the death of his son in the rebel cause; and those two villains, Gandara, with his truculent eyes and brutal mouth, and Hilario, who had insinuated himself into the control of the Peralta household and lay coiled to strike. The pure-blooded negro, little owl-like Nepomucino, who presided over the orchard and paddock of the Casa Blanca, also lingers in the memory, as does that genial bewhiskered Scotsman, Carrickfergus, who had fled overseas from all the scourin' and the scrubbin' and the unco guid. The group portrait of a small colony of shiftless, rum-drinking Englishmen, whose evil genius was the purple-faced Cloudesley Wriothesey, is done with the pungency of a Rowlandson.

There probably is, as Hudson himself thought, too much amorous dalliance, and the dialogue in some of the episodes does not, at least to English ears, ring entirely true; but the women are all carefully differentiated from each other and so arranged in the narrative as to secure the most effective contrasts. Thus fat, slatternly Señora Juez, whose advances could be deflected only by the opportune appearance of a snake, is placed between two maidens: spirituelle Marguarita, who had been hidden away by Coloma lest her gift of beauty prove as fatal as her mother's, and willowlike Monica, who, though very shy, lay in wait for Lamb in a lonely spot. After

Dolores, who, with her glowing dark eyes and pouting red lips, would have made an excellent model for a Uruguayan Rossetti, we meet Candelaria, whose generosity springs from a disinterested heart. And in the midst of painting the full-length portrait of sorrow-laden Demetria, Hudson pauses to sketch, with Chaucerian piquancy, that irresistible little jillflirt, Cleta. Usually, the more sprightly and ironic the touch, the more successful is the portrait: thus that of Dolores, whose beauty struck the hero with the force of a *pampero* and wrought havoc in his heart, seems somewhat theatrical, and those of Paquita, which come at the beginning and the end of this group, somewhat wooden.

As becomes a book of this sort, the immediate and panoramic background of all these men and women is evoked with a minimum of details. In the ranchos and around the estancias are to be seen ostriches lingering inside the kitchen ready to gobble down any "little metallic *bonne bouche*"; a hen, with her brood, scattering about papers that concern the safety of the nation; a pack of fierce dogs ready to spring upon the unhorsed stranger; a garden with an aloe hedge and many Old World flowers; gauchos preparing a heifer for roasting and stitching up a gored horse with a few hairs plucked from its tail; women boiling meat in immense cauldrons and skimming off the fat for tallow; the offal of cattle being devoured by gulls, hawks and vultures; in the evening, men and women singing and dancing to the music of the guitar or telling tales round a campfire; and venomous vinchucas (those "little things that go about") making miserable a traveller's rest. Between the ranchos or *pulperías* stretch leagues upon leagues of wild landscape: undulating plains, moors with forests of dwarf thorn, and gaunt, naked hills, with their various fauna—cicadas and fireflies and spiders, orioles and siskins, magpies and owls, snakes and armadillos and herds of cattle with fiery bulls. The thunder and lightning of revolutionary strife, mostly of a harmless mid-summer variety, does much to animate the picture as a whole. With the coming of large masses of Italian immigrants later in the century, the landscape as well as the inhabitants of the Banda Oriental changed in some of its most essential characteristics. Only in *The Purple Land*, the novels of Acevedo Díaz, the sketches of Cunninghame Graham, and a few other writings are both preserved in all their wild flavor against the onrush of time and "razure of oblivion."

The theme of the book, which strengthens one's suspicion of autobiography, is that life in the Banda Oriental, by and large, is more rewarding than that in a mechanized society, with its unnatural rhythms. In an arresting passage in the opening chapter, Lamb bemoans the loss of this land by "the holy cross of St. George," which might have put an end to the crimes caused by continual political turbulence. But after mixing intimately with the natives, he soliloquizes in quite a different vein.

Rather than see the ostrich and deer chased beyond the horizon, the flamingo and black-necked swan slain on the blue lakes, and the herdsman sent to twang his romantic guitar in Hades as a preliminary to security of person, I would prefer to go about prepared at any moment to defend my life against the sudden assaults of the assassin.

We do not live by bread alone, and British occupation does not give to the heart all the things for which it craves. Blessings may even become curses when the gigantic power that bestows them on us scares from our midst the shy spirits of Beauty and of Poesy. Nor is it solely because it appeals to the poetic feelings in us that this country endears itself to my heart. It is the perfect republic: the sense of emancipation experienced in it by the wanderer from the Old World is indescribably sweet and novel. . . . The unwritten constitution, mightier than the written one, is in the heart of every man to make him still a republican and free with a freedom it would be hard to match anywhere else on the globe. The Bedouin himself is not so free. . . . If this absolute equality is inconsistent with perfect political order, I for one should grieve to see such order established. Moreover, it is by no means true that the communities which oftenest startle us with crimes of disorder and violence are morally worse than others. A community in which there are not many crimes cannot be morally healthy. There were practically *no* crimes in Peru under the Inca dynasty. . . . Brazil, . . . an orderly country, yes, and the people in it steeped to their lips in every abominable vice! Compared with these emasculated children of the equator, the Orientals are nature's noblemen. . . .

Beautiful land of sunshine and storm, of virtue and of crime, . . . may the blight of our superior civilisation never fall on your wild flowers, or the yoke of our progress be laid on your herdsman—careless, graceful, music-loving as the birds—to make him like the sullen, abject peasant of the Old World!

Such eloquence, extravagant though it is when we recall the experiences that inspired it, touches some of the deepest impulses in us, those embedded in our residual primitive nature.

The increasing industrialization of England and America led, toward the end of the nineteenth century, to unparalleled activity in the realm of utopian fiction. Those who, like Bellamy and Wells, saw great possibilities in the machine once it was brought under social control prognosticated technological advances and a political reorganization that would lead, in the foreseeable future, to a far superior civilization. Those who, like Morris and Howells, were revolted by the growing regimentation of the masses and vulgarization of taste that industrialism brought with it and saw even greater dangers in its further development, clung to the handicrafts as the soundest basis of economic life. As might be expected of a son of the pampas and the author of *The Purple Land*, no one was more revolted than Hudson, and in *A Crystal Age* he adumbrated a society in the immeasurably remote future, after the industrial age had been consumed by "a sort of mighty Savonarola bonfire"—a society that had reverted finely to forest life.

To span this immense chasm of time, he made use of the familiar device of a traveller, who, while botanizing in the mountains, is rendered unconscious by a landslide, and, after milennia of suspended animation, awakens into a new world—the Crystal Age. The clumsiness of the device—what an unconscionable period of unconsciousness!—becomes especially pronounced near the end of the book when we become aware that the traveller is being forced to record his own death. Since Wells had not yet appeared on the literary scene to point out a better way of reaching Utopia, it would have been well had Hudson, like Bacon and Howells, found some island unknown to the geographer, or, like Morris, employed the framework of dream. Such a procedure need not have eliminated the use of the first person for the recording of the romance between Smith and Voletta, which, besides giving a certain dramatic palpitation to the pages, skilfully holds together many observations on the customs of the Crystallites (at times, however, it seems to keep us from the fuller information demanded by our curiosity) and illuminates their chief distinguishing characteristic.

Sufficient individuality is given both Smith and Voletta to lend some sense of reality to their romance—a strange one, in which an affectionate yet passionless woman is persistently wooed by an ardently amorous man. There is in Smith the relish of salvation from philistinism, but the impulsiveness of youth brings him to disaster. Some of the qualities, besides a transfiguring love of nature, that make Voletta a spiritual cousin of Rima are her nimble gait, her spurts of anger, and her uneasiness in the presence of passion. Another figure of some interest is Chastel, with her pale, suffering face, the result of long brooding on her barrenness; but, after a while, that interest begins to wane. Most of the other Crystallites, with their green eyes, their melodious voices, their purity of heart, and their serene enjoyment of life, have little more individuality than the figures of a Puvis-de-Chavannes mural. This is not, however, a serious fault, for in a utopian novel the description of the way of life of a people counts for more than characterization.

Though barely more than sketched, the society depicted gives one the impression of having been completely realized. The social unit is that of the whole family group, living together in a spacious mansion, built so long ago as to seem "coeval with the human race." The father preserves the traditions and administers the laws; but the mother, exalted above the law, is the real head—almost an object of worship. Each of these groups has its own special distinction, that spotlighted in *A Crystal Age* excelling in harvest melodies. The economic unit is that of farmsteads, which, like the estancias on the pampas in Hudson's youth, are thinly scattered over the face of the earth. Some members of the group do the work of the fields and others practice the various crafts; thus all of them have an opportunity for exercising their creative instincts. In the evening they gather for concerts of ethereal, soul-stirring music; and on the finest days of the year, all work is suspended and they give themselves wholly to the enjoyment of nature, some of the best hours being spent "careering over the surrounding country" on horseback.

As Hudson realized, a number of the ideas in *A Crystal Age* were in the air of his own time. The furnishings of the mansion— the illuminated books, the stained-glass windows, some of the furniture and other interior decorations—were surely designed by Morris' firm. Of more general origin are the vegetarianism, the abstention from alcoholic beverages (to both of which the Crystallites probably owed some of their serenity), and the length of the life-span, which gave ampler opportunity for ripeness of mind and spirit. The idea

of punishment for illness that is the result of "wantonly or care-
lessly" endangering one's life was no doubt borrowed from *Erewhon*. The absence of any social distinction between the various
kinds of workers reflects not only his own experience on the pampas
but an aspect of Morris' socialism, and the holding of most things
in common has been a part of utopian tradition from the time of
Plato. The process by which society was able to reach its crystalline
state, as well as that by which dogs and horses developed enough
intelligence to take over more of the work of the farm, is, of course,
explicable in terms of the theory of evolution.

There are other ideas more peculiarly Hudsonian. "The House
of the Harvest Melody" has been designed to harmonize well with
its setting, the domed roof giving the effect of "a cloud resting on
the stony summit of a hill." No shaven lawn or ornamental garden
mars its immediate surroundings, the wilderness coming up to its
very doors. And within the house there roam no "corpulent, blear-
eyed, wheezy pet dogs." The rights of animals are fully protected:
the women do not deck themselves with "feathered skins torn from
slain birds," and when Smith works the horses overtime, they wriggle
loose from their harness and, "flinging up . . . disdainful heels so
as to send a shower of dirt" over him, gallop off. The manner in
which Chastel is given relief from her suffering was prompted by
Hudson's belief in the healing power of the human hand when
charged with love. The religion of the Crystallites is a form of
nature-worship, God being felt as a beneficent force behind the
visible world, particularly at the time of sunset and of the rainbow
and during the most glorious part of autumn. Their wordless songs,
inspired by the sounds of nature and sung to a Theremin-like accompaniment (the chief instrument being surely of Hudson's own
invention), are the highest expression of that worship.

The most original and compelling idea in the book is that the
perpetuation of each family group devolves upon only one of the
women. On the death of the chosen one, another to succeed her is
appointed by the community, and, after a year of preparation, during
which the books sacred to her calling have been consulted, she se-
lects one of the men to be the father of her children. (Yoletta, it
seems, will be chosen to succeed Chastel and, until the fatal draught
from the mysterious phial, she will choose Smith for husband.) The
offspring, growing up into "angelic women and mild-eyed men with

downy, unrazored lips," are affectionate toward each other but know nothing of animal passion. It was largely by this method of biological selection that Crystallite society has been able to evolve. Though anticipated, to a certain extent, by Benjamin Kidd, Hudson owed the inspiration for this purest form of matriarchy to his observations of the sociology of the beehive. (Later, while reading *Kreutzer Sonata,* he must have been pleased to find that the idea also appealed to his favorite author.)

Believing as he did in the essential rightness of most of our emotions and hymning romantic love in much of his fiction, it is doubtful whether Hudson wished humanity to pattern its morality strictly after that of the Crystallites. Even though Smith regards their society as far superior to that of our time, he does not, like the author of *Back to Methuselah,* approve of a life without passion. And the very fact that the House of the Harvest Melody is in danger of extinction indicates a defect in their way of life. What he primarily wished to convey was that the "violence of the sexual rage" must burn itself out before mankind can hope to develop much further. Nature has accomplished much by combining reproduction with sex, and it was of great value to *Homo sapiens* in his early struggles; but for a long time now he has been oversexed, and industrialism, with the uncreative tasks it imposes, has accentuated this weakness. If much of the energy consumed in sexual indulgence— think of the "millions and millions" of prostitutes "just to satisfy men's ferocious desire"!—could be directed toward cultural ends, the individual would lead a fuller and more harmonious life and the world as a whole (so runs the argument) would be the better for it.

Looking back upon his "romance of the future," Hudson realized that he had left out of his calculation Nature's decree that "the ending of . . . strife is the beginning of decay." A serious defect in the eyes of the many who insist that all utopias lie within the realm of the immediately possible is that this one not only dips too far into the future but points in a direction diametrically opposite to that of contemporary tendencies. Yet it makes us aware of some of the chief dangers that beset our path, particularly those inherent in industrialism, and keeps reminding us that there are other goals, more beautiful and more deeply satisfying. Since man learns much by contrast, even with a dream as a counter, it is indeed a poor map, as someone has remarked, that boasts of no Utopia. And *A Crystal Age,* which is nearer to poetry than most of them, is one of the fairest of all such provinces.

Fan, the story of a girl who rises lotuslike out of the London slums, is very different from anything else Hudson ever wrote. Though familiar with her milieu and with some of the writings depicting it, he was probably led to this uncongenial subject ("uncongenial" because of his attitude toward the "city-soiled") only through his friendship with Gissing. Proceeding thus from no strong inner compulsion, he could hardly be expected to be at his happiest, no matter how great the effort. Yet his versatility and the original cast of his mind enabled him to make of *Fan* something better than journeyman's work.

The story itself has many of the conventional elements of its genre: the illegitimacy of its heroine, a "drink-degraded" mother, a drunken, cursing brute of a foster-father, brawls in the home and on the street, and an unexpected legacy from the real father that establishes the heroine on Easy Street. The influence of Gissing is apparent in the opening chapters, in those picturing the Chances in East End, and, especially, in the conception of Fan herself, who twice is made to declare her kinship to Thyrza. Except in the ending, the plot differs little from the average; and so large a rôle is played by coincidence, as in Fan's retention of Horton's telegram and her father's telepathic dream shortly before death, that it arouses some question as to its credibility and thus its value as a reading of life. Yet, despite these defects, there is much that attracts the attentive reader of this novel. The relationship between Fan and Arthur Eden is developed with unusual psychological insight, most notably in her response to his letter of repentance. The chief focus is not, however, as one would expect, upon this relationship, but upon that between Fan and her benefactress, Mary Starbrow. (If Hudson got a hint from *Esther Waters* for such a focussing, it was no more than a hint.)

Although there is some awkwardness in the sketching—largely the result of a deficiency in presenting a scene dramatically—the main characters are psychologically well-constructed, giving one the impression (there is reason to believe that in the case of Constance it is more than an impression) of having been studied from life. Fan herself, with her flowerlike beauty and her Pippa-like power of evoking the best in people, is an appealing figure; but, as Hudson himself realized, she is too much the gentle dove, and, toward the end, particularly when we see the humdrum future that stretches before her, our interest begins to slacken. Though not so fully or so clearly drawn, Mary Starbrow, with her variability of temper, her possessive love for her protégée, and her tumultuous passion for Horton (in the end, so unexpectedly brought under control), is a more complex and powerful creation. In Constance Churton, as in her admirer Northcott, there is embodied, somewhat in the manner of *Robert Elsmere*, the religious conflict caused by Darwin's reorientation of thought. The male characters have a rather faded daguerreotype air about them. Only when Arthur Eden suddenly finds himself in a situation similar to that of Byron and his half-sister, does he hold our attention. Chameleon-minded Merton Chance, easily intoxicated on his own rhetoric, is a figure that the author of *New Grub Street* could have drawn more expertly.

Though the medium did not allow for the expression of the whole man, there are glimmerings from some of the facets of Hudson's personality. The number of similes from nature is noticeable, some of them distinctly those of a naturalist: thus a magazine editor is likened to a spider, "against whose huge geometric web there beats [such] a continuous rain of dipterous insects of every known variety" that, being "unable to eat and digest more than about . . . a dozen . . . every month, [is] forced to spend his whole time cutting and dropping his useless captures from the web." The usual settings for the outdoor London scenes, such as the recriminatory one between Fan and Mary and those between Fan and Arthur, are the places that attracted the author of *Birds in London*—the Kew, the Kensington, and the Zoological Gardens. The background for one of the first scenes between Fan and Constance—the fields bordering a Wiltshire village—might well have been a high-light in one of his essays. Some of the characteristics of Fan, girl though she was and product of the London streets, are also those of Hudson. Her "feathers," like his, were "well oiled" against the teachings of socialism and, in spite of a strong religious nature, against creeds or doctrines. Especially are they akin in their love of nature, a love that was also an ache. Not many Victorian heroines would have found so much pleasure at having a green tree-snake coiled twice around her waist!

For its conception, *Green Mansions* owes something, though not so much as has been claimed,[2] to Lady Morgan's *Missionary*. Since the present age does not find nymphs in streams or dryads in woods, one of the chief means of giving human poignancy to an experience that belongs essentially in the realm of fantasy, as scarcely any artist need be told, is to set it in a region that will stimulate the imagination without sacrificing the sense of reality—preferably one just beyond the farthest reach of exploration. For the enactment of his story, Hudson chose an outlying part of the Guayana jungles, which had long captivated the European imagination, both scientific and literary, and improvised its topography to suit his special purposes.

Of great help in creating the illusion of reality is the choice of the hero as the teller of his own story. Though the restriction of the point of view has its disadvantages—Rima's death, for instance, cannot be presented dramatically—the feeling of intimacy that it gives makes the plotting seem less palpably invented. The introduction of the narrator is rather awkwardly managed, but, besides evoking an immediate sense of mystery with the mention of an ornamented cinerary urn kept in a darkened room, it provides, as in the novels of Conrad, an occasion for the telling. The choice of Abel as the hero is also a happy one, for he is well oriented to social and cultural life and, though young, competent as a naturalist, both in the

---

2 In a general sort of way, there is a structural similarity between the two novels, and, as Carlos Baker points out (*PMLA*, LXI [1946], 252-7), the cavern scene of the one probably owes a good deal to that of the other. But there are more differences in their settings than Baker leads one to believe: for example, the few really barren places near Rima's paradise are insignificant when compared to the desolate plains adjoining the Vale of Cashmire. To say that Hudson's heroine is "closely modelled on Luxima," who represents the luxuriant beauty and profound culture of the East, is to mistake a few externals for essentials. (The literary origin of Rima is to be traced, of course, to such romantic children of nature as Wordsworth's Lucy, Meredith's "wild one" of "Love in a Valley," and the heroine of Charles Roberts' *Heart of the Ancient Wood*, who has the "incalculable celerities" of a bird, a "mysterious ascendency in the forest," "semi-occult" experiences with animals, and a "mystic and uncanny wildness." Her most likely immediate progenitor, as Hoxie Fairchild has suggested [*PMLA*, LXVIII (1953), 357-70] is O'Shaughnessy's Colibri.) One so absorbed in ornithology certainly did not need the obscure detail of Hilario's mistaking the whistle of a birdcatcher for the voice of Luxima in order to endow a character with a birdlike language. It is true that the funerary urn in *The Missionary* appears also in *Green Mansions*, but to say that it gave Hudson the "idea for the cremation of Rima by the hostile tribe of Runi" is, I think, to interpret influences too positively.

observation of plants and animals and in that of such human fauna as the Indians of the jungles. Who could be better qualified to report accurately a unique experience?

In order to make some of the sensational elements in his story less nakedly romantic, Hudson gives a good deal of attention to the accumulation of circumstantial details. Each of the various stages of Abel's journey from Quarico to the Parahuari mountains is carefully motivated. He flees to the jungle because of complicity in an abortive revolution. His wanderings as a naturalist, which take him to the headwaters of the Orinoco, are brought to an abrupt end by a severe bout of fever and the loss of his journal. After he convalesces at one of the Maquiritari settlements, the old conquistatorial lust for gold lures him toward still more remote outposts. Upon reaching the small village of Runi and his tribe, Abel realizes that his pursuit has been that for a will-o'-the-wisp, but, impressed by the "rare loveliness" of the landscape, the poet that is also in him takes possession, and he decides to give himself up, for a season at least, to the pure enjoyment of nature. The Indians with whom he now fraternizes are made psychologically real—sullen Runi, thawed out of his hostility by casserie and the desire for revenge on a neighboring tribe; impetuous Kua-kó, an easy target at foils; and, especially, garrulous old Cla-cla, youthful in spirit despite her snow-white hair and innumerable wrinkles. Thus, before Abel crosses over the savannah to the patch of woodland under the *pax rimae,* our disbelief has been completely suspended.

As should be, there is little description of nature until Abel arrives at Runi's village. The depiction of its setting (the stream fringed with verdure and scattered dwarf trees, the brown savannah sloping upwards to a rocky ridge, the forests and mountains beyond) and particularly Rima's enchanted paradise (the clouds of greenery, the glades filled with mysterious half-lights, the impenetrable, creeper-laden undergrowth, the great variety of plant and animal life) is one of the chief attractions of *Green Mansions.* In such descriptions as those of the song of the campanero and the vista from the dominating landmark of the region, the "dark cone of Ytaioa," Abel shows himself very much the poet, and hence precisely the person to be most sensitive to Rima's preternatural beauty. The primitive vastness of the landscape, as well as the constant threat of the savages, gives poignancy to the brief drama they enact together.

Since Hudson had never seen the tropical jungles, his picture of them, which has impressed no less an expert than Beebe, is indeed a triumph of the imagination.

Rima, who is more a passion than a woman, is very subtly introduced. Her status in the savage mind as "the daughter of Didi" prepares us for an extraordinary creature, one enveloped in an aura. To Abel, she is at first only a mysterious bird-melody coming from a tangle of bushes. Later, after detecting with his keen ears an element of human feeling in it, he suspects a human embodiment. When the song keeps accompanying him on his saunterings about the forest, he becomes conscious of being an object of friendly interest. Yet, until actually getting a glimpse of her behind a "light leafy screen," he is uncertain whether the possessor of the song be human or avian; and that ambiguity, emphasized by her search for an interpreter of her ancestral tongue, is never allowed out of our consciousness. Gradually we come to see and to know Rima better—her Ariel-like figure; her arachnidian silk dress; her loose-flowing, iridescent hair and dark eyes lighting up with the fire of the ruby; the transparency of her skin, reflecting the shifting colors around her; her childlike innocence and birdlike brightness of mind; the reflection in her character of all that is best in wild nature—but her full story, like that of her spiritual cousin, Atala, is withheld until it is necessary to provide a motive for the tragic ending.

The portrayal of so elusive a figure as Rima, particularly when done in detail, is extremely difficult; yet, on the whole, Hudson succeeds. As in many oriental tales, the difficulty is to some extent overcome by the use of imagery from nature, especially from bird-life. Thus, her "quick, passionate gestures" are likened to the flirting of a bird's wings; her swift and soundless gliding about the forest, to that of a great low-flying owl; her anger, to that of a wasp, "every word a sting"; her appearance as she lay in a deathlike swoon in Abel's arms, to that of the Hata flower, whose transcendent beauty has given rise to a legend. The comparison most employed and, except for the want of song, the most appropriate is to the humming-bird: in the hut, this wood nymph is like one of these "fairy-like" creatures perched on a twig in the shade; in the forest, like one "moving about in an aerial dance among the flowers—a living prismatic gem that changes its colour with every change of position. . . . " So thoroughly is she identified with nature that we feel no discordancy when she is even likened to a snake. Essentially, of course, Rima is indescribable, and best imagined through the incandescent passion she inspires in Abel.

Up to the time of the dramatic scene on Ytaioa, which is the turning-point of the plot, the action of *Green Mansions* progresses leisurely. It takes a while for Abel to become acquainted with so shy a creature as Rima, and to remove the barriers between their love. Though the dialogue is at times formal and even operatic, Hudson shows considerable skill in the unfoldment of love within her—an unfoldment complicated by an imperfect medium of communication and her inability to comprehend the meaning of the tumult in her heart. To prevent too continuous a strain upon the romantic sensibilities, relief is provided by shifting the scene either indoors, where Rima loses much of her charm, or to the Indian village, toward which Abel occasionally turns his steps, and by the sardonic portraiture of cunning old Nuflo, with his harpings on "God's politics." In the meantime, Hudson has been carefully preparing, as with Kua-kó's eagerness to train Abel in the use of the blow-pipe, for the tragedy that is soon to close in upon them.

With the inclusion of Riolama in the Whitmanesque panoramic survey from "everlasting Ytaioa's granite throne," the action gathers momentum and intensity. The eighteen-day journey to the cave where Nuflo discovered Rima's mother is indeed interrupted by the insertion of the story of these last two survivors of a mysterious race, but, actually, it serves to increase our sense of the distance being traversed. Hudson does not shirk the difficult scene that soon takes place: Rima's anguish and despair at not finding her people, who might have given her guidance, her long, deathlike swoon, and her awakening to the realization that love is "the flower and the melody of life." Beseeching Abel not to regret the journey to Riolama, she touchingly declares that all she wished to know of her kinsfolk she has now found in him. There is some mere capriciousness in Rima's resolve to return alone to her forest home and in those familiar surroundings prepare for the coming of her bridegroom, but it is not inconsistent with her character. The scene of her appalling death, though of necessity presented indirectly, has in it "the pang of all the partings gone, and partings yet to be."

One of the chief merits of *Green Mansions* is its intensity, an intensity rare in English fiction, and comparable to that in *Wuthering Heights*, in many Elizabethan plays, and in some of the oriental romances made popular by F. W. Bain about the time of its writing. There is passion in the appreciation of nature, as when Abel drops to his knees in thankfulness for the beauty of the enchanted woods, and throughout the love scenes, especially that in which Abel identifies his beloved with the mystic Hata flower. The intensity that makes the greatest impression comes after Rima has fallen, with her lover's name upon her lips, into the voracious sea of flames. Abel's grief, sharp as a dagger-thrust, is so excruciating that it drives him to the killing of Runi and all his kindred and even to the cursing of God. Night after night, like Heathcliff, he embraces in waking visions a spirit-bride, the wraith of Rima. Pangs of remorse for his killing of the Indians and the animals sacred to his beloved, epitomized in the recurring images of dead Cla-cla's staring eyes and blood-dappled hair and the lidless white eye of a serpent's severed head, bring him to the verge of madness, the feeling that he has been "dwelling alone" for thousands of years "on a vast stony plain in everlasting twilight. . . . " Extraordinarily effective is the incident in which a moth flutters into his hut and, after resting for a while on the thatch directly over the fire, falls into the white blaze—an incident that has the power of the sleep-walking scene in *Macbeth* to revivify the most terrible part of the previous action. The intensity is superbly sustained: the main thing supporting Abel on his headlong, Orestean flight to the coast, pursued by phantom Indians and a tremendous ophidian head, is his resolve to find a repository for Rima's ashes, so that his own might ultimately be mixed with them. Since Hudson had the same instinct as the Greeks for the quiet ending,[3] the novel comes to a close with the hero's re-discovery of the "everlasting freshness and beauty" of the earth.

Without doubt, there is profound autobiography in *Green Mansions*, Rima being for her creator the incarnation of his longing for a woman who would be "the sustentation" not only of his body but likewise of his "higher winged nature." But, by the transmuting power of poetry, she becomes at the same time something more

---

[3] Note also the endings of "El Ombu" and "Marta Riquelme."

universal.[4] She is, indeed, *das Ewig-Weibliche* that draws men to her and leads some of them on to a higher plane of being. (This is perhaps the reason that *Green Mansions* means more to men than to women.) And implicit in Rima's death is a tragic vision of the world as a whole. In the life of man, so exquisite a love as that between her and Abel cannot be more than a brief interlude. In the life of nature, much that is most admirable—especially the more ethereal elements—is continually being destroyed by the evil in the heart not only of man but of Nature herself. Whenever a Rima, in whom "all the separate and fragmentary beauty and melody and graceful motion found scattered throughout nature [are] concentrated and harmoniously combined," arouses the resentment of a Runi and the likes of him, her fate is sealed. Such a belief brings to a piercing note a leading motif in all of Hudson's writings: the beautiful vanishes and returns not.

A Little Boy Lost is a fantasy of the author's own experiences as a child roaming about the pampas, with the addition of "a few dreams and fancies thrown in and two or three native legends and myths" that he had learnt from his gaucho companions. It primarily seeks to arouse its youthful readers to a greater awareness of the fabulous beauty of the natural world—one of the highest aims in writing for children. Insects, flowers, trees, hills, the sea, and such phenomena as marsh echoes, mists and mirages, are intimately or picturesquely presented; and birds, beasts, and the most primitive of men are readily accepted as companions. Strong is the sense of the animateness of all nature—Martin feeling at times, like Jefferies' Bevis and Kipling's Mowgli, that everything is "alive and [intently] watching him . . . —the passion-flowers, the green leaves, the grass, the trees, the wide sky, the great shining sun." The strangeness of nature, as in the eerie hooting of the owl, may occasionally be frightening, but there is in the book little of the terror to be found in the poem of Blake from which it takes its title. Martin recognizes in the Lady of the Hills his truest mother; and she is, as

---

4 Elmer G. Suhr, in his *Theme and Variations* (Boston, 1944, pp. 251-5), gives a good analysis of the representative qualities to be found in both her and Abel. Those that Epstein embodied in his highly stylized bas-relief reflect much more certain aspects of the character of Hudson and the elemental forces of the earth than of Rima.

Hudson would have his readers regard nature as a whole, ever solicitous for his well-being.

There are in the telling of the story many of the concrete details that delight children—various foods to be savored (including mare's milk), wood-shavings to be wrapped around arms, legs and neck, new clothes to be donned, shells to be gathered along the beach, vultures, a grey burrowing owl, serpents, seals, a doe and her fawn, and even a puma for playmate. Exciting, too, are many of Martin's adventures: emptying a bucket of cold water on the snoring old shepherd, Jacob, a creature as much out of wonderland as of the pampas; meeting with Indians, with a wild man and his troop of horses, and with gnomes; conversing with the people of the Mirage and the Old Man of the Sea; and being rescued by fishermen from a raft awash on the ocean. *A Little Boy Lost* is richest of all in the qualities that appeal to the imagination, in which realm the child, living so close to the unconscious, can freely wander. It is, indeed, more compact of poetry than most books for the young. Since, however, many of the children of our urban civilization are deprived of intimacy with the wilder aspects of nature, they may find difficulty in "piping ['cross] the [pampas] wild."

Hudson is better in the weaving of tales than in the shaping of novels. Measured by the "well-constructed story," particularly those carrying an idea swiftly to its logical conclusion or focussing upon the dénouement, his may appear somewhat elementary in technique. But so likewise would the stories of Irving, Gogol and Turgenev, who, like Hudson, needed "ample room and verge enough" to secure their effects. Most of them sound like tales told around a campfire by one who has had some part in the action and is, like the born story-teller, creatively re-imagining it. The beginnings are quiet and leisurely; the modulations of the speaking voice, well-conveyed; the flow of events, sinuously chronological; and so deeply marked are the stories with the "erosions of contour" which life gives to human experience that only upon reflection does one become aware of their artistry. It is tale-telling *sub specie simplicitatis*, as practiced by minstrel, scop, and caveman; and, though wanting in the aesthetic appeal of the latest techniques, it provided Hudson with a vehicle appropriate to his material.

The situations in his stories, whether they be of English or South American life, are powerful: captivity amongst Indians; frustrated love ending in madness; black magic spelling disaster; revenge, remorse, and, in all but one of them, death. Yet there is no suggestion of mere sensationalism, for the emotions and actions are rooted in the blood and bone of the people, who, living in a wild land where violence is continually lurking, are elemental in thought and feeling. Penetrating is the insight into the lives of these people, and, though restrained in expression, profound the sympathy. Much of the personality of Hudson is revealed in these tales, most instant of all, his sense of tragedy—tragedy that is the consequence not only of flaws in human character but, as in the experiences of Valerio and Marta, of the very composition of life. As the old shepherd in "El Ombú" chorically remarks, "We often say that He who is above us is too great to concern Himself with our small affairs. There are so many of us; and how shall He, seated on His throne at so great a distance, know all that passes in His dominions!"

The "Story of a Piebald Horse" is concerned with the rivalry between two foster-brothers for the hand of their foster-sister—a rivalry that destiny soon resolves. Elaria, the sister, is in love with Anacleto, who has likewise been adopted as a child, but the dying wish of their benefactor that she marry his son Torcuato creates scruples in their minds. The story-within-a-story technique allows Hudson to begin the action near the end. Suspense is created by whetting the reader's curiosity as to the identity of the stranger, elegantly attired and mounted on a piebald with silver trappings, who came to assist in a cattle-marking and whose inexperience, coupled with the deviltry of his partner, resulted in his death—a death that occurred before he could complete a message to the lovers beseeching forgiveness. Though rather awkardly introduced (the narrator shifting from third to first person), the account that clarifies the mystery is also not without suspense, for we do not know until the rivalry between the foster-brothers breaks into the open that Elaria is not actually Torcuato's sister. The accents in the telling are those of the horse-tamer Lucero, whom one may meet in *The Purple Land* holding forth on fate versus free will, and his introductory philosophizing sets the tone not only of this tale but of the group that follows: "I can laugh, . . . knowing that all things are ordered by destiny; otherwise I might sit down and cry. . . . Bones of a dead horse and a nettle; a bird that falls from its nest in the night and is found dead in the morning; puffballs blown about by the wind; a little lamb left behind by the flock bleating at night amongst the thorns and thistles, where only the fox or wild dog can hear it! Small matters are these, and our lives, what are they?"

In "Niño Diablo" the emphasis is more upon character. Orphaned at six by Indians and held in captivity five years before effecting his escape, Niño possesses, along with many admirable qualities of his own, their stealthiness and preternatural sensitivities. "He stoops like a falcon," says Gregory, his anxious prospective father-in-law, "makes his stroke and is gone—Heaven knows where!" Considering the urgency of his mission—the rescue of a woman being carried off by Indians—and the provocative remarks of Polycarp, we readily forgive him, as does Gregory, the appropriation of the highly-prized geldings. Swashbuckling "Polycarp of the South," who belligerently asserts that in all matters concerning his horses he is "a whirlwind, a conflagration, a river flooded in winter, and all wrath and destruction like an invasion of Indians!" makes an excellent foil to Niño—a Bobadil to a Puck. The scene of a rancho interior upon which the story opens—the flames from the fireplace casting shadows on the walls; the prongs of deer heads hung with "bridles and lassos, ropes of onions and garlic, bunches of dried herbs"; the large pot of bubbling mutton broth, around which are gathered Gregory's marriageable twin daughters, his florid wife, his old-maidish sister, and his vacant-eyed, aged mother; and, disposed about the floor in the outer circle, four children at play and various cats and dogs at doze—is worthy of the brush of a Teniers. The articulation of the three scenes of the ending is skilfully done; but, so out of proportion is the last of them to the opening one of the story, it leaves a sense of abruptness. Taken as a whole, "Niño Diablo" is diverting rather than deeply moving—the spritely scherzo of a volume whose parts, as someone has put it, are like those of a tragic symphony.

"Pelino Viera's Confession," which belongs to the tradition of Poe and Machen, is the story of a man who becomes involved in black magic. Viera has been sentenced to death for killing his wife, and, in order to justify himself in the eyes of his parents, who have returned to Spain, he commits to paper a full account of their relationship. "Accidentally I set my heel on the head of a venomous serpent, and crushed it," he says in conclusion; "that was my only crime." The suggestion of evil in the woman he married against his better judgment produces a certain tension in the reader; but, in spite of the exciting scene in the hall ot the witches and the one around her dead body, that tension slackens soon after she grows feathers, sprouts wings, and flies away into the night. It is not the presence of the supernatural that is at fault—its powerful effect upon the primitive in us makes it an excellent key for a story—and Hudson does well in not rationalizing it in the manner of Hawthorne. What does disconcert, for it narrows rather than gives free scope to the imagination, is the sudden realization that most of the magic is contained in that old stock-in-trade, an unguent, which anyone can apply effectively. As Hudson seems to perceive in his introduction and as demonstrated by Machen in "The Inmost Light" and Walpole in "Tarnhelm," these incredulous times demand a more subtle use of diablerie. The "Confession" is therefore the weakest movement of the symphony.[5]

"El Ombú" and "Marta Riquelme," longer than the other "tales of the pampas," are decidedly the best. The former relates the experiences of the successive occupants of a rancho named after the massive tree that cast its ominous shadow upon it—a rancho that is now only "a bed of nettles." The characters are powerfully drawn, particularly the *caudillo* Santos, with the strength of an ox and the temper of an autocrat, and gentle Valerio, who, though brought up amid luxury, embraced poverty because it brought peace of mind. Terrible are the crises in their lives: Santos killing a favorite slave for laying aside gratuities for the purchase of his freedom; Valerio flayed almost to death for acting as spokesman for his disgruntled fellow-soldiers; and Bruno, his son, seeking out the cruel general, and wreaking upon him, indirectly, a horrible revenge. (Goyesque is the sketch of this general, dripping with the blood of a living bull inside of which he had been placed, and rushing stark mad at his men, "yelling and whirling his sword round so that it looked like a shining wheel in the sun.") These various happenings are loosely held together by frequent references to the half-buried foundations

---

5   The narrative poem, "Tecla and the Little Men," which has something of the eldrich quality of "Goblin Market" and *The Land of the Heart's Desire*, is a more successful handling of the supernatural.

of the rancho and to the mighty, solitary ombú, under which the story is being told.

Pervading the whole story is a sense of inexorable tragedy, tinged with irony. Poignant is the sight of Santos, his face like that of "a dead man who had died with wide-open eyes," gazing from the shores of Uruguay toward his homeland in daily expectation of a pardon; Valerio sinking down from exhaustion near the threshold of his home and dying before his wife, Donata, and little Bruno could respond to his cry; grief-stricken Donata faithfully watering, year after year, the barren spot where he had expired until it became carpeted by "a creeping plant with small round malva-like leaves, and little white flowers like porcelain shirt buttons"; and Monica, her mind turned by the news of Bruno's death, finding her only solace in life the sight of flamingoes "moving like a red line" across Lake Chascomús. The feeling of actuality is strengthened by having the story told by one whose life had touched all these characters. Restrained though his account is, we are aware of his hatred for the cruelties of man and his compassion for the downtrodden. Like Lucero in the "Story of a Piebald," he holds that "when misfortune has singled out a man for its prey, it will follow him to the end, and he shall not escape from it though he mount up to the clouds like a falcon, or thrust himself deep down into the earth like the armadillo." The death of Valerio causes him to exclaim: "There are things about which we must be silent, or say only, turning our eyes up, Has He forgotten us!"

"Marta Riquelme" is the pitiful story of a strangely attractive girl caught in a coil of calamities: five years of abysmally cruel captivity among Indians, the loss of her four children, and, after her beauty had been permanently marred, the desertion of her husband, whom she "loved only too well." Brooding constantly upon her memories, which brings her to the conviction that she is being persecuted by God, Marta withdraws more and more from human society—in the end, sequestering herself in a dense wood on a cliff. Native to that region is the belief that anyone borne down by intolerable suffering may be transformed by compassionate spirits into a Kakué; and so skillfully does Hudson lead up to the dénouement that, after looking upon her crouched on the trunk of a fallen, creeper-entangled tree, her short hair standing "like an immense crest on her head" and her widely opened eyes glaring furiously like those of "some hunted savage animal," we are persuaded, even as is the priest, that she has really undergone such a metamorphosis. This horrible climax, dominating the successive crises more than any event in "El Ombú," gives to the intensity of the story as eerie a quality as that in one of Marta's own piercing cries or in the shriek of the Kakué, expressing as it does "a degree of agony and despair surpassing the power of any human soul to feel."

In order to give credibility to the climax, a good deal of attention is given to the setting—a village on the northwest border of the remote Jujuy province, hemmed in by gigantic mountains and "vast gloomy forests, whose death-like stillness" is broken only "by the hoarse thunders of a distant waterfall" or "the savage screams of some strange fowl." The terrifying experience that the priest has at the outset of the narrative, establishing the imaginative key, prepares us for the transformation scene. We are more immediately prepared for "some unimaginable calamity" by the condition of the weather, which, with days of storm and then with an overcast sky, has charged Marta's retreat with the deepest gloom. The narrator, so much in love with his heroine that he almost forgets his priestly vows, is more a participant in the story than the old shepherd of "El Ombú." Thus the concluding section, in which he wages spiritual battle against Pachacanac and the other powerful gods of this primeval region not only to preserve his own faith in God but to effect the ultimate redemption of Marta, is justified, though it might have been done more trenchantly and in smaller compass. In the drawing of his portrait, the irony is at times too obvious, as when, upon reading in the memoirs of a predecessor that the natives welcomed the idea of an unquenchable fire in hell for it would save them much wood-gathering, he exclaims, in the manner of a character out of Anatole France, "So hard it was for their heathen intellects to comprehend the solemn doctrines of our faith!" On the whole, however, he is sympathetically presented, his struggle with the powers of darkness reminding one of those of the Christian missionaries in ancient Greece and Rome and in modern Africa.

The other two stories, "An Old Thorn" and "Dead Man's Plack," are laid in England—the one preserving a strange incident in the rural life of a century earlier and the other vivifying a page of pre-conquest history. In "An Old Thorn," which has in it much of the quality of the essay, Hudson tells of the feeling of reverence that grew in him for a hawthorn snaked with ivy, standing solitary beside a road across the South Wiltshire Downs—the "green disc" of ivy on the topmost boughs looking like the crouched head of a serpent. When he learnt that his feeling was shared by many in the neighboring villages, the folklorist in him was aroused; and, from various scraps of information elicited from them, he pieced together the sad history of Johnnie Budd, an unemployed laborer who, having stolen a sheep in order to feed his hungry wife and children, blamed his arrest and subsequent death sentence upon the enmity of this old thorn, whose bark had been "hurted" when, as a child, he played "crows" upon its branches. Since the story is as much concerned with the tree as with the man—how, better than the thorn of Wordsworth's poem, it was able through "unconscious intelligence and cunning" to secure a firm roothold on the sheep-mown turf of the downs and how it acquired a power over the lives of men—the characterization of Johnnie and his human milieu is too meager to give him full substance in our mind. Yet the sight of him kneeling before the thorn, pressing his face against its bark and murmuring a prayer "for its forgiveness and for deliverance from the doom which threatened him," etches itself upon the memory. The rest of his history is told by flashbacks, which, according to present-day standards, are somewhat awkwardly managed. "An Old Thorn" is certainly a strange tale—one peculiarly adapted to Hudson's genius and, like "Marta Riquelme," unique.

"Dead Man's Plack," which is almost long enough to have been considered with the novels, is primarily a study in remorse. Had Hudson allowed himself more room he might have secured the effect aimed at: the portrait of a "woman who was capable of a horrible crime and who was yet essentially noble in spirit." As it is, too much time is devoted to Elfrida's crimes and too little to psychological explanation. The sense of deep wrong that, in large measure, led her to acquiesce in the murder of Athelwold could have been made more convincing had we—perhaps by means of flashbacks—been given more of her earlier life. We are supposed to believe that it was the perfidy of Athelwold and the "desertion" of Edgar that turned a yearning for love into one for "power and splendour"; but how can we be certain that she ever aspired to anything better? By identifying her with elemental forces of nature—the fire in the hearth, the river Test, and "the sea of rounded hills" on Salisbury

Plain—Hudson seems to think that, especially considering the violence of the times, we will judge her actions in somewhat the same light we should those of a hawk or a puma; but this too is not done thoroughly enough to produce the desired result. Elfrida remains, in the end, with still too many veils about her.

As a study in remorse, "Dead Man's Plack" is not however without a certain impressiveness. After the murder of young Edward, whose image comes back persistently to haunt her, she fears only the revenge of Dunstan and of the masses, who, like "a frantic bellowing herd" might "gore and trample her to death"; but with the passing of all fear of earthly punishment, there comes the "terrible thought" that ultimately, "at God's judgment seat," she will have "to answer for her . . . dark deeds," and even her wanderings over the downs and her meditations at Stonehenge cannot rid her of this greatest of fears. The ministrations of saintly Editha and many benevolences to the church bring some respite, yet she knows that, even though final pardon may be granted, her journey through purgatory will be a long and arduous one. The occasional rebellions by the unregenerative elements in her nature—as when, in the midst of a conference with some clergy, she bursts out with a cry of joy at the announcement of Dunstan's death—help to give vitality to the characterization. For this and other reasons, "Dead Man's Plack," unlike most historical fiction, is more than a series of tapestries. Though the minor characters scarcely come to life, the shade of Elfrida becomes substantial, and what Hudson has her say and do seems to the reader just what she must actually have said and done a thousand years ago in the flesh.

Thus, despite shortcomings in technique and a comparatively small expenditure of effort, Hudson was able to secure a niche for himself amongst the lesser masters of English fiction—a niche larger than those of Jefferies and Williamson, his only rivals among the major out-of-door essayists. Few though his books are, one is impressed by their variety: tales of the pampas, the English countryside and Saxon England, a fantasy for children, a realistic and a utopian novel, a romance against the background of Buenos Aires, another against the Banda Oriental, and still another within the stupendous shadow of the tropical jungle. At least four of them are memorable: "El Ombú" and "Marta Riquelme" deserve to rank close to such masterpieces of the short story as "Heart of Darkness" and "The Death of Iván Ilych"; *The Purple Land* belongs to a small but very select group; and *Green Mansions* is one of the best fantasies in our language. Most of Hudson's tales and novels not only bring new material to literature and a new and a strange beauty, but illuminate certain aspects of his personality that otherwise would not have found full expression, particularly his tragic vision of life.

Religious Atheist

We build our crumbling nest
Beneath the dark eaves of the infinite.

—MARY WEBB

Of Earth are we stripped or crowned.

—MEREDITH

While the earth remaineth, seedtime and
harvest, and cold and heat, and summer
and winter, and day and night, shall not
cease.

—GENESIS

ALTHOUGH IT IS customary to distinguish between two kinds of knowledge, that of the heart and that of the brain, the distinction is somewhat arbitrary, for the two are but the inner and outer aspects of the same experience and inextricably intermingled. At the core of the most abstract logic, there is an inborn emotional bias, and within the most instinctive or the most mystical experience, there exists a skeleton of logic. As embodied in empirical philosophy and well exemplified in *The Prelude* and *Far Away and Long Ago*, the senses are the ultimate sources of the material upon which each of them works. The brain and the heart are indeed both invaluable in the experiencing of life, and the wise man is he who keeps them in equipoise, their many ramifications interpenetrating one another richly and profoundly.

If the word *reason* could be completely dissociated from the purely logical faculty of the mind, and made to signify, as it does for many, the thinking that seems to be done by the entire body—rising with the pyramidal arrangement of the data of the senses and resting upon its edifice like a vertex—Hudson would surely have had nothing to say against it. "I live the life of Reason and common sense," he writes in one of his letters, "but it is the lower sort of reason based on instinct"—reason that relies largely upon the intuition for its insights. So high an estimate did he in fact place upon this kind of intelligence that (as has already been pointed out) he considered it a guiding principle in all life. The very vividness of his own sense impressions may at times have made intellectual reflection difficult—the experience also of Thoreau, Muir and many another field naturalist—but, as his numerous contributions to natural science attest, he was able to make more than commonly good use of it.

For the discursive or analytical reason—what Wordsworth calls "our meddling intellect"—he had a certain instinctive distrust. The appearance of reality seems to invite apprehension by such an instrument, but, operating cinematographically and often mechanistically, it is likely to give a devitalized or false idea of reality. And when, despite the paucity of its material and the finiteness of its perspective, logic hastily constructs a complete system of life, it tends to open a chasm between the mind and the concrete facts of existence.

With such a proclivity, the science of his day seemed to Hudson to be formulating a new and more labyrinthine scholasticism and thus (in Whitehead's phrase) bifurcating the universe. He himself touched reality in too many ways ever to become enamored of any science or philosophy insufficiently aware of life's multifariousness. The very movement of his thought, as reflected in the choice of the out-of-door essay as his vehicle for expression, was not, in any strict sense, a logical one. Instead of crossing the ocean of Being aeronautically with deftly articulated abstractions, he preferred the long tact of clipperlike thinking, which, never a slave to charts nor exclusively intent upon the discharging of a cargo of baled philosophy on the docks of some great city, could, on the way, sport with the elements. What cargo he did occasionally unload was first proved upon his own pulses and oriented to his whole personality.

As indicated by his elevation of the poet above the naturalist in the presentation of nature, the kind of knowledge which he regarded as decidedly superior was that of the heart—that gained through the feelings and the intuition.[1] Feeling is of course the primal mode by which the mind, in its original unconscious state, stored experience and shaped it into patterns. Our less fundamental intellectual consciousness, evolved out of the same matrix in order to deal with a more complex milieu and frequently distorted by the concepts amongst which it moves, is a later and more fallible development. The universal spirit seems more akin to our earlier, unconscious mind, and thus our communion with it in its constant flux is more attainable through the intuition than through discursive reasoning. What logic achieves only laboriously, intuition, as illustrated even in the experience of such abstract scientists as Archimedes, Newton, Poincaré and Einstein, grasps in a flash. Without this power, so Hudson was convinced, art and religion would wither away, and the individual and society would no longer be able to co-operate with Nature in their further evolution.

The disparagement of the rational faculty and the exaltation of the feelings and intuition are characteristic of the mystic, and such,

---

[1] Though occasionally using the word *intuition* himself in its accepted meaning, Hudson objected when he found it in Bergson. The objection was, however, largely a verbal one, for most of the qualities Bergson ascribes to intuition are included in Hudsonian instinct.

he essentially was. As we saw earlier, the mystical experience was often evoked by certain natural objects and forces. Sometimes it simply brought him a clearer perception of the objects themselves and their relationships; but at other times, particularly when evoked on the top of a down, along the shore of the sea, or in the midst of a vast wilderness, where one is more receptive to an impression of nature as a whole, it expanded his consciousness over all the surrounding region and made him feel that he was in communion with the Spirit "that penetrates and clasps and fills the world." Because his kinship with nature was so intimate and deep as to become in itself almost a sort of mysticism, many of his experiences were probably little more than moments of heightened awareness. (His statement "that all true poets are in some degree mystic" confirms one in this view.) Some of them, however, especially those rare ones in which he felt matter to be "but a disguise, a shadow and delusion" and the physicist's "force" or energy "but a semblance and shadow of the universal soul," have the air of authenticity about them, and, though occupying no such prominent place in his total experience as in that of Wordsworth or the greater mystics, they became for him "moments big as years."

To some extent at least, Hudson erred in his evaluation of the discursive reason, for one can discover truth by thinking about life as well as by living it (who can perceive the fourth dimension?) and surely this faculty would never have developed to its present state if it habitually distorts experience. His emphasis upon the prime importance of the feelings and the intuition has, however, the support of many philosophers, among them, Hume and Schopenhauer, James and Bergson and Whitehead. Yet, as might be expected of one with his scientific training, he never went to the extreme of Rousseau, Blake, and Lawrence in their assault upon the intellect nor genuflected before the shrine of Unreason. Realizing how great is the margin of error in all the instruments of knowledge and how subject the feelings and intuitions are to personal vagaries, he respected the processes of logic for their disciplinary rôle—for making the various feelings and impulses keep good company. He himself took to task those mystics who report in too specific a manner their essentially ineffable experiences, for they run the risk (particularly if their reports are colored too obviously after their own idiosyncrasies) of polluting the purest mountain stream of feeling. Hudson's deficiencies in epistemology (so to speak) are not, therefore, so great as they seem at first glance—his general approach to life being indeed very congenial to the spirit of our age, which, while making considerable use of scientific and logical processes in its thinking has come to question their complete adequacy and, in order to obtain a sense of the wholeness of truth, frequently turns to mysticism.

Not only his distrust of discursive reasoning and an unwilling- ness to remain long in its rarefied atmosphere but also a certain innate scepticism of all dogmas and of all the elaborate systems yet constructed kept him from formulating in any detail a philosophy of his own. And even had he been to the idiom born and possessed with an eagerness to build, he would never have presumed to read so fully as have many theologians and philosophers the mystic codex of Nature. Truth marries no one, says the proverb, and Hudson realized that the mystery would remain as long as Nature continues to exist as a living organism, immutably mutable, and man stands within her processes. His scepticism, like that of Montaigne, was not, however, inherently negative. As indicated in the discussion of his artistry and his biology, he did try to achieve, in a tentative sort of way, a fairly coherent idea of nature as a whole. Depending largely in its construction upon the intuition, the resulting philosophy is substantially that of a speculative poet, with some of the incon- sistencies that arise from an occasional shift in mood. And many of his utterances, like the melodies that came to Keats while gazing at a Grecian urn, are "unheard," and imagination must help guide the pen of logic in order to transcribe them into an explicit key.

Essentially unimpressed by the mechanistic philosophy prevalent among the biologists of his day, Hudson remained true to his deep- est intuitions and looked upon Nature as an immense organism, which, like the human body, is composed of myriads upon myriads of smaller organisms. The world as a whole is pervaded by one unifying spirit, and each of the component organisms, no matter how minute—every earthworm, wasp, aphid, alga, cell, and even (as is implicit in his thinking) every molecule and every atom— possesses, like any of the vertebrates, a distinct psyche or spirit of its own. In "its attribution of [man's] own sentient life and intelli- gence to all things," such a philosophy is akin (so we are reminded) to the animism of primitive man, though it is without his materialistic conception of "souls" surviving "the bodies and objects they inhabit." As already noted, it found expression in the mythopoeic imagination of the Greeks and, in a more sublimated form, in many modern nature poets. Bringing with it, as it often does, a sense of awe as well as of beauty, Hudson believed animism to be the root and essence "of all nature-worship, from fetishism to the highest pantheistic development."

Since he was aware not only of the unique individuality of many plants, animals, and places but also of the universal spirit immanent in varying degrees in each of them, and since, as with many mystics with a strong sense of the external world, direct communion with this spirit usually came as an extension of a feeling of rapport with some particular object or creature or while under the influence of some special aspect of nature, he might best be called a panpsychist. "There are beautiful moments in our converse with nature," he remarks after listening to a blackbird, "when all the avenues by which nature comes to our souls seem one, when hearing and seeing and smelling and feeling are one sense, when the sweet sound that falls from a bird is but the blue of heaven, the green of earth, and the golden sunshine made audible." The sight of "a great spread of thinly growing viper's bugloss" on a down near Burlington Gap and the glittering, fiery gold of the sky and of the sea during an evening spent near Abbotsbury brought his spirit flying "out of its nest over all nature." Though his phrasing at times seems to imply a certain transcendentalism—most of all when using the figurative language of early nineteenth-century romanticism or picturing Nature as "the great Artist-Mother"—he was careful to explain that the sense of someone behind the outer show of things acting with a given purpose, such as Maeterlinck perceived behind the hive, is "not assuredly of 'someone' outside of or above the natural phenomenon, but in and one with it, just as the act of a man proceeds from him, and is the man." Nature as a whole is like a vast orchestra, each organism, from the simplest to the most complex, with its instrument to play, and, though its infinitely diverse choirs perform together with marvellous precision and, for the most part, in general harmony, they do so, nonetheless, without a maestro.

There is something of panpsychism, so he maintained, in all men, for at least a remnant of the primitive persists ineradicably at the core of even the most sophisticated. Though forced to alter its outer form periodically during its long career, it has been able to weather many assaults, from the time of Thales, Anaximenes and the other Greek hylozoists to Bruno, Gassendi, Spinoza and the Cambridge Platonists, and hence on to Schopenhauer, Lotze, James, and Bergson of our own era. As the fountainhead of vitalism,[2] which has been especially productive in recent years in the exploration of the processes of evolution and in various fields of psychic research, panpsychism has appealed to many scientists who have not been afraid to go beyond the ambit of the measurable and the strictly logical or to make a comprehensive survey of Nature—Fechner, Butler, McDougall, Du Noüy, Eddington, and (if he may be included here) Smuts. This philosophy, it should be remembered, was held by Hudson only tentatively, for, as implied in his definition of animism ("the mind's projection of itself into nature"), he thought it possible that it may be merely an expression of the pathetic fallacy—the all-too-human tendency to expand our ego throughout the universe.

As he was well aware, one of the chief characteristics of the universe and all it contains is that of ceaseless and endless change. Though considerable use is made of the leitmotif and the refrain in the music played by the cosmic orchestra (to vary the Heraclitean figure), the performance goes on and on *ad infinitum*, those themes or melodies not dropped being continually varied or developed and new ones introduced. What is it that keeps the composition from becoming amorphous or merely repetitious? Why should there be any motifs at all? Or, to drop the analogy, how is the flux of things given some pattern? Like Bergson and many other evolutionists, Hudson came to the conclusion that there exists in the midst of change a creative driving force, which is constantly shaping life.

As to whether any purpose guides this creative force—one of the most fundamental and baffling problems confronting the human mind—he was persuaded that (as has already been indicated) there are at least such formative principles as beauty and intelligence. Surely, one of the most obvious aspects of this world of ours, as recorded again and again in the arts, from the time of Homer and

---

[2] Since, in Hudson's thinking, there is no unbridgeable gulf between organic and inorganic matter (just how it is to be spanned, biophysics may one of these days discover), some of the chief defects of vitalism cannot be charged against him.

Plato to that of Keats and Bridges, is the infinite variety and harmony of its beauty. And, though suffering many defeats (some of
the bitterest of them administered by man), the "unconscious aestheticism" of Nature seemed to Hudson to be exerting a steady
influence on this globe. Since the intelligence inherent in life does
not appear to operate consistently according to human standards, its
presence is not so obvious; but, though disturbed by certain of
its manifestations (as in insect life)[3] and by its many lapses, he was
continually aware, especially when in an unusual psychic state, of
its formative power. And, feeling at times even a certain reciprocity
on the part of Nature to man's endeavor to understand her, he would
most assuredly have approved, in regard to both organic and inorganic evolution, Jeans's belief that the universe is closer to a great
thought than to a great machine.

The evidences of beauty and intelligence as constitutive principles, adding much to the power and quality of consciousness, did
not, however, lead him, as they probably did Darwin (or was it
rather, as Hudson thought, because of "kindly and compassionate
feelings"?), to take refuge in teleology—that "poor, hastily made
straw shelter, which lets in the rain and the wind." Even though
the creative force, as manifested in animal life, seems to be moving
in a definite direction, it is doing so, he felt, only in a groping sort
of way. Perhaps it is evolving itself while at the same time shaping
life as a whole, or does not have the cosmic organism under sufficient control to enforce its impulses completely on the refractoriness
of matter. Looking back upon the vast succession of steps by which
mankind has ascended from the dark, one may be prompted to read
into nature some primal purpose, but, actually, as Hudson realized,
life cannot be explained apart from its temporal flux, and the most
comprehensible ontology vouchsafed the human intelligence is history—what has happened to man and his fellow-creatures and to the
world in which they move and have their being.

Many phenomena seemed to him to indicate a want of purpose
—that the imprints upon the sands of our little rotatory island in

---

3 "If we be of animistic mind we become when watching [insects] uncom-
fortably conscious of a spirit, an entity, in or behind nature that watches us and
our watching with an unfathomable look in its eyes and a challenging and mocking
smile on its lips" (*Adventures among Birds,* p. 208).

the sidereal ocean are those not of a goodman Friday but of some monster. Many risky and seemingly useless experiments are performed in the creation of new species, which, if they fail in adaptation, are discarded as readily as an artist does his unsuccessful sketches.[4] As he noted in the armadillo family and in all those animals quickly paralyzed by fear, many of the species that have succeeded in gaining a foothold in some particular environment have later been injured and even destroyed by the selfsame instincts that originally led to their adaptation. Not only is Nature, in spite of a certain emphasis upon individuality, notoriously reckless of the individual life, but, for no apparent reason, she allows species after species, and even whole orders and phyla, to die out of existence. The universality of death, which so profoundly disturbed Hudson, is perhaps proof enough of a general failure in adaptation. The fact that amidst this extravagant expenditure of life, *Homo sapiens*, Nature's highest achievement and in a way a recapitulation of her whole history, is no more exempt from such a fate than any other species, can be disquieting to anyone with religious sensibilities.

Nature's occasional cruelty was especially repugnant to him, for it made her seem at times terrifyingly alien. By "an unconscious iniquity," he tells us, the parasitic instinct of the cuckoo and the cowbird has perverted "maternal affection," making it "subservient to the very opposing agency against which it was intended as a safeguard!" Of the many cruelties animals, even of the same species, inflict upon each other, the one that repelled Hudson most was the way wasps and ichneumon flies paralyze their victims in order to provide their young with live food—an experience, like that of the duel Turgenev witnessed between an adder and a toad, almost enough to drive out of one's mind "the idea of a beneficent Being who designed it all." The cruelty incarnate in men and women, which, through the invention of traps and cages and guns, goes beyond "nature's ordinance," was to him a continual source of bitterness. The occasional utter wantonness of Nature, shattering in a few moments the labors of centuries, is illustrated on a grand scale in

---

4 "One can imagine," observes Hudson, "some Principality or High Intelligence, a visitor from Aldebaran, let us say, looking on at" Nature's experiment with the bat (which, unlike millions of others, has turned out to be a success) "and remarking: 'My dear, what a silly fool you are to waste so much energy in trying to do an impossible thing' " (*The Book of a Naturalist*, p. 35).

pamperos and blizzards and tornadoes, floods and famine-producing droughts and pestilences, vast forest or prairie fires, and volcanic eruptions and earthquakes. A severe cold wave, which wrought great havoc upon the bird life in Cornwall, made him think, for a while at least, "that the darkest imaginings of men—the blackest phantom or image of himself which he has sacrificed to—was not so dark as this dreadful unintelligible and unintelligent power that made us. . . ."

Despite his doubts as to the purposiveness of the creative force and his hatred of all cruelty, Hudson, calling himself a "religious atheist," came to a general acceptance of the conditions of life. Though never accepting quite to the extent of Thoreau or Rilke the enormous amount of killing involved in the struggle for existence, he did find some justification for it when regarded as a means of forcing the pace of evolution. "Owing to the softness and sensitiveness induced in us by an indoor artificial life, . . . we have come," he says, "to a false or an exaggerated idea" of the painfulness of pain; and rending beaks and talons, steeled paws and poisonous fangs, are not so ubiquitous in fact as in seeming. As to the ways of wasps, ichneumon flies and cuckoos, he recommended the passage in *The Origin of Species* in which Darwin "said that [even if] it was not perhaps a logical conclusion, . . . it seemed to him more satisfactory to regard such things 'not as specially endowed or created instincts, but as small consequences of one general law'— the law of variation and the survival of the fittest." While never minimizing the agony involved in many forms of death, such as those from starvation and long infirmity, he kept pointing out that some of them are not particularly painful. The death that comes swiftly and unexpectedly, with the swoop of a hawk, is an easy one —the mere prick of a needle. The newly-hatched robin that the cuckoo ejected from its nest "is no more conscious than a chick in the shell; take from it the warmth that keeps it in being, and it drops back into nothingness without knowing and, we may say, without feeling anything."

The principle of Nature that only by means of struggle can strength be maintained and life evolved—a bitter and depressing draught, in some of its implications, to the "happy clan" of Victorians—was as much a stimulant to Hudson as it was to Meredith. "No sooner is any species placed above it, or over-protected, than degeneration begins." "For the healthy man, or for the man whose virile instincts have not become atrophied in the artificial conditions we exist in, strife of some kind, if not physical then mental, is essential to happiness." From time to time he even exalted pain into one of the supreme instruments for the sculpturing of life into greater significance.

As things are designed in this world of sentient life there can be no good, no sweetness or pleasure in life, nor peace and contentment and safety, nor happiness and joy, nor any beauty or strength or lustre, nor any bright and shining quality of body or mind, without pain, which is not an accident nor an incident, nor something ancillary to life, but is involved in and a part of life, of its very colour and texture.

We should indeed welcome most of Nature's buffets and bruises.

For human beings, he accepted an ethics informed, like Nature's, with what is best for the maintenance and the further development of the race. As stressed in the discussion of his social philosophy, evil will result not only from the transgression of her laws but likewise from any attempt on the part of mankind to divorce itself from her influences. It is all very well to erect a high superstructure of ethical and spiritual values, but, as Montaigne, Meredith and many others have also cautioned, the foundations must be anchored deep in the primitive subsoil. If these values are detrimental to survival, the edifice, like the Tower of Babel, will come toppling to the ground, with man and all his achievements under it. "The cruel instinct of the savage," Hudson contends, "is less painful to contemplate than that mistaken or perverted compassion which seeks to perpetuate unfitness, and in the interest of suffering individuals inflicts a lasting injury on the race."

So much did he believe Nature depends upon struggle to force the pace of evolution that he even accepted the necessity of occasional war. Peace may bring with it "all sweet and gentle feelings, all virtues [and] all graces," but it also, from time to time, can become, he says, "like a secret, unfelt malady which is slowly consuming a beautiful woman's life." Just as a person gains vigor through struggle with a hostile environment and in competition with his fellows, so tribes and nations cleanse racial blood and forge strength in their struggle with one another for survival or for a

larger measure of the earth's resources. Civil wars were to Hudson
the more beneficial, and when one broke out in Uruguay, the thought
that "there still exist[ed] one nation of the globe [unwilling to]
have peace at any price" was exhilarating. "The more good old-
fashioned throat-cutting there is in the Banda the better I shall like
it." [5] Thinking that England had become, at the end of the nineteenth century, a "peace-rotten land" and that the "flame of war"
might be the only remedy to purify her "of many hateful qualities
—of our caste feeling, of our detestable partisanship, our gross
selfishness, and a hundred more"—he was in a mood to "thank the
gods for a Wilhelm and a whole nation insane with hatred of England." And when, after the war, he observed how quickly his
country was wrapping herself up again in a false sense of security
even though "a million million bi-coloured souls" of Africa and
Asia might one of these days seek to overrun the mere promontory
that is Europe, he struck a final note of warning: "Dreaming of
peace on earth, everlasting peace, since to understand is to despair;
does not the aspiration itself signify decay?"

This attitude toward the prime evil of our age, though comprehensible and, in a way, courageous, is yet, so it must seem to all
those sympathetic to the ideal of peace under law (one of the most
fundamental concepts of Western culture), not a particularly wise
one. It has, of course, been shared by many: Thoreau, who prophesied a moral regeneration from the War Between the States; Burroughs, who readily supported the entry of the United States into
the first World War; Keith, who even opposes a world federation
on the grounds that it will contravene biological necessity; and
Ortega y Gasset, who, like von Hartmann before him, asserts that
"every other kind of discipline . . . arises out of the [one] which
man invented in order to fight." Recent studies in biology have,
however, invalidated the basic premise of their argument: fighting
has been found to be non-essential in the retention of racial vigor
—in fact, some of the largest and most "important groups of species
. . . have been evolving their pacific régime, and thriving under it,
for millions of years, and are today in a state of progressive evolu-

---

5 Hudson's general attitude was probably influenced by his South American
background, where revolution often takes the place of balloting.

tion. . . . " [6] (Among the various peoples of the earth, the comparatively peaceful Chinese have been able to maintain their racial strength in spite of frequent invasions.) And, except here and there amongst the lower orders of the animal world, as with certain species of fish and bees and ants, fighting to the death between large masses of the same species is practically unknown. In short, war is essentially an aberration of instinct.

Besides, what was good for primitive tribes, which were usually small and economically self-sufficing, is not necessarily good for the large, complex nations of contemporary society, which have become so dependent upon one another that the spark of war anywhere can quickly ignite a world-wide conflagration. Though the World War should have been lesson enough, Hudson apparently did not realize that modern weapons have been developed to such a degree of destructiveness that they not merely thwart the seeming purpose of evolution but may actually lead to the suicide of the human race. Yet, it should be said for him that he never glorified soldiering, even to the extent of Santayana in "Tipperary"; he was convinced that England's entry into the war was justified because she had been attacked and that it would be unmanly to stand by and see "men[,] women and children" murdered "in cold blood" without returning "blow for blow and bullet for bullet"; and, as much as anyone, he looked forward to the day when "the human race will discover some means of saving itself from rotting without this awful remedy of war." [7]

"Death is a reality," so Hudson tells us, "only when it is very near, so close on us that we can actually hear its swift stoaty feet rustling over the dead leaves, and for a brief bitter space we actually know that his sharp teeth will presently be in our throat." Yet the hardest thing of all for him to accept was the fact that Nature's "only provision" for the dead is that they "shall be speedily devoured." Coming upon a wheatear lying dead on the turf of White-

---

[6] Wallace Craig, "Why Do Animals Fight?" *International Journal of Ethics*, XXXI (1921), 278. A better article is Julian Huxley's "War as a Biological Phenomenon" (*On Living in a Revolution*, New York, 1942).

[7] One of the chief faults Hudson found in Tolstoy was "his insane delusions about non-resistance" (letter to Garnett of November 25, 1917). There is, of course, no evidence in the animal world to support Tolstoy's argument.

sheet Hill, he was brought up short by the thought of the myriads
of birds that die annually in migration.

> [That] they die in [such numbers] is not strange; the strange, the
> astonishing thing is the fact of death; what can they tell us of it—
> the wise men who live or have ever lived on the earth—what can
> they say now of the bright intelligent spirit, the dear little emotional
> soul, that had so fit a tenement and so fitly expressed itself in motions
> of such exquisite grace, in melody so sweet! Did it go out like the
> glow-worm's lamp, the life and sweetness of the flower? Was its
> destiny not like that of the soul, specialised in a different direction,
> of the saint or poet or philosopher! Alas, they can tell us nothing!

Though he never would have agreed with Meredith that the yearning for personal immortality is a "cry of unfaith," Hudson refused
to be comforted by a belief in an afterlife—"the faith and hope of
reunion with our lost" ones. As has already been dwelt upon, it
was largely his sense of oneness with the human family—with its
innumerable generations from time immemorial—that occasionally
reconciled him to "the mortal hillock." Being without issue, he
realized that the only immortality lying in store for him was the
feeling evoked in others that, because of his presence in their midst,
the earth has become endowed with greater beauty and perhaps with
something of his own spirit.

In imagination, he faced squarely the probability (now fairly
well established by the second law of thermo-dynamics) of the
ultimate extinction of all human, animal, and vegetable life and of
the earth itself, together with its fellow-planets and sun—all of
them mere thistledown afloat in the Milky Way! By the time that
Nature has buried the cancerous cities of men, as she did the Roman
remains in England, beneath the loam accumulated by earthworms
and bacteria, Western civilization will have followed the passage
of the Egyptian, the Babylonian, the Hellenic, the Aztec and the
Incan. After all the pale, restless people of the towns have become
mixed with the earth, and in England the swart Iberian has sup-
planted the Anglo-Saxon, there will remain for a long while under
the slackening sun, toilers of the sea, plowmen moving to the slow
rhythmic tread of oxen, and solitary shepherds minding flocks on
plain and down. These Hesiodic figures, too, will in the fullness of
time go their way—their villages, the last and sturdiest of human

outposts, swallowed up by the wilderness—and so will the various animals and plants, until the flanks of the earth become as snow-bound as are now its poles. Flowers and butterflies, spiders and snakes and birds, pumas and shepherds and emperors—all will have returned to the same indistinguishable dust.

Whenever our deepest feelings are touched, so Hudson remarks, there is a resulting melancholy—Keats's wakeful anguish of the soul. An important simple compounded in his own melancholy, it will be recalled, was the sense of being a stranger amongst those who now possess the earth—one of "a dying remnant of a vanished people." Another, which he shared with the Lake poets and a number of his contemporaries, was a sometimes wistful and sometimes tragic sense of the doom that awaits many graceful and noble creatures and many of the wild places on this globe. Much of his melancholy was, however, of a philosophical cast—the inability to accept with the sanguinity of a Meredith or a Whitman or a Have-lock Ellis the *Weltanschauung* of naturalism, particularly the universality of death ("a monstrous betrayal, a thing unnatural, almost incredible") and the apparent cosmic indifference as to the ultimate destiny of humanity and of all the other broods of life.

Yet the tragic drift of the world did not lead him, as it has many, to the conclusion that "the old, proud pageant of man" is essentially a vain spectacle. There is, after all, far more good than ill in most of our lives, and often a joy "sweeter than honey and the honeycomb." The sheer beauty of the world, particularly to one with such a sensuous temperament as his, is itself an incomparable gift. And there comes at times, when submitting ourselves to the mysterious creative force within us, a profound feeling of fulfilment. Thus it was that he could criticize, though not without some inconsistency, the theme of "Dover Beach": "That desolation . . . which made [Arnold] so unutterably sad, was due to the erroneous idea that our earthly happiness comes to us from otherwhere, some region outside our planet. . . . The 'naked shingles of the world' is but a mood of our transitional day. . . . " And while never conscious of a "providence who . . . recompenses us according to what our lives are," he felt at times, like one of his own characters, "that something outside of [him]self sustain[ed him]. . . . It may be God."

Whatever be the true cosmology, Hudson was convinced that Nature should be regarded as the supreme guide to mankind. The instability of contemporary society—the mounting psychoneurotic disturbances and the inner emptiness—he attributed, as we saw, to its loss of contact with the fields and woods and the folk of the wild, together with its increasing subjection to the machine. In order to lead his fellowmen back to the wellsprings of vitality and joy, and thus reintegrate their personalities and make them more responsive to the beneficent influences of Nature, he sought to convey through his writings, as he puts it, "some faint sense or suggestion of the wonder and delight which may be found in" her and the harmony that exists between all her creatures and their earthly matrix. Though he never donned prophetic robes in his essays, it is this underlying purpose, as well as his more theoretic philosophy, that gives to them a unity often wanting in this form of literature.

Not only does Nature, through her various forms, colors, sounds and movements, quicken and enhance the sense of beauty but she may bring, as she did to the heroes of *A Crystal Age, Green Mansions,* and *Far Away and Long Ago,* balm to the bruised spirit and a "new insight and comprehension." As Hudson says and many poets have demonstrated, flowers

> . . . Subtle things [can] teach—
> (Not like harsh lessons writ with pen)—
> And inner sense oft reach,
> That wakes not in the haunts of men.

An old thorn can inspire reverence, and a grove of ancient yews, the feeling of a cathedral "older and infinitely vaster" than any built by man, "fuller of light and gloom and mystery, and more wonderful in its associations." The lifting up of the eyes unto the hills has brought help to many besides Wordsworth and the psalmist. It is from experiences like these, so Hudson felt, that our hearts and minds and spirits are nourished "even as old King Nebuchadnezzar nourished his body" on grass.[8] (If only contemporary civilization could turn itself out to pasture for a while!)

---

8 "It seems that English landscape, the beauty of Nature in England," says W. J. Turner, "is still a source of real inspiration" to the composer, "whereas English life," which is "almost completely suburban," is "fatal to inspiration" (*Music and Life,* London, 1921, p. 50).

Like Thoreau and Muir, Hudson continually stressed the value of the wild. Not only does it bring us close to Nature—its unfathomable mystery and its inexhaustible power—but, by stripping away all mere complexities, it allows us, as the plains of Patagonia did him, to become aware of our deepest intuitions and to weigh the values of society with detachment. Though the larger, more epic, wildernesses are given the greatest prominence in his panoramas, he did not overlook the small waste places in the midst of cultivated districts.

> Like the ocean and the desert they[, too,] revive a sense and feeling of which we have been unconscious, but which is always in us, in our very marrow; the sense which . . . comes down to us from our remote progenitors at a time when the principal activities of the race were in woods and deserts. Given the right conditions and it springs to renewed life; and we know it is this which gives to life its best savour, and not the thousand pleasures or distractions which civilised dwellers in towns have invented as substitutes.

No other out-of-door essayist and few other writers have made so insistent the call of the wild.

More than pure landscape ("trees and grass and water"), it is the "wild and glad animal life" that excites and refreshes us. Is not the presence of animals in such large numbers and variety (he might well have asked with Cardinal Newman) "as mysterious as any thing which Scripture says about the Angels"? Since the elements of their beings, particularly those of beasts and birds, are similar to our own, we can readily enter into the rhythm of their lives, and, if this sympathy is heightened by the realization of their sharing in our destiny, they can be deeply companioning. It is largely the sight and sound of animals that make us feel toward any landscape, as Hudson felt toward Salisbury Plain, "that we are not aliens here, intruders or invaders on the earth, living in it but apart, perhaps hating and spoiling it, but . . . like them living and seeking our subsistence under her sky, familiar with her sun and wind and rain." One of the reasons he devoted a large portion of his life pioneering for laws to protect wild animal life was that with its diminution—especially with the loss of any species of vertebrates—some of the fascination and the beauty of the outdoors would vanish.

The keenness of the senses of animals and the sureness of their instincts were so much a source of wonder and admiration that occasionally he could not help thinking "it would have been better" had animal life "continued till the time of the dying of all life on the earth with no such development as that of the large-brained being who walks erect and smiling looks on heaven." This bitter thought was strengthened by an appreciation of such other qualities as those already mentioned: their want of self-consciousness (a quality that attracted him also to children), their ability to live in the present untroubled with moral problems, and (what has inspirited many a man) their zestfulness even in the face of the severest hardships. Most admirable was the integration of their lives—an integration that comes, in part, from a closer relationship with nature and the ability to synthesize their experiences more completely than we do. Through intimacy with our horizontal brethren, Hudson thought man might regain some of the faculties he has lost or perverted since the childhood of the race, and, without the help of psychoanalysis, become an integer again.

This emphasis upon man's kinship with animals—inherent in a panpsychic or pantheistic philosophy and much dwelt upon by its poets—is also of value, so it seems to me, in helping to eliminate the belief still widely held that man is somehow of a different substance from animals and that there is thus a fundamental opposition between him and the rest of nature—a belief that has done and continues to do much damage in the realm of thought. To divorce human from natural history is not only to interpret man in too limited a perspective but to keep him beating his wings forever over the patrimonial confines of some obsolescent religion or in the intense, yet blighting, inane. Indeed, as Huxley contended against Arnold, it may be said that, with the right approach, the study of natural history does as much as many of the humanities to bring one to the attainment of real culture.

It was almost as much his admiration for animals as for primitive man (the usual starting-point in the romantic argument) that led Hudson to stress the value of keeping oriented to the instinctive life. The instincts, embedded as they are in the unconscious, put us, he believed, in closest touch with the existential processes and are the primary creative forces in our lives—the inspiration of love, religion, and art and the goads driving us along the road of destiny.

The intellect, which has no such sense of direction, is a less trustworthy guide and, through its pride, may keep us from "all that is sweetest and most precious in life." However deep our respect for the accomplishments of the intellect may be, it is the instinctive or involuntary act, the *acte gratuit*, as Cunninghame Graham, Pirandello, and Gide have also emphasized, that calls forth our most fervent applause.

Why are we, children of light—the light which makes us timid—so strongly stirred by a deed like this [he has been describing how an Indian, in a spirit of defiance, sprang from his mount to the side of an unhorsed comrade, even though knowing it was to his death], so useless and irrational, and feel an admiration so great that compared with it that which is called forth by the noblest virtue, or the highest achievement of the intellect, seems like a pale dim feeling? It is because in our inmost natures, our deepest feelings, we are still one with the savage. We admire a Gordon less for his godlike qualities— his spirituality, and crystal purity of heart, and justice, and love of his kind—than for that more ancient nobility, the qualities he had in common with the wild man of childish intellect, an old Viking, a fighting Colonel Burnaby, a Captain Webb who madly flings his life away, a vulgar Welsh prize-fighter who enters a den full of growling lions, and drives them before him like frightened sheep. It is due to this instinctive savage spirit in us, in spite of our artificial life and all we have done to rid ourselves of an inconvenient heritage, that we are capable of so-called heroic deeds. . . .

The frustration or maladjustment of the instincts, since it betrays the most vital experiences of the race, was to Hudson one of the main drawbacks to the flowering of life.

An important therapeutic value to be had from an appreciation of nature, whether of animals or of landscape, is, he thought, its liberation of a person, for a time at least, from his super-ego— "that second self which he has unconsciously acquired" and which is responsible for many mental disturbances. As is well known, an excellent deterrent to morbidity is an interest in something outside of self, be it one's garden, a horse or dog or cat, birds, or a member of one's own species. Recently a distinguished criminologist "made the statement," so Ditmars informs us, that, as "far as he had been able to discover, no child that had been fond of pets had ever turned out to be a professional criminal." When a person lives (as Hudson puts it) fully *in* nature—with a sense of oneness toward life "in all its appearances, in all organic shapes, however different from the human"—then he not only learns, as did the Chinese landscapists, his rightful place in the total scheme of things, but, slipping the noose of the super-ego, can range in the domain of a greater self, even that of the universal spirit, and thereby achieve a fuller, more complete personality.

One of the reasons Hudson advocated a rural society in which the habitations of men are scattered at comfortable distances over a countryside was that, like Wordsworth and Emerson, he thought "the love of our kind cannot exist" in crowded communities "unmixed with contempt and various other unpleasant ingredients." "A human life" (George Eliot says in words he would have applauded)

> should be well rooted in some spot of a native land, where it may get the love of tender kinship for the face of earth, for the labours men go forth to, for the sounds and accents that haunt it, for whatever will give that early home a familiar unmistakable difference amidst the future widening of knowledge: a spot where the definiteness of early memories may be inwrought with affection, and kindly acquaintance with all neighbours, even to the dogs and donkeys, may spread not by sentimental effort and reflection, but as a sweet habit of the blood.

The author of *The Purple Land* was as fully aware as Thoreau and Tolstoy that the fraction of life can be increased in value by lessening the denominator. Not only does plain, open-air living, particularly if it has wide margins of leisure, bring with it "the old common happiness which Nature gives to all her children," but it reduces to a minimum the danger of one-sided progress or over-specialization, which (to extend Hudson's thought) is now the greatest of handicaps to all the other species.

Since we are "all of us at times hermits in heart," he, like most of the romanticists, stressed the importance of solitude in the communion with Nature. The proverb "You will grow only where you are alone" may be but partially true, for, as Hudson realized, much of one's character is the product of the give-and-take of social life, yet it emphasizes the necessity of withdrawing now and again, like the prophets of old, from the hubbub of society in order to hear the still small voice of the soul and thus be able to shape oneself from within. "Precisely as my life ceases to be solitary," confesses Gosse in his autobiography, "it ceases to be distinct." If one can achieve, when alone with nature, the state of alert passiveness, he may become aware of some of the deepest truths of life, and if to that is added the mystical experience, there will come an intuition of the eternal.

Some of the chief weaknesses in this programme of a return to nature—a programme that is continually being given fresh currency, most notably by Rousseau, and more recently by Thoreau and Tolstoy and Lawrence—stem from Hudson's attitude toward society and art and the capacity of the mind. It is well to counsel men not to elaborate their lives beyond their needs, but the needs of some of us go beyond what life brings directly and include the creations of Mozart and Sibelius, El Greco and Rodin, Shakespeare and Hazlitt and Yeats, Mann and Whitehead and Santayana. We find such works life-enhancing, for they not only clarify our experience and unite us in sympathy with others, but by showing the inadequacy of our present way of life and the finer possibilities in our nature, open up new areas of being. Much of the creative power of our greatest artists would be lost in the sort of society Hudson envisioned. As with the aesthetic faculty, there may be many things wrong with civilization, but surely they are much more the result of a want of balance between its various components than the advanced stage of its development.

Moreover, to an extent greater than he realized, it is possible to penetrate close to the heart of Nature, as the orientals have done, through pure contemplation, which can function outside the limits of space and time. His attitude toward all elaborate systems, theological as well as philosophical, was in part responsible for this deficiency; but even more to blame was his scepticism toward any intuitive or mystical experience that did not have its origin deep in the sensuous world. A large body of knowledge and wisdom has, however, been accumulated (to use the phrasing of the Bhagavad-Gita) by drawing the five senses turtle-like from the world under the spirit's buckler, and the fact that it has furnished much of the foundation of the cabala, the long dynasty of mystics and sages, and the various religions, shows how greatly it has appealed to some of the profoundest instincts of man. Many indeed have found in this sort of spiritual tradition the most enduring therapeutic value. Had

Hudson given more credence to it—had it seemed less dictated by
the all-too-human yearnings of mankind—it might have evoked in
him a stronger faith in the more purposive forces of the universe,
perhaps even to the extent of perceiving behind history the outlines
of a Divine Comedy.

The question also arises in one's mind as to whether long and
close contact with nature is really of great profit to most men. Evil
being so interwoven with the good, will the average person (who
after all is not endowed with Hudson's fine sensibilities) choose the
right things to admire and emulate? The worst traits of animals—
their ruthlessness, their violence, and their enthrallment to each
passing sensation—may merely provide him with a justification for
his own. "If lecherous goats [and] serpents envious cannot be
damn'd," Leopardi might well have asked with Donne, "alas, why
should I be?" As in the use of the biological argument for war,
some of the most repellent of the evolutionary processes may be
regarded as giving sanction to certain of the brutalities of society,
such as that of "power" politics. Yet, as abundantly illustrated in
his fiction as well as his essays, Hudson was aware that much of
the value to be derived from nature depends upon the individual
(solitude, for example, is of benefit only to the imaginative) and
to the sort of society in which he moves. Though the minds and
senses of country folk are often lulled and blunted by saturation
in the outdoors, they seemed to him, nonetheless, definitely superior
to their town and city brethren, with a fuller understanding of
their relationship to the whole of life. Their appreciation of nature,
like the love between those long married, may not be particularly
vocal, but he was certain of its genuineness. Under a more equitable
economic balance amongst the various groups of society, nature
would be appreciated to a greater degree and, in turn, its effect
on them would be more enriching.

A way of life oriented to the instinctive requires, surely, a fuller
and more closely reasoned statement than Hudson gave it. Some of
the primitive impulses—murder, cannibalism and incest, one should
not forget, are among them—have been frightfully destructive. If
no restraints were placed upon many of our instincts, such as those
enforced by that product of the collective experience of the race, the
conscience, men would soon become merely zoological again. Yet,
as indicated in his attitude toward the sex impulse and erotic litera-

ture,[9] he was not a "brutalitarian." Just as he could not bring himself to the reverencing of all the manifestations of the universal spirit, he did not wish men to give free rein to all the irrational forces within them. Even though some of the emphasis upon instincts must be attributed to his belief that the leaders of contemporary society were becoming too preoccupied with the things of the mind, he had, as has already been stressed, a considerable respect for the corrective power of the rational faculty. Distressing as the combat between the centaurs and the Lapithae would have been to Hudson, there can be no doubt as to which side would have enlisted more of his sympathy.

A more serious weakness in his justification of the ways of Nature to man—not so serious, however, as Arnold's sonnet and Huxley's essay would lead one to suppose—is the failure to realize sufficiently, except perhaps while writing some of his fiction, that Nature is deficient in what man now needs most—ethical values. True though it may be that, as Wordsworth likewise felt, all the possibilities of our moral being are to be found in her, ethical standards play only a minor rôle in the evolutionary processes and in the universe as a whole—the chief cause of Hudson's feeling of something awry at the heart of things. When man looks for moral guidance, he turns far less to the natural order, in which reason itself does not seem to have a dominant place, than to the code he himself has formulated out of his own experience. It is well, of course, that this code, as Hudson counselled, be correlated with the laws of Nature, since it must embody principles that will insure the survival of the group and the individual; but, for its further development—particularly necessary in this day of atomic power—man must rely upon his own creative intelligence.

Though weak from an ethical point of view, the programme is not neglectful of spiritual values. When the senses have been subtilized and the emotions heightened, one may feel himself in rapport with all visible nature; and, at rare moments, it may seem to him, as it did to Wordsworth near Tintern Abbey and to Hudson on a beach in Norfolk, that there is no "matter nor force in sea or land nor in the heavens above, but only spirit," and that he is in the

---

9 He deplored, for example, D. H. Lawrence's "relapses into the old sty" (letter to Garnett of November 2, 1913).

company of spiritual entities. With the world extended at wings and at dome, one can then experience an all-sufficing *recueillement* of the soul. The frequency and the quality of these moments of rapport and illumination, which are of the essence of religion, vary, to be sure, with the individual (to Hudson they brought primarily a sense of the beauty of the earth and the aesthetic order of the universe); to miss them, so he felt, is to miss the highest values Nature can give. There are, no doubt, other approaches to the spiritual forces of life, but they will become more reliable and stable if they are accompanied by experiences of natural mysticism.

Almost all philosophies are more useful for their occasional insights than for their success in logical consistency and elaborate schematization. Those of out-of-door essayists or poet-naturalists are often of special interest, for, of all manner of men, they appear to be in most intimate contact with the ever-changing flux of life—with the world as it is perceived and enjoyed as well as analyzed by the mind. Their philosophic conclusions may be scattered about in their volumes and, when gathered together, not easily arranged into a systematic pattern, for, knowing that life cannot be explained apart from its continual development, they are more concerned with its many different rhythms and with what lies pregnant in matter than with static or abstract concepts; but among these conclusions is to be found some of the most valuable material with which to fashion a tentative philosophy of one's own—indeed, the sort of material that no philosopher, particularly should he be temperamentally inclined toward idealistic abstractions, dare ignore if his system is to have any semblance of reality. All towers and spires must begin from the ground.

Out-of-door essayists have kept us in touch with such elemental and enduring things as the awful continuity and primal energy of protoplasm, the perennial cycle of birth, growth, decay and death, and the amazing diversity of life along with its archetypal embodiments. Salient in their pages are the glittering prairies of the Arctic and Antarctic; the pinnacled walls of the Andes, the Sierra Nevadas, the Alps and the Himalayas; the deserts of Patagonia and Sahara and Arabia; the vast plains of America, the steppes of Asia, and the bush-veldt of Africa; the shifting sand-dunes, elusive even to the roots of wild rice, and the great salt meadows and marshes bordering many of earth's shores; the illimitable ocean, with its blossoms of crested waves; the procession of the seasons along the Plata and the Amazon and the Mississippi, the Thames and the Rhine and the Danube, the Nile and the Ganges and the Yangtze, with their ploughed fields and pastures and woodlands, their herds of sheep and cattle and horses, their many communities of wild animals, and their insect and bird choirs—all probably more permanent, treaded more lightly by the centuries, than the fame of Hannibal and Caesar, of Phidias and Michelangelo and Rembrandt, of Buddha and Plato, and of Homer and Shakespeare and Bach. Certainly, few have been able to make us feel more at home in the midst of "this wonderful various world" than Hudson.

Documentation

The first number indicates the page on which a quotation ends, and the second, after the colon, the line. The following abbreviations have been used for the various volumes of the collected edition of Hudson's works, the three volumes of letters, and the biography:

PL—*The Purple Land*
CA—*A Crystal Age*
BLP—*Birds of La Plata*
NLP—*The Naturalist in La Plata*
FAN—*Fan: The Story of a Young Girl's Life*
IDP—*Idle Days in Patagonia*
BTV—*Birds in Town and Village*
BL—*Birds in London*
ND—*Nature in Downland*
B&M—*Birds and Man*
EO—*El Ombu and Other South American Stories*
HD—*Hampshire Days*
GM—*Green Mansions*
LBL—*A Little Boy Lost & Various Poems*
LE—*The Land's End*
AIE—*Afoot in England*
SL—*A Shepherd's Life*
AAB—*Adventures among Birds*
FAR—*Far Away and Long Ago*
BN—*The Book of a Naturalist*
DMP—*Dead Man's Plack, An Old Thorn, & Miscellanea*
TLT—*A Traveller in Little Things*
HRP—*A Hind in Richmond Park*
MBB—*Men, Books and Birds*, ed. M. Roberts
GAR—*Letters from W. H. Hudson, 1901-1922*, ed. E. Garnett
C-G—*W. H. Hudson's Letters to R. B. Cunninghame Graham*, ed. R. Curle
ROB—M. Roberts' *W. H. Hudson: A Portrait*

When a quotation has been included merely to give more of the flavor of Hudson's style, or when the particular essay in which it appears is indicated, documentation has been omitted. If the passage quoted is taken from some other book listed in the bibliography, only the author's surname has been given.

14:5 *FAR* 328.
14:18 *ROB* 20.
14:20 *ROB* 19.
14:28 *LE* 142.
14:33 *ROB* 25.
15:3 *ROB* 25.
15:14 *FAR* 126.
15:23 *FAR* 204.
16:4 *FAR* 336-7.
16:27 *NLP* 24.
16:31 *NLP* 347.
17:8 *FAR* 145.
17:12 *FAR* 130, 131.
18:12 *FAR* 11.
19:5 *FAR* 249.
19:22 *FAR* 62.
20:3 *HRP* 230.
20:8 *BN* 154.
20:18 *FAR* 198-9.
20:29 *AAB* 22.
20:30 *FAR* 219.
20:36 *FAR* 182.
21:3 *FAR* 220.
21:17 *FAR* 238-9.
21:36 *FAR* 242-3.
22:11 *FAR* 243.
22:22 *HD* 196.
22:24 *FAR* 243.
22:27 *FAR* 283.
23:25 *FAR* 150.
23:36 *FAR* 151.
24:39 *Journal,* 1850.
25:6 *FAR* 306.
25:36 *FAR* 306.
26:23 *FAR* 316-17.
26:34 *FAR* 45.
27:3 *FAR* 306.
27:16 *FAR* 319-20.
27:35 *BN* 202.
27:37 *FAR* 346.
28:12 *LE* 185.
29:17 *FAR* 340.
29:36 *NLP* 5.
30:18 *IDP* 5.

30:30 Letters to S. F.
Baird of June 3,
1868 and Sept. 5,
1866.
31:14 *Proceedings,*
1870, pp. 158-60.
31:39 *IDP* 204.
33:7 *AIE* 264-5.
33:25 *HRP* 65.
33:28 *LBL* 155.
33:34 *PL* 304.
33:36 *AAB* 265.
34:14 *BTV* 53.
34:16 *AAB* 10.
34:37 *EO* 185.
34:38 *LBL* 152.
35:12 *MBB* 312.
35:26 *ROB* 14.
36:11 *AIE* 25.
36:15 *TLT* 202.
36:26 *ROB* 28.
37:10 *ROB* 39.
37:31 *AIE* 33-4.
37:36 *MBB* 255.
38:4 *C-G* 30.
38:8 L e t t e r to his
brother of Dec. 28.
38:25 Letter to his sis-
ter Margaret of Oct.
10.
38:26 *ROB* 52.
38:34 Letter of Gissing
to his brother of
July 27, 1902.
39:36 *C-G* 30.
40:8 *AAB* 151.
40:12 *ND* 7.
41:3 *ROB* 71.
41:14 *AAB* 177.
41:29 *GAR* 239.
41:39 *ND* 275.
42:5 Curle 190.
42:8 *ROB* 21.
42:11 Ford 43.

42:20 "A Note on
Hudson," *Lit. Rev. of
the N. Y. Evening
Post,* Sept. 16, 1922.
43:1 Letter to G. Bot-
tomley of Feb. 26,
1908.
43:10 *FAR* 327.
43:16 *ROB* 1-2.
43:19 Curle 190.
43:28 Curle 191.
44:10 *AIE* 87.
48:27 *HRP* 70.
48:30 *Birds and Poets*
(Riverby ed.), p.
124.
48:36 *HRP* 72-3.
49:2 *AIE* 213.
49:39 *Journal,* Feb. 17,
1860.
50:15 *ROB* 269.
50:34 *ND* 51-2.
51:10 "The Timber."
51:12 "Man."
51:26 "Of Gardens."
51:39 "An Apology of
Raymond Sebond."
52:5 *Religio Medici,* I.
xvi.
52:37 *AAB* 232.
54:15 *Religio Medici,*
I. xvi.
55:4 *An Essay on Man,*
I. 119, 86-7.
56:12 *The Castle of
Indolence,* xxxviii.
58:3 Letter to R. West
of Nov. 16, 1739.
59:8 *ND* 216.
59:13 *Journal,* April 1,
1852.
60:4 Letter to Barring-
ton of April 12,
1770.

60:15 *B&M* 248.
60:21 Letter to Pennant of Oct. 8, 1768.
61:7 Letter to Pennant of Nov. 4, 1767.
62:4 *B&M* 249.
66:12 *The Voyage of the Beagle* (Everyman ed.), p. 363.
66:21 *The Naturalist on the River Amazons* (Everyman ed.), p. 365.
69:33 *Birds in a Village* (London, 1893), p. 190.
70:9 *Journal*, Nov. 3, 1853.
71:13 *Journal*, Jan. 2, 1842.
71:18 *Walden* (Walden ed.), p. 155.
71:25 *Ibid.*, pp. 159, 166, 162.
72:6 *Ibid.*, p. 101.
72:10 *Ibid.*, p. 232.
72:15 *Ibid.*, pp. 349-50.
72:30 *Journal*, June 16, 1840.
72:34 *A Week* (Walden ed.), p. 319.
73:3 *Excursions and Poems* (Walden ed.), pp. 227-8.
73:6 *Journal*, Jan. 7, 1857.
73:12 *Speaker*, March 3, 1906.
73:22 *Walden* (Walden ed.), p. 149.
74:11 *B&M* 245.
75:29 C. Barrus, *Our Friend, John Burroughs* (Boston, 1914), pp. 137, 142-3.
75:32 *Journals*, Jan. 1860.
76:23 *The Summit of the Years* (Riverby ed.), p. 31.

77:9 *Journals*, May 27, 1865.
77:34 Barrus, *op. cit.*, p. 117.
79:3 *AIE* 75.
81:6 "Footpaths," *Nature near London.*
81:39 *Journals*, Oct. 20, 1904.
82:30 *The Story of My Heart* (London, 1883), p. 64.
87:5 Nov. 7, 1889.
88:34 *BLP* 86.
88:37 *BLP* 290.
89:10 *Nature*, April 14, 1892.
89:19 *NLP* 233.
90:19 C. Barrus, *The Life and Letters of John Burroughs* (Boston, 1925), II, 86.
91:4 *NLP* 364.
91:22 *NLP* 358-9.
92:14 Gardiner, xii.
94:2 *IDP* 17-19.
94:23 *HRP* 255.
95:4 *C-G* 92.
95:6 *Afoot in England* (N. Y., 1933), p. 219.
96:27 Aug. 27, 1892.
96:34 July 16, 1892.
99:17 *DMP* 216.
99:33 *BN* 179.
99:39 *DMP* 314.
100:30 *Birds in a Village* (London, 1893), p. 188.
101:13 *Ibid.*, pp. 188-9.
101:24 *ND* 6.
101:36 *BLP* xiv.
102:27 *Nature*, March 23, 1893.
104:3 *IDP* 6.
104:18 *IDP* 24-5.
104:23 *IDP* 195.
104:30 *IDP* 209.
105:2 *BTV* 6.
105:10 *BTV* 116.

106:17 *BTV* 33.
107:2 *BTV* 30.
108:12 *BL* 64.
108:21 *BL* 14.
108:29 *BL* 169.
109:28 Letter to Barrington of Dec. 9, 1773.
110:24 *ND* 55.
111:33 *ND* 9.
112:31 *ND* 52.
113:8 *B&M* 41.
113:28 *B&M* 109.
114:9 *B&M* 232-3.
114:15 *B&M* 68.
114:22 *B&M* 52.
116:17 *GAR* 272.
117:9 E. Thomas, *A Literary Pilgrim in England* (London, 1917), p. 197.
117:15 *HD* 53.
118:21 *HD* 287.
121:2 *LE* 182.
121:5 *LE* 157.
121:7 *LE* 135.
121:28 *LE* 142.
122:27 *AIE* 192.
123:10 *AIE* 86.
123:14 *AIE* 261.
124:14 *SL* 137-8.
124:22 *SL* 43.
125:2 *SL* 235.
125:23 *SL* 317, 318.
125:28 *SL* 147.
125:33 *SL* 90.
126:16 *SL* 144.
127:8 *AAB* 2.
128:13 *AAB* 51.
128:16 *AAB* 66.
128:25 *AAB* 265.
129:9 *FAR* 2.
129:19 *FAR* 236.
129:25 *FAR* 237.
130:8 *FAR* 298.
131:36 *FAR* 315.
132:37 *C-G* 102.
133:3 *BN* vii.
133:26 *BN* 273.
133:28 *BN* 228.
134:3 *BN* 329.
135:12 *TLT* 12.

135:35 *TLT* 204, 205.
136:22 *ROB* 69.
136:37 *HRP* 228.
137:3 *HRP* 55.
137:22 *HRP* 320, 300.
137:26 *HRP* 317-18.
137:33 *HRP* 255.
138:4 *HRP* 261, 312.
140:7 *AAB* 103.
140:10 *BTV* 195.
140:18 *FAR* 238.
140:26 *NLP* 177.
140:31 *AAB* 150.
141:3 *NLP* 374.
142:17 *HD* 15-20.
143:2 *LE* 37.
143:17 *ND* 236-7.
143:25 *FAR* 238.
143:30 *B&M* 15.
143:37 *ND* 40.
144:8 *AIE* 223, 222.
144:11 *BN* 29.
144:16 *BN* 309.
144:27 *ND* 271-2.
144:38 *FAR* 60.
145:2 *ND* 143.
145:6 *ND* 153.
145:10 *FAR* 40.
145:15 *LE* 196.
145:18 *ND* 219.
145:27 *AAB* 260.
145:30 *AIE* 16.
147:6 *HRP* 274-5.
147:15 *FAR* 7.
147:22 *IDP* 219.
147:25 *HRP* 64.
147:30 *HRP* 65.
148:5 *HRP* 76-7.
148:18 *HRP* 65, 66.
148:21 *ND* 35.
148:24 *HRP* 81.
148:34 *HRP* 61, 63.
149:20 *HRP* 37, 38-9.
149:25 *BTV* 108.
150:4 *AIE* 66.
150:9 *NLP* 203.
150:22 *BN* 183.
151:6 *BN* 176.
151:11 *AIE* 5.
151:15 *DMP* 302.
151:21 *B&M* 22.
152:3 *BN* 210-11.

152:10 "Rules and Lessons."
152:12 *The Prelude,* III. 127, 131-2.
152:24 *BN* 315.
152:32 *IDP* 111.
153:2 *B&M* 71.
153:7 *HD* 123-4.
153:9 *BN* 211.
153:34 *TLT* 256.
154:10 *HD* 124.
154:17 *IDP* 199.
155:31 *B&M* 113.
156:6 *AAB* 140-1.
156:19 *HD* 254.
156:22 *ND* 258.
156:31 *AIE* 55.
157:7 *SL* 150, 151.
157:13 *IDP* 223-4.
157:27 *IDP* 218.
157:33 *LE* 224.
158:7 *Journal,* July 2, 1852.
158:18 *HRP* 219.
159:3 *B&M* 6.
159:5 *HRP* 113.
159:18 *HRP* 130.
163:12 *LE* 292-4.
164:7 *HRP* 318.
165:30 *HRP* 318-19.
165:34 *ND* 98.
165:39 *BN* 142.
166:15 *HRP* 306.
166:22 *AAB* 180.
166:36 *HRP* 174.
166:38 *SL* 20.
171:3 *ND* 261.
171:12 *HD* 54.
171:15 *ND* 156.
172:4 *LE* 57.
172:7 *AAB* 261.
173:28 *BN* 318-19.
174:13 *ND* 28.
174:30 *AIE* 44, 53.
175:11 *AIE* 263.
175:26 *IDP* 42.
176:20 *HD* 242-3.
176:37 *LE* 35.
177:2 "The H u d s o n Centenary," *F o r t - nightly Review,* CL (1941), 163.

178:9 *B&M* 70.
178:13 *HD* 38.
178:28 *ND* 26, 27.
178:34 *HD* 38.
179:9 *AAB* 92-3.
179:14 *AAB* 93.
179:26 *AIE* 83.
179:39 *AIE* 81.
180:2 *LE* 51.
181:11 *B&M* 156.
181:19 *BN* 308.
181:30 *AIE* 258.
182:12 *LE* 287.
183:7 *NLP* 9.
183:26 *BLP* 310.
184:32 *TLT* 246.
185:13 *SL* 150, 151.
185:20 *ND* 177.
185:33 *HD* 244.
186:4 *AIE* 255.
186:12 *TLT* 233.
186:15 *TLT* 105.
186:26 Jefferies, *Field and Hedgerow* (London, 1889), p. 60.
187:7 *B&M* 239.
188:10 *GM* 159.
189:1 *B&M* 57.
189:8 *AIE* 168.
190:22 *BN* 22.
191:15 *HRP* 6.
191:24 *HRP* 262.
192:3 *NLP* 194.
192:24 *Ways of Nature* (Riverby .ed.), p. 126.
193:8 *ND* 65.
193:27 *IDP* 213.
193:35 *ND* 159.
194:7 *AAB* 65-6.
194:13 *NLP* 343.
194:17 *HRP* 261.
194:19 *IDP* 53.
194:31 *HRP* 272.
194:34 *HRP* 280.
195:2 *NLP* 276.
195:9 *NLP* 276.
195:19 *BLP* 351.
195:27 G. Eckstein, *Canary: The History of a Family* (N. Y., 1936), p. 175.

196:10 *NLP* 283.
196:18 *HD* 151.
196:25 *Apes, Men, and Morons* (N. Y., 1937), p. 23.
196:32 *FAR* 346.
197:18 *HRP* 33-4.
197:22 *IDP* 206, 208.
198:4 *NLP* 209.
198:22 *BN* 22, 23.
199:7 *DMP* 298.
199:12 *TLT* 170.
199:33 *DMP* 298.
200:11 *DMP* 299-300.
200:33 *HRP* 99.
201:11 *LE* 60.
201:29 *HD* 45.
202:6 *Birds in a Village* (London, 1893), p. 193.
202:12 *BTV* 189.
202:15 *BN* 22.
202:20 *BTV* 190.
202:31 *B&M* 14.
204:9 *BTV* 197-8.
204:19 *HD* 112.
205:4 *ND* 66-7.
205:13 *HD* 113.
205:24 *BN* 200.
206:10 *BN* 199.
206:17 *NLP* 177, 178.
206:35 *NLP* 182.
207:38 *BN* 205.
208:9 *HD* 126.
208:16 *HD* 124.
208:33 *NLP* 171-2.
209:21 *HD* 65-6.
209:30 *HD* 170.
210:20 *HD* 138-9.
210:32 *HD* 131.
211:17 *ND* 194-5.
213:10 *NLP* 312-13.
213:31 *BN* 32.
214:12 *HRP* 7.
214:23 *NLP* 353, 356.
215:8 *LE* 84.
215:28 *HRP* 238.
215:37 *AIE* 189.
216:12 *BTV* 208.
217:4 *FAR* 41-3.
217:25 *BN* 122.
218:27 *BN* 281, 282.
219:38 *BN* 53.

220:9 *BN* 51.
220:22 *BL* 208.
220:23 *DMP* 365.
220:35 *DMP* 371.
220:39 *TLT* 188.
221:14 *LE* 240, 241.
221:21 *BN* 215.
222:13 *HD* 7.
222:19 *HD* 98-9.
222:38 *BN* 81-2.
223:9 *BN* 173.
223:16 *FAR* 230-1.
224:4 *NLP* 374.
224:14 *AAB* 40.
224:21 *B&M* 28.
224:23 *B&M* 11.
224:26 *AAB* 117
225:17 *HRP* 165.
225:23 *HRP* 170-1.
225:26 *HRP* 163.
226:11 *AAB* 219.
227:7 *LE* 59-60.
227:26 *HD* 43.
228:18 *IDP* 5.
228:31 *AAB* 6.
229:2 *B&M* 15.
229:8 *HRP* 283.
229:15 *The Story of My Boyhood and Youth* (N. Y., 1913), p. 143.
229:19 *Journal,* July 5, 1852.
229:29 *BN* 87.
231:8 *AAB* 44.
231:17 *ND* 227.
231:37 *AAB* 47.
232:24 *ND* 228.
232:36 *LE* 84-5.
234:11 *HRP* 190-1.
234:19 *AIE* 52.
234:26 *IDP* 30.
234:32 *BLP* 298.
234:36 *HRP* 169.
235:15 *AAB* 41.
235:39 *NLP* 224.
236:11 *AAB* 305.
236:31 *DMP* 151-2.
236:37 *Summer Studies of Birds and Books* (London, 1895), p. 96.
237:8 *B&M* 132, 134.

237:24 *BLP* 279.
237:28 *BN* 97.
237:38 *AAB* 275.
238:15 R. Jeffers, "Hurt Hawks."
239:17 *IDP* 176-7.
239:34 *DMP* 241.
240:19 *HRP* 119-20.
242:4 *LE* 78.
242:14 *LE* 250, 251.
242:21 *LE* 80.
243:4 *LE* 23-4.
243:27 *B&M* 175.
244:17 *B&M* 177-8.
244:29 *NLP* 226, 227.
245:8 *B&M* 217.
245:11 *BTV* 169.
245:36 *B&M* 208.
246:9 *NLP* 203, 209.
248:3 *HD* 272, 274.
248:7 *BTV* 35.
248:11 *LE* 93.
248:24 *AAB* 126, 125.
248:34 *BTV* 133, 134.
249:26 *B&M* 14, 15.
249:37 *IDP* 138.
250:18 *IDP* 138.
250:26 *IDP* 139.
251:10 *ND* 144.
251:21 *BTV* 28.
252:3 *AAB* 205.
252:14 *AAB* 205-6.
252:32 *BL* 87-8.
253:4 *NLP* 272, 273.
253:17 *AAB* 135.
253:39 *IDP* 137.
254:8 *B&M* 110, 107.
254:22 *B&M* 21-2.
255:12 *NLP* 272.
255:14 *BLP* 10.
255:19 *AAB* 187-8.
255:23 *AAB* 186.
255:38 *BTV* 99.
256:10 *ND* 153-4.
256:15 *ND* 152.
256:22 *ND* 231.
256:35 *ND* 234.
257:1 *IDP* 147-8.
257:21 *AIE* 200, 199.
257:27 *HD* 251.
257:36 *AAB* 127-8.
257:39 *BLP* 385.

258:2 *NLP* 254.
258:6 *BLP* 46.
258:11 *NLP* 268.
258:15 *NLP* 271.
258:19 *BLP* 152-3.
258:27 *B&M* 102.
258:32 *AAB* 173, 174.
258:34 *B&M* 89.
259:29 *B&M* 95-7.
260:32 *B&M* 170-1.
261:1 *DMP* 276.
261:24 *ND* 98.
261:38 *HRP* 233.
262:25 *SL* 150-1.
262:38 *ROB* 110.
263:13 *SL* 250.
263:18 *SL* 285.
263:38 *SL* 254-5.
266:8 *FAR* 14-16.
266:17 *FAR* 110.
267:2 *TLT* 35.
267:8 *AIE* 26.
267:12 *AAB* 177.
267:38 *AAB* 181.
269:38 *ND* 97.
270:8 *SL* 31.
270:15 *HD* 229.
270:36 *LE* 231.
271:6 *TLT* 219.
271:13 *HD* 114-15.
271:17 *TLT* 217, 216.
271:31 *SL* 291.
272:14 *BN* 153.
272:28 *TLT* 155.
275:20 *TLT* 66, 62-3.
275:37 *LE* 293, 292.
278:27 *FAR* 303.
278:30 *B&M* 30.
279:22 *FAR* 307-8.
279:26 *AAB* 284.
280:12 *AAB* 284.
280:15 *HD* 160.
280:38 *LE* 113.
281:2 *AAB* 307.
281:5 *Afoot in England* (N. Y., 1933), p. 219.
282:20 *AAB* 106.
284:8 *GAR* 241.
284:16 *ND* 132.
284:31 *MBB* 221.
284:32 *GAR* 233.

284:37 *ND* 133.
285:5 *HRP* 312.
285:8 *ND* 236.
285:15 *ND* 155.
285:18 *ND* 132.
286:2 *ND* 135.
286:8 *HRP* 317-18, 319.
286:14 *HRP* 315, 322-3.
286:22 *HRP* 316.
288:6 *BTV* 194-5, 196.
288:21 *B&M* 170.
288:26 *AAB* 200.
288:30 *HD* 281.
289:4 *BL* 58.
289:22 *SL* 18.
291:4 *NLP* 29.
291:9 *CA* 222.
292:29 *AIE* 228-9.
292:36 *BL* 194.
293:7 *AAB* 182.
293:31 *HD* 185-6.
294:4 *AIE* 139.
294:14 *TLT* 22.
294:30 *AIE* 229-30.
295:3 *HRP* 320, 321.
295:16 *TLT* 23-4.
295:37 *GAR* 215.
296:4 *GAR* 61-2.
296:30 *C-G* 71.
296:32 *GAR* 258.
296:34 *Bookman's Journal*, VII (1922-3), 92.
297:4 *HRP* 320.
297:9 *GAR* 258.
297:12 *HRP* 262.
297:14 *AIE* 272.
297:18 *HRP* 301.
298:6 *HRP* 263-4, 265, 267.
298:11 *HRP* 247.
298:17 *HRP* 250.
298:31 *HRP* 259.
299:1 *HRP* 304-5.
299:16 *HRP* 300.
299:33 *HRP* 249.
299:38 *HRP* 299.
300:6 *HRP* 270.
300:12 *HRP* 303.
300:16 *ND* 154.
300:25 *GAR* 216.

300:28 *BTV* 71.
300:32 *Birds in a Village* (London, 1893), p. 195.
300:38 *AIE* 275.
301:1 *AIE* 292.
301:19 *AIE* 276, 278.
301:28 *GAR* 245.
301:34 *AAB* 222.
301:39 *MBB* 220.
302:8 *MBB* 250.
302:31 *GAR* 109-10.
305:13 *HD* 47-8, 51-2.
305:31 *IDP* 206.
305:36 *HRP* 228.
306:2 *BN* 153.
306:33 *LBL* 153.
307:27 *AIE* 82, 86.
308:1 *ROB* 71.
308:14 *LE* 106.
308:20 *GAR* 257.
309:17 *SL* 215, 227.
309:25 *LE* 300; *SL* 104.
309:29 *ROB* 273.
309:32 *AIE* 47.
310:1 *SL* 5, 30.
310:5 *SL* 5.
314:2 *GAR* 281.
316:6 *MBB* 45.
316:10 *BN* 191.
316:15 *GAR* 241.
316:17 *MBB* 262.
317:31 *GAR* 267.
318:15 *EO* 259.
318:18 *EO* 208.
318:20 *CA* 107.
318:22 *PL* 173.
319:18 *PL* 118, 119.
319:26 *FAN* 561.
319:35 *PL* 273.
319:37 *CA* 85.
320:4 *GAR* 80.
320:7 *EO* 184.
321:22 *PL* 205.
321:31 *PL* 37.
322:6 *PL* 215-16.
324:39 *PL* 344, 345-6, 347, 349-50.
325:18 *CA* 228.
328:25 *GAR* 237.
328:30 *CA* vi.
330:24 *FAN* 289.

334:1 *GM* 99.
334:17 *GM* 104.
334:31 *GM* 242-3.
335:20 *GM* 304.
335:35 *GM* 151.
336:12 *GM* 132.
336:19 *A Little Boy Lost* (N. Y., 1919), p. 221.
336:29 *LBL* 57-8.
338:17 *EO* 4.
339:5 *EO* 61.
341:23 *EO* 21.
341:25 *EO* 29.
342:7 *EO* 145.
342:31 *EO* 149.
343:14 *DMP* 104.
343:29 *GAR* 273.
344:13 *DMP* 67, 71.
348:21 *GAR* 281.
350:13 *DMP* 316.
350:17 *AIE* 65.
352:2 *IDP* 110-11.
352:7 *FAR* 243.
352:20 *TLT* 95.
352:21 *ROB* 179.
352:27 *BN* 270.
352:32 *IDP* 112.
353:14 *IDP* 110.
354:20 *BN* 203.

355:24 *BLP* 91.
355:30 *BN* 201-2.
356:8 *LE* 222.
356:11 *MBB* 153.
356:17 *HD* 25.
356:25 *BN* 203.
356:34 *HD* 25.
357:4 *IDP* 75.
357:13 *HD* 26.
357:29 *IDP* 166.
357:35 *ND* 198-9.
358:6 *C-G* 39.
358:12 *GAR* 180, 201-2.
358:18 *HRP* 30.
358:30 *Invertebrate Spain* (N. Y., 1937), p. 184.
359:25 *GAR* 281, 282, 202.
359:29 *AIE* 256.
359:32 *HD* 86.
360:11 *AIE* 153.
360:15 *TLT* 204.
361:19 *TLT* 202.
361:25 *TLT* 202.
361:34 *TLT* 205.
361:38 *EO* 259.
362:11 *AAB* 285.
362:20 *CA* 140.

362:25 *LBL* 157.
362:29 *ND* 211.
362:33 *AAB* 104.
363:17 *AAB* 273.
363:21 *BL* 12.
363:24 "The Invisible World" (a sermon).
363:34 *SL* 40.
364:6 *HRP* 132.
365:3 *LE* 286.
365:25 *IDP* 214-15.
365:32 *TLT* 201.
365:39 R. Ditmars, *Strange Animals I Have Known* (N. Y., 1931), p. 86.
366:3 *BN* 23.
366:12 *TLT* 245.
366:23 *Daniel Deronda*, I. iii.
366:28 *PL* 261.
366:32 *B&M* 68.
367:2 E. Gosse, *Father and Son* (N. Y., 1907), p. 245.
368:15 "Holy Sonnets," ix.
369:1 *MBB* 288.
369:36 *AIE* 67.
371:12 *PL* 1.

Select Bibliography

THE WRITINGS OF HUDSON

Curle, Richard, ed. W. H. Hudson's letters to R. B. Cunninghame Graham, with a few to Cunninghame Graham's mother, Mrs. Bontine. London, 1941.

Dewar, David R., ed. Letters on the ornithology of Buenos Ayres by W. H. Hudson. Ithaca, New York, 1951.

Gardiner, Linda. Rare, vanishing & lost British birds: compiled from notes by W. H. Hudson. London and New York, 1923.

Garnett, Edward, ed. Letters from W. H. Hudson, 1901-1922. New York, 1923.

Hudson, W. H. The collected works. London and New York, 1923. 24 vols.

Roberts, Morley, ed. Men, books and birds. London, 1925.

Wilson, G. F. A bibliography of the writings of W. H. Hudson. London, 1922.

————. W. H. Hudson as an explorer: bibliographical notes on his contributions to the academic and scientific press. Bookman's journal and print collector, VII (1922-23), 111-12.

BIOGRAPHY

Chapman, Frank. W. H. Hudson. Audubon magazine, XLV (1943), 264-9.

Curle, Richard. Caravansary and conversation. New York, 1937.

Ford, Ford Madox. Portraits from life. Boston and New York, 1937.

Hunt, Violet. I have this to say. New York, 1926.

Roberts, Morley. W. H. Hudson: a portrait. New York, 1924.

————. W. H. Hudson. Virginia quarterly review, VI (1930), 507-21.

Salt, H. S. W. H. Hudson, as I saw him. Fortnightly review, CXXV (1926), 214-24.

Teale, Edwin Way, and Wasson, R. Gordon. W. H. Hudson's lost years. Saturday review of literature, XXX (April 12, 1947), 15-17.

CRITICISM

Antologia de Guillermo Enrique Hudson: precedida de estudios criticos sobre su vida y su obra por Fernando Pozzo, E. Martinez Estrada, Jorge Casares, Jorge Luis Borges, H. J. Massingham, V. S. Pritchett y Hugo Manning. Buenos Ayres, 1941.

Baker, Carlos. The source-book for Hudson's "Green mansions." PMLA, LXI (1946), 252-7.

Canby, Henry S. Definitions: essays in contemporary criticism. Second series. New York, 1924.

Charles, Robert H. The writings of W. H. Hudson. Essays and studies by members of the English association, XX (1935), 135-51.

Fairchild, Hoxie N. Rima's mother. PMLA, LXVIII (1953), 357-70.

Fletcher, James V. The creator of Rima. Sewanee review, XLI (1933), 24-40.

Garnett, Edward. Friday nights. First series. New York, 1922.

Goddard, Harold. W. H. Hudson: bird-man. New York, 1928.

Gorman, Herbert. The procession of masks. Boston, 1923.

Hamilton, Robert. W. H. Hudson: the vision of earth. London, 1946.

Hewlett, Maurice. Extemporary essays. London, 1922.

Hilton, Ronald. Recuerdos de un criollo: William Henry Hudson. Bulletin of Spanish studies, XXV (1948), 19-26.

Hughes, Merritt Y. A great sceptic: W. H. Hudson. University of California chronicle, XXVI (1924), 161-74.

Liandrat, Francisque. W. H. Hudson, naturaliste (1841-1922): sa vie et son oeuvre. Lyon, 1946.

Locker, Samuel J., ed. William Henry Hudson: a tribute by various writers. Worthing, Sussex, 1947.

Manly, J. M., and Rickert, Edith. Contemporary British literature: outlines, indexes, bibliographies. New York, 1928.

Massingham, H. J. Untrodden ways. London, 1923.

———. Centenary of W. H. Hudson. Nature, CXLVIII (1941), 187-9.

Mendoza, Angélica. Guillermo Enrique Hudson (1841-1922). Revista hispanica moderna, X (1944), 193-222.

Rosenbaum, Sidonia C. William Henry Hudson: bibliographia. Revista hispanica moderna, X (1944), 222-30.

Swinnerton, Frank. The Georgian scene. New York, 1934.

Thomas, W. Beach. The Hudson centenary. Fortnightly review, CLVI (1941), 163-9.

Weygandt, Cornelius. Tuesdays at ten. Philadelphia, 1928.

Index

G.

H.

I.